The Smaller Rhododendrons

Peter A. Cox

THE SMALLER
RHODODENDRONS

Timber Press, Portland, Oregon

© Peter A. Cox 1985
First published 1985

First published in the USA by
Timber Press
P.O. Box 1631
Beaverton, OR 97075
USA

ISBN 0-88192-014-2

Printed in Great Britain

Contents

List of illustrations

6

Maps. *Distribution of the following subsections*

Acknowledgements

Once again, very special thanks are due to the staff of the Royal Botanic Garden, Edinburgh, and especially to Professor D. M. Henderson, the Regius Keeper, for allowing me full access to the herbarium, library and the private parts of the garden, as well as for writing a foreword to this book. Also many thanks are due to Dr D. F. Chamberlain, Dr J. Cullen, Dr R. Watling, Dr A. P. Bennell, Dr G. Argent, Mr I. Hedge and Mr M. V. Mathew.

My thanks go to many friends in Britain, Ireland, USA, Canada, Europe, Australia, New Zealand, and Japan who have helped over hardiness, lists of nurseries, providing catalogues and for my many visits to gardens, nurseries and horticultural and botanical institutions.

I should like to thank the Royal Botanic Garden, Edinburgh, for the re-use of several of the photographs.

My deepest gratitude to Mrs Rosemary Wise for her lovely colour plates and line drawings and to Margaret Stones for allowing me to re-use plates and drawings from *Dwarf Rhododendrons* and the Botanical Magazine; also to the Royal Botanic Gardens, Kew for the use of the two plates from the Botanical Magazine.

Very special thanks are due to my great friend, co-gardener and traveller, Sir Peter C. Hutchison for his excellent distribution maps.

My thanks go to the Chinese for allowing me the great privilege of visiting Yunnan in 1981, to investigate and collect wild rhododendrons there; and to Dr R. T. A. Cook for his great help on powdery mildews.

Lastly, but above all, I thank my wife who has given me constant help and advice from the beginning to the end of writing this book.

Foreword

by Professor D. M. Henderson
    Regius Keeper
    Royal Botanic Garden, Edinburgh

When the horticultural press pours out a continual stream of trivial writing so often based on secondary sources, how fortunate we are to have still some writers who work from their own observation and deep knowledge of their subject. Such is Mr Peter Cox on *The Smaller Rhododendrons*.

Some years ago he published a first book entitled *Dwarf Rhododendrons* and followed it with *The Larger Species of Rhododendron*. Many years ago he realized that, while the larger rhododendrons have their own attraction especially for extensive gardens, the smaller were somewhat neglected and could be developed considerably for the more modest garden. He has studied and grown and talked about smaller rhododendrons for many years and this volume is full of good information on these plants. He is so refreshingly direct. If he disagrees, or has strong opinions, he certainly says so and backs his remarks up with strong reasoning. And he needs to do so for, in the rhododendron world, it seems there are rarely as few as two opinions on any subject.

By travelling widely where rhododendrons grow naturally and where they are extensively cultivated, Peter Cox has gained an unrivalled understanding of them in the wild and in cultivation. He has also collected them assiduously so continuing the tradition of the great rhododendron collectors of the first half of the century. His father, E. H. M. Cox, a notable writer and traveller and great promoter of good plants would surely have approved his holistic approach, wherein he discusses the complex biological interactions of frost, winds, soils, pests and diseases, hybridization and propagation always with a lively pen. However, he does not confine himself to the information from the past. He looks forward to the future and it is fascinating to have, towards the end of the book from such a successful hybridizer, an assessment of what new hybrids should be sought in future programmes. Clearly a man who is still as young and active as Peter Cox will produce yet another book on the subject 10 years hence and it will be fascinating to see then what report he can make of his own success if he follows all his own good advice.

D. M. Henderson
1984

Introduction

Much has happened in the rhododendron world since *Dwarf Rho-dodendrons* was published in 1973. This being so, there was little point in attempting to revise that book; so I decided to rewrite it from beginning to end. Since 1973, the now almost completed Edinburgh Revisions have appeared. So has Mr H. H. Davidian's first volume of *The Rhododendron Species* on Lepidotes (excluding Vireyas). China has to some extent re-opened to western visitors and botanists. The micro-propagation of rho-dodendrons is now firmly in production in North America and may soon be in Britain. Interest in rhododendrons the world over has greatly increased with multitudes of new hybrids becoming available, especially in North America. The American Rhododendron Society is spreading its wings far afield with the formation of a Danish and now a Scottish Chapter. The Rhododendron Species Foundation is going from strength to strength. Many new nurseries specializing in rhododendrons have come into being.

The Smaller Rhododendrons attempts to incorporate many of these developments into one volume. As in *The Larger Species of Rho-dodendron*, I follow the Edinburgh Revisions. This is not to say I agree with all the changes that have been made as will be seen in the text. There is certainly room for further improvements, especially from a hor-ticultural standpoint. From tentative enquiries and discussions with fellow enthusiasts the world over, I get the feeling that while many people are not happy with parts of the Revisions, most are willing to accept broadly the Subgenus to Subsection system. I feel confident that opposition to this will soon melt away.

As in *Dwarf Rhododendrons*, I have drawn a line at about 1.52m (5ft) and only include plants normally under this height. This is an average maximum height which may often be exceeded under favourable and/or heavily shaded conditions. I have covered the same species with the addition of descriptions of those not in cultivation, plus numerous new hybrids. Alas, there is not room to do justice to the Vireyas. The ever-green azalea cultivars would need a volume of their own to cover them fully so I have just selected a few of the most popular and the most promising. The rhododendron hybrid lists endeavour to include all dwarf hybrids established in commerce plus some of the best newer ones.

Lastly (as mentioned in *Dwarf Rhododendrons* p.12 and *The Larger Species of Rhododendron* p.10) I am including a brief description of climate and conditions here at Glendoick, near Perth, Scotland where I base most of my comparisons. Conditions are not ideal but we can grow a large percentage of the plants mentioned in this book with some

success. The winters are relatively mild, only just dropping below −18°C
(0°F) and the summers are cool, rarely over 27°C (80°F). The real
bugbear is the frequency of autumn and, more so, spring frosts which can
do appreciable damage to buds, flowers, growth and wood. Rain is often
inadequate during the growing season. The yearly total is just below
76cm (30in), falling spasmodically through the year. Recently, dry spells
of a month or more have occurred. Snow rarely lies long and frost is
frequent without a snow cover.

Elevation is between 15 and 60m (50–200ft) above sea-level. Shelter is
fairly good from the north but Dutch elm disease has made us more
vulnerable to wind in recent years. Soil is a medium to medium-heavy
loam, moderately or occasionally very acid, and short in organic matter.
Drainage is generally good. Aspect is south with all too rapid drying out.

It is hoped that people buying this book in addition to *Dwarf Rhododendrons* feel that the different and new information contained made
their purchase worthwhile. Also, that those who have failed to obtain
Dwarf Rhododendrons feel that this is a worthy substitute and that the
wait was not in vain.

Abbreviations

The following abbreviations have been used in the text.
+ or − greater or lesser (more or less)
NSEW north, south, east, west
F flower
L leaf
H hardiness
Ht height
Inflor inflorescence
USDA U.S. Dept. of Agriculture Hardiness Zone

Collectors

F G. Forrest
KW F. Kingdon Ward
L&S F. Ludlow & G. Sherriff
L, S&T Ludlow, Sherriff & G. Taylor
R J.J. Rock
SS&W J.D.A. Stainton, W. Sykes, J. Williams
W E.H. Wilson
C&H P.A. Cox & P. C. Hutchison
Sch A.D. Schilling
BLM L. Beer, C. R. Lancaster & Morris
SBEC Sino-British Expedition to China

Awards

FCC First Class Certificate
AM Award of Merit
PC Preliminary Commendation
HC Highly Commended

T (after award) award at trials
AGM Award of Garden Merit
AE Award of Excellence
PA Preliminary Award

Publications

AMRS-QB American Rhododendron Society Quarterly Bulletin
AMRS-J American Rhododendron Society Journal
RHS-RYB Royal Horticultural Society Rhododendron Year Book
RHS-RCYB Royal Horticultural Society Rhododendron & Camellia
  Year Book
RHS-RMC Royal Horticultural Society Rhododendron with Magnolias
  and Camellias
RHS-RSHB Royal Horticultural Society Rhododendron Species Hand-
  book
RHS-RHHB Royal Horticultural Society Rhododendron Hybrid Hand-
  book
SP of RH The Species of Rhododendron edited by J. B. Stevenson

Measurements

m metres
ft feet
cm centimetres
mm millimetres
in inches
F·Fahrenheit
C Centigrade

1 *Dwarf Rhododendrons in their Natural Habitat*

Distribution of species

The genus *Rhododendron*, with approximately 800+ recognized species now, is one of the largest in the plant kingdom, and, it might be added, one of the most diverse. This is true for difference in form, even though it hardly equals the genera Senecio and Euphorbia. None the less, species on the one hand grow to 30m (100ft) high with leaves up to 90cm (3ft) long and, on the other there are creeping prostrate shrublets with leaves 8mm ($\frac{1}{3}$in) long. It is their natural requirements that are similar: moisture-retentive soils, a temperate climate, plus rain and mist during the growing season. Bearing these requirements in mind, it becomes obvious that only certain regions of the world have such habitats to offer these plants. While a few species have managed to survive or gain a foothold at low levels, it is to many of the world's great mountain ranges that we must look to for the ideal conditions.

Nobody knows exactly where rhododendrons originated. It is obvious, though, that where natural conditions are at their most suitable, they have evolved and proliferated to the multitude of species and forms that are to be seen today.

I am not going into details here of their history of distribution and why certain seemingly ideal areas have few or no native rhododendrons. I attempted to cover this subject in *The Larger Species of Rhododendron*. It is certain that continental drift, the various ice-ages and warmer periods between, together with the rising and falling of the world's mountain ranges have all had a considerable bearing on present distribution.

Space does not allow me to cover the tropical or so called Malesian species in this volume. These are mostly found in the area between and including the Malay Peninsula and the northern tip of Australia with their centre of distribution and the greatest density of species on the island of New Guinea. The Malesian species nearly all belong to the Section Vireya. None of these can be successfully grown out of doors in Britain or any other country that has more than a degree or two of frost.

The rest of the genus is widely scattered through the Northern Hemisphere with far the greatest concentration in the area where the Himalayas, the Xizang (Tibetan) Plateau and the mountain ridges of Burma and south-west China meet. Geographically, this is one of the most striking areas of the world with steep high ridges and narrow gorges between, gouged out by tremendous rivers. This type of country has a remarkable effect on the flora, with each valley virtually isolating one ridge from the next. The result is that many ridges have their own endemic species, subspecies and/or varieties. Each species only grows within a limited altitudinal range so has no chance of travelling down a mountain side and up the next, other than with the help of an animal or bird carrying seed, perhaps adhering to its fur, feathers or clothes (man!). Certain versatile species may be able to grow over an altitudinal difference of as much as 2,700m (9,000ft) while others are confined to as little as 150m (500ft) or even less. These versatile plants are generally those which are also common over a large area while those confined to narrow belts of hillsides may be rare. It could be said that on the whole, the widespread versatile plants are easier to grow than those more particular as to their habitat.

Few species are really distinct. The genus is really a botanist's nightmare and no two botanists would come out with anything like a similar classification. So many merge into one another botanically although their typical form may appear distinct enough. As more is found out about distribution and variation, further changes are likely to be made in classification. Species which merge into one another may be referred to as aggregate species. A 'cline' is a little different. In an area between two points, the typical form of one species gradually changes into the typical form of another closely related one.

When I visited the Cangshan Range (formerly Tali) in 1981, we found relatively clear-cut species although some were extremely variable. This might be considered a contradiction, but in reality it is not.* These variations are what we have come to expect within certain common and widespread species such as *R. decorum* and *yunnanense* (but not, of course, dwarfs). What especially interested me was that in the case of *yunnanense*, we saw virtually the same variation wherever we went. It is apparent from the field notes of collectors like Forrest and Rock that these variable species may be fairly uniform in one place and extremely variable in another for no obvious reason. Cangshan is fairly isolated with no other comparable peaks near by. Further north in Yunnan where there is a much greater area of high country, collectors tell of extraordinary mixtures and muddles of species and probable natural hybrids. We saw surprisingly few natural hybrids and what we saw were mostly hybrids between distinct as opposed to closely related species. In N.W. Yunnan where many related species meet, it is often impossible to ascertain what is a natural hybrid and what is a part of a cline or other intermediary.

As mentioned earlier, elevation plays a big part in distribution. Taken the world over, rhododendrons are to be found from sea-level to a remarkable 5,900m (19,000ft). The widespread Lapponica subsection which contains many of the dwarfs with tiny leaves and purplish flowers, covers this whole altitudinal range. This is because *R. lapponicum* itself is found well within the Arctic Circle at sea-level and *nivale* survives as one of the highest of any plant life in parts of the Himalayas. *R. lapponicum* spreads southwards to N.E. USA, central Siberia and northern Japan

* A surprising percentage of natural hybrids have appeared amongst the Cangshan seedlings, including many crosses not seen in the wild.

where it may achieve the altitude of 2,000m (6,000ft). So I would like to bet that taken the world over, some member of the Lapponicum sub-section can be found the whole way from sea-level to 5,900m (19,000ft).

A rather strange altitudinal occurrence takes place in China. As one proceeds eastwards from, say, the northern tip of Burma, similar (though not the same) species are found at progressively lower altitudes at the same latitude. Presumably this is due to the climate becoming more and more a continental type resulting in harder winters at lower altitudes. Although the actual distance from the sea is not all that different, these more easterly areas get further from the prevailing S.W. monsoon.

Doctors David Chamberlain and James Cullen of the RBG, Edin-burgh, while revising the subgenera Hymenanthes and Rhododendron respectively, have been paying far more attention to distribution than other botanists have hitherto done. Not only have they plotted the known distributions of each species where locations can be identified onto maps, but they have divided the main rhododendron area of S.E. Asia into zones. The divisions of these zones are where the greatest number of species reach the edges of their distribution and it is surprising how many species do in fact fit neatly into each zone. Chamberlain points out how, although we regard N.W. Yunnan as perhaps the centre of the genus, the great majority of species growing there belong in the subgenus Hymenanthus and to only four subsections: Neriiflora, Talien-sia, Glischra and Selensia. He also points out that where there is such a conglomeration of different and merging species, much speciation is taking place.

Ecology

In the first part of this chapter I mentioned how rhododendrons are found within a certain climatic zone and that they require rather special-ized conditions to be able to flourish. By 'flourish', I mean perpetuate themselves in a more or less healthy state indefinitely. It can be said that rhododendrons transferred from the wilds of China, Japan and North America flourish in Britain but, except in a very few gardens, they are unable to perpetuate themselves to any great extent. In other words, without the hand of man, they would soon be ousted and replaced by native flora and certain alien plants that have naturalized themselves successfully. Considering how well they grow in Britain, it is indeed surprising that only one or possibly two species can be regarded as truly feral in this country. These are, of course, *ponticum* and *luteum*. Both are native to Europe and western Asia where the conditions are somewhat akin to our own. Also *ponticum* has been found as fossils in Britain.

In China, I have seen species apparently adaptable to all sorts of conditions and pressures there and yet these seemingly robust and aggressive species are not capable of fully establishing themselves in Britain. Why? The answer as I see it is simple: climate. We are reputed to live in a temperate climate where rain falls all the year round and according to some, never stops. Yet rhododendrons will not establish because our climate is too dry. Their minute seedlings just cannot put up

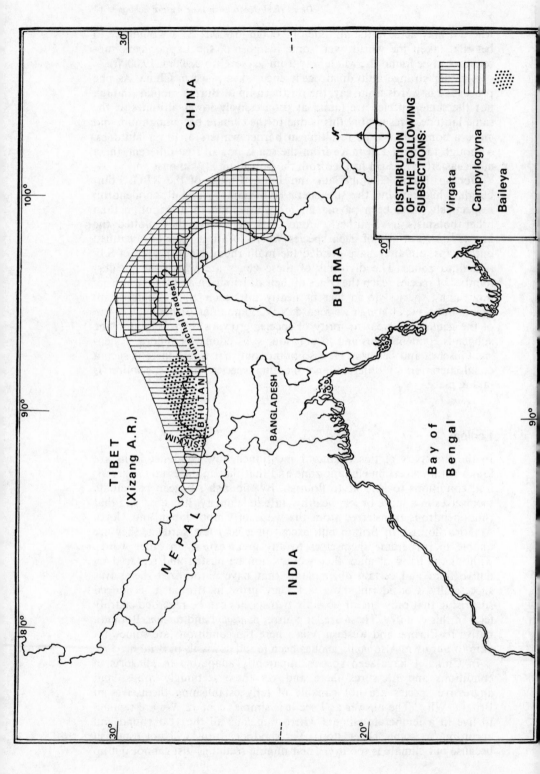

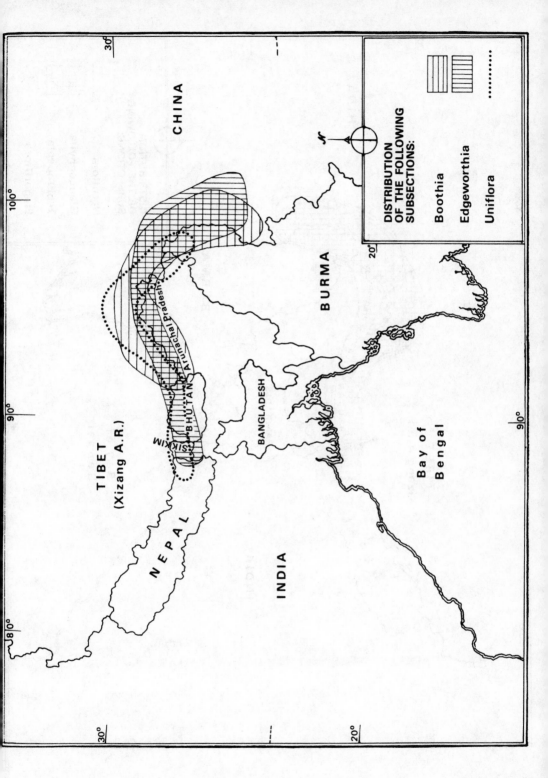

DISTRIBUTION
OF THE FOLLOWING
SUBSECTIONS:

Boothia

Edgeworthia

Uniflora

CHINA

TIBET
(Xizang A.R.)

NEPAL

INDIA

BHUTAN

SIKKIM

Arunachal Pradesh

BANGLADESH

BURMA

Bay of
Bengal

30°

10°0°

9°0°

8°0°

20°

9°0°

30°

20°

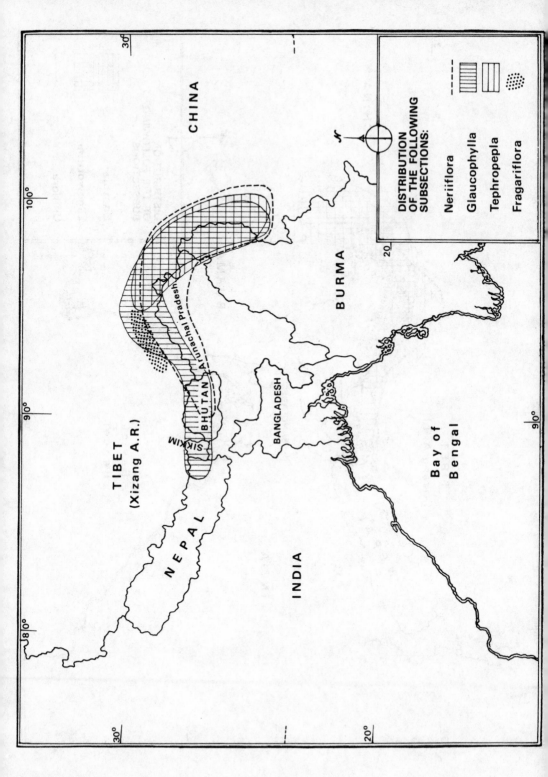

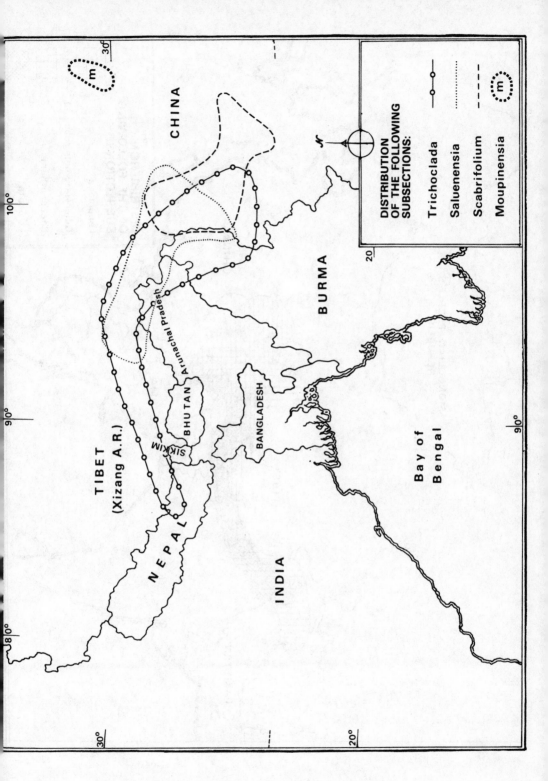

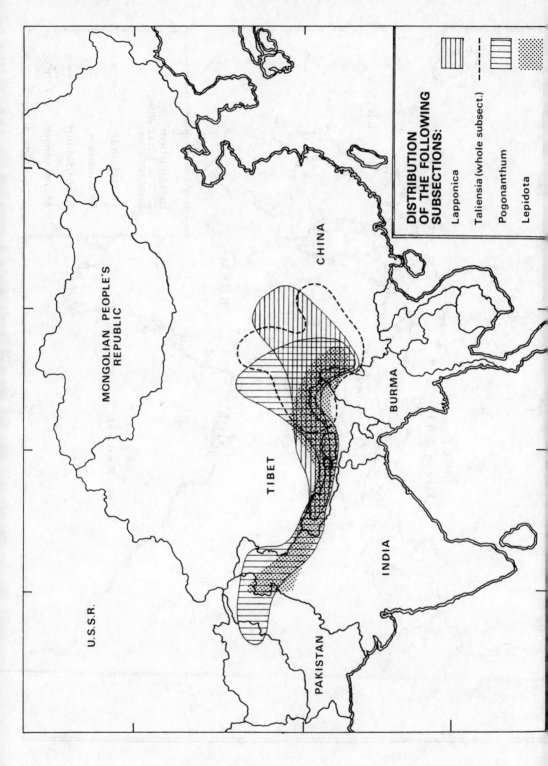

DISTRIBUTION
OF THE FOLLOWING
SUBSECTIONS:

Lapponica

Taliensia (whole subsect.)

Pogonanthum

Lepidota

U.S.S.R.

MONGOLIAN PEOPLE'S
REPUBLIC

TIBET

PAKISTAN

INDIA

CHINA

BURMA

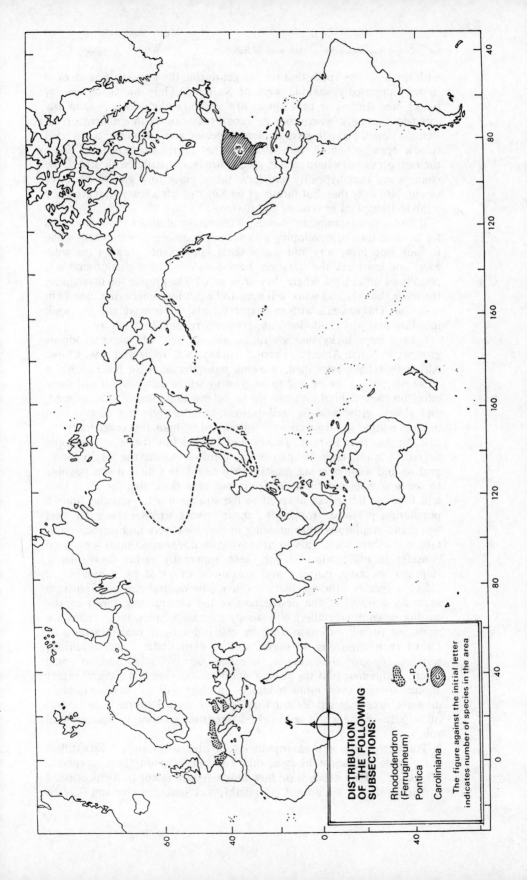

DISTRIBUTION
OF THE FOLLOWING
SUBSECTIONS:

Rhododendron
(Ferrugineum)

Pontica

Caroliniana

The figure against the initial letter
indicates number of species in the area

with the long, dry spells that we *can* get during the growing season, even in the supposedly soaking west of Scotland. Only on shady, mossy banks, tree stumps or peat blocks are seedlings likely to appear in any numbers. Actually, where they do occur, they can be an embarrassment. Being a purist, I like to have authentic species, and anyone who has tried to sow open-pollinated seed will know that except where isolated or on the rare occasions where certain species are incompatible with others, the chances are that hybridity will have taken place to a greater or lesser extent. Not only that, but forests of seedlings (if left a few years) are quite a job to transplant or remove and destroy.

If one is to contemplate growing a collection of dwarf rhododendrons for the first time or developing a new area, I consider it well worth while to look into how, why and where these same plants grow in the wild. First one must ask the question, how does one's own climate and soil conditions differ from where they grow wild? The greater the divergence, the more thought and work will need to be put into improving the site in question. This is dealt with in chapters 2 and 3. Here we will just look into how and why rhododendrons grow where they do in nature.

I have been lucky enough to be able to see wild rhododendrons growing in North America, Europe, Turkey, N.E. India and S.W. China. Although I have seen them growing naturally in these places, only a small percentage can be said to be growing where man has not had some effect on their habitat. We are led to believe that rhododendrons need, and always grow wild in, well-drained, moisture-retentive soil, rich in organic matter; in virgin country untouched by man, this is generally the case. In America, Europe, Turkey and India I saw the results of some degree of interference by man in the form of cutting the virgin forest, grazing and some burning, mostly fairly recent. In China, it was possible to see how man and rhododendrons had been coexisting for some time and how the latter had adapted to the strains of a tremendous human population pressure. Admittedly, those species which require the best woodland conditions were growing in comparatively undisturbed habitats, but others seem able to at least exist under conditions we would consider totally inadequate for these apparently rather fussy plants. Repeated hacking, burning and grazing is tolerated by a number of different species although there is often little natural regeneration from seed. As a result of the destruction of the surrounding forest or the cutting down of everything else woody over large areas, these plants are subjected to full exposure and on easily dried-out near-mineral soil. Dwarf rhododendrons we found able to exist under these conditions were *racemosum, trichocladum, virgatum* ssp. *oleifolium* and to some extent *fastigiatum*, plus the azaleas *simsii* and *microphyton*. Several bigger species seemed even more tenacious in their will to survive, notably *decorum, arboreum* ssp. *delavayi* and *pachypodum*. Reports from several other parts of the world tell of rhododendrons growing in near mineral soil.

Transferred to a new environment with almost certainly a very different climate and most likely a different soil, how do these adaptable plants fair? Much depends on how different each factor is. As mentioned earlier, in Britain we do not get reliably wet summers, our soil is often too heavy or too alkaline, and our winters are often too mild leading to precocious growth and severe damage from spring frosts. In parts of the world like S.E. Australia and coastal California, the climate is even further removed from S.E. Asia with virtually no frost. In S.E. USA, the soil is invariably heavy. The further removed are the conditions in a garden from those found in the wild, the more trouble has to be taken to create micro-climates and near perfect soil conditions for rhododendrons to succeed. These adaptable species mentioned above plus many others from different localities are far more likely to succeed in difficult localities than those fastidious species only found growing in specialized habitats. People have only recently started to wake up to the real value of these tough, tolerant species and their use for hybridizing. I believe that in time, rhododendrons will be raised and selected to grow easily in far more diverse climates and soils than have ever been imagined. I for one am preparing to plant some of these stalwart species in certain dry, exposed positions I had considered unsuitable for any rhododendrons. Also I intend to use them for hybridizing.

Most dwarfs and semi-dwarfs are found naturally just below, about and above the line where trees peter out. While some may be located under a thin tree cover, the majority seek the open, be it a forest clearing, on isolated rocks or on great expanses of open moorland where trees are unable to survive. These are social plants, forming huge carpets or thickets, often to the exclusion of all other plants. The higher up the mountains, the more rugged the climate becomes with stronger winds, lower temperatures and a shorter growing season. Here, most plants including rhododendrons are forced to retreat into hollows, behind rocks and into crevices. In north-facing hollows the snow may linger long and in those wet areas of the Indo-Xizang (Tibetan) frontier, snow may lie for as much as eight months. Species growing here have to burst into bloom as the snow melts and ripen their seeds in these four months although some do their final ripening under a blanket of snow. In contrast, species in the warm temperate forest have little need to hurry. While some do open their flowers early, they may take nine months to ripen fully their often sizeable seed capsules. Species from N.E. Asia and Siberia, while undeniably winter-hardy, burst into growth and flower quickest of all. These can be devastated by spring frosts in a fickle climate.

Why can we not naturalize these alpine species which grow on Chinese moors as heather does in Scotland and cassiopes and phyllodoces do in western North America? Once again climate is the answer. Here, snowfall is unreliable and winters often mild. Icy blasts may occur with no snow cover as well as the same mild spells mentioned earlier inviting early bloom, while growth can be followed by ghastly cold east winds. Our heather has become used to these conditions although even it can be severely browned some seasons. Dwarf rhododendrons would take many centuries of natural selection and evolution to adapt to the rigours of our Scottish hills.

To finish this chapter, a few quotations from plant collectors to emphasize my points in this section:

Reginald Farrer in *Gardener's Chronicle* (23 August 1919, p.101)

Indeed, I continue to be even more struck than I had expected with the numbers and variety of rhododendrons in these ranges (Upper Burma) where any little outcrop or open slope may yield a distinct species!

My own notebook in China, 18 May 1981

Rounding the corner a glorious sight unfolded, the whole immediate hillside covered with creamy-white *cephalanthum* and the purplish-blue *fastigiatum*; the best sight of the whole expedition except perhaps the *Primula sonchifolia*. At first rather stunted plants (of *cephalanthum*) grew out of lime rubble (soil sample taken). Although heavily grazed, fine specimens of both species grew together.

Roy Lancaster in *Plant Hunting in Nepal* (p.111)

Beer and I were slowly searching on opposite sides of the river when each found a new *Rhododendron* species. Our shouts were simultaneous and I crossed the water carrying a small twig of my find to match that which Beer was busy photographing. It proved to be *R. nivale* . . . The whole plant was aromatic when bruised, in common with *R. anthogogon* and *setosum*, both of which accompanied it. Although we searched for some time, these appeared to be the only woody plants at this height . . . 5,100m (16,500ft) . . .

E. H. Wilson in *Horticulture* (March 1910)

In coniferous forests, from 9,000–12,000ft they [rhododendrons] form usually the only undergrowth and with their gnarled stems form an almost impenetrable jungle. No wild animal appears to eat or destroy them—indeed, the Tibetans declare they are poisonous; and the wood, though hard, is little used even for fuel, consequently, these Rhododendron thickets remain unmolested by man or beast [alas this is not so now (*P.A.C.*)]. There is nothing in the nature of Ling or Heather in these regions, their place being taken on the moorlands by dwarf growing, tiny leaved species of Rhododendron.

J. G. Millais in *Rhododendrons and the Various Hybrids 2nd Series* Notes from G. Forrest comparing the dwarf rhododendrons of China with the heather of his native Scotland (p.17) . . .

Forms of the dwarf *intricatum* and *fastigiatum* were simply legion and clothed all the uplands giving a very home-like touch to all the higher altitudes. Take the moors and hills surrounding the head waters of any of our principal Highland streams in the early spring, those in full flood with patches of snow around: for heather and heath imagine mile upon mile of dwarf rhododendrons, at that season almost the exact brownish shade of dry heather, and you have the scenery of the summit of Beima-Shan, altitude 15,000ft . . . The moorlands of the Chungtien Plateau were covered with many forms of *fastigiatum* in fullest flower and in many shades, from the deepest purple through lavenders to bright rose-pink. At these lower altitudes the shrubs seem to thrive best in marshy situations and some of the boggy flats on the margins of the pine forests which clothe the surrounding hills were ablaze with the blooms of *R. hippophaeoides, scintillans* of what I took to be the true form of *fastigiatum*. Those flats are generally bordered by birch saplings and again the charming combination drove my thoughts homewards for comparisons, reminding me, bar the colour, of just such flats as we have in the Highlands where heather and birch grow in company.

Introduction into cultivation

Few people realize, when looking at rhododendrons growing in gardens, where they come from, let alone the trials and tribulations that collectors have gone through to introduce them into cultivation. Having been brought up as a child with rhododendrons and been told much of their history by my father, I am inclined to look with amazement at people who have hardly heard of Yunnan and Sichuan, and are certainly not able to pin-point them on a map.

My father was very much involved in horticulture in and around London when the bulk of new rhododendrons were coming in from China, Burma and Xizang. He was gardening editor of *Country Life*, editor of the *New Flora & Silva*, the writer of various gardening and plant-collecting books, and owner of a bookshop specializing in gardening literature. Thus he kept abreast of all that was new. He frequently visited the great gardens like Tower Court, Exbury and Caerhays where thousands upon thousands of seedlings were being raised from seed just sent back from Asia. He knew all the great collectors of the day: Forrest, Farrer, Wilson, Kingdon Ward, Rock and Ludlow and Sherriff. Being brought up in these circles, I either had to fall completely for the thrills of going on plant-hunting trips myself, or turn against plants and gardening altogether, and I have never regretted going for the former.

My father went to N.E. Burma with Farrer in 1919. Having been bitten by the collecting bug, I have always been a little surprised that he never went out east to collect again. As a child, I still have a vivid memory of being introduced to Kingdon Ward, by then a tiny, wizened old man with the most wrinkled face I ever saw, and to Rock who once visited the garden here at Glendoick. Ludlow and Sherriff and Mrs Betty Sherriff I had the good fortune to know very well and all three gave me great encouragement to collect in the east myself. I remember Ludlow telling me that while he always wore boots when travelling and collecting, Sherriff always wore gym shoes (plimsolls). Ludlow lived to a much greater age than did Sherriff but I doubt if their different choice in footwear had much bearing on their longevity!

Much has been written on the history of plant-collecting, on the French missionaries, botanical collectors like Hooker and Henry and professional collectors like Fortune, Forrest and Kingdon Ward. It is strange how these collectors either wrote little or nothing of their exploits (like Forrest or Ludlow and Sherriff) or must have spent their entire time between expeditions writing their many fascinating works (like Wilson, Farrer and Kingdon Ward).

Being a professional collector was extremely hard work and often ended in early death—such were the fates of Farrer and Forrest, both dying in the field. A few, such as Farrer and Sherriff, were wealthy, and were able to pay their own way, leading lives of comparative luxury even while travelling. However, those who had to do it for a living were very poorly paid or rewarded. Forrest was given bonuses for each new species he sent back and there is little doubt that this induced Sir Isaac Bayley Balfour of the Royal Botanic Gardens, Edinburgh (who felt sorry for Forrest), to name rather more species than he would have otherwise done. Likewise Kingdon Ward had to keep collecting and writing to the end of his days to make ends meet—all this on top of frequent hardship and even danger while out on expeditions.

In the early part of this century, these collectors went for a whole year or more on collecting trips. Although politically things were much different from today, some countries and areas like Nepal and Xizang (Tibet) were hard to get into and there were frequent mini-wars, rebellions and so on, although this did not deter these intrepid explorers. Nowadays, political barriers have closed many of the remaining promising collecting areas. Parts of China have been opened and a few lucky people (myself included) have got into semi-remote areas, while tours have reached Omei-shan and have limited access to other places. Alas, our thoughts of Xizang and even N.W. Yunnan are not too hopeful at the time of writing.

People may ask, 'why bother? Are there not enough rhododendrons and other plants in cultivation to satisfy everyone?' No, even fresh introductions of old favourites are welcome to many enthusiasts, but the chances of new species or forms or something lost to cultivation spur one on to try and try again. It is a challenge to collect and grow seeds and plants from the wild and only those who do it know of the thrills involved from the moment an expedition is born to the first flowering in cultivation.

Collecting expeditions have changed much. No longer are year-long spells in the field possible. Neither can they be afforded, nor are they politically acceptable. It is a question of a quick 'in and out and grab what you can, whatever the season'. But plant collecting has become a sensitive occupation. Governments, in many ways quite rightly, frown on wholesale stripping of their indigenous flora even though they may do little to conserve it themselves. I certainly do not approve of any large-scale collecting of wild plants, and certainly no plants (as opposed to seed) should be gathered commercially. Likewise seed should never be collected by the pound as Forrest did. We had permission to collect a very limited quantity of live material in China and we were most careful to obey these rules. We did see one very inviting bank of seedlings by the thousand but we left them to grow in peace. One more recent trip to China I know of met with endless frustrations, and even though in theory they had permission to collect a few plants and herbarium specimens, these were removed from them before returning home and they only just got away with their seeds.

The pounds of seed Forrest collected with the aid of native collectors must have largely gone to waste. What percentage of this was ever sown and how much that was sown grew to flowering size? Let us not be greedy. It is the greed of some that is ruining the chances of others.

With the boon of air travel, these quick trips in and out *can* be very successful and collecting can be fruitful even in the growing season. Spring collecting of rhododendron seed is by no means a waste of time; in N.E. Turkey, the European Alps, N.E. India and now China, I have managed to collect viable seed of most species I found. In some cases it is possible to gather seed off a plant actually in flower and thus select the best forms, although of course these do not necessarily produce seedlings of equal merit. In autumn, cuttings are very much a possibility and well worth a try.

What are the most promising areas left to explore? China is so large and the flora so diverse that any temperate parts are still worth a visit regardless of how well known they are reputed to be. For a really virgin botanists' paradise, try the huge area consisting of N.E. India (Arunachal Pradesh), S.E. Xizang, N. Burma and adjoining N.W. China, that is if you can get there. Few have ever succeeded in getting into that border region of perpetual dampness, knife-edge ridges and periodic earthquakes.

Successful collecting of seed is not quite so simple as it may seem. Some plants, including certain dwarf rhododendrons, shed their seed all too rapidly once it is ripe and it may ripen at funny, unexpected times. Much rhododendron seed does not ripen until well on in the autumn when travelling is very difficult due to snow. September may be too early even though green capsules once fully developed usually give viable seed. We were lucky in China in 1981, in that 1980 had been a bumper flowering season, and for the bigger species there was abundant seed. Dwarfs usually flower every year but anyone looking for seed of large species in autumn 1981 must have had a sad disappointment.

Reginald Farrer, in the *Gardener's Chronicle* (4 December 1920, p.276) wrote:

In a sunless climate like this [Upper Burma], it is very difficult to forecast the arrival of harvest-time and I have been afraid to be as much too early for some of my treasures as I was too late for others in the torrid summer of Siku [Gansu formerly Kansu]. Nature however, makes her own pace and seeds have their moments of maturity precipitated by the arrival of frosts, rather than any interposition of the sun. For a long time, indeed, I viewed the persistently green capsules of the Rhododendron with dismay; they never seemed to change or develop in the smallest degree and I began to fear that I might have to sit among the snows far beyond Christmas, when I hoped the year's work might be over. I did not realise how the seeds and woody valves of rhododendrons continue desiccating and ripening inside, though the fleshy outer envelope remains as green as ever, 'till the frosts, by nipping this into dryness, split it open.

Rhododendron seed is easily collected and dried. As long as it is not kept in polythene and is dried off naturally (without too much artificial heat) and stored in paper packets, it should give excellent germination. One special plea. However and wherever seed is collected in the wild, please see that it is given a collector's name and number and that field notes are made giving location, altitude and habitat plus (if possible) some description of the plant. Better still, collect corresponding herbarium specimens and a photograph.

Collecting live plants and cuttings requires infinitely more care. Plants are best kept healthy by wrapping the roots in moss which is held in place by rubber bands or cotton thread. Try to ensure a decent root system in the first place where possible. Store in a light but sunless position and watch the watering with the utmost attention. Over- or under-watering spells disaster. Transportation over any length of time should be in aerated trays or baskets. For a very short duration, polythene bags are good, but in hot conditions rot will quickly set in. Cuttings can be stored in polythene in the dark for a week or more but try to keep them cool. Generally, these are better kept dry but must be turgid when placed in the polythene. Again moisture plus heat is a killer.

The bringing home of live plants is becoming more and more difficult owing to importation restrictions and, in many ways, quite rightly so. We have enough pests and diseases already without bringing in any more. Enquiries should be made to the Department of Agriculture and Fisheries, Plant Health Branch, about permits and quarantine, and to similar bodies in other countries. Importation into North America, Australia, New Zealand and Japan is even more difficult, due to the necessity for roots to be washed clean of all soil. In addition, plants often have to withstand fumigation.

2 Dwarf rhododendrons in the garden

Choice of site

The ever decreasing size of gardens and lack of experienced hired labour has made dwarf plants of all kinds more popular than ever before. Even if space is available, few people have the time or the energy to look after large areas of garden. What plants can give more pleasure all year round and year after year than a well thought out collection of dwarf rhododendrons? These plants are often attractive at all times with the added bonus of showy flowers in season. Many people are becoming fed up with annuals, herbaceous borders and roses which all need constant attention and often only look good for short spells in the summer. The great majority of dwarf rhododendrons are long-lived, easily accommodated plants, remarkably free from pests, diseases and other ailments and will grow well in a variety of sites provided the ground is carefully prepared before planting.

Being used to full exposure in nature (see Chapter 1, p.25), many will grow happily in full sun in all but the hottest climates or positions and put up with a fair amount of wind. The great majority of suburban gardens up and down Britain are perfectly suitable and even if the soil is clay or limy, raised beds can be made above the natural soil level. In south-east USA, raised beds are essential.

Each country or district has some limiting factors of climate or soil, affecting what is likely to succeed. Here in eastern Scotland, our worst enemy is spring and to a lesser extent, autumn frosts and some allowances need to be made to afford special protection for early flowering (and growing) kinds. Other places, like parts of North America and Australia, may suffer excessive summer heat or drought, salt spray, very low winter temperatures or atmospheric pollution. Whatever the problem, some degree of modification can be achieved by creating microclimates by the use of shade, shelter or overhead protection, either temporary or permanent.

For rhododendrons to flourish, they need an acid, moisture-retentive, well-drained site with a climate lacking in extremes of heat and cold. Almost anyone can grow some rhododendrons if they are prepared to put a little thought and consideration into the initial site. Not all dwarfs like the same conditions, so if space and choice of habitat permit, different types can be selected for different positions (see lists of recommendation; pp.247–52).

The majority of dwarfs become leggy and out of character if grown in too much shade, especially under ideal conditions in the best climates. In warmer, drier climates, north-facing banks are definitely more desirable than locations facing the midday and afternoon sun. The famous north peat walls in the RBG, Edinburgh are a good example of a suitable site. These face north with trees and larger rhododendrons to the south, and the soil is light and sandy.

Also in the RBG are comparatively new beds situated to the west side of the Rock Garden. These dwarfs are in full exposure and sun, the only shelter being the Wild Garden with its trees to the west. On the whole, these dwarfs, mostly belonging to the Lapponica and Saluenensia subsections, have done well but the hard winter of 1978–9 severely damaged many plants. Most recovered but it took almost two years before they looked happy again. One thing it accomplished was sorting out the hardiest clones which will be those most valuable for gardens.

Certain plants require special habitats such as species often epiphytic in the wild. Half-rotten tree stumps, moss-covered rocks (in wet areas) or specially prepared raised beds can be ideal. Others such as *R. forrestii* and many of its forms like to creep up or down steep banks, rocks or even north-facing moist walls. Evergreen azaleas enjoy more sun than any other rhododendrons and full sun in Scotland is essential for a regular show of flowers. In hotter climates they appreciate some shade. Semi-dwarf species of the Neriiflora and Taliensia subsections appreciate some shelter and shade and exceptionally good drainage. Really early flowerers (and growers) need very special siting. Not only is shade from early morning sun desirable but aspect is all important. For instance, a few yards often makes all the difference between constant frosting and frequent, successful flowering. The delay of a few days by facing away from the sun during the warmest part of the day can be a great help. Also, back-lying parts where the snow may linger long after it has melted on southerly banks, give excellent winter protection. In 1978–9, most of our main nursery was under snow from 1 January to mid-March and the winter damage even to the smallest plants was almost nil. Only those with their branches above the snow suffered. Similarly in 1982, snow saved us.

Some people are lucky enough to have or beg, borrow or steal a piece of rough woodland, even at some distance from their residence. We share a garden in Argyll, 135 miles away, which gets almost no maintenance other than what little scything, spraying and mowing we can manage between us. Part is a natural rock garden with peaty pockets. Many dwarfs were planted in these pockets where at first they flourished. Gradually some started to languish and die, either partially or completely. We found that the roots had completely filled their respective pockets and that only by mulching and/or lifting and replanting with some extra soil underneath, can their good health be helped to continue. Another lesson learnt in this heavy rainfall area (150–175cm [60–70in] a year) is to plant on mounds and not in hollows. This prevents the roots becoming too wet over long periods. In much drier east Perthshire (73cm [29in] a year rainfall) we never plant on mounds (see *Soil preparation*, p.49).

Another important point is the availability and quality of water. Many big British gardens have managed without any water laid on over most of their expanse and until the great drought of 1976 they got away with it. Of course, some people with small gardens (and larger), were not allowed to use water anyway. If one's garden is very dry, provided the dryness is due to soil structure and/or low rainfall, mulching or the preparation of deep peat beds can alleviate the need to water much in most seasons. If the dryness is due to tree roots, mulching is of little use unless one is prepared to pour on water. It is really better to plant items that tolerate dry, shady conditions rather than struggle with unhealthy plants that will never flourish. Dwarfs should rarely be planted near large trees anyway. Only where special protection is needed from ultra-hot sun, or from winter sun with frost, and for early flowers and young growth, should dwarfs be associated with large trees. Not only does too much shade make them grow out of character but overhanging branches keep the rain from reaching the soil. Very hard, dry ground can be difficult to re-wet and losses may occur after a long, dry spell.

Another site it may be better to avoid is one full of tree stumps where honey fungus (*Armillaria*) can be a killer. This disease normally attacks only dead wood but all too frequently affects live plants as well. It seems to be much worse in wet areas and when plants have been stressed due to poor drainage, wind-shake, bark-split or damage by an implement. Also broad-leaved trees may be more frequent hosts than conifers.

Do not plant the dwarfest selections as individuals into grass or other herbage. Well-prepared beds are a must where they can eventually grow into each other as they do in nature.

Fitting dwarf rhododendrons into an existing landscape may pose a problem for some people. I admit that where we grow many of our dwarfs at Glendoick, near walls and greenhouses and the house itself, hardly constitutes a natural looking setting for plants that grow wild on moorland, cliff and pasture. But what plants grow naturally on or near walls anyway unless these are supposed to represent cliffs? So long as the plants are happy and the overall effect is pleasing, is the lack of a 'natural' setting too vital? In small suburban plots, it is nearly impossible to get away from the view of 'unnatural' walls, hedges and fences anyway. Surely a closely mown lawn with neatly cut edges is just as man-made looking as anything made of brick or glass.

Shelter and shade

I mentioned under *Choice of site* that shade and shelter are not generally so essential for dwarfs as they are for the bigger species and more tender hybrids. My advice is, do not give dwarf rhododendrons too much shelter and especially shade unless they are necessary to serve some special function. This may mean some protection against the elements which may come as blasting cold east winds or hot dry winds (as experienced in parts of Australia for instance) winter sunshine and frost (a killer combination in N.E. North America) or endless days of scorching summer sun. Rhododendrons of all kinds appreciate moderation in everything (except perhaps rainfall as long as the drainage is adequate). Any excessive amounts of heat, cold, wind, sunshine, salt spray, atmospheric pollution and so on need to be regulated and the best way is by the careful use of a combination of shelter and shade. Common sense, you might say, but it is astonishing how many experienced gardeners may neglect this side of the well-being of their plants or put the cart before the horse and not establish shade and shelter *before* planting their rhododendrons.

Buildings, solid hedges or windbreaks and walls tend to deviate the wind or lift it, only to have it blow harder than ever in some supposedly sheltered corner. We have made a new bed by the corner of our house facing south-west, mainly for evergreen azaleas and dwarf Ericaceae like the creeping *Arctostaphylos* species and hybrids. I wondered why a daphne was blown flat and why the arctostaphylos always grew one way only until I happened to look at the bed during a south-west gale. I had moved the arctostaphylos branches to face the other way and now all were shifted back facing the same way as before by the ferocious gusts coming round the corner of the house. No other part of the garden seemed to have such strength in the wind at that time. Likewise areas near the walls of the walled garden suffer deviating winds. In Argyll, winds from almost any direction blow down the side of the straight edge of the next-door sitka spruce plantation and often swirl around. It is these swirling gusts that do the damage and may necessitate staking certain upright plants, which is always a nuisance.

Various artificial windbreaks are now available, some very strong and effective but the majority hardly attractive in a garden. Windbreaks of hedges or carefully placed shrubs which filter the wind rather than attempt to shut it out are much the best and most attractive forms of shelter in the long run. Do not plant trees and shrubs such as sitka spruce or certain large pines that soon become bare underneath. Anyway these are hardly suitable either for small gardens or to associate with dwarf rhododendrons. × *Cupressocyparis leylandii* in its various clones has become ubiquitous, over-produced and is not an entirely satisfactory shelter plant. It grows too densely, too large and is often unstable on its roots, partly due to being confined to containers too long. The Leylandii hedge around our main nursery was grown in the open ground and transplanted at 1m (3ft). In 20 years a few have blown down but many more would have if it had not been topped, an expensive and laborious task. At wider-than-usual planting distance, enough air blows through to avoid down draughts.

As mentioned in *Ecology*, dwarf rhododendrons are communal plants, growing in the wild like heather on our Scottish hills. In nature, there is often little or no shelter from larger shrubs and trees, only the topography to lessen or deviate the wind from certain directions. These plants have to rely on a sheltered hollow, rocks or their own neighbours to protect them from the ferocious blasts which often occur at high altitudes where they make their home. Dwarf rhododendrons should not be planted as isolated specimens. Follow nature and let them protect each other by planting in bold groups or to form a continuous undulating ground cover. I find they are always happiest when grown this way. With the dwarfest types at the outside gradually building up height to the middle of a bed, and the process repeated on the other side, it is possible to create a self-sheltering island community. Likewise, a one-sided bed, backing a wall, hedge or border of trees and shrubs can end with the highest growing rhododendrons at the back.

If shelter is essential, due to adverse weather conditions as mentioned earlier, care must be taken not to plant over-vigorous trees and shrubs too close to dwarf rhododendrons. Not only will too much shade soon be cast but greedy root systems rapidly compete with the rhododendrons, robbing them of nutrients and the moisture so necessary for their well-being.

In the coastal belt of the Pacific north-west of North America, the natural vegetation is usually dense conifer forest. Unless the forest has recently been cut over or been cleared and used for some time for farm land, the shade is usually far too dense for any rhododendrons. On a visit there during 1982, I was astonished how many knowledgeable gardeners attempt to grow all kinds of rhododendrons in a ridiculous amount of shade. Slight thinning is no use as the canopy soon closes in again as the trees grow. The result is leggy plants and little or no flower. This is usually second or third growth (from virgin) forest and must be very severely thinned, preferably *before* any planting has been done.

When considering what trees and shrubs to associate with the smaller leaved dwarf rhododendrons, try to avoid those with large leaves. My father and I made the fundamental mistake of planting magnolias between our groups. Actually the magnolias generally came first and the dwarfs were an afterthought, but they are not a happy combination. The large magnolia leaves have to be cleared after each leaf fall as they can smother most smaller dwarfs. Their shade is too dense to plant underneath. Magnolia root systems are extensive and should not be disturbed and, last but not least, they need constant pruning to stop them from spoiling the rhododendrons nearest to them. As I happen to be almost as fond of magnolias as I am of rhododendrons, the two just have to coexist in imperfect harmony.

The above error of planting leads one to consider what is the right combination of dwarf rhododendrons and their shade and shelter. Climate often dictates, but generally the smaller and finer the leaves that may fall amongst dwarfs, the better, both aesthetically and practically.

Conifers are usually good from the leaf fall angle but are inclined to make the soil over-dry within their root area and overhang. Slow-growing conifers are frequently planted with dwarf rhododendrons. Personally, I have not made this association and I know of others who violently object to this mixture. As they often grow together in nature about the tree-line where there are many dwarfed conifers, I see no real objection to this type of planting, either as low hedges or more informally.

Suitable plants for either shade or shelter or both are the smaller leaved cotoneasters, Triflorum-type rhododendrons, evergreen loniceras and euonymus, tree heaths, bamboos, small leaved hollies, box, eucryphias, enkianthus, and stuartias.

For shade only, evergreens may be needed in severe continental climates to keep off winter sun but for most of us, rowans (*Sorbus* sp.), smaller leaved cherries, maples, dogwoods and southern beeches (*Nothofagus*) are suitable examples. Widely spaced, high pruned oaks can be regarded as the best for open woodland conditions with their good leafmould-making leaves and deep root systems. Trees to avoid are those with greedy roots, large flabby leaves and those that create deep shade such as elm, sycamore, horse chestnut and beech. Birch unfortunately have greedy shallow roots while large conifers such as douglas fir dry out the ground and shed their branches all too readily.

Coastal conditions may cause rather different problems of shelter with frequent really ferocious winds and/or salt spray. Low shelter can be provided by *Phormium tenax* and *P. cookei*, now available in many colour forms, various lower senecios and olearias, sea buckthorn, *Rosa rugosa*, escallonias, fuchsias, and *Arbutus unedo*, *Eleagnus* varieties and *Rhododendron ponticum*. Higher shelter for the coast is *Pinus radiata*, *P. muricata*, *P. nigra*, *P. mugo*, sitka spruce, sycamore, cypresses, taller olearias, griselinia. Climates like those experienced in California, southeast Australia and New Zealand will enable many other shelter plants to be grown. Really dwarf *Ulex* sp., *Hebe* sp. *Cistus* sp., tree heaths and other low shrubs can be placed near to rhododendrons on the windward side.

Be careful to avoid solid windbreaks on the down side of a planting across a slope. This can check frost drainage. Frost flows like water down a hill and a solid belt acts like a dam. Damage from this cause is especially likely during early autumn or late spring frosts.

Hardiness and climate

Hardiness

The longer one lives, the more the subject of hardiness both intrigues and infuriates. We all say, if only we lived in a better climate such as . . . , how well we could grow . . . . A touch of jealousy creeps in when we visit gardens, areas or countries that can succeed with plants which we fail with. In fact, *everyone's* climate has its drawbacks and its compensations.

In Britain our weather is never predictable; if it were it would not be such a topic of conversation. No two seasons are ever alike. Maybe we never suffer the extremes found in continental climates. Maybe we have rain spread over the year. But most people living on large continents know when to expect their summers, autumns, winters and springs. I suppose we always have something of a spring and autumn but some years we certainly have no winter and/or summer. All too frequently our winter comes in April (as in 1981), May or even June while our summer may not come until October if at all. This ghastly uncertainty can affect plants in all sorts of ways, mostly unpleasant. Whenever unseasonable weather hits us as it does in one way or another almost every year, we find ourselves unprepared. In theory, we do not suffer really cold winters or prolonged droughts. When they do come, severe losses occur. To be fully prepared for all nature can throw at us at *all* times of the year, is, in most circumstances, virtually impossible and prohibitively expensive. So we just carry on, hoping for the best.

Droughts, spring frosts and other hazards *do* occur where rhododendrons are found wild and create havoc. G. Forrest reported dead rhododendrons for miles (from drought) and Kingdon Ward reported everything frosted. In nature, these supposed disasters are not necessarily as serious as they appear. These native species have been growing in the same areas for perhaps thousands of years and are capable of repairing damage caused by natural upsets and even man with his hacking and burning. The climate and soil suits them, otherwise they would not be growing there. They regenerate by sprouting from the root or a fresh generation grows from seed.

In gardens, our introduced plants have not had a chance to evolve to suit our conditions and only rarely are able to naturalize themselves to any extent. So many rhododendrons are not in tune with our climate and may start flowering and/or growing when the first hint of mild weather appears, even as early as January or February while others may go on growing into the winter. Even some of our hardier (winterwise) plants may grow out of season. In April 1981, we had rows of young plants (two–three years old) capable of surviving winter lows far below any ever recorded here, yet killed stone dead with the bark split from top to base even under the protection of plastic. We often have spring frosts which spoil early blooms following a mild winter but on this occasion the frost was so severe that every flower, or expanding growth bud (even right under the shelter of trees) was reduced to a black pulp while many plants were completely defoliated. Some have recovered by sprouting from the base, others have not. Some that recovered took two years to regain their former size.

I have gone into some details of the vagaries of our climate because it is this very uncertainness which makes the hardiness of certain plants so impossible to assess. Generally, the older a plant becomes the hardier it is. Growth tends to come later, wood becomes tougher and less easily split and the plant has more reserves of strengh to overcome extremes of weather. Surprisingly, some very small seedlings appear to have a sort of built in hardiness which they may lose a year or two later. But this only applies to mid-winter frost. Early frost before growth is ripened or late frost after growth has started can kill little seedlings of normally hardy species.

There is not room here to go into details of why plants are frosted and what actually happens inside a plant. I will, though, mention a few possible precautions which may be taken to minimize damage. The most obvious is to give some form of visible protection, be it live or artificial. The use of windbreaks and shade was covered in the previous section of this chapter. Live protection is always more satisfactory, although it may vary at different seasons of the year, especially with deciduous or herbaceous subjects. Temporary shelters such as frames, lath houses, polythene tunnel houses or cloches are a great help, especially to young plants (see Chapter 5, *Propagation*, *Growing on of young plants*). It is surprising how just a sheet of glass can make all the difference between severe damage and none at all. In future, as a lesson from the April 1981 frost, I intend to protect small rooted cuttings and seedlings more carefully, even if it means putting *on* glass or plastic lights in April-May.

Many of my more tender rhododendrons are planted on partially shaded walls and I often cover these from October to May with an old frame light or similar structure. Be careful to be sure the soil does not dry out and if there is danger of this happening, uncover for a while during mild, wet weather. In milder climates, this winter and spring protection is of course unnecessary.

Several high alpine and some not so high elevation dwarfs can greatly benefit by a cloche over them from September to May. In nature, a snow cover is more or less assured. In some funny way, a cloche seems to make a satisfactory alternative to a winter blanket of snow as well as protection from unseasonable frosts.

Overhead or side protection against winter sun in continental climates and spring sun in climates like that in Britain definitely does help minimize desiccated plants or flowers. Buildings, hedges, shrubs or trees can all be used with effect. While evergreens are likely to provide more protection than deciduous items, the latter in the form of large shrubs or trees do help in cases of slight frost.

Smudge pots, usually burning waste oil, are often used to keep frost off fruit plantations or nurseries, especially in the USA. Even the heat emitted from buildings in towns can raise the air temperature a degree or two. Other people use sprinklers during danger periods from spring frosts. Blossom or tender young shoots encased in ice are less likely to be damaged although sometimes the sheer weight of ice can cause breakages, even to whole trees or branches.

Bare soil gives off a more gradual amount of heat than soil insulated with a mulch, hence damage is more likely to occur on heavily mulched soil during radiation frost.

Damage from icy blasts as occurred in western USA in 1955 and 1972 can be reduced by good shelter from north and east.

Bark-split is covered at the end of Chapter 3. For some unknown reason, we appear to suffer from this complaint more than anywhere else I know of, both on young and older plants. This is certainly not due to any over-fertilizing as many of our plants subject to splitting never receive fertilizer while others that do are equally prone.

Climate

Britain
Maritime climate. Rainfall plentiful to barely adequate, falling intermittently throughout the year, greatest in the west, least in east and south.

Western coastal areas and islands. Mild winters with temperatures rarely below −10°C (15°F), summers cool, rarely above 27°C (80°F). Islands and coastal margins especially favourable if sheltered. Rainfall moderate to heavy 1–2.5m (40–100in). Little snow. Months of May–October inclusive usually frost free. Subject to severe winds, particularly in north, and danger from salt spray near coasts.

Southern England. Milder in west, more continental in Kent. Temperature rarely below −15°C (5°F) and may exceed 32°C (90°F). Rainfall 50–75cm (20–30in), often inadequate. Good for evergreen azaleas but too hot for some dwarfs to flourish.

Eastern England and Scotland. Moderate winters, minimum about −18°C (0°F) but can suffer cold easterly blasts in spring. Snow rarely prolonged. Rainfall often light and inadequate 50–75cm (20–30in). More suitable for lepidote dwarfs than the west where they may grow too vigorously. Frost-free spell usually late May to late September but often longer.

Central areas. The nearest to a continental climate. Winter frosts can be severe, especially in valleys among hills with temperatures liable to drop below −18°C (0°F); maximum temperatures to 30°C (85°F). Rainfall light to moderate, sometimes inadequate, snow sometimes heavy and prolonged. Only late June to late August reliably frost-free.

Europe

Western and southern Scandinavia. Some coastal influence, especially on coastal south Norway but all colder than most of Britain. Away from coasts, temperatures may drop to −30°C (−22°F). Rainfall usually adequate, higher on west coast. Much snow but not always reliable. Few species hardy in colder areas. Summers fairly cool. Growing season May–October.

North-west and north coastal Europe: Belgium to Germany. Winters similar to above minimums except near coasts. Moderate snow and rainfall, sometimes inadequate. Summers warmer, to 38°C (100°F). Growing season as above.

East Baltic. Very severe frost with very few species or hybrids hardy. Snow usually stable through winter. Minimum down to −42°C (−43°F).

Southern central Europe around Alps. Minimum temperature around −12°C (10°F). Few late frosts and little snow at lower levels. Valleys may be rather warm with dwarfs tricky and sometimes subject to root-rot. Rainfall heavy to moderate, usually adequate.

Southern Europe. Generally too dry and hot, and soil unsuitable.

North-west Spain, north Portugal, north-west France. Very little frost and moderate summer temperatures. Rainfall inclined to fall in winter with summers often dry. With a little care, suitable for many rhododendrons.

Australia

South-east. The mountain areas are good for many rhododendrons with little frost and only occasional light snow. Rain mostly in summer, 1.3–1.5m (50–60in). Hot winds can cause trouble. Mulching and watering desirable. Early bloomers best as heat may spoil those that open later. Low elevations rather hot. Higher altitude dwarfs rather difficult.

Tasmania. Good, mild climate and mostly adequate rainfall. Often good for rhododendrons.

New Zealand

North Island. Little frost. West moist, east dry. Low elevations rather hot. Hardly suitable for dwarfest rhododendrons.

South Island. Up to two months longer growing season than in Britain but inland subject to spring frosts. West wet, east dry. Often conditions are very good for rhododendrons with most of the genus being possible out of doors.

Africa

Evergreen azaleas good in Cape area of South Africa. Many parts of Africa with high elevations and rainfall could be good for the more tender kinds but with seasonable rainfall, watering will be needed at times.

North America

Most parts of North America are capable of growing at least a few rhododendrons successfully but in such a large continent, extremes are liable to be rather more noticeable than in Britain, New Zealand and for that matter, in their native S.E. Asia.

North-eastern coastal areas. Moderate rainfall over most of the year. Coastal areas such as eastern Long Island are favourable with a $-18°C$ ($0°F$) minimum but further north, temperatures can be much more severe where only the very hardiest rhododendrons will grow. Maximum about $32°C$ (low 90s $°F$).

North-eastern inland. Moderate rainfall. Liable to very severe winters down to $-34°C$ ($-30°F$) or lower where very few dwarfs will survive. Some modifying influence by the Great Lakes. Summers can be hot. Avoid winter sun.

South-eastern areas. Moderate to heavy rainfall. Climate and soil conditions tricky with cold blasts and often hot summers. Bad combination of heat and high humidity. Few alpine types are likely to survive for long. Diseases can be troublesome. Raised beds desirable.

Gulf region. Moderate rainfall throughout year. Moderate winters to $-15°C$ ($5°F$) but summers hot. Few dwarfs likely to succeed but many evergreen azaleas satisfactory. Raised beds desirable.

Southern coastal California. A few of the more tropical lepidotes may succeed, otherwise evergreen azaleas are the best bet. Little or no frost and summers not exceedingly hot. Low rainfall so much watering needed.

California inland. Two parts. Sacramento Valley, moderate frosts to $-8°C$ ($18°F$) but very hot summers to $45°C$ ($113°F$). Very few dwarfs possible. Little rain from June to October. Sierra Nevada foothills, colder winters but summers still hot and dry. Some dwarfs possible with care.

California north coastal. Very little frost. Immediate coast under fog influence, cooling summers. Good for rhododendrons from low elevations of S.E. Asia which can flourish when well irrigated. Many dwarfs outgrow themselves and die young.

North-west coastal areas. The nearest to ideal for most dwarfs in North America with moderate winter frosts, rarely below −12°C (10°F) but icy blasts as in 1955 and 1972 can cause severe damage. Summers warmer than Britain but rarely exceed 38°C (100°F). Rain mostly in winter so summer irrigation usually necessary. Rhododendrons very popular.

North-west inland. Greater extremes of cold and heat than on coast and much less rain. Therefore more shade and watering needed. Raised beds desirable.

South America

Southern Chile. Ample rainfall, mostly in winter. No extremes of cold or heat. Should be very suitable for lowland rhododendrons from S.E. Asia.

Argentina. Buenos Aires area. Rainfall all the year round but predominantly in summer which is hot. Heavier rain towards Chilean frontier. More tropical kinds and evergreen azaleas should succeed.

Asia

India. Himalayan foothills. All parts where rhododendrons grow wild should be suitable for a fair range except real alpine types. Rain mostly in summer with little or no frost.

South China area, Sri Lanka, Philippines, etc. Very suitable for all sub-tropical kinds as rhododendrons are wild throughout this region. Rain mostly in summer.

Japan. Lowland Japan has difficult conditions with hot summers including hot nights. Heat-resistant types necessary. Mountains and Hokkaido much more suitable for most dwarfs where many natural rhododendrons grow.

Rest of the world
Anywhere else where rhododendrons grow naturally is of course suitable for a good proportion of the genus, tender or otherwise. Many tropical and subtropical islands which have heavy rainfalls, especially if mountainous, may have eminently good locations for Malesians and the Maddenia subsection. For instance, sheltered parts of the Azores and the middle altitudes of Madeira should be ideal.

Plant associations

As mentioned previously, dwarf rhododendrons are primarily social plants and should therefore be planted in groups rather than as individuals. For grouping these together, all four seasons should be considered for overall effect. These are the flowering season, mostly from April to

June in Britain, the summer when young growth is being produced, autumn when many evergreen as well as deciduous kinds produce autumn colour, and winter when many evergreens change their foliage colour to various browns and purples. In addition, the best foliage plants are often beautiful all the year round except when their foliage is curled up due to frost or drought.

Personally, I do not object to combinations of bright-coloured pinks and reds as they do not really clash. With evergreen azaleas where the strongest colours are usually met with, so many bloom together that the overall effect can be rather over-powering. Bold masses of one or two colours are preferable to singles or small groups all in one bed or area, especially in larger gardens. There are many opinions as to colour combinations. Dwarfs do not generally contain the somewhat harsh colours of some of the evergreen azaleas, the preponderance being shades of purplish-blue, pink, white and pale yellow plus rather waxy flowered reds. Also, dwarfs tend to open over a longer period. Early varieties can flower during mild spells from January onwards—mostly purples, whites and pinks. In a good spring, we can have a fine show from mid-April to the end of May with a pretty balance of colour throughout. I have made little effort to harmonize or group colours other than dividing up groups of say yellow with pink or blue. Some people might like to have one group opening together with other groups, blooming earlier or later or both. I just mix all together (in groups where possible) to give the best overall show over as long a period as possible.

I have two hobby horses with regard to rhododendrons and their associations with other plants. There are two extremes of gardener (and planner), the one who always considers landscaping first with little thought to the welfare of the plants involved as to where they will grow best, and the pure collector and plantsman whose one and only aim is to have healthy plants and to hell with the layout. Some compromise should be made by both sides but to me, the desirability of really flourishing plants takes definite preference.

My second hobby horse is ground cover. In nature, rhododendrons have neither lower-growing plants as ground-cover under their branches nor do they have vigorous herbaceous plants growing up amongst their foliage. The larger species invariably associate with mosses of various kinds plus perhaps ferns and they form such a tight canopy that little else can grow underneath. Most dwarfs and semi-dwarfs grow above the tree-line or in open glades or on rocks and cliffs. A few bigger species may have to compete with shrubs and trees. Bamboos can be a different matter and are often capable of defeating all other plants that dare get in their way. Rhododendrons have shallow root systems with much of their nourishment being obtained from the rotting leaf litter trapped by or lying over their roots. Ground-cover not only competes with the rhododendron roots for nourishment but makes it nearly impossible to add a mulch of, say, leafmould, pulverized bark or wood chips. Also it competes for moisture and a thick mat takes all of any light showers that might fall during a dry spell.

Even groups of primulas and meconopsis, often closely associated with rhododendrons in the wild, can, if planted too near to dwarfs, cause rotting of foliage, especially when rotting leaves cover shoots in the autumn and winter.

I am not advocating gardens of pure rhododendrons. Groups of primulas, meconopsis, lilies, incarvilleas and so on make ideal companions if planted in patches *between* groups of rhododendrons. If you must grow individual rhododendrons as specimens, make sure the ground is *really* well prepared (see Chapter 3, *Soil preparation*), apply a periodic mulch and if possible, ensure the plant is clothed with leaves and shoots right to the ground. Rhododendrons do not like sun on their roots and there is no better way of keeping roots shaded than from a plant's own canopy.

The best plants to grow with rhododendrons are other members of the family Ericaceae with the one big exception, heathers. Rhododendrons and heathers mixed together are a disaster. Wherever I have seen this combination, the rhododendrons could not compete with their quicker growing, greedy, moisture-consuming relations and looked sick and miserable. By all means grow both—heathers are excellent plants—but never mix them.

Under shelter and shade (p.33) I suggest certain trees and shrubs to grow with dwarf rhododendrons with the accent on those with small leaves which do not smother the smaller-leaved rhododendrons underneath or near by. Some of the larger-growing deciduous ericaceous shrubs are ideal for breaking up or forming a background to groups of dwarfs. Not only do they look well together but they appreciate the same soil conditions such as prepared peat beds or the raised beds needed in some localities. These include species of *Enkianthus, Menziesia, Tripetaleia, Lyonia, Gaylussicia, Vaccinium* and *Oxydendron arboreum*, plus some of the smaller deciduous azaleas. All these create a contrast of foliage and most have glorious autumn colours.

As mentioned under shelter, the association of dwarf conifers and dwarf rhododendrons or evergreen azaleas is not universally appraised. In fact some detest it. Personally, I prefer dwarf conifers and heathers together or the former used as a background. A subtle mixture of colours of both conifers and small, autumn-colouring (and spring-flowering) shrubs at the back with dwarf rhododendrons or azaleas at the front can be very suitable for a small garden. I say rhododendrons *or* azaleas (evergreen) deliberately as yet again, these do not go well together. Plant groups of each near each other but not all mixed up. Evergreen azaleas appreciate hotter, drier situations than most dwarf rhododendrons and are capable of growing in hot climates totally unsuitable for the latter. Dwarf rhododendrons make a perfect foreground to an open stretch of woodland full of larger rhododendrons and/or azaleas. A fine example of this is the north peat walls backed by the wild garden in the RBG, Edinburgh.

Beds of gentians along path sides make an excellent edging for dwarfs as do creeping cassiopes and gaultherias. Do not plant dwarfs with the more vigorous gaultherias like *G. shallon, Pernettya mucronata* or their hybrid × *Gaulnettya* Wisleyensis. These are too invasive and vigorous and will soon run about through the rhododendrons. *Pernettya mucronata* varieties are better planted on their own in full sun to produce abundant crops of berries.

Varieties that bloom together in one part of any country do not necessarily do this everywhere. For instance, I read that *R. poukhanense* and *keiskei* bloom together at Winterthur (Delaware, USA) while in Scotland, *keiskei* would be over long before *poukhanense* opens (except for *keiskei* 'Yaku Fairy').

Rhododendrons for special purposes

Pot plants

Many keen rock gardeners, especially if space is very limited, grow some or even all their dwarf rhododendrons in containers. These are ideal for showing. The hardier varieties do not even need a greenhouse or frame and can be plunged outside. Here, they will need more careful and frequent watering than in the open garden but are basically trouble free and easy. The beauty of having them in a container is of course that they can be placed under cover if spring frosts threaten. Also, plants lifted for shows and then replanted do receive a check and may violently object (even fatally) to this treatment.

Many different composts are used in these containers such as various combinations of loam, grit, sand, peat, pulverized bark, oak and/or beach leafmould and conifer needles. Slow-release fertilizers suit all but the most nitrogen-sensitive kinds. In a season when no re-potting is done, two top dressings a season or two weekly liquid feeds are beneficial. With the exception of the most vigorous, re-potting every second year is often enough. Do not over-pot as this can lead to sour, stale soil and an unhealthy plant. Do not re-pot after July.

More tender dwarfs and semi-dwarfs including those too tender for growing outside do of course need slightly different treatment in containers. Many need to be kept just frost-free, and I mean 'just'. If the temperatures are held too high in winter, they may abort all their flower buds. Likewise, if they become too dry, buds may die. Any container which becomes really dry is hard to re-wet thoroughly from above so should be soaked in a bucket or trough. Even more damaging is over-wet soil for any length of time. Normally (in nature) epiphytic species and their hybrids need a particularly free draining medium.

All rhododendrons with yellow and pink flowers are prone to lose some depth of colour when opened indoors, even for the last day or two of opening. Leaving them outside during the day and bringing them in at night should get over this problem.

Plastic or earthenware containers are suitable but make sure in the case of plastic that drainage is really adequate. Some people make extra holes, even up the sides of the pot. Pans are generally better than pots as a dwarf plant in a tall pot looks ridiculous.

Most people want scent from indoor rhododendrons when not for show purposes. Unfortunately, the majority of suitable kinds are either scented and straggly or not scented and compact. The scented hybrids may be trained around stakes and wires and these are fine when in full flower but otherwise look hideous. I feel there is much work needed here for the hybridizer to produce dwarf growers with scented flowers, opening early in the season. Some at least could and should be well-coloured. My previous efforts at this have failed but some promising seed has set this year. Few of the present scented species or hybrids can really be classed as dwarfs. *R. edgeworthii* with its superb foliage, flowers and scent is one of the best.

The indoor types of evergreen azaleas are so well known I will not go into details here. Sadly, few survive to live and flower another year after purchase and yet keeping them going for many years is not really difficult. Several friends with no greenhouse succeed admirably. These plants cannot put up with the dry heat of full blast central heating for long. If kept in a relatively cool, well-windowed room over winter until the flowers open, returned to a cool room until June when they are plunged outside in a partially shaded position until September and kept well-watered, they should live and flower. Re-potting into a good peaty compost every two to three years into a slightly larger pot each time and feeding, especially when in growth, should ensure a lasting pleasure year after year with little trouble. Any of the many pot-plant feeds available should be suitable. Do, though, remove all the dead flowers with a pair of scissors just after the flowers have all gone over. A slightly heated greenhouse from the time the flowers are over to June is of course preferable to a cool room.

I know a few people who have extensive collections of tender rhododendrons planted in surprisingly small greenhouses. Given a mixture of local soil (if light and acid), peat and/or leafmould and conifer needles, the majority should do well. The dwarfer types will appreciate raised beds made up in one or two tiers with peat blocks as in the Malesian rhododendron/tropical ericaceous house in the RBG, Edinburgh. Again, the great majority will survive so long as the temperature is kept just above freezing and the soil remains open and well drained. Never tread on the beds.

Showing

Showing dwarfs does not present quite so many problems as many of the larger varieties do although the same basic principles do of course still apply. Container grown plants give few difficulties except to mention that over-forcing leads to poor, out of character blooms. Likewise with cut trusses or sprays. It is rarely worth bringing in cut branches more than two days prior to a show unless frost is imminent. These are best cut early in the morning and placed as soon as possible into deep water in a cool, sunless place under cover. Is hammering or splitting the stem really much help? I doubt it. I prefer the latter if either. Try to select upright shoots, usually found on the top of a bush. Hanging side branches are hard to show successfully. Only pick pieces where there are still a few buds to open. Certain dwarfs, notably Lapponicums, shed very quickly so perfect timing is critical with these and handling with extreme care. A thorough clean up of dead flowers, seed capsules and bad foliage is always worthwhile.

Various proprietary brands of additives for use in water with cut flowers are now available and these really do work. An alternative is to use one's own mixture of some form of carbonated water and citric acid.

These reduce the growth of bacteria which clog up the stems and reduce water intake. Aspirin in the water or hot water at 43°C (110°F) also help to revive wilting trusses.

Many are the methods of transportation. Endeavour to avoid water-loss and crushing. If transporting by car, place trusses in bottles held in position by sectioned wine boxes. Do not allow tall branches to bash against each other. Alternatively, wrap ends of stems in moss, place in polythene bags and tie tightly on to stems. Place carefully into flower boxes using sticks inserted firmly across and use tissue paper to keep them from moving about.

Good staging wins prizes. See that trusses or sprays face the right way and fix stems in position in vases *full* of water with newspaper topped with moss. Ensure that exhibits are properly labelled and placed in the correct classes. Surely a well-managed and staged show full of first class exhibits is worth every effort.

Much the same applies for exhibits for awards. For cut material, select the appropriate size of vase and arrange carefully. Showing is fun and no one, however small a collection they have, should be frightened of competing with those with large gardens. A few shoots cut off even quite small plants does them no harm.

Foliage

The beautiful foliage of many rhododendrons, large and small, is not appreciated nearly as much as it should be. So many people when thinking of rhododendrons, never get further than *ponticum* and 'Pink Pearl' and may possibly stretch to 'Nobleanum' and 'Praecox'. All these have dowdy foliage at all times of the year. Visitors to rhododendron gardens see them in April–May and so often completely ignore the superb young foliage during the months of June to September.

What could be better for their foliage than fine specimens of *R. lepidostylum, mekongense* Viridescens or Rubroluteum Groups or *campanulatum* ssp. *aeruginosum* with their gorgeous glaucous young leaves, *tsariense* with its brown indumentum on the leaf upper surface or *williamsianum* and *moupinense* with their brown and bronzy or chocolate coloured young growth? Many other species and hybrids are a joy to see in young foliage and produce a great variety and contrast in colour and form. Other species have curious narrow leaves which give almost a porcupine effect. The best examples are *roxieanum* Oreonastes Group and *makinoi*. Still others have beautiful woolly indumentum on the leaf underside. Usually this starts pale white to fawn and turns to dark fawn to rufous-brown with age. Good examples are *haematodes, tsariense, beanianum, yakushimanum* and *recurvoides*. Several turn interesting shades during the winter such as *saluenense* ssp. *chameunum, dauricum* dwarf and hybrids like 'P.J.M'.

Autumn colour may not normally be associated with dwarf rhododendrons. The new introduction of dwarf *mucronulatum* is especially fine with combinations of scarlet and gold, *trichocladum* may turn a nice yellow while many evergreen azaleas shed a portion of their leaves, those with *kaempferi* blood often turning lovely shades of red or purple.

Aromatic foliage is found in the majority of dwarf lepidotes. A gentle rub or brush against the leaves may be all that is needed to give off the scent. The Pogonanthums (Anthopogons) are the best and often the strongest with *kongboense* perhaps prince of all. Members of the Glauca subsection are strong too. Not all are necessarily pleasant to everyone's nose!

The bark of dwarfs does not of course have the impact that the larger species may have and bare stems usually mean badly grown plants. None the less, a few dwarfs do have attractive bark such as *glaucophyllum*, *brachyanthum*, *moupinense* and some of the smaller members of the Maddenia subsection.

Photography

When a party visits our garden during a good season for bloom, it is amazing how much film is expended. Camera and film manufacturers should pay homage to the genus Rhododendron without which many could be out of business!

Before attempting to photograph rhododendrons, ask the question: 'What do I want the results for?' Slides are best for lectures and black-and-white prints for many articles. Personally, I do not think that cheap coloured prints, such as are commonly taken of flowers, are worth looking at. These require very expensive equipment for first-rate results. While a good average camera (single lens reflex) will give good enough pictures, the best processing, printing plus colour reproduction for books is decidedly expensive. Japan leads the world in this, as in the production of relatively cheap first-rate cameras.

My advice is to use only one camera at a time. When in China recently, I took two, only to lose both in Hong Kong. At the time, I could only afford to buy one replacement but I had intended to use the two cameras for coloured slides and black and white prints respectively. Maybe I would have cursed having the wrong one in the wrong place.

Cameras are becoming more and more fool-proof. Yet most experienced photographers prefer to be able to use manual adjustments to aperture, speed and focus when they wish. When in China, I had no accessories; those that I took were lost too. My results with a new untried camera were on the whole passable and only on occasions did I miss having a telephoto or wide-angle lense or close-up rings. These accessories can be heavy to carry and can take time to set up even resulting in the best shots being lost. So consider these points before spending a lot of money.

The chief difficulty of photography using a built-in exposure meter is to decide what part of the picture should be given the correct exposure. So many shots are spoilt by important parts of the foreground or background being either over- or under-exposed. Some expensive cameras, lenses and filters do help to compensate these errors but for most of us, much film gets wasted and potentially good shots spoilt. When plenty of film is available, the best answer is to take two or more different exposures and the chances are that one will turn out right. Get to know your camera and film. Nothing can compensate for this.

Light-coloured flowers are always troublesome, particularly in sunlight. It is often impossible to get a correct exposure for both flowers and foliage. Usually the foliage has to suffer as over-exposed flowers lack definition and may turn out as a blur. When taking single trusses, try to get the background out of focus. With overcast conditions, the meter often lies, resulting in under-exposure. Allow at least one extra stop. Many experienced flower photographers never take their photographs in bright sunlight.

Good, well-composed photographs taken with correctly adjusted cameras, take more time and effort than random holiday snaps. On trips to the wild or on garden tours, time is often short and precious. For shots good enough for reproduction, a quickly adjusted light telescopic tripod is a must, especially under poor light conditions. But while a good photographic record is most desirable, some people go nuts and end up seeing virtually nothing through their own eyes, looking only through the camera's lens. Garden visitors of this type can become distinctly unpopular, often treading on valuable plants. My advice is to take a camera and take some trouble and care but do not become an accessory and clicking addict!

3 *Planting and maintenance*

Soil preparation

The better (for rhododendrons) the soil is before planting, the happier the rhododendrons will be. This principle applies to the soil preparation for any plant; but while most rhododendrons will tolerate many types of soil, few soils are good enough without at least some preparation.

Above all, rhododendrons like a light soil, acid, rich in organic matter, well-drained yet moisture-retentive. Many soils have some of these requisites while occasionally they have none. A few lucky people have the lot. All these fortunates need do is to dig a hole, shove in a rhododendron, lightly firm it up and perhaps water it in, then sit back and wait for it to grow.

Obviously, the further from ideal the soil is, the more thought and work will have to be put into it to give good results. There is a strong interaction between soil and climate. The better the climate for rhododendrons, the less perfect the soil has to be. At one extreme, only drainage may be needed. Many parts of the west of Scotland fall into this category. At the other extreme, raised beds are a must, made above the existing soil. In some cases, a proportion of the native soil can be mixed in but in others, for instance on lime or certain clays, completely fresh material has to be brought in and placed on top of the natural soil.

Peat is best drained by open ditches as it is difficult to drain satisfactorily with draining pipes below ground. Clay is really tricky stuff. For most of the year it is like glue or concrete, with perhaps only a handful of days when it can be handled properly. If water lies for long on the surface of any site, especially on a new building site, the soil will almost certainly have been compacted with heavy machinery. Beware of made up soil. Our garden centre was made on top of rubbish and spoil off the making of the Perth-Dundee dual-carriageway. We were delighted at the time to have this done for nothing but have in many ways regretted it ever since. Although drained, the compacted rubbish on top made an almost impervious layer which is a devil after heavy rain and overhead watering. Other than starting again, there is not a great deal that can be done about this sort of problem. Many new gardens suffer a similar fate, especially if the ground is naturally clay.

Silt can be troublesome too, and hard to stop filling and so blocking any drains. Medium loams are easier to deal with and are ideal for the majority of plants. For rhododendrons, plenty of peat, leafmould and/or conifer needles and suchlike substances have to be added and well mixed in for the best results. Sandy soils, especially so-called greensand and

Bagshot sand, are in many ways the best for rhododendrons. Although they often dry out easily, wonderful root systems develop and once the plants are thoroughly established and organic matter has been added or had a chance to accumulate, they generally flourish with little or no attention.

Here at Glendoick we have a great depth of sandy silt on the flat 'carse' ground and medium to heavyish loam, often very shallow, on the south-facing hill slopes. The former grows good plants and splendid root systems but dries out horribly easily and is subject to very late spring frosts. Plenty of organic matter, two feeds a year and a good mulch help enormously. The loam over rock likewise suffers from drying out. The addition of organic matter is of course again greatly beneficial but up to now mulching has just allowed elm roots to do their worst underneath in robbing the soil of all its moisture and goodness. I say up to now because our multitude of elms are now all dead and nearly all are felled and cleared away. Apart from letting in much more wind and causing endless work and disturbance, we now have a chance to redevelop much of the garden and establish new areas. Drainage is rarely a problem and hopefully, with no elms, we shall be able to grow better plants more easily. I have mentioned our own experiences because many others must have had similar problems.

With friends, we have, for our sins, another garden (very wild) in Argyll, west Scotland. Here, with double the rainfall of Glendoick and a rather impervious rock, drainage presents various problems. The rock often has saucers above it and if plants are placed too deeply into these pockets, they will grow for a while and then suddenly collapse and die, presumably of waterlogging which rots the roots. Surface water can also cause problems and if not quickly removed by drains and ditches, can also cause root rotting and death. We now plant everything on mounds with (so far) much improved results. This is something we would never dream of doing at Glendoick, in fact we often plant in saucers (see *Planting*, p.56). These comparisons between our two gardens show how conditions can vary and how each needs its own special treatment.

On a small scale, intensive cultivation is possible. All tree stumps and dead or unwanted shrubs should be dug out, roots and all. Not only are these a nuisance if left in but they can act as a source of honey fungus (see p.67). Except on very light soils, do not attempt to prepare or plant during wet weather. It just puddles the ground and spoils the soil structure. If there is a hard pan, break this as much as feasible. As mentioned earlier, beds are always preferable to single holes, especially for the smaller dwarfs and evergreen azaleas. These should first be dug or tilled, as deeply as possible. Then fork in organic matter, preferably peat, oak and/or beech leafmould, old sawdust, conifer needles or other similar materials provided they are reasonably acid. Which is used depends on local availability. Mix in thoroughly. With heavy soils, gypsum (calcium sulphate) at 454g (1 lb) per 10sq m (100sq ft) can be added to flocculate the soil, sprinkled on the surface, not dug in. All sorts of loosening materials can and should be incorporated such as sand, gravel, wood or bark chips, old ashes plus organic matter. I like to add as much as 50 per cent organic matter to existing soil where there was little or none before.

Conifer needles are especially good for loosening and aerating the soil. In western North America really coarse sawdust is used with the addition of nitrogen (for applications see p.52).

For larger dwarfs in woodland, beds may be out of the question. The size of hole to be dug really depends on the nature of the soil. If it is at all heavy or compacted, it is desirable to dig an area large enough to accommodate the roots for many years or even to their expected ultimate spread. If only a small hole is prepared, the roots will soon hit inhospitable soil; the plant will languish, even if well mulched on top. Try to avoid a sudden change from a well-prepared mixture to a wall of hard, uninviting terrain. The addition of a relatively slow-acting fertilizer can be beneficial although with rhododendrons, it is always better to err on the cautious side when applying these substances (see p.57).

Rhododendrons can be a success in areas with moderately alkaline soil provided special beds are prepared. The use of plenty of acid peat on preparation and an annual mulch of peat plus a sprinkling of sulphur (flowers of sulphur or ferrous sulphate) can reduce the pH (see pp.58–9) and give satisfactory conditions for most rhododendrons. Some though, are much more tolerant of alkalinity than others (see lists of recommendations, ·p.248). Alternatively, individual holes may be successful if the following formula, described by Judith Berrisford in *Rhododendrons and Azaleas*, is followed. She lived with a pH of 7.5 and made holes lined with flowers of sulphur, filled with acid peat and rotted bracken (alternatives should do) which were also mixed with the surrounding soil at the edge of the holes. The plants, once in situ, were mulched with conifer needles and chopped bracken to a depth of 15cm (6in) twice a year. Many lepidote dwarfs grew well having been treated this way. She also applied magnesium sulphate (Epsom salts) at two tablespoons to nine litres (two gallons) of water over the root area of each plant three to four times a year during the growing season. Manganese sulphate was used as a leaf spray, 28g (1oz) to nine litres (two gallons) applied in the evening on a dull day.

Pure chalk is really out for rhododendrons. If you live on chalk and must have rhododendrons, grow them in containers and water with rainwater or move house!

At Glasneven Botanic Garden, Dublin, they dig out beds 38cm (15in) deep and cover the bottom 10–15cm (4–6in) with clinker or other rough material. Then they add a layer of really coarse lumps of peat and loam, after which they fill the beds with half peat and half local loam which in this case should not be broken too fine. The beds are not raised (as it is a dry area and the local water is alkaline) to avoid drying out rapidly. Only rhododendrons showing some degree of lime tolerance have grown well for a number of years under these conditions (see lists of recommendations, p.248).

Raised beds are a necessity where soil conditions and/or disease problems dictate that rhododendrons will otherwise fail. This includes much of the S.E. USA. Half-raised beds are those where a proportion of the local soil, usually clay, is incorporated into the prepared planting mixture. This method should work in many areas. Failing this, totally fresh ingredients have to be brought in and set above the level of the clay. Many different ingredients are satisfactory, depending on local availability. Acid leafmould and/or acid peat, conifer needles, ground or shredded bark, bark chips, wood chips, coarse sawdust, forest litter, cones, rotten wood, crushed corn cobs or similar materials are all suitable although some of these may be too coarse to use individually. Beware of very dry peat, especially if used on its own. Thoroughly soak *before* use. Coarse sawdust is much used in some areas, especially western North America. Adequate nitrogen must be added. Many people like to apply several light applications of this fertiliser rather than one heavy one. To give a guide, add 5.4kg (12 lb) of ammonium sulphate per 100sq m (1,000sq ft) for each 2.5cm (1in) of sawdust. (In western North America they frequently incorporate this sawdust into the existing soil with satisfactory results but in the east they have problems with too much potassium and not enough magnesium. This can be corrected.) One word of caution, British sawdust is too fine and should not be used unless thoroughly rotted.

A good way of disposing of litter such as paper and organic kitchen refuse is to put it under beds and holes. Avoid fat and grease. Trample it down thoroughly and if the soil is poor, add a little nitrogen. The paper helps as a reserve of moisture, and plants do well for many years. Cover rubbish with a good layer of ordinary soil mixture (as above).

Raised beds should be surrounded with peat blocks, wooden slabs or stones. Watering, of course, is needed more often with raised beds. A check should be kept on the pH, especially if using alkaline water and it may be necessary to add sulphur to counteract this.

Beds of pure peat or peat plus a little grit and other organic matter with a little mixed fertilizer such as Hortus No. 1 (Hortus Rhododendron Fertilizer) (see *Feeding and Mulching* p.58) are ideal for the dwarfest and more tricky rhododendrons and fellow Ericaceae, even where the natural soil is suitable. These beds can be built up in terraces using layers of similar-sized peat blocks as retaining walls. While any blocks will do, some types of peat break down more rapidly than others. Very dry blocks may distort the wall if packed in tightly once they soak up moisture. These beds can be made on flat or steep ground but should preferably face or slope north and be partially shaded by trees and/or shrubs. The blocks should be gently sloped inwards and do not build the blocks more than three or four high. Pack in loose peat or peat mixture below and behind the blocks. Well-laid blocks make neat and attractive beds. These beds dry out rapidly during their first season so if the weather is at all dry, frequent watering may be needed. The crevices between the blocks are ideal sites for many small and rare plants. It will be found necessary to replace individual blocks over the years especially if attacked by birds or frequently walked on. Moss may cover the surface, especially under shady conditions. This is not undesirable provided the coarse moss *Polytrichium* does not become established. This can grow several inches deep and can choke out many low-growing plants if not kept under control. Shaded blocks also act as ideal seed beds for ericaceous plants. While many interesting and desirable seedlings may appear, some can become rather an embarrassment in time.

These peat beds may be too acid for some dwarf rhododendrons and their relatives. It may be necessary to add dolomitic limestone (ground) or other de-acidifying substances such as Cornish Calcified Grit to bring up the pH level. The Pogonanthum (Anthopogons) section do not like conditions too acid.

At the Rhododendron Species Foundation, Tacoma, Washington State, USA, bark, old mushroom compost and imported top soil are mixed into natural soil and, after planting, are given a 5cm (2in) bark mulch. Bigger plants tend to be mounded to avoid the roots contacting pure local soil. Plants take about two years to settle down and may look chlorotic for a while. I can vouch that the established plants look excellent.

Selection of plants

Many are the ways of building a collection of dwarf rhododendrons. If a large collection is envisaged, first ask yourself whether you are a purist and only want a collection of authentic species, perhaps even all from known wild sources. Few, other than botanic gardens and some private arboreta are likely to go as far as this. Or is your one idea to fill up a sizeable area as quickly and cheaply as possible with everything and anything you can get hold of, including chance seedlings? Many people start the latter way only to have regrets later. Even when considerable knowledge is gained, some cannot perhaps be bothered or do not have the energy, physique or determination to root out comparative rubbish that has grown for a number of years. A happy medium is usually the solution, starting with a selection of the best species and hybrids from a reputable source, be it a nursery, garden centre or friend. Few garden centres or friends will be able to produce a really wide variety of dwarfs so it is the specialized nurseryman (see p.254) to whom one must turn. Some send by mail order while others need to be visited. Mail order firms like to send out in autumn or early spring to avoid the growing season, while at garden centres, plants are available all the year round and may be selected in flower. Established containerized or container-grown plants obtained during the growing season require more care in establishing than those planted in autumn or early spring (see p.55).

Growing one's own seedlings is always fun. Avoid open pollinated seed where possible. Although many dwarfs do not hybridize as readily as larger rhododendrons do in gardens, insects still manage to cross-pollinate the majority. While interesting seedlings can appear, most will turn out inferior. Either hand-pollinate your own plants (or deliberately hybridize them) or acquire seed from a reputable source, the best being the seed exchange of the American Rhododendron Society. Seed from wild sources is now a little more readily obtainable than a few years ago (hopefully still by publication) and may be received from the ARS or even by subscribing to an expedition. Alternatively, grow plants from cuttings, layers or even graft one's own (see p.225 for guidance on propagation).

The best forms of rhododendron species, especially those with awards if difficult to propagate, may be more expensive than non-selected species. For all but the purest, seedlings from hand-pollinated or wild source seed are generally perfectly good. Plants with awards are naturally of a high standard although clones better than award forms can be found in certain cases. When awards are mentioned in catalogues for the larger dwarfs or even some hybrids without specifying a clone, it may not be the actual award forms that are given.

Specimen plants are a mixed blessing. Not only are they expensive but they can be much more difficult to establish and keep healthy than small plants, particularly if the soil they were grown in is alien to that of their new home. Still, for those wanting an instant garden and not afraid of the price, they are worth it. For those species (and a few hybrids) that take some years to start flowering, specimens can save a long wait.

Planting

Planting carelessly or otherwise can make or break a plant almost as much as soil-preparation or the lack of it. Remember, most rhododendrons are extremely long-lived barring accidents. Certain dwarfs are even capable of outliving a person. Really fine old specimens which have had their soil well-prepared, been carefully planted, well-fed, mulched, watered and generally cared for, give endless pleasure and are admired and envied by all visitors.

Planting involves two main operations, spacing and actual planting. For those with extra (muscular!) help and those with plenty of lasting energy themselves, rhododendrons may be planted thickly and then spaced out after a few years. As previously mentioned, dwarfs are social plants and are far more likely to flourish cheek by jowl than as isolated little dots in an otherwise bare expanse of soil. As my own plants are often hard-pruned for cuttings, I attempt to keep many of them from growing into each other by removing shoots between bushes. If each variety is planted in groups, little harm may come from leaving beds over-crowded, provided vigorous ones are not swamping out those making slower growth. Remember, rhododendrons can be moved at any time in their lives and provided their roots are kept more or less intact, they receive no check whatsoever. I do not really advocate inter-planting dwarfs with temporary shrubs, perennials or alpines. Sooner or later the rhododendrons will become enveloped by something far too vigorous to be a suitable neighbour and may even disappear out of sight only to be found dead or emaciated in the winter when the herbaceous foliage had died down. My advice is not to inter-plant but to strive to move every second or third plant after five to ten years. Of course one may not be there to do the job and ultimately some of the plants may be ruined. So many people seem to move house regularly these days and with dwarf rhododendrons, one can lift the lot and take them to one's new home. They are not difficult to move five to ten years after planting and any reasonably able body should have no difficulties. For initial or subsequent replanting, 30–90cm (1–3ft) are the distances to plant apart, depending on vigour.

Many people who should know better fail to plant rhododendrons at the correct depth. No one should go wrong because there is only one correct way and that is just to cover the root ball and no more. Usually the old planting depth is easily seen and should be repeated. Occasionally, it may have previously been too deep or even too shallow with half the roots sticking out. If so, correct this. A few more rules. Never mound soil up the stem after planting (this can be a killer as can deep planting). Never trample in too firmly, especially in heavy and wet soils, as the roots like it loose and well-aerated. Gentle firming and then a good watering is much superior. On windy sites, staking may be required. Try not to damage the root ball by pushing the stake through it.

Under some circumstances, it pays to break up the root ball before planting and some people even wash most of the soil off. If the roots are pot-bound in an old container or the soil on the ball is alien to one's own, the plant may establish much better and quicker by removing most of the soil and teasing out the ball. A Danish customer told us that when he first bought plants from us, they were slow to establish. In those days when carriage was relatively cheap, we left much of the soil on the roots. When carriage became so expensive, we shook off much more soil. Our Danish friend told us that from then on they all grew much better. Another friend who grows much in troughs and raised beds containing a large proportion of gravel, bare-roots everything, including Ericaceae, before planting. Establishment is invariably superior.

When to plant is always debatable. In Britain, most people are happy to plant open ground rhododendrons in the autumn, mostly in October–November. A few insist on spring planting, rather to the annoyance of nurserymen. Winter rains and snow help to bed plants in and they are much more likely to withstand droughts during their first season. Only on exceptionally cold, windy sites would I advise planting in spring to save leaves, unaccustomed to the exposure, from being blown off during the winter. But if the site is that bad, they may have little chance of success anyway. Another drawback of spring planting is that the nursery may be situated at a warmer site than the customer. This leads to more advanced growth and flowers than a plant that over-wintered in the customer's garden, leading to more likelihood of spring frost damage. Also soil is usually in a better state for planting in the autumn; in spring it is invariably too wet, too dry or too cold.

The late Captain Collingwood Ingram of Japanese cherry fame, who died in 1981 aged over 100, had many astute ideas. One is to cover late-planted dwarfs with an inverted flowerpot for a week or more to help establish them in hot weather. Another idea is to cover the roots of certain dwarfs with stones to keep them cool in summer and also to peg down branches to get them to develop roots and form a thicket. I recently saw his *R. ludlowii*, perhaps the only plant now remaining grown from wild seed. This had been repeatedly layered and rooted with the use of stones and is a flourishing specimen, unusual for this rare and difficult species.

In damp, mild climates, tree trunks, rocks and stumps (stumps may be used in dry climates too) can be used for certain kinds, largely species which are naturally epiphytic such as *edgeworthii*, *megeratum* and *valentinianum*. I tried several of these in Argyll on mossy forks or holes in trees, mossy rocks and tree stumps. Even with 150cm (60in) rainfall, long,

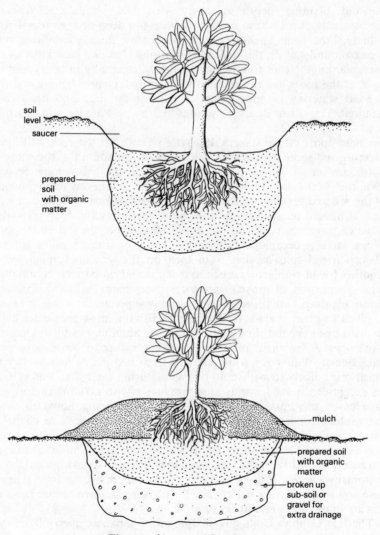

soil
level
saucer

prepared
soil
with organic
matter

mulch

prepared soil
with organic
matter

broken up
sub-soil or
gravel for
extra drainage

The use of 'saucers' for planting

dry spells can occur. Three *megeratum* placed on a leaning mossy oak
only lived a year or so and died in a drought. On the other hand, several
valentinianum on rocks have flourished and one *kawakamii* has survived
too. The moss should be carefully peeled back over quite an area and
slabs of peat or natural bedded leafmould placed on the now bare rock
or trunk. Make a little hole for the plant, firm up by hand and replace
the moss, adding more if necessary. It is desirable to keep the moss in
position with stones or string. Old tree stumps can be used in drier
localities, especially if there is a nice bed of semi-rotted wood in the
middle which conserves moisture well. I have grown *forrestii* in this way.
Hollowed-out logs, both vertical or horizontal are equally good. A friend

in Washington State, USA, has many treasures planted in these logs such as *proteoides, pumilum* and *megeratum.*

Mention was made under *Choice of site* (p.31) and *Soil preparation* (p.49) of the way we plant most of our rhododendrons in Argyll on mounds due to heavy rainfall and inadequate drainage. The depth at which the plant is placed should be such that the base of the root is only just below the top of normal soil level. As the plant grows, more leaf-mould will be placed around and over this mound, thus encouraging the roots to expand at and above normal soil level and not below where the drainage may at times be faulty. In the USA, I saw a public park with heavy soil where all the plants were mounded and covered with a deep mulch of bark. In contrast, on dry, well-drained sites, plants may be placed in the base of 'saucers'. This was done on a large scale in the Valley Gardens, Windsor Park when the species collection was moved from Tower Court. I do likewise on our steepest and dryest banks at Glendoick. These saucers help collect natural leaf fall, retain a mulch and enable a hose to be used for filling the saucer with water in dry weather. Saucers may also be used for grafted plants to encourage rooting above the union.

If initially planted in a deep saucer, this can gradually be filled up with organic matter and/or a soil mixture until the union is covered. The depth of the saucer depends on the height of the union above soil level.

Feeding and mulching

Feeding

Most rhododendrons grow naturally in soil poor in mineral plant foods. In fact, they are extraordinarily efficient at extracting elements from soils where only minute quantities exist. This gives us a clue to the correct approach in cultivation.

The majority of large rhododendron collections in Britain are never given any fertilizer at all or certainly not after they are planted out in their final position. This may come as a surprise to those in America who pile on fertilizer year after year, reckoning their plants will succumb if not fertilized regularly. The above may make you think I am anti-fertilizer. In fact, I am not, as long as it is used in moderation. As a nurseryman, I want to make a good saleable plant in two–three years and the careful use of a little fertilizer as a supplement to other cultural requirements does help speed up growth, improve foliage and in some cases, encourage the production of flower buds. But remember, fertilizer never compensates for any other lack of care and attention over soil and water.

Many dwarfs, especially those of the Neriiflora and Taliensia sub-sections, have a very low tolerance of nitrogen and can all too easily be scorched or even killed by doses which may suit others perfectly. Many dwarfs may lose their character and grow straggly if treated too well.

Many bigger rhododendrons, especially hardy hybrids and deciduous azalea hybrids, will respond luxuriantly to fairly heavy applications of mixed fertilizer and with these it is quite easy to work out recommended amounts. With dwarfs, we are dealing with such a diverse group of plants that to give a precise dose for all is impossible. In Britain, if you live in a relatively dry area with good soil and plenty of good leafmould, there may be no reason to use fertilizer at all. On the other hand, if plants seem slow to get away, as may be the case where the soil is poor in nutrients due to excessive rainfall or leaching from heavy watering, fertilizer should be beneficial. Specially balanced proprietary rhododendron fertilizers are now generally available, but do go easy, even on doses recommended for dwarfs.

Rhododendrons do of course need some of all the major elements—nitrogen (N), phosphorus (P), potassium (K), calcium (Ca), sulphur (S), and magnesium (Mg); and the minor (trace) elements—manganese (Mn), boron (B), copper (Cu), zinc (Zn), iron (Fe), and molybdenum (Mo). Under some circumstances, it is necessary to apply these individually but take expert advice on this, particularly with the trace elements which are needed only in minute quantities by the plants and excessive doses can create unfortunate complications.

N should be applied in ammonium, not nitrate form. This promotes good growth and is likely to help plants survive drought. It is available in compound fertilizers (safest) as ammonium sulphate, or in organic fertilizers like cotton seedmeal, hoof and horn and so on.

P is available as superphosphate or in compounds. It is beneficial for flower-bud production and ripening wood combined with K. Bonemeal is a good slow-acting source of P.

K is not needed in any quantity by rhododendrons.

S is usually available naturally in sufficient quantities but may be added to acidify soil (see p.51).

Mg is needed for chlorophyll formation and probably helps stop excessive intake of Ca and K.

Ca, contrary to the so called lime-hating theory, is certainly needed but only in very small quantities. Certain very acid sands or peats are short of Ca which is best added in the forms of dolomite (magnesium limestone) or gypsum (calcium sulphate). The latter, scattered on the surface, we find a very effective cure for chlorosis in our Argyll garden.

Trace elements are generally available as fritted trace elements or are included in many compound fertilizers or can be added in the form of seaweed extracts.

Do not apply N after July as it is important to harden off growth before autumn frosts. P, or P and K, may be applied late for bud set and ripening growth.

I like to add fertilizer in spring (April–May here) and give a light dressing to all young plants except to those most sensitive to N (Neriiflora and Taliensia subsections especially). I use an organic-based compound called Hortus GOC No. 1, now available in small packs as Hortus Rhododendron Fertilizer, analysis 12N 6P 6K. Another popular mixture is 5N 10P 10K. K is unnecessarily high in both. If growth is sluggish, I give another application in June-July, especially on those plants that make a secondary growth. An average application would be 30g (1oz) per sq m.

The term pH is a measure of soil acidity and alkalinity. pH 7 is neutral, 6 slightly acid and 8 slightly alkaline. Five is ten times more acid than 6 and 4 a hundred times more acid than 6 and so on. An ideal pH for rhododendrons is around 5 to 5.5, but 4 and 6 are generally suitable for most. Over 6 can be treated with extra acid peat, sulphur or ferrous sulphate to reduce the pH, while under 4.5 may need magnesium limestone or even ordinary lime. We found wild rhododendrons in China growing on pHs between 3.7 and 8.1 but these seem to be extreme cases and were populated with respectively highly acid- and alkaline-tolerant species. It might be a valuable exercise for future expeditions to the wilds to take whole sets of soil samples among different species. The results could be valuable for selecting and hybridizing for different soils in cultivation.

Repeated applications of acidifying organic substances *can* lead to over-acid conditions for certain species and their hybrids. These plants are evidently intolerant of either ultra-low acidity (say below pH 4.5 or 5) and/or of soil with especially low levels of calcium and/or magnesium. Intravenal chlorosis and poor growth often accompanied by scorching are the symptoms. This is easily cured by adding dolomite (magnesium limestone), Cornish Calcified Seaweed and in some cases gypsum (calcium sulphate). The amount to apply is about 28g (1oz) of gypsum or 14g ($\frac{1}{2}$oz) of dolomite per square metre (sq yd). Make sure this is evenly distributed over the area. (May need to be repeated if soil is very acid.)

It is now apparent that high pH soils with a high Mg content may be better tolerated than those with very high Ca only. As mentioned earlier, rhododendrons are particularly efficient at absorbing Ca and if too much is present, they take up an excessive amount and poison themselves.

Some methods have already been suggested to counteract alkalinity (see p.51 and above). Aluminium sulphate is occasionally recommended. While it reduces the pH, it is definitely harmful to rhododendrons. People on alkaline soils sometimes tell us of the benefits of Chelates (sequestrines). On normally acid soils like ours, they appear to be of little or no use in curing chlorosis. Not only have they failed to improve the leaf colour but they have burnt and even killed certain sensitive plants. New formulations may have removed this danger.

I have seen several people use a top dressing of farmyard manure. If loose and strawy, I feel it does little good as it can all but disappear in dry weather in spring or summer. Hen manure is usually too rich in ammonia and/or lime and may cause scorching. Well-made cattle manure dug into the ground is sure to do good to larger more vigorous rhododendrons but I would not advise it for dwarfs as an alternative to the substances already mentioned.

Mulching

The purpose of mulching with the various organic substances available depends on what part of the world one lives in and on various local conditions. Mulching can be used for any one or a combination of the following:

1 to retain moisture;
2 to modify surface soil temperatures;
3 to check erosion;

4 to control weeds;

5 to provide organic matter and nutrients.

Few gardens or even individual plants can fail to benefit from mulches in one form or another. I like to give all young individual plants and as many beds as possible an annual dressing of leafmould, preferably well made beech and/or oak. Any leaves taken off alkaline soil are likely to be alkaline themselves, as are leaves like apple, horse-chestnut, elm and sycamore off moderately acid ground. Anyway, their leafmould is of poor consistency, soggy when half-made and powdery when well-rotted. Oak and beech leaves should either be old stuff dug out of hollows or should be stacked for two years to rot. Turning helps speed up the process. If used fresh, they need holding down with a good covering of twigs, wood chips or such like material. Leafmould acts both as a feed and as a moisture-retainer.

Any mulch applied deep enough helps to retain moisture but beware of those that form an impervious layer which will just run off the rain or irrigation water. This includes fine sawdust, fine peat and grass cuttings. The last named should *never* be used fresh as a mulch. I know of a case where a part-time handyman dumped his grass cuttings in heaps on an azalea bed. Fresh cuttings heat when decomposing, and the following year all the azaleas whose roots were under the cuttings were completely dead.

Mulches depend much on local availability. A few lucky people may have a good supply of leafmould or conifer needles. The latter are good in any form. Sweepings off the floor of a conifer forest contain needles of various ages plus a mixture of small twigs and moss. This makes an ideal loose material which lets through air and water and yet keeps the ground moist, discourages weeds, maintains an even soil temperature and, when rotted, feeds the rhododendrons—in other words it does everything a good mulch should do without the necessity of adding the extra fertilizer needed in the case of sawdust. A layer of 7.6–10cm (3–4in) should last for three–four years but this depth would not be suitable for really low growers.

The most usually available mulches these days are wood wastes in the form of pulverized or chipped bark, wood chips and sawdust. In America, these are used in huge quantities. They can also be misused. I once saw a garden with mostly dead or dying plants in all directions, knee-deep in sawdust. Elsewhere in western North America, I have seen large collections with sawdust where a proportion of the plants were healthy while others looked horribly chlorotic. I feel that even the best coarse douglas fir sawdust can be over-used if it is relied on entirely for organic matter, both in the soil and as a mulch. Used this way, the correct application of the necessary nitrogen becomes very difficult, especially for those dwarfs which are intolerant of more than a little nitrogen (see *Soil preparation*, p.52).

Bark as chips or more often pulverized or shredded is readily available in retail packs and by the load. This is usually pre-composted (heated) and therefore should be free of any harmful effects from tannin, weeds, pests and diseases or the need for extra nitrogen. Unfortunately some barks tend to err on the alkaline side but do not seem to give off enough calcium to harm rhododendrons when used as a mulch. With wood and bark chips, the breakdown is very slow. These make an excellent, long-term mulch but do little to feed the plants directly until decay is well-advanced. Chippers are now made in various sizes. Small ones which will chop up leaves, twigs etc. and are hand-operated, are relatively inexpensive and suitable for small private gardens. Large heavy-duty machines, usually run off a tractor power take-off, are much more expensive and are capable of chipping quite sizeable thicknesses of wood. Chips can also be hopper-fed into wood boilers, so for those with large houses and gardens, a chipper can be worthwhile and used to full advantage. Also, chips apparently have no noxious effects if worked into the soil. In Britain, wood chips *could* encourage honey fungus, especially in ground already affected but little is known about this to date.

Peat, especially fine dusty peat is not the best of mulches. Not only does water have difficulty in penetrating dry peat but the roots are encouraged upwards too rapidly.

I like to use twigs around individual plants which would only include the largest dwarfs. These twigs help to trap falling and blowing leaves and eventually rot down and assist in feeding the plants. Paraquat weed-killer can be used to spray amongst the twigs although where hand weeding is necessary (to pull brambles and nettles for instance) these twigs can be a nuisance.

Non-organic mulches are rather ugly in a garden if not completely hidden. Some gardeners use black polythene and cover it with old sawdust or pulverized bark. Other mulches are aluminium foil and mats made with material such as roofing felt. The latter are good for establishing many shrubs and trees but are unsuitable for newly planted rhododendrons as the soil immediately under the mat dries out and remains dry. Polythene should have little holes or slits made to let the water through. Black polythene can be very good for smothering and preventing the growth of weeds.

Maintenance of rhododendrons

Rhododendrons are associated with abundant moisture in their native habitat, with frequent rain during their growing season and dripping mist. How is it that most can put up with the fickle British climate, which can occasionally produce a month or more of dry, hot weather during the growing season, and can also tolerate extraordinarily hot conditions in places like Australia and California? The fact is most rhododendrons are much tougher climate wise than we realize. My trip to Yunnan, S.W. China in spring 1981 gave me a few surprises and one was to see how some rhododendrons put up with adverse conditions far beyond what most are likely to meet in our gardens. Admittedly, we were not there during the monsoon period which does usually bring a thoroughly wet spell. Burning, hacking, grazing and often bone dry, practically mineral soil was the lot of some species and I suspect that at least a few of these have had to put up with this treatment for many a year.

I am not suggesting that we abuse our cultivated rhododendrons, only that a great many are not so fragile and particular as is generally thought. Losses in southern England in the great drought of 1976 were severe but I was delighted to see how many seemingly near dead specimens in gardens like Borde Hill, Sussex are making a good comeback.

I have come to believe that the only time when it is really vital for a rhododendron to have abundant moisture is when it is actually growing. Life would be easy if they all grew only at the same time of year. They do not, and far from it. Given an early spring and no frost, growth here at Glendoick may start in early April or even late March. A dry spell in late summer followed by plentiful rain in September, and growth will start up again, some with first, others with secondary growth and this late growth is horribly vulnerable to early frosts. If we plant early and late growers all mixed up together and the spring and summer is dry, we should water for several months to get good early growth on all our plants. Few people in Britain attempt to do this and yet, somehow, most plants survive. In climates that can *rely* on a really dry summer, it is necessary to install really efficient watering systems laid throughout the garden with none of that awful hauling about of hoses. Properly used, good early growth can be almost guaranteed, barring frosts, with a good watering system as plants need never reach the droughted stage which checks their growth.

Where hoses and sprinklers have to be dragged around, it is hard to water sufficiently during really dry, hot weather, even with plenty of water available. The time sprinklers are left on depends partly on what is being watered and partly on the type of sprinkler. Small plants on bare ground require much less water to soak in thoroughly than do old-established plants, especially in woodland where there are tree roots. Likewise, heavy mulches like that of bark or wood chips require a large amount of water to penetrate the mulch, let alone soak the ground underneath. A really good soaking is much more desirable than just a superficial wetting. The latter may dry out again in under a day and never reach the dry roots.

There are now many types of sprinklers on the market. Most wet a circular area, which means overlapping, and frequently parts get more or less missed out. We have largely changed from a variety of sprinklers that cover circular and rectangular areas to pulsators. The diameter these cover can be altered simply and many have breaks enabling one to do an arc as well as a full circle. The wider the circle covered, the longer it takes to water an area properly. A small area of bare ground may be soaked in three hours but a large area of woodland can take eight hours or more which means it can be left on overnight. We are in the lucky position of having our own water supply but we did actually empty our pond on the hill during the autumn of 1982. We have now installed a small reservoir and pump for part of the nursery. We may be considered lucky when so many people are restricted over using hoses and have to pay water rates. In fact, most of our system is old and is very expensive to maintain.

Once watering has been started, it must be continued until the drought breaks or the plants will suffer more than if not watered at all. American growers often water right on into the autumn, many people saying that turgid plants overwinter better than wilting ones. A customer told us that following the drought of summer 1983, he had an excellent set of flower buds while his neighbours had few. He managed to water continuously while they gave their plants little or no water. Poor growth due to drought or other causes does not generally lead to an abundance of flower.

Water is obviously necessary for newly planted areas and is desirable for plants suffering severe distress from drought, but as a guide, it is better to stop after September. Of course, in the case of nurseries, it may be essential to soak open ground stock before lifting.

I have never seen watering in sunshine with sprinklers do any harm. Trickle irrigation can be used in some places although it may be hard to get an even spread of water. Do not use water softeners. The sodium used is poisonous to plants. Alkaline water can be better than no water. Little harm may be done as long as the pH does not rise drastically due to calcium.

The use of deep mulches can minimize the use of water. In Vancouver, in the University of British Columbia Asian garden, they try to avoid watering as much as possible as they reckon constant watering spoils the well-being of the plants (and the soil) once established. By using 12.5cm (5in) of leaves from the Vancouver corporation as a mulch, they produce splendid growth in their 1.4m (55in) rainfall which does occur mostly during the winter. In 1981, they managed to avoid all artificial watering. Growth of dwarfs there can even be too vigorous, resulting in out-of-character plants.

Deadheading

There is no doubt that regular deadheading does lead to better growth and improved flowering. As most dwarf lepidotes flower freely every year regardless, the majority of these can be ignored. Also many dwarf hybrids are infertile and so set no seed. It is the big species, not covered in this book, that respond most to deadheading as soon as the flowers have finished. The larger dwarfs, such as members of the Neriiflora and Taliensia subsections, do definitely benefit from the prompt removal of their seed capsules. Another group of plants easily dealt with are those with long pedicels which hold the flowers (and capsules) clear of the foliage. These include R. *calostrotum, campylogynum, hanceanum, keleticum, lowndesii, ludlowii* and *pumilum*. Most of these lack vigour and set an abundance of fat, energy-sapping capsules if given the chance. I go over most of these if I can every year with a pair of scissors and do both stock plants and those for sale. It does not take long.

With larger growers, it is quicker to use finger and thumb, nipping or snapping out the entire truss, being careful to avoid taking or breaking leaves, shoots and young growth buds.

Pruning

If grown in an open, fairly sunny site, dwarfs rarely if ever need to be pruned, either to shape them or keep them in bounds. All have natural habits of their own, be it a mound, prostrate carpet, erect or umbrella shape. It is only when plants become drawn up by neighbours or too much shade that they become leggy. Most dwarfs, particularly lepidotes, will break into a mass of young shoots from the base if moved and then cut back. It is usually better to cut back in stages rather than being too severe in one go. Many, notably Lapponicums and their hybrids and evergreen azaleas may start dying back when old and are frequently covered with lichen. These will often refurbish themselves if cut back but should be helped along with a good soil and mulch. All too commonly, dwarfs are seen with their roots half-exposed and poor, sickly growth. This is usually due to constant removal of weeds leading to loss of soil, hence the bare roots. These, if worth saving, should be replanted at the correct level into freshly made up beds and pruned as above.

All pruning of live wood should be done preferably in early spring. After flowering, autumn or winter are second-best, summer or early autumn worst. Vigorous young shoots made late in the growing season are vulnerable to early or hard frosts and this is one of the reasons for not cutting back too hard all at once which may encourage this soft growth and result in death if frosted.

A few dwarfs naturally produce stout, sappy 'water sprout' shoots. If they spoil the shape of a bush, they can be removed.

Most rhododendrons sooner or later start to develop dead wood, usually in the form of suppressed shoots under the canopy of leaves. Their removal should be tackled every year or two. Always cut close to but not into the trunk or up to the nearest live shoot. Dead wooding helps to keep plants healthy by letting in light and air and giving space for fresh young growth to emerge. This can be done at any time. Snags are a sign of bad pruning.

The best tools for pruning are a combination of a narrow pruning saw, loppers and secateurs.

Weeding and weedkilling

I rather enjoy weeding for a while although I do find constant kneeling and stretching severe on the rheumatics. The end product of weeding is a nice clean bed. If the bed contains well-grown plants that one is proud of, there is pleasure to be had admiring the fruits of one's labour.

Whenever it is necessary to walk, kneel or otherwise go near rhododendrons, it should be remembered that soil compaction is anathema to them. Therefore, easy access by way of paths, stepping stones or rocks should be made to all parts of a dwarf rhododendron garden. I like to do most of my pruning when the ground is frozen solid and the weeding when it is dry, but of course this is not always possible. I always instruct my staff to avoid walking on beds and woe betide any visitor who is caught trampling between plants, even to look at a label or take a photograph! On light, sandy soils, the damage caused by over-compacting is not likely to be as serious.

I do not normally advocate hoeing amongst rhododendrons, especially dwarfs. The roots are so near the surface, that however shallowly one hoes, valuable surface roots are sure to be damaged. In summer 1981, we had with us a Dutch student for a few months, son of a well-known Boskoop rhododendron nurseryman. He told us that in their flat ground intersected with sluggish canals, they have gone back to the hoe to a large extent. The canals, which they rely on for water for irrigation, are becoming so polluted with pesticides that in dry weather (as in 1976 when it was so badly needed), they are unable to use water from them. So weedkillers are at least partially banned. They use a type of hoe that just scuffs the surface sufficiently to kill small weed seedlings. Perhaps this hoe could be adapted for general use.

As mentioned earlier, rhododendrons do not like competition with their shallow root systems so the ground should be kept as clean as possible. We still have not managed to reach a routine with weedkillers that keeps our nursery clean through the year and far too much hand weeding still has to be done. Certain species of rhododendron, their forms and hybrids, are susceptible to certain weedkillers and twice we have landed in trouble with different substances affecting different related groups. I hope to try other herbicides shortly but the following is a short list of well-tried ones in descending order of usefulness. Read all instructions very carefully and only spray among one's best plants oneself.

Cleensweep, Gramoxone, or Weedol (paraquat)
Very useful for burning off top growth of weeds between plants and is quickly broken down in the soil. Can be applied up to rhododendron stems but should not touch green wood or foliage on which it makes black spots. Cleavers, ground ivy and nettles rather resistant. Apply two–three times a year. Encourages moss.

Ramrod (Propachlor)
One of the safest to use among plants in its granular form but only keeps clean ground free of weeds for about six weeks. Must be applied to damp, clean ground and must be reapplied before seedlings start to appear. Ronstar (oxadiazon) may be an improvement on Ramrod but tests are needed before passing it as relatively safe. Nine–sixteen week control, best as granules.

Prefix (chlorthiamid) and Casoron G (dichlobenil)
Very similar. These should be applied as granules during winter and they act through the roots of herbaceous plants. Should be safe to use on established plants but use with caution. Some shrubs and deciduous azaleas susceptible.

Hormone weedkillers such as MCPA, 24D, and 245T
Should never be applied amongst rhododendrons while they are in active growth as the young leaves can be severely distorted. Drift or fumes can even cause damage several yards away. I like to cut over established perennial weeds in May-June and then spray them in August-September when most rhododendron growth is hardened off and the weeds have regrown. 245T is very effective on nettles but a very dry summer restricts regrowth and renders spraying less effective.

Sodium chlorate
This old favourite, now made less of a fire hazard, is still good for cleaning dirty ground before planting. Heavy applications are the most effective but do not attempt to plant anything for at least six months. May seep down the back of walls etc. so beware!

Roundup or Tumbleweed (glyphosate)
Has a similar effect to sodium chlorate in that it kills everything but planting may be carried out ten weeks after application. Is rather expensive and do not let it touch any valuable plants. Must be sprayed on to plenty of green foliage to be successful.

Asulox (asulam)
One of the few weedkillers capable of killing docks and bracken. Must be applied when the foliage of both is near maturity. Repeated applications are often necessary.

Stump killing is always difficult. 245T at 0.568 litres (1 pint) 50 per cent in 18 litres (4 gallons) diesel oil is quite effective. It can either be sprayed on or painted on to newly cut regrowth stumps, or fresh regrowth. The fairly new Krenite (fosamine ammonium) applied in autumn kills buds so that no growth appears in the spring. It only works on deciduous subjects. One problem is that it needs at least 24 hours of dry weather after application.

Diseases

In the past few years, diseases of rhododendrons have come more to peoples' notice, partly due to the stricter EEC regulations. It is now much more difficult to bring live plants into Britain. If an import permit is granted, a growing season quarantine may be insisted upon. Having seen diseases that we do not at present have here on rhododendrons and their allies both in the wild and in cultivation abroad, I feel these restrictions are necessary although they are annoying. Likewise, other countries may not have all the diseases encountered in Britain.

The more removed from perfect the conditions for rhododendrons are in one's garden, the more likely they are to suffer from diseases. The combination of excessive heat and humidity is the worst. In these circumstances, special precautions may include the use of raised beds (see p.51-2) and regular fungicide applications. Even these do not always lead to success, especially with plants from very different climates such as those from the Pacific N.W. taken to the S.E. United States.

Britain is usually fairly cool and when it is hot, it is not usually humid, so serious outbreaks are rare. None the less, recent research and perhaps more thorough observations have brought to light diseases which we hitherto ignored or which are new and spreading.

Root rot (*Phytophthora wilt*)

Favoured by conditions of abundant moisture and high temperatures, probably involving any of three species of *Phytophthora*. When temperatures and humidity are high, this disease always leads to death. It attacks young roots and gradually kills the whole root system. Leaves turn a dull yellowish-green followed by permanent wilting.

This disease has spread recently, partly due to the great increase in container growing. The roots in containers reach a higher temperature than they would in the ground and moisture is hard to control. Many other plants such as heathers and conifers are susceptible. Rhododendrons can be infected and yet not show symptoms in cool, well-drained soils but these 'carriers' may show browning of the root tips.

Control
Avoid poor drainage and over-watering in high temperatures. A very low pH may help. May be encouraged by overdoses of weedkiller such as Casoron G or eelworms. Some degree of control may be obtained by the use of heavily chlorinated water. A certain percentage of pulverized conifer bark incorporated into the container composts also helps control. Many fungicides are available such as Dynone (Prothiocarb) and Aaterra (Etridiazole), the former as a drench, the latter in composts. Nina and Aliette (both May & Baker) are claimed to be able to kill the pathogen completely. Others are Dexon, Fongarid (Furalaxyl), Terrazole, Subdue and Fubol (Metaloxyl) (the last two both Ciba-Geigy). Control eelworm with Nemagen or Nemafos (Thionazin) at high soil temperatures, over 18°C (65°F) if possible, giving a thorough drench.

Honey fungus (*Armillaria species*)

Can be very troublesome in wooded areas of Britain, especially where rainfall is heavy. The combination of tree stumps and damage from waterlogging, drought, windshake or a blow from a scythe, spade or mowing machine can enable this normally saprophytic fungus to enter a live plant. The commonest pathogenic species is not *A. mellea* as was previously thought but other species of *Armillaria*; *A. mellea* is most commonly a secondary fungus.

Symptoms are sudden collapse and death (either the whole plant at once or branch by branch) especially during the growing season. Early symptoms sometimes appear as unhealthy drooping, chlorotic or shedding foliage. Tell-tale fructifications may be seen on or near stumps in late autumn—honey-coloured smallish toadstools in clusters. The fungus spreads by brown or black 'bootlaces' called rhizomorphs. Plants in really good condition are unlikely to be attacked, as experiments with container-grown plants have shown. Wood chip or sawdust mulches *may* encourage the disease although I have no proof of this. Five species of *Armillaria* occur in Britain to which native conifers are largely resistant. Exotic conifers are often attacked, especially Sitka spruce, particularly when planted on old broad-leaved woodland. Apparently honey fungus is rarely pathogenic in the coniferous areas of W. North America.

Control
Clear all stumps and piles of dead wood where possible. I always dig out any dead or unwanted rhododendron roots. In small areas, renewing or

sterilizing the soil may be worth doing. Burying a vertical wall of thick gauge polythene may succeed in isolated groups or individual plants. The phenolic compounds Armillotox or Bray's Emulsion are worth trying on plants showing first indications of attack. There is some indication that coniferous stumps are not as bad a source of infection as are those of broad-leaved trees.

Rusts

These appear as orange powdery patches (pustules) on the leaf undersides but may initially only be noticeable as interveinal brown patches or spots. The fungus flourishes and spreads most rapidly under warm and humid conditions. Young growth is particularly prone to infection which, for example, may even spread on cuttings being rooted under polythene sheeting.

A wide range of both lepidote and elepidote rhododendrons are known to be susceptible and some hybrids are more susceptible than the parent species. Different strains or species of rust are involved which do not always attack the same hosts. For instance, the rust that attacks many dwarf lepidotes is not the same that is bad on *cinnabarinum* and its hybrids in S.W. England.

Control
Research is now being carried on in the RBG, Edinburgh, to discover which rhododendrons are susceptible, how the rust spreads and its status on the alternative hosts, species of *Picea* (spruce). Worst-affected plants should be burned or at least all diseased foliage removed and the rest treated with a systemic fungicide at regular intervals during the growing season, in order to achieve effective control. Any plants showing rust are better isolated from other rhododendrons where possible. It should be feasible to eradicate this disease completely using a combined programme of hygiene with removal of infected leaves and spraying with e.g. Plantvax (Oxycarbonate) and/or Bayleton (Triadimefon).

Powdery mildew

Several different powdery mildews are known to affect rhododendrons. One has recently become widespread in the south of England and as far north as north Wales.* In bad cases, plants can be defoliated. Symptoms are first seen when a very faint whitish mildew develops in patches, usually on the under surface of leaves during the growing season. The patches become discoloured and the corresponding upper surfaces develop yellow to purplish-brown areas. This powdery mildew also occurs in Australia but so far not in New Zealand.

R. cinnabarinum and its hybrids are particularly susceptible, also plants with Fortunea and Campylocarpa subsections blood in them. A few semi-dwarfs are susceptible such as 'Seta' and 'Tessa'. These have *moupinense* in common. Other hybrids have also been affected. Hybrids seem more susceptible than species.

* Rain after the 1984 drought brought a rampant attack of powdery mildew on hybrids and species, worst under the drips of trees. Now confirmed in W. Scotland.

Control

Sheltered gardens are the most likely to be affected and also the moister parts of Britain, although a hot, dry summer may favour its development. It probably over-winters on leaves. It is extremely important to try to halt the spread of this disease and we are endeavouring not to introduce it from the south into Scotland. Affected plants are not allowed to be exported. A spraying programme using fungicides such as Bayleton (Triadimefon) or Karathane (Dinocap) should give adequate control. Other possibilities are Fungiflor and Nimrod, the former as a preventative, the latter as a cure.

Other powdery mildews

These can affect rhododendrons and related plants under glass such as members of the Vireya section. There are probably two different mildews involved here.

Another affects deciduous azaleas in North America. Apparently these are all different species or strains of mildew which are not likely to spread from, say, indoors to outdoors or from azaleas to rhododendrons. Control as above.

Petal blight

(*Ovulinia azaleae*) and other organisms including *Botrytis cineria* (grey mould)

An unsightly disease in which flowers become brown-spotted, then collapse. The collapsed flowers stick on to leaves and branches. Often attacks evergreen azaleas but others such as members of the Maddenia subsection can be affected. Worst in damp, muggy weather and under glass. Especially severe in parts of E. USA.

Control

Avoid overhead watering during flowering. Heavy mulches limit the development of spores. Spray mulches or flowers and foliage over the flowering period with Benlate or similar fungicide or use a fungicide smoke under glass. Repeated applications may be needed.

Galls (*Exobasidium*)

Worst on evergreen azaleas and on *ferrugineum* and its hybrids. Can be a serious complaint if the infection is heavy. Green, pink or red swellings develop on leaves or shoots or even flowers and turn white when sporing.

Control

Hand pick, following where necessary by spraying monthly during the growing season with Zineb, Ferbam or Benlate.

Botrytis (*Greymould*)

See under Propagation p.244.

Bud-blast

Rarely a problem these days. Buds are killed and turn black with spore laden bristles. Mainly *caucasicum* and *ponticum* and their hybrids are affected. Leaves and shoots may be affected in damp areas.

Control
Hand pick and burn the buds. It might also be worthwhile to spray with gamma-HCH against the leaf hopper which spreads the disease and against the fungus with a sulphur-based or other fungicide.

Few other diseases are serious enough to warrant control measures in Britain. Warmer climates than that of Britain may suffer from these other diseases to an extent where spraying may be necessary. Leaf spot, Cylindrocladum wilt and blight, crown gall, stem and tip blight can all cause problems, especially in the warmer parts of the USA. Enquire locally for further details. In Britain, leaf spot is usually due to too much moisture at roots and/or too much shade. It is caused by many different fungi.

Lichen

Not really a disease, it is often seen and asked about. Frequent on old plants making poor growth. Can be very unsightly but is perfectly natural in unpolluted places and does no harm to plants in itself.

Control
Can be rubbed off small plants. Encourage vigorous growth by pruning, adding fertilizer and a mulch (see p.64). An algicide can be sprayed on, such as Algifen or Alginex.

Liverwort and mosses

These can choke young or prostrate plants by forming a tight mat on the soil surface, both indoors and out. Prevention is always better than killing established mats.

Control
Various algicides may be applied such as Alginex or Algifen. The fungicide Thiram can control both liverwort and moss. Ferrous sulphate is quite effective but beware of it burning young foliage. The herbicides Tenoran (chloroxuron) and Ronstar (oxadiazon) are good against liverwort but always wash or knock off (granules) plant foliage.

Pests

We are remarkably free of pests that damage rhododendrons in Britain and those that do are rarely serious enough to warrant routine control measures. In parts of North America they can be a much more serious problem. Pests can be divided into two groups, vertebrates and invertebrates. In the country, vertebrates tend to be the most damaging. Deer, rabbits, hares and even mice may attack plants and birds may destroy early blooms and pull out small plants. In North America chip-munks and ground squirrels can be troublesome. Dogs (as opposed to bitches) and even humans (also males!) can urinate on one's best plants and even kill them. I have even had plants broken by cats.

Roe deer (and other deer) are a real problem and are becoming more plentiful over large areas of Britain. Deer are also a problem in parts of North America, Europe and New Zealand. Only high fences, 2–2.5m (6½–8ft) depending on species, are the complete answer and they need to be well-maintained. While any rhododendron *may* be attacked, lepidotes and evergreen azaleas are amongst the most popular. We find that most damage, both rubbing and chewing, takes place between January and April. Various deterrent compounds are available but many are of doubtful value. Ones we have tried with some success are A.A. Protect and Cervacol.

Rabbits also enjoy the above plants but I find them less troublesome provided there is not a large quantity of them or a lot of snow. Likewise hares, but they seem to be becoming rare. Wire netting is the only real answer.

Moles and birds (mostly blackbirds) can be a menace on watered ground in very dry weather but they can churn up and scratch at any time when the ground is soft. Blackbirds are especially fond of attacking peat beds. Surprisingly large-rooted plants can be thrown out where they may soon dry out and die. Blackbirds are in fact our worst pest in the nursery and carefully erected nets are the only answer. For established plants, wire netting laid on the soil and slightly buried helps deter birds and even human pilferers. Moles may be trapped.

Insect pests

It is rare that these are a serious problem in Britain and that control measures need to be taken. On the other hand, in areas such as parts of North America, certain pests can cause severe injury.

Weevils

Various species can be troublesome. The adults eat notches out of the *edges* of leaves while the larvae girdle roots and stems at and below soil level. Both can cause much damage although the larvae do not normally trouble established plants in Britain. Young seedlings or rooted cuttings are often attacked and killed by the larvae in boxes, trays or pots.

Control. Difficult, partly due to resistance to insecticides, even Aldrin and Dieldrin in places. Foliar sprays from May to August of Orthene, Fenitrothion, Malathion or Diazinon to kill adults are partially suc-cessful. Diazinon we find effective on larvae in containers. Recent Amer-ican research has shown that lepidote species produce chemical compounds called terpenes which act as weevil repellents. There is a theory that a deep mulch encourages weevils and that if there is not a deep mulch, birds eat them and give a satisfactory control.

Aphids

Mostly troublesome on young seedlings and rooted cuttings indoors while a few may appear outside, especially towards the end of a long, dry summer.

Control.   Spray, fumigate or dust with Malathion, Diazinon or other insecticides recommended for aphid control.

Caterpillars

These can be found eating young leaves, particularly those of indumentumed species in woodland conditions. The damage is more of a section eaten out (as opposed to the notches of weevils) or even an entire leaf.

Control.   I usually hand pick and squish them but if the problem is severe, spray with Derris, Trichlorphon, or Diflubenzuron. Spray into opening buds and both sides of leaves. Taliensia and Neriiflora species and their hybrids are amongst the most vulnerable.

Rhododendron and azalea whitefly

These cause yellowing and mottling of foliage and a black sooty mould may form on the honeydew secretion.

Control.   With Malathion or Diazinon in early autumn.

Red spider mites

Worst indoors, especially on azaleas or during hot, dry weather outside. Leaves become whitish or grey and minute webs are formed.

Control.   Discouraged by shade and moisture. Spray regularly with water or with Dimethoate, Tetradifon or use predatory mites.

Other insect pests

Various other pests can attack rhododendrons, mostly in warmer areas than Britain. These include thrips, symphyllids, scales, mealy bug, rhododendron bug, grasshoppers.

Control.   According to local advice and insecticide availability.

Disorders

Bark-split

Frost, especially unseasonable frost, probably causes more damage to rhododendrons in Britain than every drought, gale, flood, pest and disease put together. As frost can strike in such a devastating way over such a large part of the year, one never knows where and when it will hit next.

   Apart from damaging or destroying buds and flowers, which most people notice first, it also blasts young growth, and by far the most serious injury is bark-split. Any sharp frost which strikes when the sap has started or not ceased to flow, can cause bark-split. It can occur anywhere from the base of the plant to the youngest shoots, but it is at the base that our chief concern lies as it usually results in the death of the whole plant if splitting is severe.

Very often the splitting is not noticeable until the bark dries out and peels back. Bark-split only half-way round the stem may not lead to death. Complete healing can only take place when the original centre of the stem becomes isolated and this can very often be cut out with a sharp knife after two–three years. Splitting was so bad here at Glendoick after the late April 1981 frost on young stock that hundreds of normally perfectly winter-hardy plants were killed by being split right around the stem. Severe winter frost can also damage the bark of tender rhododendrons and evergreen azaleas.

It may be possible to save plants *prior* to an unseasonable frost by protecting the base of the stem(s). This can be done by mounding up soil or some mulching material up the stem(s) or wrapping the base with fibreglass, polystyrene or a similar substance. All must be removed once the danger is over. Danger always lurks when growth comes exceptionally early due to a mild winter and/or early spring, or late, perhaps due to a prolonged summer drought followed by autumn rain. I have tried tying up split stems with polythene strips straight after a frost with little or no success.

Bud and growth damage

Sudden early autumn frosts may kill or damage both growth and flower buds as can spring frosts. Either can lead to partially killed flower buds with just a proportion of buds in a truss opening or distorted young growth which may look like insect damage or even chlorosis. Completely blackened young growth is better cut off or broken off, as it can start rotting in damp weather and affect old foliage underneath and even young secondary growth.

Chlorosis

This is a complex problem. It can be caused by drought, waterlogging and frost as well as deficiency or toxicity of some major or minor element. It can even be caused by a lack of calcium in very acid soils, particularly in those with a high mineral content. A professional soil analysis is recommended if some imbalance of major or minor elements is suspected.

4 *Species*

Classification

In recent years, much has been happening in the classification of the genus Rhododendron. Changes in the classification of such a large and complex genus are inevitable, however much gardeners and horticulturists may hate them. One reason is that botanists and gardeners tend to look at classification through rather different eyes. Another is that no two botanists, even if there were thousands working at it, would ever produce a similar classification of the genus, even if working in the same herbarium. Rhododendron species just do not fit neatly into separate cubby holes. In fact, the great majority of species not only vary enormously but merge into one another, especially those of western China.

Sir Isaac Bayley Balfour was largely responsible for the classification we have known for 50 years, with his publication of *The Species of Rhododendron*. This was written when new rhododendrons were pouring in from S.E. Asia as a result of the collections of Forrest, Kingdon Ward and Rock. Many species were described which sooner or later were found to be too similar to others already described and were therefore reduced to synonymy. Related species were grouped into 'series' and 'subseries' which were never fully validated terms and many of these series and subseries have since been proved to have few or no really distinctive characters to separate them. These series were arranged alphabetically in *The Species of Rhododendron* and there was no arranging of these series into larger units showing the relationships between the series. The Azalea series was always an entirely false group which should never have been brought together under one 'umbrella' name. The lack of botanical significance of the name Azalea does not really matter but it is a great pity that plants so diverse as the evergreen (so called, some are really deciduous) and the Pentanthera (Luteum subseries) section should all be referred to as 'azaleas'. 'Azalea' now contains two subgenera divided into six sections by the Philipsons in much more natural divisions.

Contrary to what some people may think, many of the names now used in the Cullen, Chamberlain and Philipsons Revisions, and also brought to the fore by Hermann Sleumer in *A System of the Genus Rhododendron* (1949), are not new names. In fact they are mostly very much older than Bayley Balfour's 'series'. Some of George Don's published names such as Pentanthera, Pogonanthum and Tsutsusi were published in 1834. Don also validly united Rhododendron and Azalea into one genus.

As mentioned previously, botanists themselves tend to come up with completely different answers. This is partly because each botanist has different preferences for the characters used to separate different species. Moreover, some of the recent research into flavonoids, leaf waxes and even distribution, which obviously has great taxonomic importance, is sometimes largely or completely ignored by botanists using only a purely morphological basis for their classification. Cullen, Chamberlain and Philipsons versus Davidian is a perfect example of this phenomenon. While one must greatly admire Davidian's lifelong work now being published and his exceptional knowledge of Rhododendron species, he has ignored the results of scientific studies around him. It is a major disaster in the Rhododendron world that Davidian has not co-operated with fellow workers on rhododendrons to produce a classification that would have been acceptable to all. The failure of many individuals plus some institutions and societies of the Rhododendron world to accept the Cullen, Chamberlain and Philipsons Revisions may be understandable, but it is only leading to bickering and an inconsistency in naming in nurseries, gardens and perhaps even botanic gardens. This results in confusion on the part of the beginner and even the more advanced enthusiast. The inconsistency will not help the furthering of the study and interest in Rhododendron species.

I have accepted the Revisions as far as subgenera to subsections. I do have misgivings about various changes that have and have not been done. I can see that modern taxonomy and the gardener may be drifting even further apart than before. Some botanists used to and still do take cultivated plants into account when looking for morphological evidence. Others say that cultivated plants are always unreliable. Those with collectors' numbers could have had their origin mixed up at some stage from the collection of seed to the mature garden plant. Even if a plant is under an authentic number, it could be a horticultural atypical selection. So these botanists base their morphological research purely on herbarium specimens. Unfortunately this basis also falls down on several points. So many characters cannot be seen on a dried specimen. Even on good specimens, a whole host of characters are unlikely to be discernible, such as seed (in some cases), cotyledons, juvenile foliage, habit, bark, flowering and growth time. Poor field notes may even mean loss of flower colour and time of flowering.

In my observations and writing on rhododendrons, I have attempted to bridge the widening gap betwen pure taxonomy and the gardener. The trouble is that the pure taxonomist living in his herbarium and the pure gardener in his patch are only looking at rhododendrons from their own narrow angle. Admittedly, the taxonomist has a better chance if he or she works in a large herbarium. He may have at his disposal a great many specimens collected over a wide area of one or a group of related species. Apart from the lack of characters like those above to which a taxonomist may have no access, it must be remembered that herbarium specimens are but a sample (they should be an 'average' sample) of a whole population. As the majority of species vary greatly in the wild in one place as well as over their whole distributional range, one specimen made out of a whole host of varying individual plants cannot be said to be necessarily representative of the whole. Some botanists either never have the opportunities or never want to get out into the field to study wild populations. This is indeed unfortunate but the trouble as far as rhododendrons are concerned is that several years would have to be spent in the field travelling over wide areas to be able to make a really worthwhile study. Having seen wild rhododendrons growing in several parts of the world, I have only been able to reach a very few satisfactory conclusions. Too brief a glimpse at wild plants may lead to a number of hasty and ill-judged guesses. I *have* been able to assess the variability of species within an area and the occurrence of true natural hybrids. I have *not* been able to correlate the variation of a species or related species over a large part of its or their distributional range or even been able to come to any conclusions over the extent to which speciation occurs and whether there is any clear-cut difference between a complex intra-specific variation and a true natural hybrid. It is where closely related species (or so called species, subspecies or varieties) meet that a really thorough study is required. Alas, where I have been, there were only relatively clear-cut species and clear-cut natural hybrids. Modern speedy trips to China, India and so on are hardly conducive to the amount of research required.

Gardeners tend to be narrow-minded in a somewhat different way from botanists. As more and more of the original seedlings of species collected in the wilds during the heyday of collecting die and disappear from gardens, so do the chances of a gardener being able to observe a large number of different plants of a given species diminish. Recent introductions may have made up for this to a small extent but little planting will ever be done again on the scale of Exbury, Tower Court and Muncaster in the pre Second World War era. Nor is the amount of seed sent in during that time ever likely to be exceeded. Even the huge collections at Windsor Valley Gardens or the RBG, Edinburgh gardens rarely have more than one or two of each species or collectors' number while other collections may have groups of plants propagated from one clone. This last point is all-important. Species that are easily propagated vegetatively are frequently grown from a handful or even only one selected clone. That one clone may be how a horticulturist establishes his or her knowledge of that species. It may not be an average form of that species and could have been selected for some special characters atypical of that species. What is more, many of these clones have been grown from seed off cultivated and not wild plants. It could even be that the plant is a hybrid or sport and is just masquerading under the given specific name. Gardeners should not procrastinate over the new revisions without first studying the most extensive species collections *and* herbarium collections. Their view can be so narrow taxonomically without this study that it can be of little significance.

This excellent summing up of the situation appeared in AMRS-QB (Fall 1981), p.217, by Dr Herbert A. Spady:

There does not appear to be much ground for hostility to taxonomic revision based on sound scientific principles. The species concept is a great abstract leap from the real world of plant populations. This does not distract from its usefulness to the scientist and amateur ... So the species of Rhododendron must as nearly as possible be described and classified in terms of natural populations and the advancing scientific facts about their differences.

I feel that Cullen, Chamberlain, Philipsons and Davidian have gone ahead with their respective projects without considering adequately the overall consequences of their lack of co-operation. Once Davidian's books are all published, the controversy could reach boiling point if something is not done to alleviate the problem now. The Edinburgh Revisions, for all their drawbacks, *are* combining science and taxonomy. I too suffer from *cinnabarinum* spp. *xanthocodon* Concatenans Group and do not like it. These revisions are forward-looking and not necessarily final. These revisions are not the destruction of Rhododendron classification as we have known it. Indeed, a very high percentage of specific names are as they were and if a horticultural distinction occurs, you can still use the old specific or varietal 'Group' name on its own. Nobody is forcing you to write '*cinnabarinum* ssp. *xanthocodon* Concatenans Group' on your labels. You can leave it as *concatenans*. As for botanic gardens discarding forms of *campylogynum* because they have no 'handle', they will wish to keep a collection of variations, especially those with collectors' numbers, just as much as any gardening enthusiast should.

Now let's discuss the change from series to sections and subsections. In most cases, all that is done is to alter the ending of the word. Subsections have an equal status to the majority of the old series and are in no way more flexible or inflexible. The higher divisions (subgenera and sections) are used to group related subsections together. Apart from Pogonanthum (formerly Anthopogon), Rhodorastra (formerly Dauricum) and Rhododendron (formerly Ferrugineum), the old lepidotes are the same as subgenus Rhododendron and the elepidotes, subgenus Hymenanthes. These are not new names and, as stated earlier, were published long before the 'series'. Again as I have stated, Azalea was the most unnatural series of the lot.

Further to the complaints about the Edinburgh Revisions, no reason is given for the objections to joining the Lacteum and Taliense series together into the Taliensia subsection. I assume it is because of *lacteum*, *beesianum* and *wightii*. *R. wightii* does not really belong here anyway; it is decidedly aberrant anywhere but might be happiest in the Grandia subsection. *R. lacteum* and *beesianum* might be better in their own subsection. As for the rest, they cannot be separated from most of the old Taliense series by any definite character.

To sum up, Rhododendron species are the same plants, regardless of how we choose to classify them. Now that the ARS has spread to a Scottish chapter, I feel that they (we) should give a lead to unite classification to the large majority's satisfaction. Until there is an international conference that really achieves a generally accepted horticultural classification, I propose that we all basically accept the subgenus, section, subsection concept but otherwise call our plants whatever we choose, as long as the name is or was correct for that plant. When it comes to

Classification comparisons

Edinburgh Revision	Bayley Balfour and Hutchinson	Davidian
Subgenus Rhododendron	*Lepidote*	*Lepidote*
Section Rhododendron		
Afghanica subsection	Triflorum series, s.s. Hanceanum	Triflorum series, s.s. Hanceanum
Baileya subsection	Lepidotum series, s.s. Baileyi	Lepidotum series, s.s. Baileyi
Boothia subsection	Boothii series	Boothii series
Campylogyna subsection	Campylognyum series	Campylogynum series
Caroliniana subsection	Carolinianum series	Carolinianum series
Edgeworthia subsection	Edgeworthii series	Edgeworthii series
Fragariflora subsection	Saluenense series (part)	Lapponicum series (part)
Glauca subsection	Glaucum series	Glaucophyllum series, s.s. Glaucophyllum
Lapponica subsection	Lapponicum series	Lapponicum series
Lepidota subsection	Lepidotum series	Lepidotum series
Maddenia (part) subsection	Maddenii series (part)	Ciliatum series
Moupinensia subsection	Moupinense series	Moupinense series
Rhododendron subsection	Ferrugineum series	Ferrugineum series
Rhodorastra subsection	Dauricum series	Dauricum series
Saluenensia subsection	Saluenense series	Saluenense series
Tephropepla subsection	Boothii series, s.s. Tephropeplum	Tephropeplum series
Trichoclada subsection	Trichocladum series	Trichocladum series
Triflora subsection	Triflorum series	Triflorum series
Uniflora subsection	Lepidotum series (part)	Uniflorum series
Virgata subsection	Virgatum series (part)	Virgatum series
Section Vireya		
Pseudovireya subsection	Vaccinioides series	Vaccinioides series
Section Pogonanthum	Anthopogon series	Anthopogon series
Subgenus Therorhodion	Camtschaticum series	
Subgenus Hymenanthes	*Elepidote*	
Argyrophylla subsection	Arboreum series, s.s. Argyrophyllum	
Campanulata subsection	Campanulatum series	
Campylocarpa subsection	Thomsonii series, s.s. Campylocarpum	
Fulgensia subsection	Campanulatum series (part)	
Glischra subsection	Barbatum series, s.s. Glischrum	
Lanata subsection	Campanulatum series (part)	
Maculifera subsection	Barbatum series, s.s. Maculiferum	
Neriiflora subsection	Neriiflorum series	
Pontica subsection	Ponticum series	
Taliensia subsection	Taliense series (and Lacteum series)	
Thomsonia subsection	Thomsonii series, s.s. Thomsonii	
Williamsiana subsection	Thomsonii series, s.s. Williamsianum	
Subgenus Tsutsusi	Azalea series (part)	
Section Tsutsusi	Azalea series, s.s. Obtusum	
Section Tsusiopsis	Tsusiophyllum tanakae	
Subgenus Pentanthera	Azalea series (part)	
Section Rhodora	Azalea series, s.s. Canadense (part)	

showing, the official RHS publications will need to be adhered to but the use of 'Group' names should be left to the individual.

I have arranged the subsections alphabetically purely for ease of reference. I have followed the Edinburgh Revisions almost to the letter because, if I attempted to arrange and describe the species as I personally believe, it would just add to the existing confusion rather than go any way towards solving it. The Edinburgh Revisions were done in a broadly scientific manner which has given a truer picture than before.

Species descriptions

For simple reference, the portion of the genus Rhododendron covered in this book is divided into sub-genera, sections and then subsections alphabetically within each section. I have deliberately not attempted to place closely related subsections and species together as Cullen and Chamberlain have done. This arrangement leads to difficult reference and it is rather unsatisfactory and based on surmise anyway. Otherwise the Cullen and Chamberlain revisions are followed with comments in the text on my own assessments of their classifications as well as Davidian's.

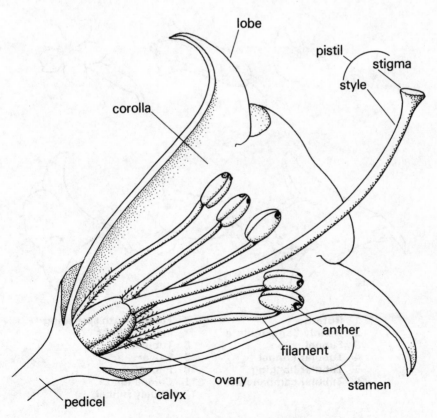

Named parts of the rhododendron flower

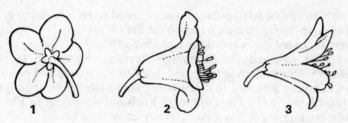

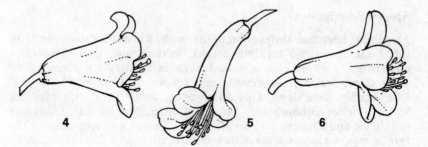

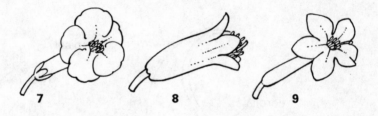

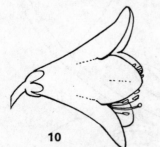

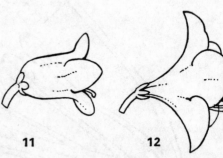

1	Rotate	7	Tubular with spreading
2	Openly Campanulate		lobes or limbs
3	Funnel	8	Tubular
4	Tubular Funnel	9	Salver
5	Tubular hanging	10	Funnel
6	Tubular campanulate	11	Campanulate
		12	Widely funnel

Flower shapes

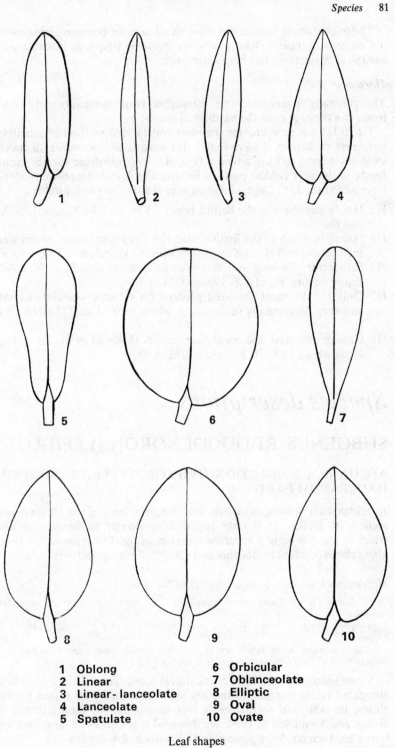

1 Oblong
2 Linear
3 Linear-lanceolate
4 Lanceolate
5 Spatulate
6 Orbicular
7 Oblanceolate
8 Elliptic
9 Oval
10 Ovate

Leaf shapes

Those characters considered most significant for positive identification are entered in italics. Descriptions are made as simple as possible while botanical correctness has been attempted.

Hardiness

This generally covers just winter hardiness, as unseasonably early or late frosts can damage even the hardiest of plants.

H1 to H4 has now become the most widely used method of classifying hardiness in Britain. I have found this unsatisfactory, owing to insufficient categories, so have added a fifth, H5, to cover those species winter-hardy in the very coldest parts of Britain. For North American readers I have added the U.S. Dept. of Agriculture Hardiness Zone numbers.

H5 Hardy anywhere in the British Isles (-5 to $-10°F$). Equals USDA 5 and 6a.

H4 Hardy in much of the British Isles, the exceptions being inland glens in Scotland and N. England where minima go below -5 to $-10°F$.

H3 Satisfactory for west and best situated in areas near E. & W. coasts. Equivalent to about 5°F. Equals USDA 7a.

H2 Only for the most sheltered gardens on extreme western seaboard and very occasionally in the south, about 10°F. Equals USDA 7b to 8a.

H1 Greenhouse and the most favourable sheltered walls in mildest areas, about 15 to 20°F. Equals USDA 8b.

Species descriptions

SUBGENUS RHODODENDRON (LEPIDOTE)

AFGHANICA SUBSECTION (TRIFLORUM SERIES, SUBSERIES HANCEANUM PART)

R. afghanicum, having no close relations, has been given its own subsection by Cullen. It is only superficially similar to *hanceanum* with which it was placed in a separate subseries of the Triflorum series. Probably related (Cullen) to Boothia and Camelliiflora subsections.

afghanicum Aitchison & Hems. 1880 H3 USDA 7a LI-2 F1

Ht to 50cm (20in). Habit rather straggly in the wild with prostrate ascending branches.
L evergreen, thick, 3–8cm ($1\frac{1}{5}$–$3\frac{1}{8}$in) long, narrowly elliptic to elliptic, pale green below.
F white to greenish-white, 0.8–1.3cm ($\frac{1}{3}$–$\frac{1}{2}$in) long, tubular base, rotate limb, racemose truss of 5–16. Calyx conspicuous, irregular, stamens 10.

A rare species of very little horticultural merit. Very distinctive with its elongated rachis but the flowers are small and dull. Introduced by Aitchison in 1880 and subsequently lost to cultivation. Reintroduced by Hedge and Wendelbo in 1969. We flowered it at Glendoick and then lost it in a hard winter. Very poisonous to livestock. Rootability low.

E. Afghanistan and its border with Pakistan only, 2,100–2,700m (7,000–9,000ft), in fairly dense forest, usually *Abies*, on gneiss or limestone rock walls and ledges.   June–July

BAILEYA SUBSECTION (LEPIDOTUM SERIES, SUBSERIES BAILEYI)

A new subsection, previously included in the Lepidotum series to which it is obviously related. Also shows relationship with the Saluenensia subsection in its crenulate scales. Has a sharply deflexed style.

baileyi Balf.f. 1919 (*thyodocum* Balf.f. and Cooper) H3–4 USDA 7a, 6b L1 F2–3

Ht 0.5–2m (1½–6ft). Habit fairly compact to leggy and scraggy.
L 2.1–7cm (¾–2¾in) long, 0.8–3.3cm (⅓–1⅓in) wide, narrowly elliptic to obovate, usually dark brown below, occasionally greenish-brown and densely scaly. Old leaves may turn yellow in autumn.
F purple to almost red, with or without darker spots, up to 3cm (1¼in) across, rotate or subrotate, 4–9 rarely to 18 per truss, long slender pedicels.

A rather neglected and unusual plant with flowers of a striking colour, often freely produced. The taller forms are best planted at the back of a border of dwarfs as their habit is rather untidy. Often cultivated under L&S 2896. AM 1960. Rootability low.

A rather limited distribution from Sikkim through N. Bhutan to S. Xizang. Found in forests, bamboo, or on dry or moist hillsides, scree or rocks at 2,400–4,300m (8,000–14,000ft).   April–May

BOOTHIA SUBSECTION (BOOTHII SERIES)

This subsection has been altered from the Boothii series by the removal of the old Tephropeplum subseries. According to Cullen, this has little relationship with the remaining members of the Boothia subsection, and I agree. Davidian has also removed subseries Tephropeplum and given it series status.

Cullen gives the closest relations to this subsection as Edgeworthia and Maddenia, especially for their epiphytic habit and seed shape and to Camelliiflora, Glauca and Trichoclada subsections. Boothia consists of small evergreen shrubs to 2m (6ft) or slightly more, often epiphytic or confined to rocks and cliffs in the wild. Leaves whitish below. Flowers usually yellow and broadly campanulate. Calyx well developed. Stamens 10. Style sharply deflexed at base.

With the exception of *micromeres*, all are good garden plants but are only suitable for the milder parts of Britain, California and like climates. Well worth trying these on tree stumps, mossy rocks, cliffs and tree trunks, the last only in really damp climates. Some are recorded as coming from as high as 4,100m (13,500ft) but I really doubt if any are to be found much over 3,700m (12,000ft).

boothii Nutt. 1853 (*mishmiense* Hutch. & Ward) H1–2? USDA 8b, 7b L1–2 F2

Ht to 2m (6ft). Habit usually epiphytic, rather straggly.
L 7.8–11.2cm (3–4½in) long, 3.8–5.2cm (1½–2in) wide, ovate to broadly elliptic, leathery.

F dull to bright yellow, unspotted, campanulate in truss of 3–10, about 3cm (1¼in) long.

The flowers of this rare species are rather small for the size of the leaves but it is none the less a fine plant. Is apparently now only cultivated in California. Plants under *mishmiense* are growing in Australia but these are seedlings so may not be true to type. Only suitable for the very mildest of British gardens and similar climates.

Limited known distribution in W. Arunachal Pradesh (*boothii* type) not Bhutan, and S. Xizang and E. Arunachal Pradesh (Mishmiense Group) in forests and scrub at 1,800–2,700m (6,000–9,000ft). April–May Mishmiense Group. Made synonymous with *boothii* by Cullen, in my opinion correctly. Flowers usually spotted.

chrysodoron (Tagg ex) Hutch. 1934 (*butyricum* Ward) H2–3 USDA 7b & 8a, 7a L1–2 F2–3

Ht to 1.5m (5ft) in cultivation. Habit bushy. Fine peeling red papery bark.
L 4.5–8.8cm (1¾–3½in) long, 2–4.5cm (¾–1¾in) wide, oblong-elliptic.
F bright canary-yellow, 3–4cm (about 1½in) long, campanulate, calyx *smaller* than *sulfureum*, 2–3mm.

A very fine plant with amongst the best-coloured yellow flowers in the genus. Needs a very favourable site in the mildest British gardens as the growth comes very early. AM 1934. Rootability medium.

Has only been found wild in two parts of Upper Burma and possibly W. Yunnan, 2,000–2,600m (6,500–8,500ft) as an epiphyte and on rocks.
February–March–April

dekatanum Cowan 1937 not in cultivation

This is probably a synonym of *sulfureum* or a geographical form of it, coming from one collection in S. Xizang. The differences appear to be purely botanical and it is likely to be of little horticultural consequence.

Found in rhododendron and bamboo forest at 3,500m (11,500ft).

leucaspis Tagg 1929 H3 USDA 7a L2–3 F3–4

Ht to 1m (3ft). Habit bushy, usually wider than high. Branchlets hairy.
L 3–6cm (1¼–2½) long, 1.8–3cm (⅔–1¼in) wide, broadly elliptic, densely hairy above and on margins.
F milky white often tinged pink, about 5cm (2in) across, 1–3 per truss, usually in pairs, *almost rotate*. Calyx large, hairy, green or reddish.

A superb plant but alas just too tender to give its best in all but the milder British gardens. We can usually keep it for several years but it eventually dies of bark split. We always replace it. It makes a fine container specimen and blooms quickly from seed. While needing some protection for hardiness and its early flowers, it loses its character if drawn up in too much shade. Rather aberrant in this subsection, its nearest relation being *megeratum*. AM 1929 to KW 6273, FCC 1944 to KW 7171. A so-called dwarf American clone called 'Midget' did not prove dwarf at Glendoick. Rootability medium.

R. leucaspis

Apparently rare in the wild, having been found only in a few river gorges of S.E. Xizang on cliff faces and grassy banks at 2,400–3,000m (8,000–10,000ft). Could it be more common as an unseen epiphytic? Found only by KW and L&S and introduced twice by KW.   March–April

megeratum Balf.f. & Forr. 1920 H3 USDA 7a L1–2 F2–3

Ht 30–90cm (1–3ft). Habit bushy, often compact. Shoots at first hairy.
L 1.5–4cm ($\frac{3}{5}$–$1\frac{1}{2}$in) long, 1–2cm ($\frac{2}{5}$–$\frac{3}{4}$in) wide, elliptic to orbicular, *glaucous* below, margins usually hairy.
F creamy yellow to deep yellow, 2–3cm ($\frac{4}{5}$–$1\frac{1}{5}$in) long, rotate to broadly campanulate, 1–3 per truss.

This is potentially a gem but rarely produces the full glory of masses of its beautifully shaped flowers. Most forms I have seen are either pale-coloured and/or shy-flowering and are also surprisingly tender. Some of a supposedly good hardy form succumbed to our severe spring frosts of 1981. Plants of two other clones have suffered repeated bark-split resulting in die-back and/or death. In Argyll we tried planting it on mossy tree trunks but long dry spells eventually killed all three plants. Might prove hardier on raised beds and on lighter soils than ours. AM 1935 deep yellow, AM 1970 bright yellow. Rootability medium.

Comes from a fairly wide area from S.E. Xizang and Mishmi country Arunachal Pradesh through Upper Burma to N.W. Yunnan at 2,400–4,100m (8,000–13,500ft), mostly on mossy rocks and cliffs and more rarely epiphytic on firs and other trees looking like great bunches of mistletoe. Its average altitude is apparently about 3,400m (11,000ft) so it should be hardier than it appears to be. The western forms are said to be superior.   March–April

micromeres described in *The Larger Species of Rhododendron*

R. sulfureum

sulfureum Franch. 1887 (*cerinum* Balf.f. & Forr., *commodum* Balf.f. & Forr., *theiochroum* Balf.f. & Sm.) H2 possibly to 4 USDA 7b & 8a, possibly to 6b L1–2 F2–3

Ht 0.6–1.6m (2–5ft). Habit quite compact to leggy and straggly, depending on form. Bark attractively smooth brown.
L 2.6–8.6cm (1–3½in) long, 1.3–4.2cm (½–1½in) wide, shape very variable, usually obovate but also broadly obovate to narrowly elliptic. Hairs soon shed. Moderately to very glaucous below.
F greenish to bright or deep yellow, 1.5–2cm (about ¾in) long and 3cm (1¼in) across, campanulate in trusses of 3–8.

A very variable species in form and hardiness. Considering the variation in elevation, this is hardly surprising. Fairly hardy and good forms are in cultivation and it is hoped that our own introductions from Cangshan, Yunnan in 1981 will prove to be amongst the toughest. This could be a case for selective breeding for excellence and hardiness combined. AM 1937. Rootability medium.

Widely distributed from S.E. Xizang and Upper Burma to N.W. and S.W. Yunnan, 2,100–4,000m (7,000–13,000ft) usually on rocks, cliffs and rocky pastures, occasionally epiphytic. All that we saw were on cliffs and crags, usually in inaccessible places.   March–April

CAMPYLOGYNA SUBSECTION (CAMPYLOGYNUM SERIES)

This subsection now contains only one very variable species made up of a host of former species and varieties. Although all may merge botanically, this is a case where it is important to retain horticultural identities.

All are neat evergreens, usually dark green above and glaucous beneath, with dainty nodding thimble-like campanulate flowers with a glaucous bloom, generally held above the foliage on long pedicels. To quote from my father's article in *The New Flora & Silva* (April 1929): '. . . the neatest and most perky and self-satisfied of all dwarfs'.

Closest relations are found in the Glauca subsection and also *pumilum* and *genestierianum*.

I have seen several plants in North America, supposedly belonging to this species with leaves and flowers much larger than average. These are undoubtedly hybrids with the Glauca subsection.

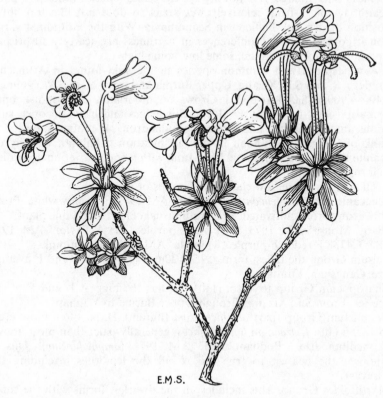

E.M.S.

R. campylogynum

campylogynum Franch. 1884 (*caeruleo-glaucum* Balf.f. & Forr., *cerasiflorum* Ward, *charopoeum* Balf.f. & Forr., *cremastum* Balf.f. & Forr., *damascenum* Balf.f. & Forr., *glauco-aureum* Balf.f. & Forr., *myrtilloides* Balf.f. & Ward, *rubriflorum* Ward, also *campylogynum* var. *celsum* Davidian. H3–4 USDA 7a & 6b L1–3 F2–3

Ht 5cm–1.3m (2in–4ft). Habit prostrate, creeping, mound-shaped or occasionally erect, with dense growth.
L 0.7–3.7cm ($\frac{1}{4}$–$1\frac{1}{2}$in) long, 0.3–1.2cm ($\frac{1}{8}$–$\frac{2}{3}$in) wide, obovate to narrowly elliptic, glaucous beneath except in Cremastum Group.
F black-purple, claret, red, purple, pink, salmon-pink and cream, about 1.6cm ($\frac{2}{3}$in) long, rarely to 2.3cm (nearly 1in) long, campanulate, 1–3 per truss. Calyx variable 4–7mm ($\frac{1}{6}$–$\frac{1}{3}$in) long, stamens usually 10, unequal. Style *thick* and *sharply deflexed*, capsule erect.

This is a splendid plant in most of its forms and it is well worth while making a collection of these. There is a great variation in foliage, flower, habit and flowering time and no collection should be satisfied with one *campylogynum*. We grow at least ten clones and I am always on the lookout for more. Some forms are a little tender here and funnily, these tend to be the dwarfest ones with us. Frost damage leads to die-back but they always make a recovery at Glendoick. The plentiful flowers may form a carpet of exquisite bells on the top of often level dense growth. Our forms with claret, black-purple and plum-coloured flowers all have splendid dark foliage. It is not always the easiest species to keep in good health. It comes from relatively wet areas so does not like too hot a position or dry soil. Difficult in Scandinavia. With the altitudinal variation it comes from, the differences in hardiness are scarcely surprising. Rootability mostly medium, some low, some high.

A widespread and common species in the wild found in Arunachal Pradesh, S. and S.E. Xizang, Upper Burma and from N. to S.W. Yunnan, 2,400–4,900m (8,000–16,000ft). Grows on moorland, often moist, open rocky hillsides, on mossy boulders, cliff ledges and clefts, in open situations among bamboo and larger rhododendrons. We found it on the E. flank of Cangshan, Yunnan in the last-mentioned habitat. Usually on granite but also on limestone. May–June with a wide variation according to form.

The following are now classed as Groups or clones.
'Leucanthum' (var. *leucanthum* Ingram) AM 1973 F creamy white. Probably grown from cultivated seed. An unusual colour and a fine plant.
'Baby Mouse' AM 1973 deep plum purple. 'Beryl Taylor' AM 1975 LS&T 4738 F reddish-purple. 'Thimble' AM 1966 salmon-pink.
Celsum Group the tallest form, 0.45–1.20m+ ($1\frac{1}{2}$–4ft+) L and F average size. Cangshan, Yunnan.
Charopoeum Group to 45cm ($1\frac{1}{2}$ft) but has the biggest L and F of the species. From S.E. Xizang, through Upper Burma to Yunnan.
Cremastum Group (part *amphichlorum* Ingram). Habit often more erect to 1.20m (4ft). *L green on both surfaces*, generally paler than most above. F medium size. 'Bodnant Red' AM 1971 (*amphichlorum*). This is amongst the nearest to true red of all the lepidotes (excluding the Vireyas).
Myrtilloides Group. This includes all the dwarfest forms with the smallest L and F. The latter are 0.8–1.8cm ($\frac{1}{3}$–$\frac{2}{3}$in) long. There is a big varia-

tion here in leaf and flower colour and hardiness, coming from a wide range of altitude; from S.E. Xizang; through Burma into Yunnan. AM 1925, FCC 1943 magenta-rose.

CAROLINIANA SUBSECTION (CAROLINIANUM SERIES)

This subsection, confined to E. USA, has now been reduced by Cullen to one species with two varieties. While one may agree that *minus* and *carolinianum* are probably the same plant botanically, the two extremes from northern and southern ends of distribution are far from the same horticulturally. Furthermore, I find it extremely tiresome to lose the name *carolinianum* which is infinitely more attractive than the ugly and misnamed *minus* (meaning 'smaller') which in its southern forms can reach 10m (30ft) in the wild! Here is taxonomy gone daft and I could only accept this change with disdain and annoyance. In practice as far as labelling and listing are concerned, I will retain the name *carolinianum* at specific rank. All northern forms should remain under this name.

Cullen has based his revision of this subsection on the work of Duncan and Pullen (Brittonia 14: 290–298, 1962). The paucity of specimens in Edinburgh makes it difficult to come to any further conclusions over the differences between *minus* and *carolinianum*.

This 'species' seems closest-related to the Heliolepida subsection but of course there is an enormous geographical separation plus the horticultural one. All require extra-good drainage in cultivation.

minus Michaux (*cuthbertii* Small, *punctatum* Andrews)

Ht 1–3m (3–10ft) in cultivation, to 10m (30ft) in the wild. Habit fairly compact to loose.
L evergreen but remaining for one year only, 5–11.4cm (2–4½in) long, 2–5cm (⅘–2in) wide, elliptic to broadly elliptic, dark to light green (in white forms) above, brown scaly below.
F mauve, pinkish purple through pink to white, 2.5–3.8cm (1–1½in) long, narrowly to openly funnel-shaped. Calyx short, unequal, stamens 10.

The above description covers *minus*, *carolinianum* and *chapmanii* as there is little difference between them in purely botanical details.

minus var. **minus** H4–5 L1–2 F1–3

L apex acuminate. Habit looser and generally later-flowering than *carolinianum*, and larger than average with rather a thin texture.

This is generally found to the south of *carolinianum* and forms a larger plant. The chief difference horticulturally in Scotland, we find, is that like all plants from S.E. USA, it is useless as it fails to ripen its growth properly and in consequence, does not flower. From lower mountains and plains from Carolina to Alabama in woodlands.

carolinianum Rehd. (Carolinianum Group) H5 L1–2 F2–3

Until the hopeful worldwide accepted classification, I am leaving this plant provisionally at specific status. This grows reasonably at Glendoick, but never looks a picture of health, and tends to have an unstable root system—the whole plant above ground is liable to wobble about. Does better in the south of England (as does *minus*) but all plants we have tried flower freely.

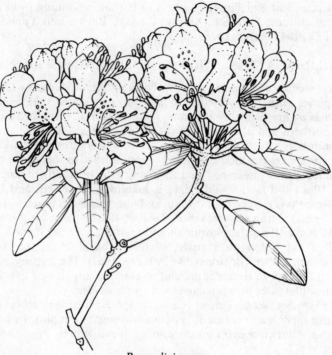

R. carolinianum

We have grown several white forms. All have paler more pointed leaves and slightly off-white flowers and (what we have grown) do not make handsome specimens, although we may not have received selected clones such as 'Gable's *carolinianum* Album Compactum'.

The great virtue with *carolinianum* is its extreme hardiness, standing −31°C (−25°F) in E. USA. It is one of the most valuable parents for hardy lepidote hybrids that we have and has produced such excellent plants as 'Dora Amateis' FCC, 'P. J. Mezitt' AM, 'Eider' AM, 'Wigeon' PC, HCT and I forecast a host of further winners. The young leaves and flowers of *carolinianum* have a built-in toughness against frost which it readily passes on to its progeny. Rootability low to medium.

Two interesting forms have emerged in cultivation. 'Epoch' is a tetra-ploid deliberately raised in the USA by treating a normal plant with colchicine. At Glendoick it develops poor foliage. I crossed it successfully with *yunnanense* and *davidsonianum* but the seedlings have hopeless spotted leaves. Some yellowish flowered clones and strains have appeared, possibly hybrids which could have a future in hybridizing.

Mountains of Tennessee and Carolinas to Georgia where it merges and/or hybridizes with *minus* var. *minus*.

minus var. chapmanii (Gray) Duncan & Pullen H3 USDA 7a L1 F1–2

Ht to 2m (6ft). Habit erect but liable to sprawl.
L broadly elliptic to orbicular, apex obtuse, usually bullate above, olive to bright green.
F pink to rose.

We grew this for many years. It always looked sick, frequently died back and never flowered. Its only virtue to us was its unusual puckered, bullate leaves. Our summers are far too cool for all S.E. American plants. Could be valuable for heat resistance and dry air tolerance in hybridizing. Some plants labelled *chapmanii* in British gardens are *minus* var. *minus*. Fire-resistant and partly stoloniferous.

Found only on a few sand dunes, open pinelands and dry creek banks in Florida gulf country. Nearly extinct in the wild due to civilization, clearing and vandalism.   April–May?

EDGEWORTHIA SUBSECTION (EDGEWORTHII SERIES)

A small and most unusual subsection which has indumentum as well as scales. The three species are not all that closely related but are retained together due to the unique indumentum made up of dense curled hairs. *R. edgeworthii* is closest to the Maddenia and Moupinensia subsections while the others come near Boothia and Camelliiflora.

All are epiphytic in nature and must have exceptional drainage to succeed in cultivation.

Leaves evergreen, often bullate above. Inflorescence terminal, few flowered. Calyx well-developed. Stamens 10. Capsule hairy.

edgeworthii Hook. 1849 (*bullatum* Franch., *sciaphilum* Balf.f. & Ward) H2–3 USDA 7b & 8a–7a L2–4 F2–4

Ht 0.3–3.3m (1–11ft). Habit usually leggy but some forms are more compact or spreading when not over-shaded. Branchlets densely woolly.
L 5–15+cm (2–6+in) long, 2.5–6cm (1–2⅖in) wide, oblong, ovate, oblong-lanceolate or rarely elliptic, strongly bullate above, moderate to dense indumentum below, rust-coloured to fawn.
F white, sometimes flushed pink or rose, with or without yellow blotch at base, 3.2–7.6cm (1½–3in) long and up to 9cm (4in) across, funnel-campanulate, 1–5 per truss, rarely more than 3, deliciously fragrant. Calyx large, deeply lobed, reddish. *Style long and straight*.

One of my favourites of all species and worth every trouble to grow well. While often seen in cultivation, few plants can be called a picture of health. If drainage is at all faulty, we find it develops leaf spot and will never flourish. I am now planting it only in raised beds full of coarse organic matter or tree stumps filled likewise. Even sand or grit may be added. I believe the hardier forms, if properly treated, will grow in many more gardens. Avoid too much shade as it all too readily becomes leggy. Has amongst the most interesting foliage, finest flowers and sweetest scents of all species. Under glass it needs the same perfect drainage whether in a bed or a pot. It is not as easy to please as its hybrids such as 'Fragrantissimum' and 'Lady Alice Fitzwilliam'. Flowers opened indoors often lack the deep rose flush of many opened outside.

While some forms may exceed our 1.5m (5ft) dwarf limit, the subsection is basically dwarf so is included here. Extremely variable in leaf size and shape and colour and thickness of indumentum. There are no significant differences between *edgeworthii* and *bullatum*, therefore the name *bullatum* is not retained.

R. edgeworthii

The eastern collections from Yunnan (formerly *bullatum*), coming from higher elevations on average than those from the west (Himalayas) (2,974m [9,760ft] as opposed to 2,377m [7,800ft]), tend to be the hardier. Two different clones have grown happily in the light sandy soil in the RBG, Edinburgh for many years. One of these forms has likewise survived at Glendoick for years up to the 1981–2 winter.

This is the only species I have seen wild both in Arunachal Pradesh and Yunnan. The collection from the former, not seen in flower, turned out to have only one large flower to the inflorescence and to be hopelessly tender for Glendoick and even our Argyll garden, not surprising coming as it did from only 2,100–2,700m (7,000–9,000ft). In Yunnan, I saw it in full bloom growing on rocks, of a more typical but excellent form, white flushed pink with about three flowers per truss. This is another case where improvements in habit, foliage flower colour and hardiness could be accomplished by selective breeding. FCC 1933 white, FCC 1937 white, AM 1923 Farrer 842 white, AM 1946 bluish-pink flushed rose. Rootability generally high.

Found wild from Sikkim eastwards through Bhutan, Arunachal Pradesh, Upper Burma, Xizang to N.N.W. and C. Yunnan, 1,800–4,000m (6,000–13,000ft), often epiphytically on oaks and other trees, sometimes on the tops of every tree. Also on rocks, steep hillsides and cliffs in forest. Occasionally recorded as having no scent in the wild by collectors.

April–May

pendulum Hook. 1849 H3 possibly 4 USDA 7a possibly 6b L2 F2

Ht 0.3–1.2m (1–4ft). Habit often sprawling but quite tidy in an open position. Branchlets densely clothed with wool.
L 2.3–5cm (1–2in) long, 1.2–3cm ($\frac{1}{2}$–1$\frac{1}{4}$in) wide, oblong-elliptic, *convex*, only slightly bullate above, dense indumentum below, whitish to beige.
F white, white-flushed pink or cream, 1.5–2.2cm ($\frac{3}{5}$–$\frac{4}{5}$in) long, openly funnel-campanulate, in trusses of 2–3. Calyx red-tinged. Style short, sharply bent.

A very distinct species, unlike any other. Not of great horticultural merit but obviously of interest to collectors. A fine old specimen was grown for many years in the rock garden of the RBG, Edinburgh in a sheltered nook. I have found it extremely difficult at Glendoick and in Argyll, due I believe to the soil not being adequately sandy. Even failed on rocks and tree stumps and raised peat beds, all having wasted away with leaf spot. The only one kept going was under a cloche during winter as winter wet is the obvious killer. The 1981–2 winter finally killed it. I intend to try it in a very sandy mixture in a raised bed. Rootability medium.

Only common locally in a few places in E. Nepal, Sikkim, Bhutan and S. Xizang, 2,300–3,700m (7,500–12,000ft), epiphytic on conifers, other trees and rhododendrons and on steep slopes, sheer cliffs and river-bed rocks in forest, sometimes pendulous. Recently reintroduced from Sikkim.

April–May

seinghkuense Hutch. 1930 H probably 2 USDA probably 7b & 8a L2 F3

Ht 30–90cm (1–3ft). Habit more or less erect and slow-growing.
L 3–8cm (1$\frac{1}{4}$–3$\frac{1}{4}$in) long, 1.6–4cm ($\frac{2}{3}$–1$\frac{2}{3}$in) wide, elliptic to narrowly ovate, more bullate than *pendulum* above, *not convex*, indumentum pale to dark brown.
F bright yellow, about 2cm (almost 1in) long, 4cm (1$\frac{1}{2}$in) across, rotate-campanulate in trusses of 1–2.

A very rare species in cultivation with probably only a handful of plants in Britain all off one clone of KW 9254. I have seen a few plants labelled *seinghkuense* which are undoubtedly just *edgeworthii* with leaves too large for the former. I think I saw the remains of two plants at Muncaster, Cumbria some years ago. Pretty and well worth more effort to propagate and distribute it. I find it hard to root and even harder to grow on. It seems to like a sphagnum moss mixture, not surprising for an epiphyte. AM 1953. Rootability low.

Cullen says that this plant and *pendulum* are very closely related, a statement I cannot accept, having grown both for a number of years. I doubt if each varies much in the wild, on the basis of my examination of the herbarium specimens. Their known distributions are quite far apart.

Probably rare in the wild only having been found in extreme N. Burma and adjacent S.E. Xizang and N.W. Yunnan, 1,800–3,000m (6,000–10,000ft), on the top of conifers and on rocks. One plant, probably this species, was found growing epiphytically on another of its kind.   April

FRAGARIFLORA SUBSECTION (PART SALUENENSE SERIES)

One species transferred from the Saluenensia subsection. Although *fragariflorum* shows its closest relationship with its former series (as it was), it was very much aberrant there and seems to lie between the Saluenensia and Campylogyna subsections. Seems to bear some affinity with *setosum*. Davidian has moved it into the Lapponicum series owing to the 'entire' type of scale. I feel it should be placed with *setosum*.

fragariflorum Ward 1929 H4–5 USDA 6b–5 & 6a L1–2 F1–2

Ht 15–40cm (6–16in). Habit tussock- or carpet-forming.
L 0.5–1.7cm ($\frac{1}{5}$–$\frac{3}{5}$in) long, 3–9mm ($\frac{1}{8}$–$\frac{1}{3}$in) wide, oblong-elliptic, rather rugose above, golden to brown below, margins usually reflexed. Occasional hairs on maturity on mid-rib above and margins.
F pinkish purple through strawberry-red to purplish-crimson, 1.3–1.8cm ($\frac{1}{2}$–$\frac{2}{3}$in) long, openly campanulate to almost rotate, 1–3 per truss. Calyx conspicuous reddish. Stamens 10, style longer than stamens.

A rare dwarf of limited merit. I have found it very difficult to propagate, in common with some other high elevation species whose leaves turn brown in winter. Far less hairy than its apparent relation *setosum*. Probably better layered or cuttings taken very late. Rootability low.

Only found in a restricted area of N.E. Bhutan, W. Arunachal Pradesh and S.E. Xizang where it is common on open hillsides, rocks, boulder screes and swamps, sometimes co-dominant with *nivale* ssp. *nivale* Paludosum Group at 3,500–4,600m (11,500–15,000ft).   May–June

GLAUCA SUBSECTION (GLAUCOPHYLLUM SERIES)

Due to the quirks of the rules of nomenclature, the species *glaucum* became *glaucophyllum* Rehder but Glaucum or Glaucophyllum series became Glauca subsection.

A fairly distinctive subsection with very aromatic leaves, a strikingly glaucous leaf underside and usually an attractive peeling bark. Closest relatives are the Boothia and Campylogyna subsections.

Semi-dwarfs, 30cm–2m (1–6ft), leaves evergreen 2–9cm ($\frac{3}{4}$–4in) long, flowers freely produced on long pedicels, campanulate to tubular-campanulate, 3–10 per truss. Calyx deeply lobed, stamens 10, style sharply deflexed.

These are generally good garden plants but the flowers are sometimes small compared with the leaves. All are relatively hardy but can suffer autumn or winter frost damage here.

It should be noted that the status of many plants in this subsection has been altered.

brachyanthum Franch. 1886 H3–4 USDA 7a–6b L1–2 F1–3

Ht 0.3–2m (1–6ft). Habit fairly dense in open to leggy in shade. Attractive peeling bark.
L 2–6.5cm ($\frac{4}{5}$–2$\frac{1}{2}$in) long, 1–2.6cm ($\frac{2}{5}$–1in) wide, narrowly elliptic to narrowly obovate, dark above, glaucous beneath.
F pale yellow through yellow to greenish yellow, 1–2cm ($\frac{2}{5}$–$\frac{4}{5}$in) long, campanulate, 3–10 per truss, long pedicel, calyx large.

Useful for its late flowering and attractive when covered in masses of semi-pendulous flowers. Very aromatic, sometimes unpleasantly. 'Jaune' AM 1966.

There are two subspecies (formerly a species and its variety). ssp. *brachyanthum* has been found on Cangshan, C. Yunnan only. We only saw a handful of plants and no flowers or seed but managed to collect live material. Much rarer in the wild and in cultivation than ssp. *hypolepidotum* although Forrest's collectors found it several times. The differences are largely botanical and geographical. Scales on the leaf underside of ssp. *brachyanthum* very sparse and distant. Found at 2,700–3,400m (9,000–11,000ft) on steep rocky hillsides amongst scrub.

ssp. *hypolepidotum* (Franch.) Cullen 1978 (*charitostreptum* Balf.f. & Ward)

Scales on leaf underside much closer, 2–3 times their own diameter apart. Little difference horticulturally. Rootability medium to high. 'Blue Light' AM 1951. Leaf size very variable in the wild.

Has a wide distribution, 160km (100m) to the north of ssp *brachyanthum* in N.E. Burma, N.W. Yunnan and S.E. Xizang, 2,700–4,400m (9,000–14,500ft), in dry, open situations in forest and scrub and on boulders, cliffs sometimes limestone and occasionally epiphytic.

both ssp. May–July

charitopes Balf.f. & Farrer 1922 H3–4 USDA 7a–6b L2–3 F2–3

Ht 0.3–1.5m (1–5ft). Habit often dense but becomes leggy with age.
L 2.6–7cm (1–2$\frac{3}{4}$in) long, 1.3–3cm ($\frac{1}{2}$–1$\frac{1}{4}$in) wide, elliptic to obovate, dark above, very glaucous below.
F clear apple blossom-pink, sometimes spotted, 2–2.5cm ($\frac{4}{5}$–1in) long, about 3cm (1$\frac{1}{5}$in) across, widely campanulate, 2–6 per truss. Stamens conspicuous, style deflexed.

A very pretty plant with quite nice foliage and the most attractive flowers of the subsection. Sometimes blooms in autumn. Swelling buds easily frosted and plant not entirely hardy at Glendoick. 'Parkside' AM 1979, pink-flushed darker pink. Rootability low to medium.

Wild in Upper Burma and just over into N.W. Yunnan. Common over a small area. Farrer remarked on its beauty and he saw pure white forms, unfortunately never introduced. 3,200–4,300m (10,500–14,000ft on rocky slopes, cliffs, thickets and stream banks. April–May

charitopes ssp. *charitopes* differs from *tsangpoense* (now classed as a ssp. of *charitopes*) in its pink flowers and larger calyx 6–9mm ($\frac{1}{4}$–$\frac{1}{3}$in) long.

R. charitopes

charitopes ssp. **tsangpoense** (Ward) Cullen 1978 H4 or possibly 3 USDA 6b.
L1–2 F1–2
F usually purplish to pinkish, 1.3–2.6cm ($\frac{1}{2}$–1in) long.

Not usually such a good plant as ssp. *charitopes* and equally bud-tender. Tetraploid. Differs from ssp. *charitopes* in its more purplish flowers and smaller calyx, 3–6mm ($\frac{1}{8}$–$\frac{1}{4}$in) long. 'Cowtye' AM 1972 pinkish purple with darker spots.

Comes from much further N.W. than ssp. *charitopes* with no known overlap. Found in a small area of S.E. Xizang only on open rocky hillsides at 2,400–4,100m (8,000–13,500ft).   April–May

The plant formerly known as *tsangpoense* var *curvistylum* Cowan & Davidian is obviously a natural hybrid between ssp. *tsangpoense* and *campylogynum*. The type resembles ssp. *tsangpoense* while the cultivated plants are hybrids. Of little merit.

glaucophyllum Rehd. 1945 (*glaucum* Hook. 1849) H4 occasionally 3 USDA 6b
L1–2 F2–3

Ht 0.3–1.5m (1–5ft). Habit rather loose and spreading with nice brownish peeling bark.
L 3.5–9cm ($1\frac{1}{3}$–$3\frac{1}{2}$in) long, 1.3–2.5cm ($\frac{1}{2}$–1in) wide, lanceolate to narrowly elliptic to elliptic, very aromatic; *very glaucous* below.

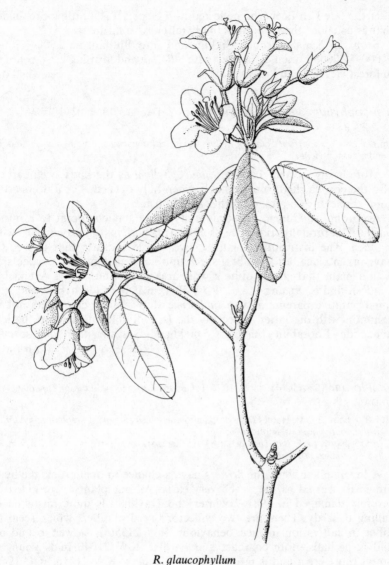

R. glaucophyllum

F pinkish-purple, rose to pale pink or creamy-white, 1.4–2.7cm ($\frac{2}{3}$–1$\frac{1}{8}$in) long, *campanulate*, 4–10 per truss. Calyx *large, leafy* and hairy, lobes acuminate, style usually *stout and deflexed*.

A fine species, long in cultivation, excellent for woodland edges. Long-lived, old specimens can eventually spread over a wide area. Quite variable in flower colour and habit. Free flowering and reasonably hardy with us at Glendoick. The fairly recently introduced creamy-white forms from E. Nepal appear to be the common type for that area. This is well worth growing for its own merit. Davidian gives this varietal status as var. *album* Davidian 1981, I feel correctly. A typical clone was named after the late Len Beer who collected it in Nepal. It is a little more tender than is usual for the type. Rootability (all) low to medium.

From E. Nepal, through Sikkim and into Bhutan, at 2,700–3,700m (9,000–12,000ft), often associated with *ciliatum* and forming large colonies in forest clearings and rocky slopes.   Late April–May

glaucophyllum var. *tubiforme* Cowan & Davidian 1948 H3–4 USDA 7a–6b L1–2 F2–3

Differs chiefly from var. *glaucophyllum* in its *tubular*-campanulate corolla and its slender straight style.

More easily frosted than var. *glaucophyllum* as the buds swell earlier, also the corolla sheds more quickly when fully opened. The flowers are a good shade of rose-pink on rather a stiff bush.

According to Cullen, the straight style and stamens point to a possibility of natural hybridity in its ancestry, perhaps *glaucophyllum* with *ciliatum*. The distribution of these two would indicate that this could have taken place but I doubt if speciation happens this way, particularly with a plant that covers quite a wide area in E. Bhutan, W. Arunachal Pradesh and S. Xizang. Also, 'Rosy Bell', a man-made hybrid with the same putative parents as var. *tubiforme*, shows many characters not in common with the latter, especially the lack of glaucousness on the leaf underside. Rootability medium. Davidian gives var. *tubiforme* specific status.   April–May

luteiflorum (Davidian) Cullen 1978 (*glaucopyllum* var. *luteiflorum* Davidian) H3 USDA 7a L1–2 F3

Ht 0.9–1.5cm (3–5ft). Habit fairly compact to erect, less sprawly than *glaucophyllum*. L as *glaucophyllum* but elliptic only. F *lemon-yellow*, 2–2.2cm (nearly 1in) long, campanulate, 3–6 per truss. Calyx lobes *rounded* at apex, *not hairy*.

A lovely plant when the flowers have a chance to open. Alas, the buds are easily frosted as they swell very early. All our plants were killed or severely damaged in 1981–2 winter and Davidian is quite mistaken in calling it hardy. There are two collector's seed numbers which seem to differ in cultivation in their behaviour. KW 21556 is slower to bud up and is perhaps more compact and hardier. KW 21040 buds younger, grows more erect and is more tender. 'Glencloy' KW 21556 FCC 1966, AM 1960. Rootability low to medium.

Only discovered in 1953 by KW in the Triangle, Upper Burma growing about the tree-line on crags at 2,700–3,000m (9,000–10,000ft).
                                                        April–May

pruniflorum Hutch. 1930 (*tsangpoense* var. *pruniflorum* Cowan & Davidian, *sordidum* Hutch.) H3–4 USDA 7a–6b L1–2 F1–2

Ht to 1m (3ft). Habit bushy. Bark brown, shredding. L 3–4.2cm (1⅕–1⅔in) long, 1.4–2.5cm (⅗–1in) wide, obovate to narrowly obovate, dark above, ± glaucous below, *scales very close together*. F *dull crimson, dusky violet* to *dull plum-purple*, 1–1.3cm (⅖–½in) long, campanulate. F *smaller* than *charitopes* ssp. *tsangpoense*.

Now given specific status once more. Cullen reckons this is closer to *brachyanthum* than *charitopes* (*tsangpoense*). The flowers, though not exciting, are of unusual shades and often cause comment. Liked by Lionel de Rothschild. Useful for its late flowers.

From Arunachal Pradesh, Upper Burma, S.E. Xizang, at 2,400–4,000m (8,000–13,000ft) in forest, rhododendron thickets and rocky hillsides.

May–June

shweliense Balf.f. & Forr. 1919 H3–4 USDA 7a–6b L1–2 F1–2

Ht 30–75cm (1–1½ft). Habit in cultivated plants, compact, often wider than high.
L 3.2–4cm (1⅖–1⅗in) long, 1.5–1.6cm (about ⅜in) wide, narrowly elliptic to narrowly obovate.
F yellow, flushed pink, about 1.1cm (almost ½in) long, campanulate, 2–4 per truss. Style pubescent. Corolla not scaly outside on herbarium specimens but with scales on cultivated plants.

A rare species. Cullen considers most if not all cultivated plants to be hybrids because of the scales on their corollas. There are only two rather poor specimens in the RBG, Edinburgh herbarium. The leaves on these look all right for size and shape compared with cultivated plants but the leaves are perhaps more glaucous below. Cultivated plants tend to lack vigour. Rootability medium to low.

A limited distribution on the Shweli-Salween divide, W. Yunnan, at 3,000–3,400m (10,000–11,000ft) on cliff ledges and rocky slopes. May–June

LAPPONICA SUBSECTION (LAPPONICUM SERIES)

This is the largest natural grouping of truly dwarf species. Apart from the aberrant *cuneatum* which Davidian has placed in a separate subseries, all normally grow under 1.5m (5ft) in cultivation.

All are small evergreen shrubs, ± aromatic, with densely scaly leaves on both surfaces and early deciduous leaf bud scales. Flowers in terminal trusses, several flowered, usually openly funnel-shaped, colour purple/purplish-blue, yellow and rarely pink. Whites are purely albino forms. Pedicels short, calyx usually conspicuous. Stamens 5–10. Capsule short and scaly.

Distribution, apart from *lapponicum*, extends from Nepal eastwards well into W. and N. China. *R. lapponicum* including Parvifolium Group is circumpolar and reaches southwards into N. USA, N.E. Siberia and Japan.

The majority grow wild in a similar habitat. Unless otherwise stated, the following covers all the various types of habitat. Open rocky hillsides, dry or moist grassy pastures, peaty moorland, limestone screes and cliffs, on or amongst boulders, by streams and waterfalls and margins of thickets. These plants, more than any others, take the place of *Calluna vulgaris* on the Chinese mountains.

Many are excellent, hardy, free-flowering and easily grown garden plants. All are hardiness H4–5. Several have been much used in hybridizing, largely to produce the so-called blues like 'Blue Diamond' and 'Songbird'. Several have relatively frost-resistant flowers. Those with an open or leggy habit stand up well to pruning, even with shears. To make a really effective display, plant in bold clumps, close together, so that they can grow into each other and form an undulating carpet.

This subsection was revised by Professor W. R. and Dr Melva Philipson of New Zealand with a few modifications by Cullen. The Philipsons record a number of probable natural hybrids. While it is hard to accept everything the Philipsons have done, a careful look through the herbarium specimens in the RBG, Edinburgh revealed that they are now far better classified than they were previously. Several species have been reported with white variants in the wild but very few are at present in cultivation. Several species are polyploids, or have mixed chromosome numbers.

There is an old rule of nomenclature which allows the use of a specific name (or former specific name) at sub-specific or varietal status for a completely different plant. The Philipsons have done this no less than three times in their revision of this subsection. While their right to do this must be accepted, it can only add to confusion in the nomenclature of the genus and from a horticultural point of view, it merely adds to the present chaos in classification. These three names are *occidentale*, *australe* and *longistylum*. If at any time somebody wishes to raise any of these to specific status, the names will have to be changed.

amundsenianum Hand. Mazz. 1921 Not in cultivation.

Only known from two collections of poor material from S.W. Sichuan.

bulu Hutch. 1932 Not in cultivation. An erect or straggly shrub to 1.6m (5ft) with L 1.2–2cm ($\frac{1}{2}$–$\frac{3}{4}$in) long. F pinkish-purple to deep violet, occasionally white, 1–5 per truss. Variable.

Known distribution restricted to a part of the Tsangpo valley, S. Xizang in open woodland and open hillsides, common in places.

burjaticum Malyschev 1961 Not in cultivation. Spreading shrub to 15cm (6in). L 0.8–1.2cm ($\frac{1}{3}$–$\frac{1}{2}$in) long. F rosy-violet, 3–8 per truss.

Probably closely related to *lapponicum* but has short stamens and style. The only other species in the subsection to occur outside the Sino-Himalayan region. E. Sajan Mountains, S.W. of Lake Baikal, Siberia.

capitatum Maxim. 1877 H4–5 USDA 6b–5 & 6a L1–2 F1–2

Ht to 1.5m (5ft). Habit nearly always *erect* (Philipsons state rounded, wrongly).
L 0.6–2.5cm ($\frac{1}{4}$–1in) long, elliptic, rather pale and shiny above.
F pale lavender to deep purple, 1–1.5cm ($\frac{2}{5}$–$\frac{3}{5}$in) long, 3–5 per truss. Stamens 10, style average length.

A rare member of the subsection and one of the earliest to bloom. Should be very hardy owing to its northern habitat. Related to *nitidulum*. Needs the introduction of better forms. Rootability low to medium.

Grows like heather in N. China in Gansu, E. Xizang, Sichuan and Shaanxi at 3,000–4,300m (10,000–14,000ft) in forests and moist meadows and on mountainsides.   March–April

complexum Balf.f. & W.W. Sm. 1916 H5 USDA 5 & 6a L1–2 F1–2

Ht 8–60cm (3in–2ft). Habit compact or erect, much branched.
L 0.3–1.1cm ($\frac{1}{8}$–$\frac{2}{5}$in) long, elliptic to ovate.
F pale lilac to rosy-purple, 0.9–1.3cm ($\frac{1}{3}$–$\frac{1}{2}$in) long, 3–5 per truss. Style usually short.

A very neat and tidy little plant as I know it in cultivation with tiny leaves. Rare. Rootability medium.

From N. Yunnan, 3,400–4,600m (11,000–15,000ft). April–May

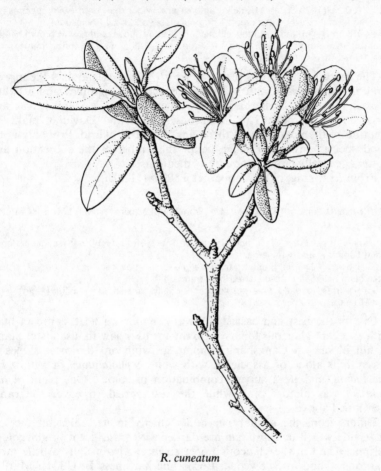

R. cuneatum

cuneatum W.W. Sm. 1914 (*cheilanthum* Balf.f. & Forr., *cinereum* Balf.f. & Forr., *ravum* Balf.f. & Sm., *scherocladum* Balf.f. & Forr.) H4–5 USDA 6b–5 & 6a L1–2 F2–3

Ht 1–2m (3–6ft), occasionally taller. Habit bushy or erect.
L 1.1–7cm ($\frac{2}{5}$–nearly 3in) long, narrowly to broadly elliptic, fawn to deep rust below, hardly to fairly aromatic.
F rose-lavender to deep rose-purple, funnel-shaped, 1.2–3.1cm (about 1in) long, 3–6 per truss. Calyx 0.2–1.2cm long, stamens 10, style average length.

The giant of the subsection and rather aberrant, lying between the Lapponica and Heliolepida subsections but having a large, deeply lobed calyx. Usually free-flowering but more easily frosted than most of the subsection. Fairly hardy in S. Sweden. Variable in leaf and flower colour. Rootability low to medium. Given its own subseries by Davidian.

From N. & W. Yunnan into S.W. Sichuan, 2,700–4,300m (9,000–14,000ft), often in forests as well as above the tree line. Common.

March–May

dasypetalum Balf.f. & Forr. 1919 H4–5 USDA 6b–5 & 6a L2–3 F1–2

Ht 30–90cm (1–3ft). Habit usually compact and wider than high (wild specimens a jumbled lot but mostly rather erect; 1 original plus 3 added by Philipsons).
L 0.8–1.6cm ($\frac{1}{3}$–$\frac{3}{4}$in) long, oblong-elliptic, often shiny above, and tawny-brown below.
F bright rose-purple, broadly funnel-shaped, 1.2–1.8cm ($\frac{1}{2}$–$\frac{3}{4}$in) long. Stamens 10, style longer than stamens. Tetraploid.

The more I look at this plant (as we grow it at Glendoick) the more I am convinced it is a natural hybrid between a Lapponica and a Saluenensia. None of the herbarium specimens show the shiny leaves and large flowers of ours. The Philipsons, Cullen and Davidian make no mention of the possibility of this being a natural hybrid. Probably not a good species anyway. Foliage better than most of the subsection and flowers generally larger. Rootability medium.

From Li-ti-ping, N.W. Yunnan at 3,500m (11,500ft).   April–May

fastigiatum Franch. 1886 (*capitatum* Franch. not Maxim., *nanum* Léve.) H4–5 L2–3 F2–3

Ht usually under 60cm (2ft), occasionally to 1m+ (3ft+). Habit *not* fastigiate, dense, mound-forming and symmetrical.
L 0.5–1.6cm ($\frac{1}{5}$–$\frac{3}{4}$in) long, oblong to ovate, *glaucous* above, scales *pale opaque* below, often giving a *mushroom-coloured appearance*.
F light purple to deep blue-purple, occasionally pinkish, 0.9–1.8cm ($\frac{2}{5}$–$\frac{3}{4}$in) long, funnel-shaped, 1–5 per truss.

One of the best and easiest of dwarfs, making a neat, compact bush with excellent glaucous foliage in many forms. I saw thousands of plants in full bloom on Cangshan, Yunnan, growing on the lower slopes of grassy hills alone or associated with white *cephalanthum* or yellow *trichocladum*, making a superb combination of colour. One plant of *fastigiatum* was almost pink while the rest varied to cover the range mentioned above.

Differs from the similar *impeditum* chiefly in its scales on the leaf underside which in *impeditum* are darker with translucent bright golden periphery and in the glaucous upper surface. Also usually a little more vigorous. Good in S. Sweden. Borderline hardiness E. USA. AM 1914 blue-lilac flowers. Rootability high.

Common in N. and C. Yunnan, 3,200–4,900m (10,500–16,000ft).

April–May

flavidum Franch. 1895 (*primulinum* Hems.) H3–4(–5?) USDA 7a–6b(–5 & 6a?) L1–2 F2–3

Ht to 2.5m (8ft) but usually to 1m (3ft). Habit erect.
L 0.7–1.5cm ($\frac{1}{3}$–$\frac{2}{5}$in) long, broadly elliptic to oblong, *shiny* above with prominent reddish scales below.
F pale yellow, 1.2–1.8cm (about $\frac{3}{5}$in) long, broadly funnel-shaped.

Differs from *rupicola* var. *chryseum* and var. *muliense* in its shiny leaves and more erect habit. Quite pretty but the clone we grow never looks happy and is liable to die back frequently. So-called white forms which grow taller with larger leaves and flowers (of unknown ancestry) are found in cultivation but there are no matching wild specimens. They are probably hybrids, perhaps with *yunnanense*. Difficult in S. Sweden.

From N.W. Sichuan, 3,000–4,000m (10,000–13,000ft), common over a limited area.   April–May

flavidum var. *psilostylum* Rehd. & Wils. 1913

This may be a natural hybrid. The Philipsons first considered it to be *flavidum* × *rupicola* var. *muliense*. Broader leaves, differing scales and a smaller calyx than type. Probably of little consequence. N.W. Sichuan, W. 3452 only.

hippophaeoides Balf.f. & W.W. Sm. 1916 (*fimbriatum* Hutch.) H4–5 USDA 6b–5 & 6a L2–3 F2–3

Ht to 1.25m (4ft). Habit erect, compact to sprawly.
L 0.8–3.8cm ($\frac{1}{3}$–1$\frac{1}{2}$in) long, elliptic to oblong, *pale slightly glaucous green above*, yellowish buff below.
F usually lavender blue, occasionally rose to bluish purple, about 1.2cm ($\frac{1}{2}$in) long, nearly 2.5cm (1in) across, broadly funnel-shaped, 4–8 per truss. Stamens 10, style variable in length.

One of the best and most cultivated members of the subsection. The many introductions are remarkably uniform for such a widespread species with only moderate variation in height, habit and flower colour. The Beima-shan forms are reckoned to be the best with fine trusses of richer coloured flowers though a little straggly in habit. Hardy in much of E. USA and has even flowered successfully in Iceland. AM 1927, lavender-blue flowers. AGM 1925. The Philipsons have shifted a number of narrow-leaved specimens into here from *websterianum*.

Fimbriatum Group

Davidian has rightly or wrongly retained this at specific status. It merges completely with *hippophaeoides* in the wild. The form with extremely long style and stamens certainly deserves some recognition. Also tends to have more purple in the flower colour. Fairly hardy in S. Sweden. Rootability medium.

From N.W., W., S.W., N. and C. Yunnan and S.W. Sichuan at 2,400–4,800m (8,000–16,000ft). One of the few species found in bogs, also on forest margins.   April–May, occasionally March

hippophaeoides var. *occidentale* Philipson & Philipson 1975

A variant with a longer style, smaller inflorescence and narrower leaf which may not be in cultivation. I cannot make out why this is not the same as Fimbriatum Group. Why banish an old name and then bring in a new one for something remarkably similar by description? N. and C. Yunnan at 3,500–4,300m (11,500–14,000ft).

impeditum Balf.f. & W.W. Sm. 1916 (*litangense* Hutch., *semanteum* Balf.f.) H3–5 USDA 7a–5 & 6a L1–3 F2–4

Ht to 90cm+ in wild but rarely over 30cm (1ft) in cultivation. Habit dense cushions, symmetrical.
L 0.4–1.5cm ($\frac{1}{6}$–$\frac{3}{5}$in) long, elliptic to ovate to oblong, *not usually shiny or glaucous above*. Scales darker than *fastigiatum* with bright golden periphery.
F mauve through violet to purplish-blue, broadly funnel-shaped, 0.7–1.6cm ($\frac{1}{3}$–$\frac{3}{5}$in) long, 1–4 per truss, usually 1–2 on the typical compact forms.

Perhaps the best known of the subsection and undoubtedly one of the finest. Somewhat variable in vigour although always compact. We find the dwarfest forms a little tender and miffy and no longer propagate them. Some forms in the trade are *fastigiatum* or hybrids. Borderline hardiness in E. USA. Fairly hardy in S. Sweden.

I am not happy with the Philipsons' interpretation of the differences between *fastigiatum* and *impeditum* nor with the inclusion of erect-growing specimens in *impeditum* formerly in *litangense*. The latter should perhaps have been retained at specific status, with a broadly upright habit and longer leaves. Two numbers, 0533 and 0557, of our own introductions from Cangshan appear to be *impeditum* and not *fastigiatum* as first thought. AM 1944 R 59263 AGM 1968. Rootability medium to high.

From N. Yunnan, S.W. Sichuan, 2,700–4,900m (9,000–16,000ft), widespread and common.
April–May

intricatum Franch. 1895 (*blepharocalyx* Franch., *peramabile* Hutch.) H4–5 USDA 6b–5 & 6a L1–2 F2–3

Ht to 1.5m (5ft) in the wild, only to 90cm (3ft) in cultivation. Habit fairly dense and twiggy.
L 0.5–1.4cm ($\frac{1}{5}$–$\frac{3}{5}$in) long, oblong to elliptic, *pale greyish-green above*.
F pale lavender through mauve to dark blue, usually pale lavender-blue in cultivation, 0.8–1.4cm ($\frac{1}{3}$–$\frac{3}{5}$in) long, *tubular* with spreading lobes often in a compact truss of 2–8. Stamens usually 10, style and stamens usually *very short*, style shorter than stamens.

A distinctive species (see characters in italics above). I have known this to be the only rhododendron in the garden to remain unfrosted. The pretty little unusual-shaped flowers are earlier than most of the subsection. Very hardy here at Glendoick but winter-killed in Washington D.C. Difficult in S. Sweden FCC 1907. Rootability low to medium according to clone.

Quite plentiful in N. Yunnan, S.W. and C. Sichuan. Also occurs on forest margins, marshes and on limestone at 3,400–4,600m (11,000–15,000ft).
March–May

lapponicum (L) Wahlenburg 1812 (*confertissimum* Nakai, *ferruginosa* Pallas, *palustre* Turczaninow, *parviflorum* F. Schmidt, *parvifolium* Adams) H5 USDA 5 & 6a L1–2 F1–2

Ht to 1m (3ft). Habit prostrate to erect, often gnarled in the wild.
L 0.4–2.5cm ($\frac{1}{6}$–1in) long, oblong elliptic to elliptic ovate, greyish to dark green above.
F pale magenta-rose to purple, occasionally white, broadly funnel-shaped, 3–6 per truss. Stamens 5–10, style longer than stamens. Said to be sometimes scented.

The Philipsons have now included *parvifolium* within *lapponicum*. While *parvifolium* as we know it and *lapponicum* probably merge botanically in E. Asia, there is a distinct difference horticulturally. The Arctic plants have been found almost impossible to keep in cultivation while those from Japan and probably nearby Korea and Siberia are comparatively easy to grow. We have one upright-growing *lapponicum* collected on the Great Slave Lake, Canada. Even this does not flourish and has yet to flower after several years. There are relic populations in outlying USA locations in Wisconsin, New York and on Mt Washington, New Hampshire at 1,550m (5,000ft). In Greenland it is generally much lower. Some success has been reported in cultivating these southern forms and a form from Labrador. Try sowing seed direct on to a peat block and establishing it in a trough.

Circumpolar distribution, often growing over permafrost where the soil is sometimes alkaline, up to pH 8.5 and also in peat, clay and moss on limestone, serpentine and igneous rocks. Even in Canada it grows at elevations of 900–1,800m (3,000–6,000ft).   January–February or later?

Parvifolium Group

We grow two forms of this, one probably from Siberia, the other from Japanese seed. The former opens its flowers in January–March according to season and can be considered a most valuable, hardy winter flowering dwarf shrub. Very hardy in S. Sweden. The Japanese form with darker flowers does not open until at least a month later. All efforts to locate a white form have so far failed. Rootability low, but easily layered. E. Siberia, Korea and Japan, only N.E. Hokkaido in a small area in clearings in *Abies* forest.

minyaense Philipson & Philipson 1975. Not in cultivation.

A rare local species with sturdy shoots and wide leaves from Minya Konka range, N.W. Sichuan. Probably related to *nitidulum* and *websterianum*, all with a large coloured calyx. Said to grow larger and sturdier than *nitidulum*. Probably 2–3 flowers per truss. Looks to me like a good species. 4,100–4,900m (13,500–16,000ft).

nitidulum Rehd. & Wils. 1913 H4–5 USDA 6b–5 & 6a L1–2 F1–2 (*nitidulum* var. *nubigerum* Rehd. & Wils.)

Ht to 1.3m (4ft). Habit usually erect.
L 0.5–1.1cm (⅕–⅖in) long, ovate to elliptic, dark above, uniformly pale lepidote below.
F rosy-lilac to violet purple, funnel-shaped, 1–2 per truss.

A little known species which I have never grown and may be lost to cultivation.

From N.W. Sichuan, 3,000–5,000m (10,000–16,000ft).   April–May

nitidulum var. **omeiense** Philipson & Philipson

Only slight botanical differences from the above: these are a more prominently mucronate leaf apex, some darker scales on the leaf underside and smaller calyx lobes. Only known from the summit of Mt Omei, C. Sichuan at 3,200–3,500m (10,500–11,500ft). This has recently been introduced and has neat little leaves. In view of the fact that specimens of var. *nitidulum* have also been collected on Mt Omei, this seems an unnecessary variety, as it is probably only a minor variation within the species.

nivale Hook. f. 1849 (*paludosum* (part) Hutch. & Ward) H5 USDA 5 & 6a L1 F1

Ht to 45cm (1½ft), rarely to 1.5m (5ft) in the wild. Cultivated plants of the typical plant are generally much lower. Habit very short growth often with thickish shoots when growth is very slow.
L only about 0.2–1cm ($\frac{1}{12}$ $\frac{2}{5}$in) long on the typical plant with *prominent dark scales on both surfaces*.
F purple, reddish purple, bright mauve to violet or pink, about 1.3cm (½in) or less long, widely funnel-shaped, 1–2 per truss. Stamens 10, style about equal or slightly longer than stamens.

It is difficult to know what to make of *paludosum*. Some specimens appear upright in habit but the field notes say only 9–12in high. I do feel the Philipsons have made a mistake here in making *paludosum* a synonym of *nivale*. Cultivated plants of *paludosum* have larger leaves as well as an upright habit.

The typical high-elevation plant from the Himalayas is difficult to grow and presents a challenge although it is not of great horticultural merit. New introductions from Nepal which could prove easier to cultivate are becoming established. Difficult in S. Sweden. Comes from the highest altitude of all rhododendrons. Rootability low.

From Nepal, Sikkim, Bhutan, S. and S.E. Xizang, 3,000–5,800m (10,000–19,000ft). April–May

nivale ssp. *boreale* Philipson & Philipson 1975 (*alpicola* Rehd. & Wils., *batangense* Balf.f., *nigropunctatum* Franch., *oreinum* Balf.f., *oresbium* Balf.f. & Ward, *ramosissimum* Franch., *stictophyllum* Balf.f., *vicarium* Balf.f., *violaceum* Rehd. & Wils. *yaragongense* Balf.f.)

Differs from ssp. *nivale* in the consistently smaller calyx lobes, the style being shorter than the stamens, and lesser contrast in scale colours. Horticulturally, this is a conglomeration of former species, some of which appear to have at least some distinction in the plants that are cultivated. Six species were recognized in the *1980 Rhododendron Handbook*: *alpicola*, *nigropunctatum*, *oresbium*, *ramosissimum*, *stictophyllum* and *violaceum*, and all are said to be in cultivation. I grow *nigropunctatum*, *ramosissimum* and *stictophyllum* and have to admit that the first and last bear little resemblance to *nivale* as I know it. This is the sort of amalgamation that really annoys gardeners and with some justification. Yet the 1980 *Handbook* made no attempt to give any of these 'Group' status. *R. stictophyllum* and *nigropunctatum* as I grow them are neat plants in foliage and flower with shiny leaves and bright mauve and pale purple flowers respectively. The former is the better plant. The point is, how many clones of these six former species exist in cultivation and are they typical of the original descriptions? The subsection badly needed a reduction in the number of former species. Most of us do welcome the reduction the Philipsons have made, but unfortunately they have done it in rather a clumsy way. *R. nivale* ssp. *boreale* now contains a huge conglomeration of specimens taken from many old species sources. The majority do appear to follow a type of low, much-branched, small-leaved plant but some are aberrant with a fastigiate habit and/or narrower leaves. Rootability mostly medium.

nivale ssp. *australe* Philipson & Philipson 1975

From examination of the scales and other characters, it would appear that although specimens have been moved from *telmateium, impeditum, drumonium, paludosum* and *idoneum,* they are a relatively uniform lot and the Philipsons have arranged the specimens much better than they were previously. The chief characters separating this ssp. from the other two are the ciliate calyx lobes and the ± acute leaf apex. From N.W. and C. Yunnan, 3,100–4,300m (10,250–14,000ft).

orthocladum Balf.f. & Forr. 1919 H4–5 USDA 6b–5 & 6a L1–2 F1–2

Ht to 1.3m (4ft). Habit erect but much branched.
L 0.8–1.6cm ($\frac{1}{3}$–$\frac{3}{5}$in) long, narrowly elliptic to *lanceolate,* slightly glaucous above.
F pale to deep lavender-blue to purple, funnel-shaped, 0.7–1.3cm (about $\frac{2}{5}$in) long, 1–5 per truss. Stamens 8–10, style equal to or *shorter than stamens.*

Some of the bluer forms are quite pretty and worth growing. Similar appearance to *polycladum* but style much shorter. Rootability various.
From N. Yunnan, S.W. Sichuan, 3,400–4,300m (11,000–14,000ft).

April–May

orthocladum var. *longistylum* Philipson & Philipson 1975

Said to differ from var. orthocladum in its longer style but how does this differ from *polycladum?* Seems rather an unnecessary taxa.
N. and N.W. Yunnan, 3,500m (11,500ft).

orthocladum var. *microleucum* (Hutch.) Philipson & Philipson 1975

Ht to 60cm (2ft). Habit compact, usually forming a mound.
F pure white, about 1.9cm ($\frac{3}{4}$in) across, 2–3 per truss.

Described from a cultivated plant, possibly from F 22108 (*polycladum*). I have found at least two apparently different clones of this but there is little difference horticulturally. As there is no known wild population and it is just an albino, it should not really have any botanical standing. It is a first-rate hardy (both plant and flowers) plant and very useful as a contrast to the usual-coloured Lapponicums. FCC 1939. Rootability medium.

April–May

polycladum Franch. 1886 (*compactum* Hutch., *scintillans* Balf.f. & W.W. Sm.) H4–5 USDA 6b–5 & 6a L1–2 F2–4

Ht to 1.2m (4ft). Habit upright and spreading with some vigorous shoots.
L 0.8–1.8cm ($\frac{1}{3}$–$\frac{3}{4}$in) long, *narrowly elliptic* to elliptic, dark green.
F lavender to rich purple-blue, 0.7–1.3cm (about $\frac{1}{2}$in) long, to 5 per truss. Stamens 10, style *longer* than stamens.

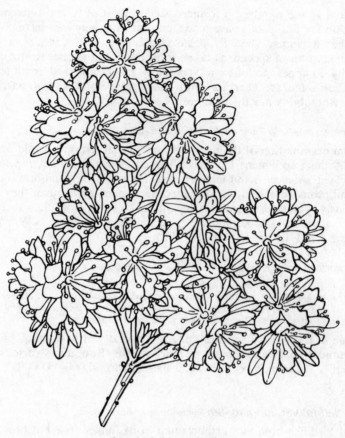

R. polycladum (scintillans)

It is sad that the well-known name *scintillans* has to go. The best blue forms, FCC and Wisley, are amongst the nearest to true-blue of all rhododendrons. A very fine plant, exceptionally free-flowering and a must for every collection. Plant in an open situation and prune or clip if necessary. Fairly successful in E. USA. Good in S. Sweden. FCC 1934 lavender-blue. AM 1924 purplish-rose, AGM 1968. In its typical form which includes most wild collections, this is quite a clear-cut species. Rootability high.

Common in N., N.W. and C. Yunnan, 3,000–4,400m (10,000–14,500ft).

April–May

rupicola W.W. Sm. 1914 (*achroanthum* Balf.f. & W.W. Sm., *propinquum* Tagg) H4–5 USDA 6b–5 & 6a L1–2 F2–3

Ht to 60cm (2ft) or more. Habit fairly compact to occasionally straggly.
L 0.6–2.1cm ($\frac{1}{4}$–$\frac{4}{5}$in), broadly elliptic to elliptic with *prominent scales on both sides, both dark and pale mixed*.

F intense purple, occasionally crimson to magenta, broadly funnel-shaped, about 1.3cm ($\frac{1}{2}$in) long, up to 6 per truss. Stamens 5–10, style usually slightly longer than stamens.

Perhaps the deepest-coloured Lapponicum and well worth growing as a result. Especially attractive with the sun shining through the flowers. Fairly good in S. Sweden. The unpublished name *luridum* of KW fits in here although Davidian says it equals *russatum*. It has extremely dark flowers. Several specimens of *russatum* (formerly under *cantabile*) with small leaves have been moved to this species by the Philipsons. Rootability low, layers easily.

Common and widespread in S.E. Xizang, N. Burma, N., N.W., W. and C. Yunnan and S.W. Sichuan, 3,000–4,600m (10,000–15,000ft). April–May

rupicola var. chryseum (Balf.f. & Ward) Philipson & Philipson 1975 H4 USDA 6b L1–2 F2–3

Ht to 60cm (2ft) or more. Habit variable, compact to open.
L as var. *rupicola* but averaging a little smaller.
F cream through pale and greenish yellow to occasionally pinkish, *calyx lobes with hairs, no scales*.

The best forms are excellent garden plants, free-flowering and hardy, and make fine companions for the purplish members of the subsection. Variable in habit and size of leaves and flowers, having been introduced many times. Difficult in S. Sweden. Sensitive to heat and poor drainage in E. USA. Hard to root from cuttings but easily layered. It would seem that there are better forms of this and var. *muliense* awaiting introduction.

Common in N.E. Burma, N.W. Yunnan and S.E. Xizang, 3,300–4,700m (11,000–15,500ft). April–May

rupicola var. muliense (Balf.f. & Forr.) Philipson & Philipson 1975.

Very similar to var. *chryseum* with which it was previously made synonymous but has now been reinstated by the Philipsons as a variety. It differs from var. *chryseum* in its hairs plus scales on the calyx lobes, narrowly oblong instead of broadly elliptic leaves and lesser contrast in the two colours of scales on the leaf underside.

Found wild to the east of var. *chryseum* in S.W. Sichuan at 3,000–4,900m (10,000–16,000ft).

russatum Balf.f. & Forr. 1919 (*cantabile* Hutch., *osmerum* Balf.f. & Forr.) H4–5 USDA 6b–5 & 6a L1–2 F3–4

Ht 30cm–1.8m (1–6ft). Habit variable, dwarf and compact to upright and leggy.
L usually 1.6–4cm ($\frac{3}{5}$–1$\frac{1}{2}$in) long but occasionally to 8.6cm (2$\frac{1}{2}$in), narrowly elliptic to oblong-elliptic to broadly elliptic, dark and light scales below.
F deep indigo-blue, deep reddish-purple to occasionally rose or white, broadly funnel-shaped, 1–2cm ($\frac{2}{5}$–$\frac{4}{5}$in) long, 4–6 per truss, stamens 10.

The colours of the best forms of this species are the most brilliant purplish-blues in the genus. Very variable in habit, flower colour and leaf size. There is a tendency for large leaves to go with straggly habit. These forms are better avoided. A must for every collection and superb in contrast with yellows, whites and pinks. Fairly successful in parts of E. USA and good in S. Sweden. An off-white form in cultivation is in my opinion not worth growing. I threw it out. FCC 1933 intense blue flowers, AM 1927 intense violet-blue, AGM 1938. Seems to hybridize (merge?) naturally with *rupicola* on quite a scale; rootability mostly medium, occasionally high.

From N. and N.W. Yunnan and S.W. Sichuan, 3,400–4,300m (11,000–14,000ft)

April–May

setosum D. Don 1821 H4–5 USDA 6b–5 & 6a L1–2 F?1–3

Ht to 1.2m (4ft) but usually to 45cm (1½ft). Habit low but often open. *Branchlets bristly.*
L 1–1.9cm (about ½in) long, elliptic, oblong to obovate, *hairy margins, underside and petiole.*
F purple to pinkish to wine-red, openly funnel-shaped, 1.5–1.8cm (about ¾in) long, 2–6 per truss. Large coloured calyx.

A very distinct species, rather aberrant in this subsection. In fact the Philipsons placed it in a separate subsection but Cullen considered its affinities with the Lapponica subsection were sufficient to move it back there. The flower colours of some forms are sufficiently bright to make them quite showy. Several new introductions have been made from Nepal and Sikkim in recent years which may give an extra colour range. Shows some affinity with *fragariflorum* and the Saluenensia subsection. Sometimes inclined to partial die-back. Rootability low.

From Nepal, Sikkim, W. Bengal, Bhutan and the Chumbi valley, S. Xizang, at 2,700–4,900m (9,000–16,000ft).

May

tapeteforme Balf.f. & Ward Probably not in cultivation.

Ht to 90cm (3ft), usually much lower. Habit matted or rounded.
L 0.4–1.2 rarely to 1.7cm (⅙–½in) long, broadly elliptic to orbicular, rufous below.
F usually purplish to purplish-blue, rarely violet, rose or even yellow, broadly funnel-shaped, 1–4 per truss. Style usually longer than stamens.

Herbariums contain many specimens under this name so it would be surprising if it has not been introduced and cultivated. Davidian says it is rare in cultivation. Resembles a more open-growing *impeditum*.

From N.E. Burma, S.W. Yunnan, S.E. Xizang, 3,500–4,600m (11,500–15,000ft).

telmateium Balf.f. & W.W. Sm. 1916 (*diacritum* Balf.f. & W.W. Sm., *drumonium* Balf.f. & W.W. Sm., *idoneum* Balf.f. & W.W. Sm., *pycnocladum* Balf.f. & W.W. Sm.) H4–5 USDA 6b–5 & 6a L1–2 F1–2

Ht to 90cm (3ft). Habit prostrate to erect. Branchlets often very slender.
L 0.3–1.2cm (⅛–½in) long, shape variable, typically *narrowly elliptic* to *lanceolate* but also broadly elliptic to orbicular.
F lavender to rose-pink to purple, broadly funnel-shaped, 0.7–1.2cm (⅓–½in) long, in trusses of 1–3. Stamens 10, style equal to or longer than stamens.

A neat little plant chiefly of interest for its very small leaves and flowers. Cultivated plants are usually erect in habit. It is evident that plants cultivated under the names *idoneum* and *drumonium* probably refer to *impeditum* and not this species. The variety *pycnocladum* was at first recognized by the Philipsons and then ignored. This is a pity as it has uniformly wider leaves and less fastigiate habit. I am happy with the inclusion of *diacritum* and *drumonium* (as in herbarium, RBG, Edinburgh) here, but not *idoneum* and var. *pycnocladum* which would have been better retained as separate taxa.

Common in the wild in N., N.W. and C. Yunnan and S.W. Sichuan, 2,900–5,000m (9,500–16,000ft), also on boggy forest margins, oak forest and dry pineclad slopes. April–May

thymifolium Maxim. 1877 (*polifolium* Franch., *spilanthum* Hutch.) H5 USDA 5 & 6a L1–2 F1–2

Ht to 1.2m (4ft). Habit *erect*.
L 0.5–1.2cm ($\frac{1}{5}$–$\frac{1}{2}$in) long, *0.2–0.5cm* ($\frac{1}{12}$–$\frac{1}{5}$in) *wide*, usually *narrowly obovate to oblanceolate*.
F pale lavender-blue to purple, broadly funnel-shaped, 0.7–1.1cm (about $\frac{1}{3}$in) long, in trusses of 1–2. Stamens 10+, style length variable.

A slow-growing (as we grow it) upright little shrub with distinctly narrow leaves and pretty little lavender-blue flowers. *R. thymifolium* and *spilanthum* are still considered distinct by Davidian. Rootability medium.

From E. Xizang, N. Sichuan, Qinghai and Gansu, 2,600–4,600m (8,500–15,000ft). April–May

tsaii Fang 1939. Not in cultivation

Ht to 30cm (1ft). Habit(?), probably erect.
L 0.6–1.2cm ($\frac{1}{4}$–$\frac{1}{2}$in) long, narrowly elliptic to oblong-lanceolate, dull grey-green above.
F pale purplish, broadly funnel-shaped, about 0.6cm ($\frac{1}{4}$in) long. Stamens 4–7 longer than style.

Appears to be like a dwarfer *hippophaeoides* with smaller leaves, flowers and number of stamens. Only known from type collection. E. Yunnan, 2,900m (9,500ft).

websterianum Rehd. & Wils. 1913 H5 USDA 5 & 6a L1–2 F1–2

Ht to 1.5m (5ft). Habit erect.
L 0.6–1.5cm ($\frac{1}{4}$–$\frac{3}{5}$in) long, ovate to oblong-elliptic to ovate-lanceolate, dull, dark greyish-green above.
F light purple, funnel-shaped, about 1.6cm ($\frac{2}{3}$in) long. Calyx large, usually coloured. Stamens 10, style longer than stamens.

The Philipsons doubt if this is in cultivation but many specimens were removed by them into *hippophaeoides* etc. Probably related to *nitidulum*.

From N.W. Sichuan, 3,300–4,900m (10,750–16,000ft).

websterianum var. **yulongense** Philipson & Philipson 1975

F yellow or white. Does not appear to differ from *rupicola* var. *chryseum* to me.

From N.W. Sichuan, 4,300–4,800m (14,000–15,500ft).

yungningense Balf.f. 1930 (*glomerulatum* Hutch.) H4–5 USDA 6b–5 & 6a L1–2 F1–2

Ht to 1.3m (4ft). Habit erect.
L 0.8–2cm ($\frac{1}{3}$–$\frac{4}{5}$in) long, elliptic to oblong, dull green above.
F deep purplish-blue to pale rose-purple, rarely white, broadly funnel-shaped, 1.1–1.4cm (about $\frac{1}{2}$in) long, 1–4 per truss. Stamens usually 10, style variable in length.

Probably near to *hippophaeoides* with smaller leaves. Apparently grows wild with *fastigiatum* as twice seed came back from F and R with these two species mixed. *R. glomerulatum* was described from a cultivated plant. Quite pretty in a modest way. Rootability medium? Herbarium specimens seem fairly uniform.

From N. and N.W. Yunnan and S.W. Sichuan, 3,200–4,300m (10,500–14,000ft).

April–May

Former species now considered by the Philipsons to be natural hybrids which have horticultural significance:

edgarianum Rehd. & Wils. H4–5 USDA 6b–5 & 6a L2 F2

This is considered a natural hybrid of *nivale* ssp. *boreale* by the Philipsons as collected under W 3467. They do not seem to give a sound reason for considering this to be a natural hybrid and state that the scales and calyx are quite different from the putative parent. F 13965, R 11098 and R 16450 have been moved into *tapeteforme*. A compact and neat plant with an upright habit.
L about 0.8cm ($\frac{1}{3}$in) long, broadly elliptic.
F blue-purple to rose-purple, about 1.3cm ($\frac{1}{2}$in) long, open funnel-shaped, 1–3 per truss.

Attractive in the better bluish forms. Useful for its later flowering than most of the subsection. Rootability low.

From S.E. Xizang–Sichuan border, 3,700–4,600m (12,000–15,000ft).

May–June

lysolepis Hutch. H4–5 USDA 6b–5 & 6a L2 F2

Ht to 1.2m (4ft). Habit fairly erect.
L up to 1.9cm ($\frac{3}{4}$in) long, oblong-elliptic, *dark and shiny above*.
F pinkish-purple, about 1.2cm ($\frac{1}{2}$in) long, broadly funnel-shaped, 2–3 per truss.

This plant, probably raised from KW 4456, appears, according to the Philipsons, to be *flavidum* × *impeditum*. The herbarium specimen of KW 4456 does look like a hybrid of *impeditum*. *R. lysolepis* itself was described from a cultivated plant at Kew and the type specimen from this suggests *flavidum* as a parent—this could be so, in view of the similar erect habit and shiny leaves. It has quite attractive foliage and flowers and is worth growing on these merits. Rootability medium.

From Sichuan, 3,700m (12,000ft). KW's description of his 4456 point to there having been a number of plants (similar), not an individual.

April–May

As would be expected with a complexity of plants such as there is in the Lapponica subsection, there are a number of intermediaries and natural hybrids among the herbarium specimens. I am sure that a visit to areas of Yunnan and Sichuan where many different species occur would reveal several hybrid swarms, particularly where man has disturbed the virgin environment.

1 *R. fastigiatum, orthocladum* var.
microleucum, rupicola var. *chryseum,*
Lapponica subsection
(painting: Rosemary Wise)

II *R. valentinianum*, Maddenia subsection
(painting: Margaret Stones)

III *R. calostrotum* 'Gigha' FCC,
Saluenensia subsection
(painting: Rosemary Wise)

IV *R. anthopogon* 'Betty Graham' AM L&S
1091, *anthopogon* apricot L&S, *laudandum*
var. *temoense*
(painting: Rosemary Wise)

V *R. haematodes*, Neriiflora subsection
(painting: Rosemary Wise)

VI *R. roxieanum*, Oreonastes Group,
Taliensia subsection
(painting: Margaret Stones)

VII *R. poukhanense*, section Tsutsusi
(Azalea section, Obtusum subseries)
(painting: Margaret Stones)

VIII *R.* 'Curlew' FCC AMT
(ludlowii X *fletcherianum)*
(painting: Margaret Stones)

LEPIDOTA SUBSECTION (LEPIDOTUM SERIES)

A small subsection which includes two rare species from central Nepal and the widespread, common and variable *lepidotum.* Leaves deciduous, semi-deciduous or evergreen, to 2m (6ft). Inflorescence terminal, pedicel long, 1–5 per truss. Flowers white, yellow, pink, reddish or purple, rotate campanulate. Calyx well-developed, stamens 10, style very short and sharply deflexed.

Often pretty in flower with neat, delicately poised, almost flat flowers.

Closely related to subsection Baileya, also related to Trichoclada and Lapponica. Distribution from Kashmir, along the Himalayas and into S.E. Xizang and N.W. Yunnan.

cowanianum Davidian 1952 H4 USDA 6b L1–2 F1

Ht to 2.4m (8ft). Habit open.
L deciduous, thin, 2.5–6.5cm (1–$2\frac{1}{2}$in) long, 2.2–3cm ($\frac{7}{8}$–$1\frac{1}{5}$in) wide, broadly elliptic to obovate, margins hairy, often colours well in autumn.
F precocious, pink, purplish magenta to deep wine, 1.4–2cm ($\frac{3}{5}$–$\frac{4}{5}$in) long, shortly campanulate, 2–5 per truss. Calyx large, reddish. The flowers in each truss open separately and the first drops before the last opens.

A distinct species, only discovered and introduced in 1954. It is of very limited garden value with small quickly shedding flowers. Not easy to grow and really only a collector's plant. As a result it is rare but obviously should not be allowed to die out in cultivation. We at Glendoick only have two plants left out of many original seedlings. Cullen considers it more closely related to *lepidotum* than to the Trichoclada subsection where it was originally placed on account of its scale type and inflorescence. Davidian has also moved it to the same subsection (series). Autumn colour sometimes good. Rootability medium from soft wood cuttings.

From Nepal, 3,000–4,000m (10,000–13,000ft), clearings or edges of forest, along rocks on river beds or in deep, wet tree-covered gorges. May

lepidotum (Wallich ex) G. Don 1834 (*cremastes* Balf.f. & Farrer, *elaeagnoides* Hook.f., *obovatum* Hook.f., *salignum* Hook., *sinolepidotum* Balf.f.) H2–5 USDA 7b & 8a–5 & 6a L1–2 F1–3

Ht 5cm–2m (2in–6ft). Habit low and compact to upright and leggy, often stoloniferous.
L 0.4–3.8cm ($\frac{1}{6}$–$1\frac{1}{2}$in) long, narrowly elliptic to obovate, rarely lanceolate, densely scaly below, evergreen, semi-deciduous to rarely deciduous.
F white, yellow through pink to purple and crimson, 1.2–2.4cm ($\frac{1}{2}$–1in) across, 1–3, rarely to 4 per truss, rotate-campanulate, pedicels slender, longer than corolla. Style very short, deflexed.

This could be the most widespread (except perhaps *lapponicum*) and variable of all species. As it comes from greatly differing altitudes, its hardiness is also very variable. Many different forms have been introduced but some of the most attractive-sounding ones have not, so careful selection in the wild when in flower would pay dividends. The dwarfest forms tend to be the hardiest and make nice, free-flowering plants and appreciate a fairly sunny position. The dwarf deciduous yellows formerly

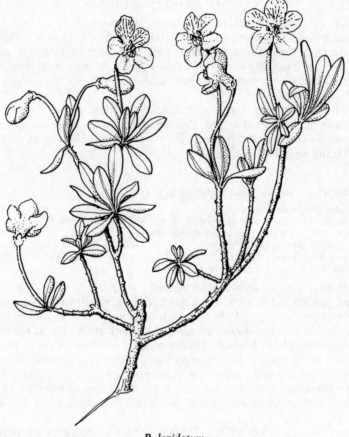

R. lepidotum

called *elaeagnoides* are closely related to *lowndesii*. Sometimes is or was burnt for incense in Xizang. 'Reuthe's Purple' AM 1967 is probably a hybrid with a member of the Saluenensia subsection. An almost white form from Caperci, USA, is also probably a hybrid. Mostly tender in S. Sweden. Rootability mostly low to medium.

Davidian has recently described the varieties *album* and *minutiforme* and says about ten or more different forms are in cultivation. This is a case where one could go on endlessly splitting hairs for leaf shape, flower colour and size, habit and so on. Herbarium specimens indicate little purpose in naming any variations at a botanical rank although 'Group' names could be useful for gardeners. Cullen confirms this.

From a huge area stretching from Kashmir all the way to N.W. Yunnan and S.E. Xizang, 2,400–4,900m (8,000–16,000ft), on a great variation of habitat from high moorland down to various types of forest plus rocks and cliffs, sometimes limestone. Can tolerate dry conditions in the wild. Common in both Himalayas and Yunnan.   May–June

lowndesii Davidian 1952 H3–4 USDA 7a–6b L1 F2–3

Ht 5–30cm (2in–1ft), usually to about 20cm (8in) in cultivation. Habit dense creeping mat, stoloniferous, *stems hairy*.
L deciduous, 1.5–2.5cm (⅗–1in) long, thin, narrowly elliptic to oblanceolate, *hairy*.
F pale yellow, lightly spotted, 1.2–2.4cm (½–1in) across, rotate-campanulate, 1–2 per truss.

A very pretty little shrublet when studded with numerous small flat flowers on erect pedicels. Unfortunately, it is rather hard to please and we at Glendoick lost all our original plants in various situations in endeavouring to discover its needs. We now cover it with cloche from September to May until the danger of frost is over and find this is the only way to avoid frosted or rotted shoots. It is well worth this trouble. Our biggest plant is now 70cm (28in) across and over 20 years old. Avoid overhanging trees or shrubs. Ideal for peat beds. Introduced in 1954 and collected again in 1983. Closely related to *lepidotum* but generally more hairy.

From C. and W. Nepal, only in drier areas, 3,000–4,600m (10,000–15,000ft), on shady rock ledges and crevices, peaty banks, grassy slopes and under boulders.   May–June

MADDENIA SUBSECTION (MADDENII SERIES)

Most of this subsection are too tall to be included here and are described in *The Larger Species of Rhododendron*. This is a large subsection of mostly tender species, the majority with white or white tinged pink, often scented flowers. Most have an epiphytic tendency and, if not in trees, are found on cliffs, rocks and very steep hillsides. They are closest-related to the Edgeworthia, Camelliiflora, Moupinensia and partly to the Triflora subsections, while the yellow-flowered species are close to the Boothia subsection. Leaves evergreen, young growth often hairy, inflorescence terminal, 1–6 rarely to 10 flowered. Stamens about 10, style longer than stamens.

Davidian has hived off these dwarfer species into a separate series (see *The Rhododendron Species, Vol. 1: Lepidotes*, 1982) called the Ciliatum series. From a gardener's point of view, this makes sense, but botanically, possibly not. In addition to the following, Davidian includes *amandum* and *crenulatum* (see *The Larger Species of Rhododendron* p.224), neither of which are in cultivation.

burmanicum Hutch. 1914 H2–3 USDA 7b & 8a–7a L1–2 F2–3

Ht to 2m (6ft). Habit usually compact but straggly in shade. Hairs on young shoots.
L to 7.5cm (3in) long, oblanceolate to obovate, dark green margins hairy, mostly shedding when L mature.
F yellow to creamy or greenish-yellow, 3–3.8cm (1⅕–1½in) long, funnel-campanulate, 5–10 per truss. Stamens 10.

A fine semi-dwarf yellow for the mildest British gardens only. Rather bud tender. Sometimes scented. Good in San Francisco. Rootability high.

From S.W. Burma only, Mount Victoria, 2,700–3,000m (9,000–10,000ft), on windward side and along forest edges on leeward slopes. Often scorched by grass fires.   April–May

ciliatum Hook. f. 1849 (*modestum* Hook.) H3(–4) USDA 7a–6b L2 F2–3

Ht to 2m (6ft) usually less. Habit compact in open, some forms straggly in shade. Bark roughish, reddish-brown, peeling. Branchlets hairy.
L 3.8–9cm (1½–3½in) long, elliptic to narrowly elliptic, hairy above and fringed with hairs.
F white or white flushed pink, 3.6–5cm (1½–2in) long, campanulate to funnel-campanulate, 2–5 per truss. Calyx conspicuous, stamens 10.

A well-known species, first found by Hooker in 1849 and reintroduced many times. Variable in flowering time, size, colour and shape of flower. Some forms hardier than others. Naturalizes itself in some gardens. Hardy enough for most parts of Britain except in winters like 1981–2. Very free flowering. L&S 17498 very early, poor, narrow flowers; BLM 314, 324 have given us some excellent forms. Rootability high. AM 1953 white tinged pink.

Often common in E. Nepal, Sikkim, Bhutan and S. Xizang, 2,400–4,000m (8,000–13,000ft), upper forest areas, rocky hillsides, beside water and boggy ground, sometimes associated with *glaucophyllum*.   March–May

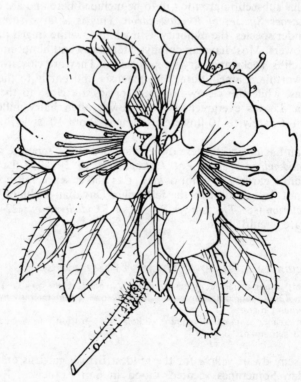

R. fletcherianum

fletcherianum Davidian 1961 H4 USDA 6b L2 F2–3

Ht to 1.20m (4ft). Habit compact when young, leggy with age. Bark roughish, reddish-brown, peeling.
L to 5cm (2in) long, oblong-lanceolate to oblong-elliptic, *bristly* margins. Narrowly *winged* petiole.
F pale yellow, nearly 5cm (2in) long and across, widely funnel-shaped, in compact trusses of 2–5. Calyx conspicuous, hairy, stamens 10.

Formerly known as Rock's *valentinianum* and considered closely related to this species by Cullen. To me it is far closer to *ciliatum* in foliage, habit and flower shape. It is easy to see from the herbarium specimens why this distinct plant was confused with *valentinianum*, and how these specimens can sometimes be misinterpreted.

A fine species, hardier than either relative but said to be tender or difficult at Windsor Park. Appreciates good drainage to avoid leaf spot. Very free-flowering and has proved to be an excellent parent for dwarf yellows. Rootability variable, low to high. 'Yellow Bunting' AM 1964.

Only found twice by R in S.E. Xizang, supposedly at 4,000–4,300m (13,000–14,000ft) (R often exaggerated his altitudes) in alpine regions and forests.

valentinianum (Forr. ex) Hutch 1919 H2–3 USDA 7b & 8a–7a L2–3 F2–3

Ht 1.3m (4ft) usually less. Habit fairly to very compact. Peeling bark.
L to 4.6cm (1¾in) long, elliptic, *rounded at both ends*, dark green above with *golden hairs* above and on margins.
F bright yellow, 2–3.5cm (⅘–1⅖in) long, funnel-campanulate, 1–6 per truss.

A very pretty plant in and out of flower with attractive dark hairy leaves and richly coloured flowers. Just hardy enough to survive in sheltered E. Scottish gardens. Good in the west, especially when planted on rocks and tree-stumps. Good around San Francisco. Sometimes shy-flowering. Very distinct. AM 1933. Rootability high.

Only grows wild in a small area on N.E. Burma–S.W. Yunnan frontier, 2,700–3,700m (9,000–12,000ft) in open scrub, rocky slopes and cliffs, sometimes limestone. March–April

valentinianum var. *changii* Fang 1939 Not in cultivation

Described from a number of collections from S.E. Sichuan which have non-bristly calyx and pedicel. The geographical disjunction is interesting.

MOUPINENSIA SUBSECTION (MOUPINENSE SERIES)

Three species, all from the same area of Sichuan. *R. moupinense* itself is well-known in cultivation, the other two have not (at least not until very recently) been introduced. They could turn out to be all one species after further population studies. None the less, *dendrocharis* and *petrocharis* would make most exciting introductions if they live up to the promise of herbarium specimens. The combination of tiny leaves and comparatively large flowers should make ideal little pot plants and might be valuable for hybridizing.

Low, usually epiphytic shrubs with hairy branchlets. Leaves very stiff and thick, margins ciliate. Flowers white to deep rose-red, 1–2 per truss.

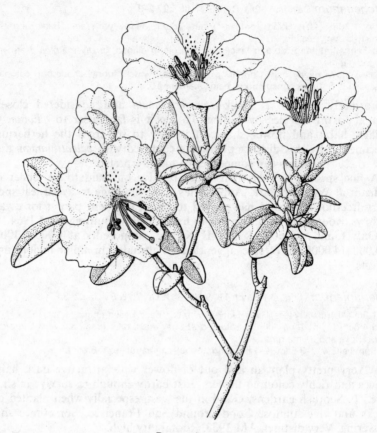

R. moupinense

moupinense Franch. 1886 H3–4 USDA 7a–6b L1–2 F3–4

Ht to 1.5m (5ft). Habit fairly compact in open to thin in shade.
L 2.5–4cm (1–1½in) long, narrowly ovate to elliptic or obovate, *stiff and thick*, dark green and shiny above, margins hairy.
F white, white-tinged pink to deep rose-red, with or without spots, 3–3.8cm (1⅕–1½in) long, up to 5cm (2in) across, openly funnel-campanulate, 1–3 per truss. Stamens 10, style longer than stamens.

This beautiful, early flowering species is usually surprisingly hardy but is prone to bark-split, especially when young. The buds and flowers are relatively tough, putting up with light frosts for a day or two. Needs perfect drainage and is remarkably drought resistant. Does well on rocks and stumps and by partly shaded walls which can help protect the early flowers. Sensitive to intense heat. Shoots very brittle. Good around San Francisco. Not hardy in S. Sweden. The parent of many early flowering hybrids. We find a white form of W 879 definitely more tender than the pink forms we have grown for years. The intensity of colour increases after hard frost particularly with late opening buds. The almost red form, still rare, is worth acquiring. AM 1914 flowers white, AM 1937 suffused rose-pink, spotted crimson. Rootability high.

Found in C. Sichuan and in Guizhou, 2,000–3,300m (6,500–10,800ft), usually epiphytic on broad-leaved trees and also on rocks and cliffs.

February–March occasionally April

dendrocharis Franch. 1886 Not in cultivation

Ht to 70cm (2¼ft). L 1.3–1.7cm (½–¾in) long.
F rose-pink. Style shorter than stamens.
Leaves very much smaller than *moupinense*.

From C. Sichuan, S. of the known distribution of *moupinense*, on old logs, 2,600–3,000m (8,500–10,000ft).

petrocharis Diels 1921 Not in cultivation

L more persistently hairy than *dendrocharis*.
F white.

C Sichuan, 1,800–2,300m (6,000–7,500ft), rocks and slopes.

RHODODENDRON SUBSECTION (FERRUGINEUM SERIES)

A small subsection confined to Europe including the only rhododendrons found in the Alps.

Small shrubs to 1.5m (5ft). Leaves evergreen, densely scaly. Inflorescence terminal, many-flowered with elongated rachis. Flowers tubular-campanulate. Stamens 10.

Useful, hardy, mostly late-flowering dwarfs, long known in cultivation. No close relatives botanically or geographically, but they show some affinity with Lapponica and Rhodorastra subsections.

ferrugineum (the Alpenrose) Linn. 1753 H4–5 USDA 6b–5 & 6a L1–2 F2–3

Ht to 1.5m (5ft). Habit usually quite compact, wider than tall, often spreading branches.
L 2.4–4cm (1–1½in) long, narrowly elliptic to elliptic, dark green above, densely reddish-brown scaly below.
F rosy-crimson through pink to (rarely) white, 1.2–1.8cm (½–¾in) long, tubular-campanulate, many flowers per truss. Stamens *at least as long* as corolla.

This well known species, often seen by visitors to the European mountains, is a most useful and hardy late-flowering species. While perhaps not as free-flowering as some dwarf species, it often provides a good show of bloom. Quite variable; we grow one interesting form with a wavy leaf (Glenarn form) while some have much deeper-coloured flowers than others. Does not tolerate high temperatures in USA or drought. There is a fine white-flowered form in cultivation. AM 1969 to white form. Rootability usually high.

Very common in the Pyrenees and Alps as far east as Austria, 900–2,100m (3,000–7,000ft) from open moorland to a carpet on the forest floor or mixed with pine scrub. I have seen whole groups of hybrids known as X *intermedium* Tausch where this species meets *hirsutum*. R. *ferrugineum* always grows over acid rocks, *hirsutum* on limestone.

June–July

R. ferrugineum

hirsutum Linn. 1753 H4–5 USDA 6b–5 & 6a L1–2 F2–3

Ht to 1.5m (5ft), usually less. Habit as *ferrugineum*. Young growth usually hairy.
L to 3cm (1⅕in) long, narrowly obovate to obovate-orbicular, usually *paler* above than *ferrugineum*, margins fringed with hairs. Scales wider apart below than *ferrugineum*.
F usually shades of pink, pale to deep or rarely white, 1.2–1.8cm (½–¾in) long, tubular-campanulate in many-flowered truss.

One of the few specimens confined to growing above or on limestone and able to tolerate fairly alkaline conditions in cultivation. Generally a neater plant than *ferrugineum* in cultivation with paler-coloured flowers but often not as easily grown. Wild collected plants show much variation in foliate and habit. Rootability high. The white form is rare in cultivation. The pretty double form known as 'Flore Pleno' has flowers like miniature rose-buds. It has only very few hairs.

Common on the limestone ranges of Europe, 360–1,800m (1,200–6,000ft) in similar situations to *ferrugineum*, particularly among dwarf pine. Occasionally found in cracks in pure limestone rock, but there it can show chlorosis. June–July

myrtifolium Schott & Kotschy 1851 (*kotschyi* Simonkai 1886) H3–4 USDA 7a–6b L2 F1–3

Ht rarely over 60cm (2ft). Habit spreading, usually very compact.
L 1.4–2.3cm (⅗–1in) long, narrowly obovate, dark green above, margins minutely toothed. Scales *wider* apart than the other two species below.
F rosy-pink to mauvy-pink, rarely white, 1.3–1.7cm (½–¾in) long. Stamens *shorter* than corolla, included.

Generally lower and more compact than the above two species and the flowers open earlier. The best forms are a delightful rose-pink. We find it occasionally suffers bark-split which can be fatal. Rootability medium to high.

From E. Europe, Hungary, Bulgaria, E. Yugoslavia, Romania and W. USSR on similar habitats to those of *ferrugineum* at 1,500–2,300m (5,000–7,500ft) but sometimes on limestone. May or later

RHODORASTRA SUBSECTION (DAURICUM SERIES)

While normally too tall to include in this book, forms of both *dauricum* and *mucronulatum* should be mentioned due to their dwarf stature. For normal forms and their descriptions, see *The Larger Species of Rhododendron*.

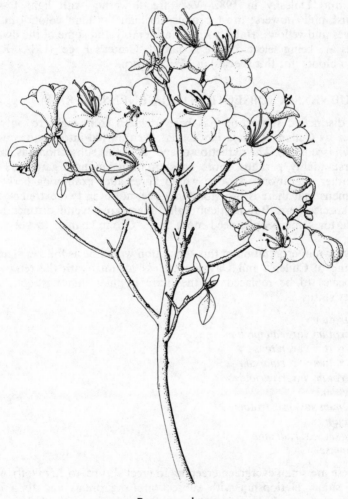

R. mucronulatum

dauricum Linn. 1753 H4–5 USDA 6b–5 & 6a

A dwarf form, largely evergreen (mentioned in *The Larger Species of Rhododendron*) has been recently introduced from Japan. It has neat shiny leaves and covers itself with rose-purple flowers in March (–April), generally later than most forms of the species. The occasional erect shoot may need pruning or pinching to retain compactness. Much used for Bonsai work in Japan. A wild population, recently reported by Doleshy on Hokkaido, may be the source of this plant, with similar purplish-bronze leaves in winter. Found from about 180m (600ft) or more, common in open scrub.

mucronulatum Turczaninow 1837 H4–5 USDA 6b–5 & 6a

A dwarf strain was introduced from Cheju Is., S. Korea, by Berg in 1976 and Doleshy in 1982. Very free-flowering with light to deep purplish-pink flowers; most produce brilliant autumn colours in reds, oranges and yellows. Habit varies considerably and some of the dwarfest clones are being selected. One is named 'Crater's Edge' (USA). Rather late to bloom (for this species) in March–April.

SALUENENSIA SUBSECTION (SALUENENSE SERIES)

This distinctive subsection has been reduced from eight to only two species by Cullen. *R. fragariflorum* has been moved into a subsection of its own (see p. 94). The reduction of species in this subsection has caused, understandably perhaps, more consternation amongst gardeners than any other alterations. Anyone would agree after examining herbarium specimens that there is probably only one, not even two extremely variable species here. But horticulturally, there are several distinct plants which, for some people, need more than 'Group' names to keep them apart.

My own interpretation of this subsection would be as follows. This is a merging of Cullen's and Davidian's classifications with the removal of subspecies to be replaced by the more popular (amongst gardeners) variety status.

calostrotum
calostrotum var. *calciphilum*
calostrotum var. *nitens*
calostrotum var. *riparium*
calostrotum var. *riparioides*
chamenum
chamenum var. *prostratum*
keleticum
keleticum var. *radicans*
saluenense

These are small evergreen creeping to erect shrubs, to 1.5m (5ft), which show some relationship with subsection Fragariflora and to a lesser extent, Uniflora. Leaves densely scaly beneath, aromatic. Inflorescence terminal, 1–3 flowered, occasionally to 7, purplish to purplish-crimson to rose-crimson to pink, openly funnel-campanulate (almost flat) flowers. Calyx usually large, coloured and hairy. Stamens 10. Style always red. Pedicels long, usually upright, 0.5–3.2cm ($\frac{1}{5}$–1$\frac{1}{3}$in) long.

These are mostly free-flowering, hardy and reliable plants. One unusual feature is that, to my knowledge, no albino has been recorded. The lower-growing selections are excellent for covering slightly shaded peat beds.

Distribution from Arunachal Pradesh, N.E. Burma, S. and S.E. Xizang, N.W. and N. Yunnan into Sichuan.

E.M.S.

R. calostrotum

calostrotum ssp. **calostrotum** Balf.f. & Ward 1920 H4–5 USDA 6b–5 & 6a L1–3 F2–4

Ht most forms 7.5–60cm (3in–2ft), others taller. Habit low and compact to more open in the taller forms.
L 1.4–3.5cm ($\frac{3}{5}$–1$\frac{1}{3}$in) long, oblong-elliptic to nearly orbicular, usually *very glaucous above*, with dense fawn, brown or cinnamon scales below. Petiole *not* bristly.
F bright rose-crimson to rich purple with deeper spots, 2.5–3.8cm (1–1$\frac{1}{2}$in) across, widely funnel-shaped or rotate, *1–2 per truss*, rarely more. Calyx coloured. Pedicels 1.6–2.7cm ($\frac{3}{5}$–1$\frac{1}{8}$in) long.

One of the finest of all dwarfs, especially in 'Gigha' FCC 1971 which has masses of rose-crimson flowers over compact glaucous foliage. Does well in full sun, especially in Scotland. Easily grown but must not be allowed to dry out. Many other clones are good. Rootability high.

From N. Burma and W. Yunnan, 3,300–4,300m (10,500–14,000ft) on stony alpine meadows and cliffs.   May *calostrotum* ssp. *riparium* (Ward) Cullen 1978 (*calciphilum* Hutch. & Ward, *kingdonii* Merrill, *nitens* Hutch., *riparium* Ward, *rivulare* Ward) H4–5 USDA 6b–5 & 6a L1–2 F1–3

Ht to 1.5m (5ft), usually less. Habit compact to more open.
L as ssp. *calostrotum* but often *not* glaucous above.
F pink to purplish, *2–5 per truss*.

The assemblage of plants put in here by Cullen is quite unsatisfactory horticulturally. So as not to upset Cullen's revision, I will describe these variants as 'Groups' hoping that in the future they will regain some botanical status. Ssp. *riparium* I feel in itself should never have been reduced as there were always (particularly as herbarium specimens) plants that did not fit happily into any of Cowan and Davidian's 1954 revision. These plants appear to lie between ssp. *calostrotum* and ssp. *riparioides* with a fairly upright but *non*-glaucous foliage. Davidian still fails to recognize ssps. *riparium* or *riparioides* as being distinct enough to merit separate botanical status. This is at least as unsatisfactory as Cullen's reduction of *calciphilum* and *nitens*.

Calciphilum Group H4 L2 F2

This neat little plant certainly deserves botanical status.
L smaller than *calostrotum* type, elliptic, rounded at both ends, to 1.3cm (½in) long.
F pink, later than the average *calostrotum*.

Often flowers in autumn. Attractive but not as good a plant as the type. Rootability high. From a small area in N.E. Burma only, 4,000–4,300m (13,000–14,000ft) and possibly N.W. Yunnan, on limestone screes, locally plentiful.

Late May

Nitens Group H4 L1–2 F2

Ht 30–45cm (1–1½ft). Habit compact to erect, foliage can become sparse with age.
L 0.7–2.5cm (⅓–1in) long, oblong-obovate to oblong-elliptic, *shiny* above, fawn or brown scales below, not bristly. Young leaves green.
F deep pinkish-purple to deep magenta-pink.

Very useful in that it is one of the latest of dwarfs to flower although not as easy to grow as most of its clan. More erect and wider-leaved than ssp. *keleticum*. Rootability medium.

From only one KW number, 5482 from N.E. Burma at 3,700m (12,000ft), sprawling over boulders and ledges in bamboo country.

June–July

calostrotum ssp. *riparioides* Cullen 1978 H4–5 USDA 6b–5 & 6a L3 F2–3

This newly recognized subspecies has consistently larger leaves and flowers than ssp. *calostrotum* and generally makes a larger plant, 0.3–1.5m (1–5ft). The leaves are glaucous above and purplish-glaucous below, 2.2–3.3cm (1–1⅓) long.

We have grown this at Glendoick as *calostrotum* Rock for many years. It is certainly distinct from ssp. *calostrotum*. Our form with deep purple flowers, tends to flower again in the autumn. Is well worth growing in addition to 'Gigha'. Rootability medium to high.

From a restricted area of N.W. Yunnan at 3,700–4,400m (12,000–13,500ft) on alpine slopes and cliffs. May *calostrotum* ssp. *keleticum* (Balf.f. & Forr.) Cullen 1978 (*keleticum* Balf.f. & Forr., *radicans* Balf.f. & Forr.) H4(–5) USDA 6b(–5 & 6a) L1–2 F2–3

Ht 2.5–40cm (1in–1¼ft). Habit completely prostrate to mounded.
L 0.7–2.1cm (⅓–⅞in) long, oblong to elliptic to lanceolate, petiole *rarely* bristly.
F pale to deep purplish-crimson with crimson spots, up to 3cm (1¼in) long and to 3.8cm (1½in) across, widely funnel-shaped or rotate, 1–3 per truss.

From a horticultural point of view, this plant together with *radicans* as a variety should have full specific status. Botanically, it does seem to merge with *calostrotum* ssp. *riparium* and certainly merges with *radicans*. In fact, I have seen plants in cultivation that would easily pass as either *keleticum* or *radicans* using the old descriptions. I have also seen groups of seedlings ranging completely from typical *keleticum* to typical *radicans*. So the fuss made about this amalgamation stems from ignorance.

This is an extremely useful plant. It is easily grown, free-flowering and makes splendid ground cover. There are various forms in cultivation, some mound-forming, others more prostrate. R. 58 has given us excellent large flowered plants. Has proved partially successful in Germany, S. Sweden and E. USA. AM 1928 lilac flowers with red spots. Rootability high.

Fairly widespread in S.E. Xizang, N.E. Burma and N.W. Yunnan, 3,400–4,600m (11,000–15,000ft) on moist stony moorland, screes, rocks and cliffs.   May–June

Radicans Group H4(–5) L1–2 F2–3

Generally smaller than *keleticum* in all its parts. The neatest of little plants, reaching the ultimate in dwarfness in the genus. Rooting along the ground as it creeps, it is charming, studded with numerous, almost flat and usually solitary flowers on upright pedicels. Best planted in a little shade on a sloping peat bed. Do not allow bulbs to grow up through its mat. AM 1926 to form of F 19919, flowers rosy-purple. Rootability high.

Restricted to small areas of S.E. Xizang on open stony, peaty moorlands at 4,300–4,600m (14,000–15,000ft).   May–June

saluenense Franch. 1898 (*amaurophyllum* Balf.f. & Forr.) H4–5 USDA 6b–5 & 6a L1–2 F2–3

Ht 0.3–1.2m (1–4ft). Habit compact or more often *erect* to rather leggy with age. Branchlets *bristly*.
L 0.8–3.6cm (⅓–1½in) long, oblong-orbicular to oblong-elliptic, shiny to matt above, consistently *paler below* than *calostrotum* and its subspecies and not glaucous, margins bristly.
F magenta to deep purple-crimson with crimson spots, 1.7–3cm (about 1in) long and about 5cm (2in) across, widely funnel-shaped: 1–3, rarely more, per truss.

The largest of the subsection, attractive, but not the best. Variable in height, leaf surface and hairiness. Some forms are exceptionally hairy. Merges with ssp. *chameunum* and *calostrotum* ssp. *riparium*. Rootability medium to high.

Not as common or widely distributed as ssp. *chameunum* or *calostrotum* ssps. *keleticum* or *riparium*. From N.E. Burma, N.W. Yunnan and S.E. Xizang on forest margins and thickets, stony hillsides, boulders and cliffs, sometimes limestone.

April–May

saluenense ssp. **chameunum** (Balf.f. & Forr.) Cullen 1978 (*colobodes* Balf.f., *cosmetum* Balf.f. & Forr., *charidotes* Balf.f. & Forr., *pamprotum* Balf.f. & Forr., *prostratum* W.W. Sm., *sercocalyx* Balf.f. & Forr.)

Ht 12.5–60cm (5in–2ft). Habit fairly compact, often flat-topped but not creeping, branchlets bristly.
L 0.5–2cm ($\frac{1}{5}$–$\frac{4}{5}$in) long, elliptic, oblong-elliptic to ovate-elliptic, shiny above. Margins often bristly. Leaves often turn an attractive coppery or purple hue in winter and the young leaves are purplish. Old leaves may turn red in autumn.
F deep purple-rose to purplish-crimson, 1.7–2.9cm ($\frac{2}{3}$–1$\frac{1}{8}$in) long, 2.5–3.8 cm (1–1$\frac{1}{2}$in) across, widely funnel-shaped, 1–6 per truss, calyx coloured.

A good plant in its deeper coloured forms and often has interesting winter foliage. Closely related to *saluenense*. Often blooms in autumn. AM 1945 to so-called *saluenense* Exbury which is really a clone of this subspecies. Rootability medium.
Very common and widespread in S.E. Xizang, N.E. Burma, N. and N.W. Yunnan, and S.W. Sichuan, 3,500–5,200m (11,500–17,000ft).

Late April–May

R. charidotes has been resurrected to specific status by Davidian on account of its bristly calyx, ovary and capsule and the green young leaves. I doubt if it is really worth more than Group status.

Prostratum Group H4 USDA 6b L1–2 F1–2

Ht 3–45cm (1in–1$\frac{1}{2}$ft). Habit prostrate with woody semi-erect shoots. Branchlets bristly, persistent bud scales. Petiole *bristly*.
L smaller than *chameunum* type.

This is a case where many specimens previously under *prostratum* in the herbarium are much closer to my interpretation of *chameunum* but there is a whole host of intermediaries. While Cullen is right botanically to reduce *prostratum*, it deserves at least varietal status horticulturally. I have two to three clones of what we acquired as *prostratum* but only one I regard as typical and which matches several herbarium specimens. This clone has creeping shoots with the habit as described above. Flowers not as freely produced as others of the subsection. Rootability medium.

April–May

SCABRIFOLIA SUBSECTION (SCABRIFOLIUM SERIES)

A relatively distinct subsection consisting of closely related species with axillary flowers only. Related to the Triflora subsection.
Small to medium shrubs, 15cm–3m (6in–10ft). Habit often rather straggly with vigorous 'waterspout' shoots. Leaves evergreen. *Inflorescence all axillary in upper leaf axils.* Flowers small, openly campanulate to tubular. Of low to high horticultural merit. *R. spinuliferum* is too tall to

include here (see *The Larger Species of Rhododendron* pp. 256–7). All grow wild on comparatively dry slopes and have the spreading root systems often associated with these conditions.

hemitrichotum Balf.f. & Forr. 1918 H4 USDA 6b L1–2 F1–3

Ht 30cm–2m+ (1–6ft+). Habit fairly compact to leggy. Branchlets pubescent.
L 1.2–4.5cm ($\frac{1}{2}$–1$\frac{4}{5}$in) long, *narrowly elliptic, pubescent above, glaucous beneath.*
F pink or white edged pink, with or without purple spots, 0.9–1.4cm ($\frac{1}{3}$–$\frac{3}{5}$in) long, widely funnel-shaped, 2–3 per leaf axil in upper most leaves.

Closely related to *racemosum* which has less pubescent leaves above and wider leaves. Not often equal to the best forms of *racemosum*. Rootability medium.

From N. Yunnan and S.W. Sichuan, 2,900–4,300m (9,500–14,000ft), common on dry rocky pastures, in scrub or forests, limestone or slate.

April

mollicomum Balf.f. & W.W. Sm. 1921 H3–4 USDA 7a–6b L1–2 F1–3

Ht 60cm–1.7m (2–5$\frac{1}{2}$ft). Habit often erect. Branchlets *densely pubescent.*
L 1.2–3.6cm ($\frac{1}{2}$–1$\frac{1}{2}$in) long, lanceolate to rarely oblong, *pubescent above and below, not* glaucous below.
F pale to deep pink, 1.7–3cm ($\frac{2}{3}$–1$\frac{1}{2}$in) long, *narrowly* funnel-shaped, 1–3 per leaf axil in uppermost leaves.

Similar to *hemitrichotum* but without the glaucous leaf underside. Quite pretty but often rather tender. Lacks the bristles of *pubescens* and *scabrifolium*. AM 1931 bright rose flowers.

Fairly common in N. Yunnan and S.W. Sichuan, 2,400–3,800m (8,000–12,500ft), dry bouldery hillsides, thickets or forest margins.

April

pubescens Balf.f. & Forr. 1920 H3–4 USDA 7a–6b L1–2 F1–2

Ht to 1.3m (4ft). Habit compact to leggy.
L 1.8–2.4cm ($\frac{2}{3}$–1in) long, *very narrowly elliptic to very narrowly lanceolate,* margins strongly recurved, very hairy above and below.
F rose-pink, 0.6–1cm ($\frac{1}{4}$–$\frac{2}{5}$in) long, funnel-shaped.

This resurrected species (was a synonym of *spiciferum*) has remarkably narrow hairy leaves. The flowers are very small and the plant is often rather scrawny. 'Fine Bristles' AM 1955.

From N. Yunnan and S.W. Sichuan to the north of the distribution of *scabrifolium* and its varieties; on open rocky places.

March–April

racemosum Franch. 1886 (*iochanense* Lév., *motsouense* Lév.) H3–4(–5) USDA 7a–6b(–5 & 6a) L1–2 F1–4

Ht 15cm–4.6m (6in–15ft). Habit low and compact to tall and leggy. Even dwarf forms often produce 'waterspout' shoots. Branchlets generally *glabrous* and frequently *red.*
L 1–5.4cm ($\frac{2}{5}$–2$\frac{1}{5}$in) long, broadly obovate to oblong-elliptic, *more or less glabrous above, glaucous and glabrous below.*
F deep rose to pink, white-tinged pink to white, 0.8–2.3cm ($\frac{1}{3}$–almost 1in) long, widely funnel-shaped, 1–4 per axil in uppermost leaves.

This very well known species is extremely variable in hardiness, habit, flower colour and horticultural value. While the freer-flowering dwarf

E.M.S.

R. racemosum

forms like F 19404 are the most desirable, some of the taller forms should not be ignored. Some dwarf forms invariably abort their flower buds for some unknown reason and these forms should be discarded. A good tall form is 'Glendoick' with particularly deep-coloured flowers. Narrow-leaved forms are closely related to *hemitrichotum*. Both tall and dwarf forms have suffered winter damage at Glendoick, especially the tall. Barely or not hardy in S. Scandinavia.

Versatile as to situation and climate, standing quite dry conditions, the hardier forms succeeding in some of the warmer parts of E. USA. The flowers are relatively frost–resistant. Long stems covered with capsules are decidedly ugly and some pruning of these and other long shoots is beneficial. FCC 1892; 'Rock Rose', AM 1970 a fine taller-growing clone; 'White Lace', AM 1974, white flowers, also tall; AGM 1930. Some forms are resistant to root rot, others not. Rootability medium to low. According to Joseph Gable, the hardiest forms are from R 59717 (much hardier than F 19404) collected Lichiang Range, 3,500m (11,500ft). Guy Nearing grew several generations of seedlings for hardiness and compactness.

One of the most plentiful species in N., N.W., W., & C. Yunnan and S.W. Sichuan, often covering rather dry hillsides or valley floors for miles with a long flowering season. All the plants we saw on Cangshan, Yunnan had fine rose-coloured flowers but were heavily grazed and hacked with never a chance to grow normally, and so their habit was hard to discern. Often associated with *trichocladum*. From 800–4,300m

(2,500–14,000ft), dry stony foothills, often limestone, mountain meadows, bogs, in forests or on cliffs; in near-mineral to peaty soil.

March–May with odd flowers earlier and later

scabrifolium Franch. 1886 H2–3(–4) USDA 7b & 8a–7a(–6b) L1–2 F1–3

Ht 30cm–3m (1–10ft). Habit bushy to tall and ungainly.
L 2.3–9.5cm (1–3¾in) long, narrowly elliptic to oblanceolate, *bullate* above and usually *bristly and pubescent* below.
F white to deep pink, 1–1.7cm (⅖–¾in) long, widely funnel-shaped, usually 2–3 per axil in uppermost few leaves.

The flowers are rather small in comparison with the rather large leaves. Most introductions are too tender for Glendoick.

From N. and C. Yunnan, 1,500–3,400m (5,000–11,000ft), common in open scrub in oak or conifer woodland on dry hills.   March–April

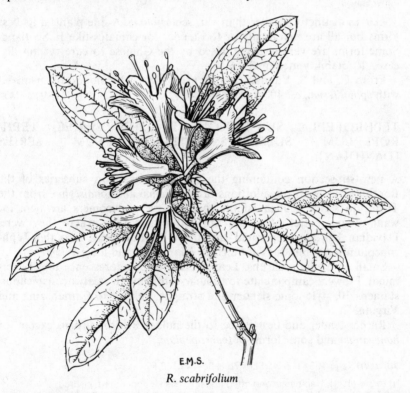

E.M.S.

R. scabrifolium

scabrifolium var. *pauciflorum* Franch. 1898 (*dielsianum* Hand. Mazz. nomen nudum [*scabrifolium* × *spinuliferum*])

This so-called variety is a range of natural hybrids or intermediaries between *scabrifolium* var. *scabrifolium* or var. *spiciferum* and *spinuliferum*. When in Yunnan, we found two of these hybrids among the latter two plants. Unfortunately we did not have the opportunity to investigate further as to whether whole colonies of these hybrids or intermediaries occurred elsewhere or not. There are nine herbarium specimens in Kunming and no less than about 30 in the RBG, Edinburgh, herbarium, and so it must be extremely common. Botanists in Kunming call the hybrid × *duclouxii* Lév. which Cullen gives as a synonym of *spinuliferum*. These hybrids are extremely variable in leaf size and shape, habit, and flower colour and shape. From C. and S. Yunnan, 2,000–2,600m (6,500–8,500ft), amongst scrub on rocky slopes.

scabrifolium var. **spiciferum** (Franch.) Cullen 1978 H3(–4) USDA 7a(–6b) L1–2 F1–3

Ht 15cm–1.8m (6in–6ft). Habit bushy to tall and leggy.
L 1.2–3.5cm ($\frac{1}{2}$–1$\frac{3}{8}$in) long, narrowly elliptic to oblanceolate, hairy like var. *scabrifolium*, often recurved.
F rose to pink to white, 1.2–1.5cm ($\frac{1}{2}$–$\frac{3}{8}$in) long, *widely* funnel-shaped, 1–4 per axil in upper leaves.

Leaves distinctly smaller than var. *scabrifolium*. A fine plant in its best forms but all are marginally or too tender for climates like E. Scotland. Some forms are very straggly. Used by the Chinese to cure certain diseases. Rootability medium.

From C. and S. Yunnan, common on dry rocky slopes, often mixed with *spinuliferum*, *c*.2,400m (8,000ft).   March–May

TEPHROPEPLA SUBSECTION (BOOTHII SERIES, TEPHROPEPLUM SUBSERIES; TEPHROPEPLUM SERIES [DAVIDIAN])

A new subsection containing the old Tephropeplum subseries of the Boothii series with the additions of *hanceanum* and *longistylum* from the Triflorum series. Cullen admits that the two newcomers are here for want of any better place but are better here than where they were. Davidian has also separated this from Boothii series into the Tephropeplum series but does not include *hanceanum* and *longistylum*.

Small to medium shrubs. Leaves evergreen. Inflorescence mostly terminal. Flowers campanulate to tubular-campanulate. Calyx conspicuous, stamens 10, style long, slender and straight. Related to Cinnabarina and Virgata.

Rather tender and best suited to the milder British gardens except for *hanceanum* and some forms of *tephropeplum*.

auritum Tagg 1934 H2–3 USDA 7b & 8a–7a L1–2 F2

Ht to 3m (10ft). Habit erect and often ungainly. Bark coppery-red, peeling.
L 2.5–6.6cm (1–2$\frac{3}{8}$in) long, narrowly elliptic to elliptic, covered with brown scales below.
F *very pale yellow to cream often tinged pink on lobes*, 2–2.5cm (about 1in), long, tubular-campanulate, 3–7 per truss, sometimes axillary. *Calyx lobes reflexed.*

Closely related to *xanthostephanum* but flowers are decidedly inferior in colour. Attractive bark. Did survive at Glendoick for several years but was very bud-tender here. AM 1931. Rootability medium.

Only found in the Tsangpo Gorge, S.E. Xizang, 2,100–2,600m (7,000–8,500ft) on sheltered cliffs and open stony banks.   April

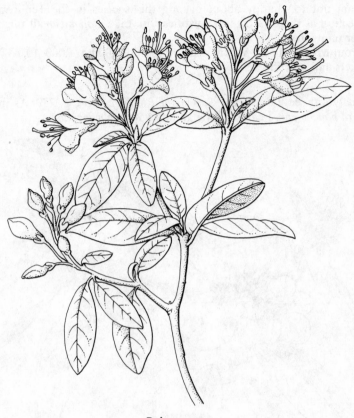

R. hanceanum

hanceanum Hemsley 1889 H(3–)4(–5) USDA (7a–)6b(–5 & 6a) L1–2 F2–3

Ht 15cm–2m (6in–6ft). Habit low and very compact to tall and sprawly.
L 2.5–12.8cm (1–5in) long, narrowly ovate to oblong-elliptic, *thick and rigid*, young leaves bronzy-brown.
F white to yellow, 1.3–2.1cm ($\frac{1}{2}$–$\frac{7}{8}$in) long, funnel-campanulate, in *elongated* truss of 5–15.

The forms usually seen in cultivation make compact to very compact low bushes but the common form in the wild is evidently much taller and sometimes sprawly with larger leaves. The one clone I have attempted of the latter I have found difficult to cultivate. The clone known as 'Canton Consul' AM has cream-coloured flowers and attractive bronzy young leaves. This is sometimes wrongly named 'Nanum'. The correct 'Nanum' is a very dwarf plant with *clear yellow* flowers and although very slow-growing, is a beautiful, free-flowering little gem. According to Davidian, this came from W 4255. There may be more than one clone of the true 'Nanum' and the cream-flowered form. Rootability high. 'Nanum' is later-flowering than 'Canton Consul'.

I am not too happy about placing this species in the Tephropepla subsection as there seems little justification. Like *afghanicum*, it might be better on its own.

From Mt Omei and Mupin, Sichuan, 1,500–3,000m (5,000–10,000ft), in thickets and on cliffs.   May-June

longistylum see *The Larger Species of Rhododendron*, p. 279. As in the case of *hanceanum*, I can see little affinity with *tephropeplum*.

R. tephropeplum

tephropeplum Balf.f. & Farrer 1922 (*deleiense* Hutch. & Ward, *spodopeplum* Balf.f. & Farrer) H3(–4) USDA 7a(–6b) L1–2 F2–3

Ht 60cm–1.5m (2–5ft). Habit bushy to upright or sprawly. Bark brownish, peeling.
L 3–13cm (1⅕–5in) long, narrowly oblanceolate to narrowly elliptic to oblanceolate, very variable, usually dark and shiny above, densely scaly brownish-grey below.
F purplish through carmine-rose to pink, pale pink and rarely white, 1.7–3.2cm (⅔–1¼in) long, campanulate to tubular-campanulate, 3–9 per truss, style longer than corolla, calyx large, leafy.

This fine plant has become somewhat neglected lately, probably because of its general lack of hardiness and often straggly habit. At its best it is free-flowering and most attractive. Here is another case for breeding for selection, making use of the many cultivated forms and their variability. An excellent subject for a sheltered woodland edge. Rather bud-tender. The Arunachal Pradesh form previously known as *deleiense* has larger, wider leaves and larger flowers than usual. Variable in hardiness. AM 1929 pale pink flowers, AM 1935 (*deleiense*), 'Butcher Wood' AM 1975 KW 20844. Rootability medium to low.

From wide areas of E. Arunachal Pradesh, S.E. Xizang, N.E. Burma and N.W. Yunnan, 2,400–4,300m (8,000–14,000ft), on crags, rocks, cliffs, screes and meadows, sometimes on limestone. There seems to be some correlation between large wide leaves and low elevation and smaller, narrow leaves at high elevations.   Late April–May

xanthostephanum Merrill 1941 (*aureum* Franch.) H2–3 USDA 7b & 8a–7a L1–2 F2–3

Ht 30cm–3m (1–10ft). Habit loose, upright or spreading. Bark smooth, reddish-brown.
L 5–10cm (2–4in) long, oblong-narrowly elliptic to elliptic, glaucous below.
F bright to creamy-yellow, 1.8–2.8cm ($\frac{3}{4}$–1$\frac{1}{8}$in) long, narrowly campanulate, 3–5 per truss, sometimes axillary. Calyx lobes *erect, not reflexed*.

A pretty, free-flowering species suitable for the mildest of British gardens along the western seaboard. The taller forms are rather beyond our size limit for a dwarf but can be pruned to keep them tidy and from becoming too large. The potentially hardiest forms from high elevations may not have been introduced or have been lost. Attractive bark. Easily separated from *sulfureum* by its long, straight style. 'Yellow Garland' AM 1961. The average altitude according to herbarium specimens should be about 3,000m (10,000ft). We unfortunately failed to find it on Cangshan, Yunnan although recorded from there.

From N.E. Burma, S.E. Xizang, N.W. and C. Yunnan, 1,600–3,900m (5,000–13,000ft), in forests and their margins, scrub, pastures and cliffs.
                                                              April–May

TRICHOCLADA SUBSECTION (TRICHOCLADUM SERIES)

This is a subsection with yellow flowers, leaves mostly deciduous and hairy leaves and stems. Terminal inflorescence, 2–5 flowers per truss funnel-campanulate. Stamens 10. Style sharply deflexed.

A closely related group in which the deciduous ones can horticulturally be considered one very variable species. Sleumer placed great emphasis on the deciduous nature of these plants, regarding them as belonging to a subgenus of their own, but as Cullen says, some vary in this respect or are always evergreen which totally defeats Sleumer's theory.

The deciduous species are attractive *en masse* as seen in the wild but are not really showy as individuals in a garden.

caesium Hutch. 1933 H3 USDA 7a L1–2 F1–2

Ht to 2m (6ft) usually less. Habit erect and spreading. Bark pale brown and shiny.
L semi-evergreen, 3–5cm (1$\frac{1}{5}$–2in) long, ± oblong-elliptic, slightly glaucous when young above and glaucous below.
F greenish to pale yellow, green spots, about 2cm ($\frac{4}{5}$in) long, widely funnel-campanulate, 1–3 per truss.

Rather early into growth and prone to bark-split at Glendoick. Some killed in 1981–2 winter. Not of great merit. Rootability medium.

From S.W. Yunnan, 2,400–3,000m (8,000–10,000ft), on rocky slopes.
                                                              May

lepidostylum Balf.f. & Forr. 1920 H4–5 USDA 6b–5 & 6a L3–4 F1

Ht 30cm–1.2m (1–4ft). Habit compact and dome-shaped. Branchlets bristly.
L evergreen, 3–3.3cm (1⅕–1½in) long, obovate to oblong-elliptic, bristly below and on margins, *very glaucous-blue above when young*. Petiole hairy. Aromatic.
F yellow, about 2.5cm (1in) long, widely funnel-shaped, 1–3 per truss.

When growing vigorously, this is one of the most beautiful foliage plants in the genus with glaucous-blue young leaves which retain their colour well into autumn. The flowers are rather ungainly in shape and do not blend with the foliage. There are splendid specimens in the RBG, Edinburgh and Brodick, Isle of Arran. Suffered in 1981–2 in very cold gardens. Reasonably hardy in S. Sweden. A very distinct plant. AM 1969 for foliage. Rootability high.

From a small area of S.W. Yunnan only, 3,000–3,700m (10,000–12,000ft), on boulders, cliffs and crevices. June

mekongense Franch. 1898 (*viridescens* Hutch., *rubroluteum* Davidian) H4–5 USDA 6b–5 & 6a L1–3 F1–2

Ht to 2m (6ft). Habit erect or spreading.
L ± deciduous, ± obovate or occasionally obovate-elliptic. Young and old leaves below and petioles covered with bristles. *Scales below markedly unequal, dark.*
F yellow to greenish-yellow, 1.7–2.3cm (¾–1in) long, 2–5 per truss, Calyx bristly.

Cullen has placed two former species *viridescens* and *rubroluteum* under *mekongense*. As we know them horticulturally, they are totally different from the typically deciduous *mekongense* or its variety *melinanthum* (see below). The usual deciduous plant varies considerably. That collected under KW 21079 from the Triangle, N. Burma, is a very useful late-flowering variant. Very remarkable distribution with an isolated occurrence in E. Nepal. AM 1979 to KW 406. Rootability high (best from soft cuttings).

From E. Nepal, S. and S.E. Xizang and N.W. Yunnan, 900–4,500m (2,900–14,500ft), in scrub and forest margins. April–July

Viridescens Group

Ht to 1.2m (4ft). Habit erect but spreading outwards.
L evergreen, up to 5cm (2in) long, oblong-elliptic, very glaucous above, less glaucous with age.
F pale yellow with green spots, about 2cm (¾in) long, 4–5 per truss.

Many gardeners are unhappy with the synonomy of this former species into *mekongense* var. *mekongense* and with reason. The trouble is that this plant and *rubroluteum* were described from cultivated material and not the type wild material they are supposed to have originated from. In the case of *viridescens*, the wild herbarium specimen is nearly deciduous. This was only described because L. de Rothschild pointed out plants growing at Exbury to Dr Hutchinson who had previously considered this plant KW 5829 to be a form of *trichocladum*. In *The Riddle of the Tsangpo Gorges*, KW describes this plant:

In the bog were tufts of an inferior species (KW 5829) with hairy smelly twigs and leaves and jaundiced flowers breaking into an unhealthy rash of greenish spots. This, however, did not flower until the end of June. It is evidently a variety of the Chinese *R. trichocladum*.

No mention of evergreen leaves or glaucous young foliage.

In cultivation, this plant has really fine glaucous young leaves and quite pretty flowers produced late in the season. 'Doshong La' AM 1972. Rootability medium to high.

From Doshong La Pass, S.E. Xizang, 3,000–3,400m (10,000–11,000ft).

June–August

Rubroluteum Group

This, as we cultivate it at Glendoick, is identical to Viridescens Group apart from the reddish tinge to the flowers. Davidian in his description (AMRS-QB, July 1975, pp. 144–5) makes no attempt to compare it with *viridescens*. Either he did not know *viridescens* or chose to ignore it. *R. rubroluteum* was reputed to have come from KW 5489, given in the 1980 Handbook as *mekongense* (as *melinanthum*). In *From China to Hkamti Long*, p. 204, KW writes of KW 5489:

At the foot of the first steep pitch we came to an open boggy pasture where grew scattered bushes of a 'Trichocladum' Rhododendron (KW 5489). They are seedy-looking objects, these Trichocladums, with deciduous leaves and pallid yellow flowers, often with an unhealthy green flush and a rash of poisonous spots. The flowers open before the leaves appear, when they look the most starved and twiggy skeletons imaginable. However, some people approve of them.

Again, no mention of evergreen or glaucous young leaves or red-tinged flowers.

In cultivation, the foliage of this clone (?) is at least equal to the Viridescens Group but I am not so keen on the combination of yellow and reddish colour in the flowers. KW 5489, which I doubt is the real source of this plant, is from Taru Tra, above the Taron, N.E. Burma at about 3,400m (11,000ft). I feel Rubroluteum Group most likely came from Doshong La, also out of KW 5829, being virtually identical to Viridescens Group. The only morphological differences between Davidian's descriptions of *viridescens* and *rubroluteum* are small—the size of scales on the leaf underside and the fact that the upper surface of *rubroluteum* is slightly more glaucous; also the small differences in shape and colour of the corolla. My own examination of one (the only?) clone of *rubroluteum* and two of *viridescens* shows no significance in scale size or corolla shape and the difference in glaucousness is very slight.

mekongense var. **melinanthum** (Balf.f. & Ward) Cullen 1978 (*chloranthum* Balf.f. & Forr., *semilunatum* Balf.f. & Forr.).

Differs from var. *mekongense* in its glabrous calyx, non-bristly pedicels or only bristly at base. While we gardeners have come to regard var. *melinanthum* as the best of the deciduous Trichocladums with the largest leaves and flowers, there is no evidence of this superiority in the herbarium specimens.

From S.E. Xizang, N.E. Burma and N.W. Yunnan.

mekongense var. *longipilosum* (Cowan) Cullen 1978

Differs from var. *mekongense* in its bristly *upper* leaf surface. Like var. *melinanthum*, this variety does not appear to be of any horticultural consequence.

From N. Burma, S. and S.E. Xizang and N.W. Yunnan.

mekongense var. *rubrolineatum* (Balf.f. & Forr.) Cullen 1978

The type specimen of Forrest's has no number but is said to come from Cangshan, C. Yunnan. Forrest writes, 'Yet another species new to me. Shrub 2ft, flowers creamy (ivory) yellow, lined and flushed rose on exterior, open pasture, Tali Range alt. 11,000ft, May 1917. Very rare! G. Forrest.' I am convinced that this is the same cross of *trichocladum* × *racemosum* we saw (SBEC 0717) with pink flowers, tinged yellow. The colour was a little different but this variation would be expected. The terminal and axillary inflorescence would again point to *racemosum* influence.

Other specimens classified as var. *rubrolineatum* in the RBG, Edinburgh herbarium do not appear to be the same hybrid, merely variants of *mekongense. R. mekongense* var. *rubrolineatum* in cultivation has deciduous or semi-evergreen leaves and yellow flowers lined and flushed with rose. This would appear to be the hybrid that Forrest and I saw on Cangshan. Davidian makes no suggestion that this is a hybrid.

E.M.S

R. trichocladum

trichocladum Franch. 1886 (*xanthinum* Balf.f. & W.W. Sm., *lithophilum* Balf.f. & Ward, *oulotrichum* Balf.f. & Forr., *lophogynum* Balf.f. & Forr. nomen nudum). H4–5 USDA 6b–5 & 6a L1–2 F1–2
Ht to 1.5m (5ft). Habit usually open and erect but bushy in full sun.
L deciduous, 2.4–4cm (1–1½in) long, obovate to obovate-elliptic, dense hairs on lower surface and midrib; *scales below ± equal, golden.*
F usually precocious, yellow to greenish-yellow, 1.8–2.3cm (¾–1in) long, funnel-campanulate.

Although they are not all that showy, KW's great dislike of these plants (see Viridescens and Rubroluteum Groups of *mekongense*) is rather hard as they can be quite attractive. On Cangshan, Yunnan, this was one of the commonest species we saw and was always in full bloom, covering whole hillsides with a haze of pale yellow. When seen with a foreground of *fastigiatum*, the blue-purple and yellow combination was quite delightful. Many have the added attractions of bronzy young growth and autumn colour, usually yellow. AM 1971 under *lophogynum*. Best grown in clumps in a sunny situation. Rootability as *mekongense*.

From N. Burma, C. and S.W. Yunnan, separated geographically from other members of the subsection, 2,400–4,000m (8,000–13,000ft), slopes, rocky places, scrub, cliffs and forest margins, sometimes on limestone.

April–May

TRIFLORA SUBSECTION (TRIFLORUM SERIES)

Only *keiskei* is small enough to include.

keiskei Miquel 1866 (*kuromiensis* Ingram, *laticostum* Ingram, *trichocalyx* Ingram) H4–5 USDA 6b–5 & 6a L1–2 F1–3
Ht 5cm–3m (2in–10ft). Habit open and leggy, bushy and compact to prostrate and creeping, sometimes epiphytic.
L evergreen, 2.5–7.5cm (1–3in) long, lanceolate to oblong-lanceolate to narrowly elliptic, olive to medium to dark green above, partly puberulent above, greenish below with large brown scales.
F pale to lemon-yellow, unspotted, widely funnel-shaped, 2–6 per truss. Calyx variable, usually small, style slender.

Plants in cultivation can be divided into three forms which make entirely different garden plants.
1 Long narrow or broader leaves, often bronzy, loose, sometimes tall habit. I include W. Berg's epiphytic form here. This often makes a poor plant in Britain and certain introductions are barely worthy of cultivation. This is apparently by far the commonest form in the wild. A few have leaves glaucous below known in Japan as var. *hypoglaucum* Makino. One form found by Hideo Suzuki has a red stripe on the outside of each corolla lobe.
2 'Dwarf form' often a good plant, especially in E. USA, where it is the only hardy dwarf yellow species. G. G. Nearing raised several generations from seed for hardiness. At Glendoick it grows best in a peat bed. We find the flowers of some forms to be of rather poor substance and easily frosted but we like W. Berg's 'Ebino' form. Does not succeed in lowland Japan where it is too hot. Some are reported to be almost as dwarf as 'Yaku Fairy'.

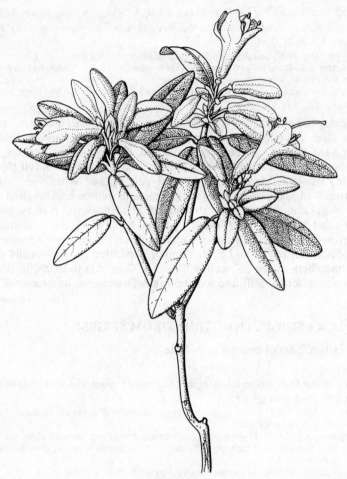

R. keiskei

3* Prostrate form from Yakushima generally known as 'Yaku Fairy' (AM 1970) in Britain. This is the same as *kuromiensis* Ingram, var. *cordifolia* in Japan and var. *prostratum* in parts of USA. This is a first rate, free-flowering plant, one of the most valuable new introductions. Flowers rather later than its taller relatives. Is proving to be one of the best of all parents of dwarf hybrids, producing low, vigorous, compact, free-flowering progeny with excellent foliage and flower quality. Hardy to $-3°C$ ($-2°F$) in E. USA. According to Suzuki there are two forms, one with leaves 2.5×0.6 cm ($1 \times \frac{1}{4}$in), the other 3.8×1.3cm ($1\frac{1}{2} \times \frac{1}{2}$in). 'Yaku Fairy' could be worth specific status. *keiskei* all forms: wild in

* As there are now numerous clones and seedlings of this plant in cultivation, it is important to have at least a Group name in regular use. Var. *cordifolia* seems to be used most often, so I propose that, until its status is reconsidered, we call it the Cordifolia Group.

Japan only from Yakushima northwards to C. Japan in hilly country on lava, sandstone or shale, often between boulders or on cliffs or rarely as an epiphytie on Yakushima.   March–May

UNIFLORA SUBSECTION (UNIFLORUM SERIES)

A small group of very dwarf species which appear to be related to the Saluenensia subsection, but also have similarities, according to Cullen, with Tephropepla, Campylogyna and Cinnabarina subsections. The last (Cinnabarina) I fail to see much connection with. With the exception of the distinctive and widespread *pumilum*, all come from politically sensitive localities in an area largely unexplored. Until more material is collected, the status of *pemakoense* and *uniflorum* will remain in doubt.

Beautiful, free-flowering little plants, often mat-forming. Leaves evergreen with revolute or crenate margins. Inflorescence terminal, 1–3 flowered, flowers funnel-campanulate. Stamens 10, style straight.

ludlowii Cowan 1937 H4 USDA 6b L1–2 F2–3

Ht to 30cm (1ft). Habit spreading or creeping.
L 1.2–1.6 cm ($\frac{1}{2}$–$\frac{3}{5}$in) long, broadly obovate to oblong-obovate, margins crenate and brown scales below.
F yellow with ± reddish-brown spots, 1.5–2.5 cm ($\frac{3}{5}$–1in) long, about 2.5cm (1in) across, almost bowl-shaped in trusses of 1–2. Pedicels 1.5–2cm ($\frac{3}{5}$–$\frac{4}{5}$in) long. Calyx conspicuous, margins ciliate.

This is a superb little gem when grown successfully with very large flowers in comparison with the foliage. It is not too easy to please and rarely flourishes unless planted in pure organic matter, preferably peat, and it appreciates a few stones around its neck. Even this treatment does not always work. It does best in a cool, partly shaded site with good frost drainage. It is worth every effort to please it, and has proved to be a most valuable parent for dwarf yellow hybrids. Moderately hardy in S. Sweden. Rootability medium to high.

A very distinct species with no known relative from a small area of S. Xizang where it is locally common, 4,000–4,300m (13,000–14,000ft) on open rocky hillsides, creeping over moss-covered rocky soil amongst *Cassiope* and other dwarf rhododendrons.   May

pemakoense Ward 1930 (*patulum* Ward) H(3–)4 USDA (7a–)6b L1–2 F2–3

Ht to 60cm (2ft). Habit usually dense forming a low mound, often stoloniferous.
L 1.3–3cm ($\frac{1}{2}$–1$\frac{1}{5}$in) long, *obovate* to obovate-elliptic, margin revolute, dense unequal scales below.
F pale pinkish-purple to near pink, *2.4–3.5cm* (1–1$\frac{2}{5}$in) long, up to 5cm (2in) across, broadly funnel-campanulate, densely hairy outside, 1–2 per truss. Calyx small.

One of the most floriferous of all dwarfs, capable of hiding its foliage with a mass of comparatively large flowers. Alas, these are very frost-prone, even in the swelling bud. Easily cultivated and only occasionally suffers frost damage to foliage and growth tips from which it readily recovers (here at Glendoick). Not hardy in S. Sweden.

Plants cultivated under *patulum* are synonymus with *pemakoense*. Some variation in flower and foliage. Davidian makes *patulum* a synonym of (*uniflorum* var.) *imperator*. The form I know is better under

E.M.S.

R. pemakoense

pemakoense. Good in S. Sweden but not successful in E. USA. AM 1933 KW 6301, AGM 1968. Rootability high.

From E. Arunachal Pradesh, S.E. Xizang, 3,000–3,700m (10,000–12,000ft), forming carpets on steep moss-clad rocks and slopes.

March–May

pumilum Hook. 1849 H3–4 USDA 7a–6b L1–2 F2–3

Ht to 15cm + (6in+). Habit dwarf or prostrate.
L 0.8–1.9cm ($\frac{1}{3}$–$\frac{3}{4}$in) long, elliptic to broadly elliptic, margins revolute, rather shiny above, slightly glaucous below.
F pink to rose-purple, 1.1–2.1cm ($\frac{2}{5}$–$\frac{7}{8}$in) long, campanulate, hairy outside, in trusses of 1–3, style short and *straight*.

KW's 'Pink baby' is a dear little plant with charming small, thimble-like flowers, smaller than its allies. At Glendoick we find this plant rather hard to please, and like *ludlowii* it does best in a peat bed. Cloche protection during winter can save winter-scorching and die-back. Some old leaves colour well in autumn. AM 1935 flowers pinkish-mauve to KW 6961. I have frequently seen other plants wrongly labelled *pumilum*. Not hardy in S. Sweden.

From E. Nepal, through Sikkim, N.E. Bhutan (doubtful, probably *lepidotum*) to S.E. Xizang where it is most plentiful, E. Arunachal Pradesh and N.E. Burma, 3,400–4,300m (11,000–14,000ft), on bare hill-sides, mossy rocks, screes and grass. L&S found a group of 12 white-flowered plants. Specimens collected at the E. end of distribution tend to have larger-than-average leaves.

April–May

uniflorum Ward 1930 H4 USDA 6b L1–2 F2–3

Ht up to 1m (3ft). Habit compact and twiggy to leggy in woodland.
L 1.3–2.5cm (½–1in) long, oblong-elliptic. The type specimen has brown scales 3–6 times their diameter apart but a clone cultivated at Windsor Park and elsewhere under the type number has very small light brown scales, about their own diameter apart, plus a few large brown scales. Can this plant be passed as *uniflorum* or not? A plant with slightly larger leaves, but otherwise similar, has the correct scales. I obtained this material from Gigha, W. Scotland.
F mauve pink or purple, about 2.5cm (1in) long, 1–2 per truss (Windsor 1–3), broadly funnel-shaped.

KW reported this as being a very rare species which leads one to be suspicious of its being a species at all. Could it be a hybrid? Quite pretty in flower but the foliage is sometimes poor and spotted or even semi-deciduous; in Sweden it is said to be deciduous and reasonably hardy.

The poor type specimen does not seem to agree with cultivated plants, the leaves looking too wide and blunt.

Only found so far on the Doshong La Pass, S.E. Xizang, 3,400–3,700m (11,000–12,000ft), spreading over moraines and gravel, often flowering in October. April–May

uniflorum var. *imperator* (Ward) Cullen 1978 H3–4 USDA 7a–6b L1–2 F2–3

Ht 15–30cm (6–12in). Habit usually prostrate with spreading branchlets.
L 1.3–3.8cm (½–1½in) long, lanceolate to oblanceolate, *darker* green above than *uniflorum*.
F bright purple or pinkish-purple, narrowly funnel-shaped, about 2.5cm (1in) long, 3.8cm (1½in) across, 1–2 per truss.

Undoubtedly closely related to *uniflorum* but rather tender. If we do not cover it with a cloche between September and May, it may be cut back almost to ground level. Pretty when well-flowered. AM 1934 rosy-purple flowers KW 6884. Rootability medium.

Found at a low elevation by KW in one valley in N.E. Burma on bare granite cliff ledges at 3,000–3,400m (10,000–11,000ft), forming mats where it gets little sun and the snow lingers late; evidently rare. April–May

VIRGATA SUBSECTION (VIRGATUM SERIES)

A very widespread but distinct species with no close relations. Cullen reckons that in spite of its different inflorescence, it has some relationship with subsections Cinnabarina and Tephropepla.

virgatum Hook. 1849 H2–3 (occasionally 4) USDA 7b & 8a–7a L1–2 F1–3

Ht 30cm–2.4m (1–8ft). Habit usually ungainly and sprawling, often with long arching branches. *Terminal bud always vegetative.*
L evergreen, 1.8–8cm (¾–3in) long, narrowly oblong to oblong-elliptic, revolute, pale below with unequal scales.
F pale to deep pink or mauve, rarely white, 2.5–3.7cm (1–1½in) long, funnel-shaped always axillary, 1–2 flowers per leaf axil with flowers occurring for several inches on robust shoots. Stamens 10. Fragrant. Seed with tails at each end as in most Vireyas.

It is sad that such an easily grown and floriferous species is barely hardy in most of Britain. The most tender forms can even be killed in fairly mild W. and S. gardens. Place it on a bank where it can sprawl and

R. virgatum

be prepared to take cuttings regularly in case of loss outside. There is a beautiful white form. AM 1973. Rootability high.

The type has a wide distribution from S. and E. Nepal, through Sikkim, Bhutan, Arunachal Pradesh to S. and S.E. Xizang, 2,400–3,800m (8,000–12,500ft), forest margins and dry scrubby slopes.   March–May

virgatum ssp. *oleifolium* (Franch.) Cullen 1978 (*sinovirgatum* Hort. ined)

This, the Chinese form of *virgatum*, is generally an inferior plant with smaller, paler flowers, 1.5–2.5cm ($\frac{3}{5}$–1in) long. It is recorded as coming from as high as 4,000m (13,000ft) but this could be one of F's or R's exaggerated elevations. We found this on Cangshan, Yunnan as a scattered shrub, usually in remarkably hot, dry sites among scrub. This and ssp. *virgatum* could be valuable subjects for hot, dry areas and could be crossed with say *minus* var. *chapmanii* to accentuate heat- and drought-resistance.

From S.E. Xizang, N., N.W., W. and S.W. Yunnan, 2,000–4,000m (6,500–13,000ft).

SECTION VIREYA, PSEUDOVIREYA SUBSECTION (VACCINIOIDES SERIES)

A small group of Vireyas found on mainland Asia, Taiwan and Philippines (as previously classified). Here, we will only cover those from the mainland and Taiwan.

R. *vaccinioides* is the aberrant member of the subsection as its leaves are scattered up the stem, not in *whorls* at the ends of the shoots as in the other species. Davidian excludes the Philippines species from his Vaccinioides series.

It is likely that in the wetter temperate rain forest of the Burmese-Indo-Chinese frontier region, there are other species of this subsection as yet unknown to science.

All are tender and of limited beauty with small flowers on rather straggly plants, usually epiphytic in the wild. R. *kawakamii* is the only species without warts which cause the leaves to be 'scabrid'.

It is now considered that these Asiatic Pseudovireyas are not all that closely related to any of the Malesian species. Not only will they not hybridize but the style is consistently *not tapered into the ovary*, an important character in classifying these plants.

asperulum Hutch. & Ward 1930 not in cultivation

An epiphyte found on older trees or on boulders in S.E. Xizang at 2,000–2,100m (6,500–7,000ft). F pale flesh pink with orange anthers, 3 per truss.

emarginatum Hemsl. 1910 not in cultivation

Shrub of 60cm (2ft) found in S.W. Yunnan at 1,800m (6,000ft). F yellow in one-flowered inflorescence.

euonymifolium Lévl. 1913 not in cultivation

Small shrub found on rocks in Guizhou. F colour unknown, in one flowered inflorescence. Probably close to *emarginatum*.

insculptum Hutch. & Ward not in cultivation

An epiphyte found in S.E. Xizang at 1,800–2,100m (6,000–7,000ft) with bright orange flowers in axillary, one-flowered inflorescence. Related to asperulum.

kawakamii Hayata H2–3 USDA 7b & 8a–7a L1–2 F1–2

Ht 1–1.5m (3–5ft). Habit bushy, inclined to be straggly, epiphytic in the wild.
L 2–5cm ($\frac{4}{5}$–2in) long, obovate, thick and leathery.
F yellow or white, 1cm ($\frac{2}{5}$in) long, widely funnel-shaped, 3–7 per truss.

We and others have now grown the yellow-flowered form for several years. Some plants have been tested both at Glendoick and in Argyll. One plant, placed on a mossy rock has survived in Argyll for several years. At Glendoick, even on a wall with cloche or frame light, protection, it does not come through our coldest winters. The rather small flowers are quite attractive but not equal to the likes of *sulfureum*. All efforts to cross this with members of the Vireya section failed until Dr John Rouse of Australia crossed it successfully with its fellow Pseudovireya, *santapauii* in 1983. Dr George Argent of the RBG, Edinburgh doubts its close affinity with the Malesian Vireyas and reckons it does not really have the 'feel' of a Vireya. Rootability medium to high. Not introduced until 1969.

Endemic to Taiwan, 1,800–2,600m (6,000–8,500ft), fairly plentiful as an epiphytie in rich rain forest.   July–August

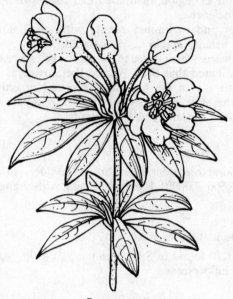

R. santapauii

santapauii Sastry, Kataki, P. A. Cox, E. P. Cox, P. C. Hutchison 1969 H probably 2 USDA probably 7b & 8a L1–2 F2

Ht to 60cm (2ft) in the wild. Habit epiphytic in the wild, hanging from large tree-trunks with little moss. Slow growing in cultivation.
L up to 4cm (1½in) long, thick and leathery, obovate-lanceolate, dark green above. Scales twice their own diameter apart.
F pure waxy white, about 2.5cm (1in) across with short tube, 0.5cm (⅕in) long and spreading lobes. Red scales on outside of corolla, 2–4 per truss, stamens white, anthers at first yellow, later brown-red. Stigma red. Long tailed seeds.

A rare species, discovered and collected by the author on the Cox & Hutchison expedition to Arunachal Pradesh, 1965. Found near Apa Tani valley, at 1,600m (5,400ft) as C&H 459. Rootability medium.

This has proved rather tricky in cultivation and inclined to die suddenly. The waxy flowers are rather attractive. Successfully introduced into Australia from Britain. Seems to appreciate a high proportion of sphagnum in its compost.   July–August

vaccinioides Hook.f. 1851 H2–3 7b & 8a–7a L1–2 F1

Ht 30cm (1ft) or more. Habit compact to straggly, epiphytic in wild, usually in moss. Branchlets *rough to touch*.
L 0.6–2.5cm (¼–1in) long, spathulate-oblanceolate, without visible lateral nerves. Shiny above. *Leaves scattered up stem*.
F lilac-pink or white-tinged pink, 1cm (⅖in) long, campanulate, 1–2 flowered.

While the flowering season is long, the insignificant little flowers are of little horticultural merit. The little box-like leaves can be confused with *Vaccinium delavayi*.

A wide distribution from Nepal, through Bhutan, Arunachal Pradesh, S.E. Xizang to Burma and N.W. Yunnan at 1,800–4,300m (6,000–14,000ft). It has a small range of altitude in the Himalayas to Burma and a much greater one in S.E. Xizang and adjoining Yunnan. The high-altitude forms have probably never been introduced. Very common epiphyte on different trees, rocks, ledges and crevices, usually in moist shady places. July–September, sometimes earlier.

POGONANTHUM SECTION (ANTHOPOGON SERIES)

This former series is so distinctive it has been given full sectional status. All are dwarf evergreens with highly aromatic leaves, pineapple-like according to Cullen. My father in RHS-RCYB, 1964, pp. 70–2, took it upon himself (I refused to help!) to associate certain species with other scents, especially in the Pogonanthums. *R. kongboense* he associated with Friar's Balsam, *sargentianum* pure crushed *Thuja*, *anthopogon* perhaps indol in human sweat, *anthopogon* ssp. *hypenanthum* bog myrtle *Myrica gale*.

The small flowers are in tight terminal trusses with a hairy throat. The corolla lobes spread outwards from the tube and may be known as spreading limbs. The leaves are densely covered with unique lacerate scales, often rufous or chocolate-coloured on the mature leaf underside, giving a resemblance to the indumentum of the Taliensia or Neriiflora subsections. The flowers are like those of a daphne.

To many, these are the élite of all dwarfs, full of character with charming little flowers and neat, often tiny leaves. The majority are hardy with us but will not tolerate hot, dry conditions; so they grow best in cool climates like Scotland. However, at least some are more tolerant of the lack of a cold winter than are the Lapponicums. The delicate flowers may be spoilt by strong sun or heavy rain, especially *anthopogon* and *cephalanthum*. The colours given for leaf undersides are for mature leaves only. The Chinese use foliage of this section in a medicine for coughs.

Several members are susceptible to interveinal chlorosis, especially *sargentianum* and *kongboense*.

The majority come from high elevations from Afghanistan in the W. to Sichuan and Gansu in the E. and are mostly found on the drier ridges in the rain shadow of the full monsoon.

Unfortunately, many species are not in cultivation and every effort should be made to collect these if and when the possibility arises.

The chief characters (easily seen) to look out for are height, habit, presence or absence of leaf bud scales and of pilose hairs outside the corolla, size and shape of leaf. Also to some extent the colour of the leaf underside although this can often vary within a species and even on one herbarium specimen where there are two or more twigs.

anthopogon D. Don 1821 (*haemonium* Balf.f. & Cooper, *anthopogon* var. *album* Davidian, *anthopogon* var. *haemonium* Cowan & Davidian) H4(–5) USDA 6b(–5 & 6a) L1–2 F1–3

Ht 30–90cm (1–3ft). Habit compact to straggly with age. *Deciduous leaf-bud scales.*
L 1–3.5cm (⅓–1½in) long, 0.8–1.6cm (¼–⅔in) wide, usually ovate to elliptic, often reddish-brown below.
F many in open-topped truss, white to deep pink, sometimes apricot-coloured buds, glabrous outside, pilose within. Flower texture like limp tissue-paper. Stamens 5–10, *usually 6–8.*

The deep pink forms are the most attractive but are often slow to bloom freely. Rather difficult to grow in some areas and may tend to die back on reaching flowering age. Several new introductions from Nepal and Sikkim in recent years. The so called var. *album* of Davidian 1980 is of little botanical or horticultural consequence. Fairly hardy in S. Sweden. 'Betty Graham' AM 1969 L&S 1091 deep pink flowers. Rootability low.

Common from E. Nepal through Bhutan, N.W. Arunachal Pradesh to S.E. Xizang, 2,700–4,900m (9,000–16,000ft), often dominant over large areas of moorland and on cliffs and rocks, frequently associated with *setosum.*   April–May

anthopogon* ssp. *hypenanthum (Balf.f.) Cullen 1979

Similar to the above but with *persistent leaf-bud scales.* Davidian makes the chief character separating ssp. *anthopogon* from ssp. *hypenanthum* one of flower colour but this does not hold with the presence or absence of persistent leaf-bud scales.

The dwarfest compact selections with small dark leaves are much the best. Very variable from SS&W 9090. 'Annapurna' AM 1974 is one of these fine selections with neat pale yellow flowers freely produced. L&S 1091 is included under this subspecies by Cullen. Rootability medium to high.

Mostly Kashmir to Nepal, also Bhutan, reaching as high as 5,500m (18,000ft).   April–May

anthopogonoides Maxim. 1872 not in cultivation (?)

Ht to 1.6m (5ft). Habit usually upright. Leaf bud scales deciduous.
L 2–4cm (¾–1⅔in) long, 1–2.1cm (⅓–¾in) wide, rounded at base, fawn to light brown below.
F white or greenish-white, rarely flushed pink in dense, many-flowered truss. Stamens 5.

One (probable) plant of this species was lost recently from cultivation. Distinct for its very dense truss or short-lobed flowers. Generally taller than *anthopogon* and leaves paler below.

Found only in Gansu and Qinghai at 3,000–3,400m (10,000–11,000ft) in scrub and forest margins.

cephalanthum* ssp. *cephalanthum Franch. 1885 (*chamaetortum* Balf.f. & Ward, *crebreflorum* Hutch. & Ward, *nmaiense* Hutch. & Ward, *cephalanthum* var. *crebreflorum* Cowan & Davidian, *cephalanthum* var. *nmaiense* Cowan & Davidian) H4–5 USDA 6b–5 & 6a L1–2 F2–3

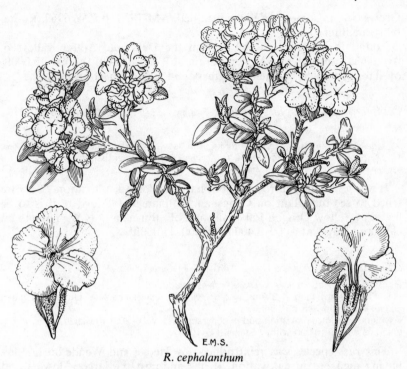

E.M.S.

R. cephalanthum

Ht 30cm–1.2m (1–4ft). Habit semi-prostrate to erect and leggy. *Leaf-bud scales persistent*

L 1.3–2.6cm ($\frac{1}{2}$–1in) *long, 0.6–1.5cm ($\frac{1}{4}$–$\frac{2}{3}$in) wide,* oblong-elliptic to broadly oblong, thick and leathery, margins recurved, dark glossy green above, usually fawn to brown below.

F white to pink, rarely yellowish to crimson, 1.3–2cm ($\frac{1}{2}$–$\frac{3}{4}$in) long, narrowly tubular in an open-topped, many-flowered truss, glabrous outside, pilose within. Stamens usually 5 rarely to 8.

There are several fine forms of this in cultivation especially a low, compact pink-flowered form. We found a compact white form mixed with *fastigiatum* on a north facing limestone bank on Cangshan, Yunnan in 1981 which should prove a good introduction. Some forms are closely related to *primuliflorum* with which it overlaps in the wild but the latter lacks the persistent bud scales. AM 1934, 'Winifred Murray' AM 1979. Barely hardy in S. Sweden. Rootability variable.

Widespread over large areas of Yunnan, S.E. Xizang and Upper Burma at 2,700–4,900m (9,000–16,000ft) on moist moorland, bouldery slopes, screes and dry limestone banks and cliffs, even epiphytic on tree trunks.   April–May

Crebreflorum Group F3

Habit compact, forming low mound or prostrate, often stoloniferous. L with margins less recurved. F pale to clear pink.

A really superb little plant and one of my favourites. We grow two clones with palish and clear pink flowers. The former is the easier grown.

Grows best in some shade in a peat bed. AM 1934 to KW 6967. Rootability medium to high.

Found in limited areas by KW in the Delei and Adung valleys of Arunachal Pradesh and Upper Burma at 3,400–4,000m (11,000–13,000ft) on slabs of rock or on sheltered grassy cliff ledges in wet districts.   April

cephalanthum var. *platyphyllum* (Franch. ex Balf.f. & W.W. Sm.) Cullen 1979

Not in cultivation.

A large-sized variant of *cephalanthum* with leaves substantially larger, *2.5–4.7cm (1–1¾in) long, 1.8–2.3cm (⅔-1in) wide.* Flowers slightly larger than the biggest size for ssp. *cephalanthum*. Variable in habit.

It was apparently introduced but has been lost to cultivation. Sadly we failed to see this plant on Cangshan, Yunnan in 1981 where it is to be found at Yellow Dragon Lake; also in N.E. Burma and N.W. Yunnan on cliffs and ledges at 3,000–3,400m (10,000–11,000ft).

collettianum Aitchison & Hemsl. 1881 H3–4 USDA 7a–6b L1–2 F2–3

Ht to 1m (3ft). Habit bushy. Leaf-bud scales deciduous.
L to 7.5cm (3in) long, 1.3–2cm (½–⅘in) wide, usually lanceolate, rather pale green above, light yellowish-buff below.
·F white, sometimes pinkish in bud in compact truss of 16–20, larger than *anthopogon*, glabrous outside, pilose within. Stamens 8–10.

This rare species was reintroduced by Hedge and Wendelbo in 1969 having died out in cultivation. It has amongst the largest flowers and leaves in the section and is attractive when well grown. Alas, it is not easy and is vulnerable to spring frosts. We nearly lost our entire stock at Glendoick in the spring frosts of 1981 and a further dying back occurred during the severe 1981–2 winter. It seems to prefer woodland conditions. Rootability medium.

Of very limited distribution on the Pakistan-Afghanistan frontier and E. Afghanistan at 3,000–4,000m (10,000–13,000ft) being locally dominant on north-facing stony limestone slopes with *Juniperus communis* above the tree line.   May

fragrans (Adams) Maxim. 1870 (*adamsii* Rehd.) Not in cultivation

Ht to 50cm (20in). Leaf-bud scales deciduous.
L 1–2cm (⅓–⅘in) long, 0.5–1cm (¼–⅓in) wide, oblong-elliptic to oblong-ovate, dark glossy green above, pale yellowish below.
F pale pink to pink with darker veins, 7–15 per truss, glabrous outside, pilose within. Stamens 5.

It has been confused with *primuliflorum* from which it is quite distinct. Only one specimen in RBG herbarium, Edinburgh.

Found over a wide area of central Asia in Siberia and Mongolia forming thickets in the alpine zone.

kongboense Hutch. 1937 H4–5 USDA 6b–5 & 6a L1–2 F2–3

Ht 30cm–2.5m (1–8ft) in wild. Habit usually fastigiate but sometimes compact. Leaf-bud scales deciduous.

L 1.3–2.8cm ($\frac{1}{2}$–1$\frac{1}{4}$in) long, 0.6–1.2cm ($\frac{1}{4}$–$\frac{1}{2}$in) wide, oblong to elliptic-oblong, often greyish-green above, fawn to brown below.
F pale pink to deep rose or even pinkish-white in the wild, about 1 cm ($\frac{2}{5}$in) long, in many-flowered fairly compact trusses, pilose *outside* and within. Stamens 5.

The deep-coloured flowered forms are quite striking flowers for their size. I always rub the strongly aromatic leaves in passing—they have a smell like pungent strawberries (Friar's Balsam according to my father). Closely related to *primuliflorum*, especially to the Cephalanthoides Group which usually has a longer corolla tube of a paler colour. Cullen has moved many herbarium specimens from *primuliflorum* var. *cephalanthoides* into *kongboense*. Needs protection in S. Sweden. Rootability medium.

Distribution in S. Xizang in the province of Kongbo and to the south of Lhasa, 3,200–4,700m (10,500–15,500ft) in oak forests, on rocky slopes, cliffs, moorland, sometimes marshy.   March to early May

laudandum Cowan 1937 Not in cultivation

Ht to 60cm (2ft) or a little taller. Leaf-bud scales usually persistent but not very conspicuous.
L 1.1–1.7cm (about $\frac{1}{2}$in) long, 6–9mm (about $\frac{1}{3}$in) wide, ovate to almost orbicular, *dark chocolate-brown beneath*.
F usually pink in a dense many-flowered truss, *tube densely pilose outside and inside*. Stamens 5–6.

Sounds a neat little plant worthy of introduction. Only three herbarium specimens in RBG, Edinburgh.
S.E. Xizang, 4,300–4,600m (14,000–15,000ft) on rocky hillsides.

laudandum var. *temoense* (Ward ex) Cowan & Davidian 1947

Differs from var. *laudandum* in the corolla being usually white, the corolla tube being only slightly pilose outside and the leaves being at least twice as long as broad as opposed to less than twice in var. *laudandum*.

A clone (H4 USDA 6b L2 F3) passed as this variety with pale lavender-pink flowers and leaves green underneath is, I believe, now the only one in cultivation. It is a most attractive plant of which I am very fond, flowering freely in March–April. There are two herbarium specimens in the RBG, Edinburgh herbarium with pale indumentum with pink or pinkish flowers which appear near to the clone described above. Two others look to me more like var. *laudandum*. There is even a variation in the indumentum colour on different shoots on one specimen. Only five specimens altogether. Needs protection in S. Sweden. Rootability medium.

S.E. Xizang, 2,900–4,700m (9,500–15,500ft) on moraines and open slopes.

pogonophyllum Cowan & Davidian 1947 Not in cultivation.

Ht a small prostrate shrub. Leaf bud scales *persistent*.
L about 1 cm ($\frac{1}{3}$in) long, 4–5mm ($\frac{1}{6}$in) wide, *whitish hairs above*, brown beneath.
F white to pink, *only 2–4 per truss*, glabrous outside, pilose within, Stamens 6.

This is obviously a neat and unusual little dwarf but with so few flowers per truss, is unlikely to give much of a show. Would appear to be the baby of the section.

From a small area of C. Bhutan only at 4,300–4,700m (14,000–15,000ft) in rocky places.

primuliflorum Bureau & Franch. 1891 (*acraium* Balf.f. & W.W. Sm., *cephalanthoides* Balf.f. & W.W. Sm., *clivicolum* Balf.f. & W.W. Sm., *cremnophyllum* Balf.f. & W.W. Sm., *gymnomiscum* Balf.f. & Ward, *lepidanthum* Balf.f. & W.W. Sm., *tsarongense* Balf.f. & Forr., *praeclarum* Balf.f. & Farrier.) H4–5 USDA 6b–5 & 6a L1–2 F1–2(–3).

Ht a few cm up to 2m (6ft). Habit often taller than broad with open upright growth. *Leaf bud scales quickly deciduous.*
L 1.1–3.5cm ($\frac{1}{2}$–1$\frac{1}{3}$in) long, 0.5–1.4cm ($\frac{1}{5}$–$\frac{1}{2}$in) wide, narrowly elliptic to occasionally elliptic, glossy and dark green above, pale brown to brown below.
F usually white, rarely rose or yellowish base, usually glabrous outside, pilose within. Stamens 5, rarely 6.

Some introductions of this species may take several years to flower freely and with the taller forms, their habit can be rather ungainly. Better plants are found in the Cephalanthoides Group. Reasonably hardy in S. Sweden. Rootability medium to high. Overlaps in the wild with *cephalanthum*, the chief difference being the deciduous bud scales.

Common in N. and N.W. Yunnan, S.E. Xizang and S.W. Sichuan at 3,400–4,600m (11,000–15,000ft), from dryish areas on alpine meadows, screes, cliffs and occasionally forest margins, sometimes on limestone.

April–May

Cephalanthoides Group. These tend to be nearest *kongboense* taxonomically and those that I grow are better garden plants than the type. I grow two forms. One has deep rose-coloured flowers and slightly greyed foliage; the other is a splendid free-flowering clone 'Doker La' AM 1980 which I obtained from the Isle of Gigha. It covers itself with clear pink flowers in late April–early May. While at first sight it resembles *trichostomum*, it blooms much earlier with less dense trusses. Cuttings difficult to root.

radendum Fang 1939 not in cultivation

Ht to 1m (3ft). Leaf-bud scales deciduous.
L 1–1.8cm (about $\frac{1}{2}$in) long, 3–6mm (about $\frac{1}{6}$in) wide, obovate, lanceolate or ovate. *Hairy leaves and pedicels.*
F purplish-white, glabrous outside, pilose within. Stamens 5.

From only one known collection in N.W. Sichuan. Near to *trichostomum*.

rufescens Franch. 1895 (*daphniflorum* Diels) not in cultivation

Ht 0.3–1m (1–3ft). Habit twisted and intricate branching. Leaf-bud scales deciduous.
L 1–2cm (about $\frac{2}{3}$in) long, 5–9mm (about $\frac{1}{4}$in) wide, usually elliptic-oblong, dark and glossy above, dark brown below.
F white, glabrous outside, tube mouth slightly pilose inside. Stamens 5.

In my estimation, this is near to *sargentianum*, only differing in the deciduous bud scales and deeper brown leaf underside. Leaf and flower size appear similar.

From C. and possibly S.W. Sichuan, 3,900–4,600m (13,000–15,000ft) in open rocky places.

sargentianum Rehd. & Wils. 1913 H5 USDA 5 & 6a L2 F2–3

Ht to 60cm (2ft) but often not over 30cm (1ft). Habit usually dense and symmetrical. Leaf-bud scales *persistent*.
L 0.9–1.5cm ($\frac{2}{5}$–$\frac{3}{5}$in) long, 5–8mm (about $\frac{1}{4}$in) wide, elliptic, dark above, pale brown to brown below.
F cream to pale yellow 1.3–1.6cm ($\frac{1}{2}$–$\frac{2}{3}$in) long, in trusses of 5–12, slightly hairy outside, pilose within. Stamens 5.

This is a most distinguished little plant forming a dense mound of the neatest dark green leaves studded with pale yellow or cream flowers. A must for every collection, preferably in both forms. Liable to become chlorotic, probably due to over-acidity and/or drought. The cream flowers of 'Whitebait' AM 1966 are slightly larger than the yellow forms as are the leaves, and it flowers freely. As in many of this section, it does not stand excessive heat. 'Maricee' AE, a beautiful American clone, probably a hybrid of *sargentianum*, has a more open habit and plentiful creamy-white flowers. Pale yellow form AM 1923. Rootability medium.

Seems rare in the wild, only found in two localities in Sichuan (so far) at 2,700–3,400m (9,000–11,000ft) on exposed rocks and cliffs.   April–June

trichostomum Franch. 1895 (*fragrans* Franch. not (Adams) Maxim., *ledoides* Balf.f. & W.W. Sm., *radinum* Balf.f. & W.W. Sm., *sphaeranthum* Balf.f. & W.W. Sm.) H(3–)4 USDA (7a–)6b L1–2 F2–4

Ht 0.3–1.2m (1–4ft) or more. Habit often loose and sprawling but becomes more compact with age in full sun. Leaf-bud scales usually deciduous.
L 1.2–3.4cm ($\frac{1}{2}$–1$\frac{1}{3}$in) long, 3–6mm ($\frac{1}{8}$–$\frac{1}{4}$in) wide, *linear, oblong to narrowly oblanceolate*, usually pale brown below.
F white to rose up to 2cm ($\frac{4}{5}$in) long, in many-flowered ± globose truss, glabrous outside, pilose within.

A superb species in its best rose and white forms, those with colours in between being inferior. Most are very free-flowering and open later than the majority of the section. Some forms are tender and suffer bark-split so should be avoided. Most forms tender in Scandinavia. Distinctive for its narrow leaves and globular truss. Some strong growing introductions, according to Cullen, may be natural hybrids of *primuliflorum*. Rootability low. The varieties previously given botanical status have been correctly scrapped by Cullen although they are retained at Group status in the *1980 Rhododendron Handbook*. 'Collingwood Ingram' FCC 1976 flowers rose, AM 1925, 'Quarry Wood' AM 1971 flowers white, 'Lakeside' AM 1972 flowers white-flushed rose—all as var. *ledoides*. 'Sweet Bay' AM 1960 soft pink F 20480, AM 1972 rose, both as var. *radinum*. 'Rae Berry' is a good deep pink American clone. Var. *hedyosmum* may be a *trichostonum* hybrid and is probably now out of cultivation.

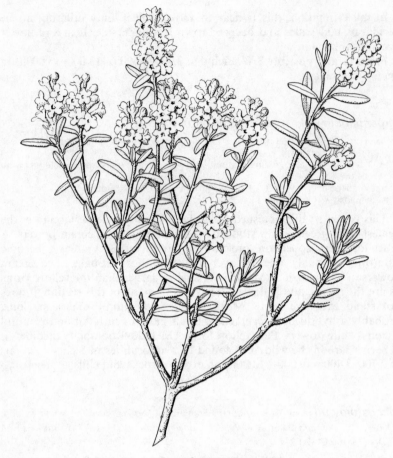

R. trichostomum

Very common in the wild in N. and N.W. Yunnan, S.W. and C. Sichuan at 2,400–4,600m (8,000–15,000ft) but usually between 3,000–4,000m (10,000–13,000ft) in forests and thicket margins and open slopes in both dry and moist situations.   May–June

IMPERFECTLY KNOWN SPECIES

chrysolepis Hutch. & Ward 1930. Probably not in cultivation

Known only from two fruiting specimens collected in Upper Burma at 2,100–2,400m (7,000–8,000ft). Formerly placed in Boothii series, subseries Tephropeplum. According to Davidian it was grown and flowered at Wisley Gardens under KW 13500 but the plant I saw at Wisley under that name was *mekongense* ssp. *melinanthum* Viridescens Group.

SUBGENUS THERORHODION (CAMTSCHATICUM SERIES)

This small subgenus was considered by many (including myself—see *Dwarf Rhododendrons* pp. 94–5) to be distinct from other rhododendrons on account of the flowers coming from young growth and not from the usual resting buds common to the remainder of the genus. Dr W. R. Philipson has pointed out that this is not in fact so and that no growth emerges from the apparent leafy flowering shoot. These 'leaves' are only bracts. So there is really no significant difference between *camtschaticum* and its near relations and the rest of the genus *Rhododendron*. Bean, Vol. **IV**, 1980, places *camtschaticum* in the genus *Therorhodion* but I am sure it will become generally accepted that it should remain in *Rhododendron*.

The deciduous leaves, persistent leafy bracts and the unilaterally split corolla tube do warrant a separate subgenus.

R. glandulosum Standley ex Small and *redowskianum* Maxim. are apparently not in cultivation. If and when the occasion arises to study them more fully, they will probably prove to be synonymous with *camtschaticum*. Seed of *redowskianum* has recently been collected in N.E. China.

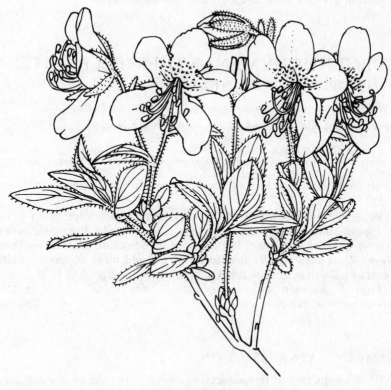

R. camtschaticum

camtschaticum Pall. 1784 H3 USDA 7a L1–2 F2–3

Ht to 30cm (1ft) but usually less. Habit prostrate, often flowing with the contours, suckering and rooting as it goes. Dense tufted branches.
L *deciduous*, 2–5cm ($\frac{4}{5}$–2in) long, 1–2.5cm ($\frac{2}{5}$–1in) wide, obovate to spathulate-obovate. Margins hairy. Thin-textured.
F purple, reddish-purple, pink, red or white, about 4cm (1½in) across with spreading oblong lobes, 1 rarely to 3 per truss. Calyx green, conspicuous.

This most intriguing dwarf prefers cool climates generally and grows better in Scotland than S. England and N.W. USA. Here in Scotland it is easily grown, quite vigorous when happy, and may flower in under a year from seed. It is very attractive when well-flowered, and the autumn colour can be good, in shades of orange and red. While extremely winter hardy, young growth is rather susceptible to spring frosts. Therefore avoid frost pockets in areas where growth comes early.

I have isolated a fine strain of red-flowered plants and I know of a similar pink strain. A beautiful white-flowered clone has recently been introduced from Alaska. Some people have had difficulty in establishing this and seedlings have all died in infancy. If white-flowered seedlings could be raised, no doubt a white-flowered strain could also be isolated. Grows best in plenty of sun. Rootability (soft) moderate to high.

From N. Japan (N. Honshu and Hokkaido only), Sakhalin through the Kuriles, Aleutians to W. Alaska. Also USSR from Ussuri to Kamtschatica in gravelly loam and crevices, often on hilltops.

May–June and often in August

SUBGENUS HYMENANTHES (ELEPIDOTE)
ARGYROPHYLLA SUBSECTION

adenopodum Franch. 1895 (*youngae* Fang) H5 USDA 5 & 6a L2–3 F2–3

Ht to 3m (10ft). Habit spreading, often wider than high. Young shoots densely tomentose.
L 9–18cm (3½–7in) long, 2–5cm (1–2in) wide, 2.6–4.5 times as long as broad, leathery, dark green above glabrous when mature, grey to fawn felted indumentum below.
F pale rose ± spotted crimson, 4.2–5cm (1$\frac{2}{3}$–2in) long, funnel-campanulate in loose trusses of 6–8.

Recently transferred back to the Argyrophylla subsection (from which it should never have been removed) from the old Ponticum series. Hardly qualifies as a dwarf but included here because of its inclusion in *Dwarf Rhododendrons*. Rather slow-growing and more commonly cultivated in USA than in Scotland. Quite attractive foliage. AM 1926.

From E. Sichuan and Hubei, 1,500–2,200m (5,000–7,250ft) in thin woods amongst rocks.

April–May

CAMPANULATA SUBSECTION

With the reduction of this subsection, only *campanulatum* ssp. *aeruginosum* remains dwarf enough to include here.

campanulatum* ssp. *aeruginosum (Hook.f.) Chamb. 1979 H4–5 USDA 6b–5 & 6a L3–4 F1–2

Ht to 6m (20ft) but usually 1.2–1.8m (4–6ft). Habit rounded and slow growing in best forms.
L 5–11cm (2–4$\frac{1}{4}$in) long, 3.5–5cm ($\frac{2}{5}$–2in) wide, margins recurved usually with a *glaucous bloom above* especially when young. Indumentum usually dense, buff to rusty-brown.
F pink, rose, lilac to purple, often spotted, about 4cm (1$\frac{2}{5}$in) long, campanulate, in fairly compact truss of 10–12. Calyx minute.

One of the finest foliage plants in the genus with beautiful glaucous metallic-blue young foliage. Unfortunately the flowers are often decidedly second-rate, often being a really hot magenta, not everyone's favourite, but luckily take many years to appear. Hardy in S. Scandinavia.

Differs from ssp. *campanulatum* in its generally smaller stature, smaller leaves with thicker often darker indumentum and deeper-coloured flowers in more compact trusses. Probably merges with ssp. *campanulatum* in Sikkim and there are (?) natural hybrids with *wightii* in Bhutan. Rootability usually low.

From Sikkim and Bhutan at 3,700–4,500m (12,000–14,750ft) on stony alpine slopes and ledges. April–May

CAMPYLOCARPA SUBSECTION (THOMSONII SERIES, SUBSERIES CAMPYLOCARPUM)

This subsection, now separated from the old Thomsonii series, includes some of the most beautiful of all rhododendrons. Only one species plus its variety and one subspecies are dwarf enough to include here.

Leaves are orbicular or nearly so. Flowers campanulate, yellow, pink or white with a small calyx. Many parts are glandular (sticky to touch).

callimorphum Balf.f. & W.W. Sm 1919 (*cyclium* Balf.f. & Forr, *hedythamnum* Balf.f. & Forr.) H3–4 USDA 7a–6b L2–3 F3–4

Ht 0.6–2 rarely to 3m (2–6 rarely to 10ft). Habit dome-shaped when young but scrawny with age, especially after die-back.
L 2–7cm ($\frac{4}{5}$ nearly 3in) long, 1.5–5cm ($\frac{3}{5}$–2in) wide, 1–1.5 times as long as broad, glabrous above, glaucous below, glandular.
F pink to deep rose ± basal blotch, 3–4cm (1$\frac{1}{5}$–1$\frac{3}{5}$in) long, campanulate, 4–8 per loose truss.

A beautiful species, free-flowering from a young age. While reasonably hardy, it does suffer bark-split and die-back after spring frosts and severe winters. Young plants cut to the ground in April 1981 grew from the base and made fine bushy plants again by autumn 1982, surviving the 1981–2 winter well. Appreciates good drainage and not too heavy a rainfall. Rootability moderate.

From W. Yunnan near Burma frontier, 2,700–3,400m (9,000–11,000ft) on open stony slopes, in and on margins of thickets, bamboo and on cliffs. April–June

callimorphum* var. *myiagrum (Balf.f. & Forr.) Chamb. 1978

Only differs from *callimorphum* in its white flowers ± spots and blotch. 3,000–4,000m (10,000–13,000ft).

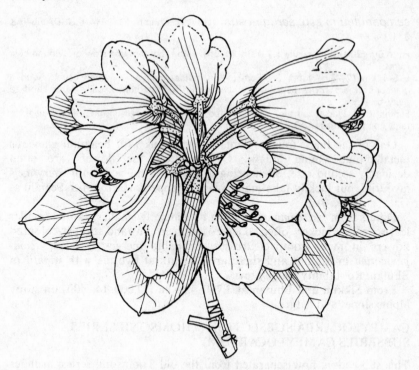

R. campylocarpum ssp. *caloxanthum*

campylocarpum ssp. *caloxanthum* (Balf.f. & Forr.) Chamb. 1978 (*telopeum* Balf.f. & Forr.) H3–4 USDA 7a–6b L2–3 F2–3

Ht 90cm–1.8m (3–6ft). Habit as *callimorphum*.
L 3.2–8cm (1¼–3⅛in) long, 2.6–5.6cm (1–2¼in) wide, 1.1–1.7 times as long as broad, orbicular, glabrous above, sometimes glaucous and glaucous below.
F creamy to sulphur-yellow, often orange in bud, 2.5–4cm (1–1⅜in) long, campanulate, 4–9 per loose truss.

A most attractive plant with the neatest foliage. Very free-flowering. Often short-lived and worth giving extra care over drainage to avoid trunk rotting at ground level. It suffers bark-split as does the closely related *callimorphum*. The eastern equivalent of ssp. *campylocarpum* and apparently intergrades with it. Distribution overlaps with *wardii* with which it hybridizes (merges?). Rootability low to moderate.

From Upper Burma and adjacent S.E. Xizang and W. Yunnan, 3,400–4,000m (11,000–13,000ft), common, often in dense masses on rocky slopes, cliffs, in and on margins of scrub and conifer forest.   April–May

GLISCHRA SUBSECTION (BARBATUM SERIES, SUBSERIES GLISCHRUM)

recurvoides Tagg & Ward 1932 H4–5 USDA 6b–5 & 6a L2–3 F2–3

Ht 1–1.5m (3–5ft). Habit usually compact and dense. *Perulae persistent for several years. Branchlets hairy*.

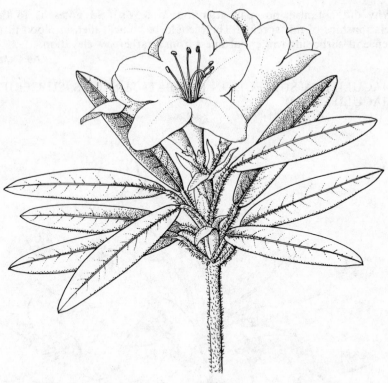

R. recurvoides

L 3–9cm (1⅕–4in) long, 1–3.2cm (⅖–1¼in) wide, 3–3.5 times as long as broad, lanceolate to oblanceolate, rugose and shiny above, dense tawny to cinnamon indumentum below. Margins recurved. Petiole hairy.

F white, flushed pink to rose with crimson spots (no blotch), about 3cm (1⅕in) long, campanulate, 4–7 per fairly loose truss.

Chamberlain has correctly moved this species from Taliensia to Glischra and it is obviously closely related to *crinigerum* in foliage and flower. When well grown, it is a superb foliage plant. It appreciates some shade and shelter, especially from spring frosts as the growth is easily frosted. One of my favourites in its best forms. Variable. Takes several years to produce its attractive flowers. Fairly hardy in S. Scandinavia. Rootability moderate. AM 1941.

Only known from type locality in N.E. Upper Burma, KW 7184 at 3,400m (11,000ft) on steep granite screes and amongst boulders in the open, flowering freely even on very small plants. Growing adjacent to *crinigerum* from which this species could have evolved. Probably little connection with *glischrum*. KW's field notes are:

Scattered about on the sunniest side of steep granite screes, amongst boulders. Closely allied to No. 7123 (*crinigerum*) and may be seen growing within a few feet of it, this species (*recurvoides*) in the open, the other in the *Abies* forest or in thickets on the sheltered slope. The two species are, however, quite distinct.

Why did botanists not pay attention to KW's field notes as to the relationships of this species? There could be some Taliensia blood in it, hence its surprising winter hardiness from a rather low elevation.

April–May

MACULIFERA SUBSECTION (BARBATUM SERIES, SUBSERIES MACULIFERUM)

R. pseudochrysanthum

pseudochrysanthum Hayata 1908 H4–5 USDA 6b–5 & 6a L1–3 F3–4

Ht 15cm–3m (6in–10ft). Habit tight and compact to upright and occasionally leggy. Young shoots tomentose. Always rather slow-growing.
L 3–8cm (1$\frac{1}{5}$–3$\frac{1}{5}$in) long, 1.5–5cm ($\frac{2}{5}$–2in) wide, ovate to elliptic, *thick and rigid*, usually glabrous above on maturity but sometimes covered with thin grey indumentum, usually glabrous and shiny below with persistent indumentum *on midrib only*.
F pink in bud opening to paler pink or white with deeper lines outside and spotted within, 3–4cm (1$\frac{1}{5}$–1$\frac{3}{5}$in) long, campanulate, 5–10 per truss.

A superb species of great character and merit. Many forms are now cultivated. RV 72003 introduced by J. Patrick from the summit of Mt Morrison, Taiwan, is producing an astonishing variation in foliage and habit. The very dwarf ones with leaves red underneath are the most sought after but these may take much longer to bloom than their taller relations and will not do so until the foliage matures and loses the red underside. Also popular are those with persistent grey indumentum above.

Beautiful in flower, this species is now gaining the popularity it deserves. Unfortunately, many are prone to a leaf-tip browning which is probably caused by too much heat and sun plus drying out at the roots during long hot spells. In W. USA, the dwarfest forms are found difficult and are particularly susceptible to burning. Try more shade and less fertilizer. The gravelly nature of its native soil points to the need for excellent drainage. The tough leaves seem resistant to severe weevil damage. It appreciates some sun in Scotland. AM 1956. Rootability moderate. This plant does appear to be related to *pachysanthum*.

Endemic to Taiwan, 1,800–4,000m (6,000–13,000ft), covers large areas in conifer forests and above the tree-line in rocky places and gravelly soil. It often grows mixed with *morii* with which it occasionally hybridizes.
April–May

NERIIFLORA SUBSECTION (NERIIFLORUM SERIES)

This is a large and important subsection containing many of the finest red-flowered species. They are mostly dwarf to semi-dwarf evergreen shrubs with only one species (*mallotum*) being excluded on account of its large size. Leaves narrowly elliptic to orbicular, glabrous or with thin to thick indumentum below. Inflorescence 1–12, occasionally more, usually in a loose truss. Flowers often red, fleshy, tubular-campanulate to less frequently campanulate, with depressed nectaries. Calyx small to large, often coloured. Stamens 10. Ovary tomentose. Style glabrous.

The majority are hardy enough for sheltered gardens throughout Britain although many are subject to bark-split from late spring frosts. Many of the lower-growing species from *forrestii* to *sanguineum* tend to be shy-flowering, particularly when young, and the freest-flowering forms should be sought after.

All are from relatively high rainfall areas, often at high altitudes, and do not tolerate excessive sunshine or high temperatures. They appreciate good drainage, abundant organic matter and plenty of moisture. Distribution is from C. Bhutan eastward through Arunachal Pradesh, S.E. Xizang, N.E. Upper Burma and Yunnan.

The former subseries of the Neriiflorum series did form relatively natural groups so I am listing them alphabetically in these groups and referring to them as 'Alliances'. These four Alliances are listed in the order Chamberlain uses in his revision (*Notes from the RBG, Edinburgh*, Vol. 39, No. 2).

Many are liable to die off partially or at least become semi-deciduous with the leaves turning yellow and dropping in autumn, especially after a very wet or dry spell. If the soil is heavy, try placing a bed of coarse gravel and sand below each plant and planting on a mound. Alternatively, plant on mounds and mulch heavily. Do not over fertilize.

HAEMATODES ALLIANCE (HAEMATODES SUBSERIES)

All have a thick woolly indumentum and most have showy red flowers.

beanianum Cowan 1938 H3–4 USDA 7a-6b L2-3 F1-3

Ht usually 1.5-1.8m (5-6ft), occasionally more. Habit fairly compact but often straggly in old age. Branchlets *bristly*.
L 6–9cm (2½–3½in) long, 3.2–4.4cm (1⅓–1¾in) wide, obovate to elliptic, dark green and *rugulose* above with fulvous indumentum below.
F usually crimson-scarlet, sometimes pink or even ivory, tubular-campanulate, in trusses of 6–10.

A fine plant in its best forms which have beautiful deep crimson-scarlet fleshy flowers in loose but well-shaped trusses. In poorer forms, the flowers hang between the leaves. The indumentum is one of the deepest-coloured in the genus. The flowers are unfortunately very easily frosted and the plant liable to bark-split when young. AM 1953 to KW 6805. Rootability low to moderate.

Uncommon in the wild as far as is known, only found in two valleys in Arunachal Pradesh and N.E. Upper Burma, 2,700–3,400m (9,000–11,000ft) in bamboo, granite gullies, alpine slopes and forest edges.

March–May

catacosmum (Balf.f. ex) Tagg 1927 H3–4 USDA 7a–6b L2–3 F2–3

Ht 1.2–3m (4–10ft). Habit fairly compact. Shoot *stout* compared with *haematodes* and ssp. *chaetomallum*. Young shoots tomentose.
L 6–11cm (2½–4½in) long, 3–5.5cm (1⅕–2⅕in) wide, obovate, leathery, dense woolly indumentum below, pale to dark fulvous.
F scarlet to rose-crimson or crimson, tubular-campanulate, fleshy in trusses of 5–9. Calyx large and petaloid.

A fine species best suited to milder gardens. Rare. Closely related to *haematodes* and ssp. *chaetomallum* but has generally larger leaves. Rootability moderate.

Limited distribution in S.E. Xizang and N.W. Yunnan, 3,700–4,400m (12,000–14,500ft) (probably exaggerated) on forest margins and cliff ledges.

March–April

chionanthum Tagg & Forr. 1927 possibly not in cultivation

Ht 0.6–1m (2–3ft). Shoots bristly.
L about 7.5cm (3in) long, and 2.5cm (1in) wide, obovate, indumentum discontinuous and patchy, tawny.
F white, about 3.5cm (1⅖in) long, tubular-campanulate in trusses of 4–6.

From its description, this could be a hybrid. Plant, leaf size and flower colour point to a close relationship with *citriniflorum*.

Rare in the wild in N.E. Upper Burma and W. Yunnan, 4,000–4,300m (13,000–14,000ft) on rocky slopes.

coelicum Balf.f. & Farrer 1922 H3–4 USDA 7a–6b L2–3 F2–3

Ht a small shrub. Habit compact to occasionally thin and erect.
L 6–8.5cm (2⅖–3⅓in) long, 3.1–4.4cm (1¼–1⅘in) wide, *1.6–2 times as long as broad*, obovate.
F crimson fleshy, 3.8–4.5cm (1½–1¾in) long, tubular-campanulate, 6–15 per truss.

Very close to *pocophorum* but smaller in all parts. Leaves shorter and broader for their size. Nice foliage. Rather tender at Glendoick. Rootability moderate.

From N.E. Upper Burma and adjacent W. Yunnan, 3,700–4,400m (12,000–14,500ft), shaded screes, cliffs and in bamboo. Farrer saw it flowering in the snow, visible for miles.   April

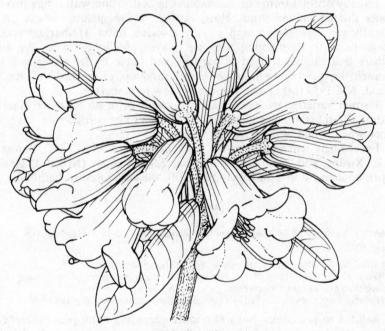

R. haematodes

haematodes ssp. **haematodes** Franch. 1886 H4–5 USDA 6b–5 & 6a L2–3 F3–4

Ht usually 0.6–1.5m (2–5ft), occasionally more. Habit dense and compact in open, looser in shade. Young shoots mostly *tomentose*.
L to 10cm (4in) long, 4.5cm (1¾in) wide, obovate to oblong, leathery, dark green above, thick woolly mud-coloured to rufous indumentum below.
F scarlet to crimson, tubular-campanulate, 6–12 per truss, 3.8–5cm (1½–2in) long. Calyx red or green.

A splendid species in foliage and flower. Will grow in sun or shade in Scotland but avoid full sun in warmer areas. Blooms freely on maturity. FCC 1926. Rootability low to moderate.

Quite plentiful in W. Yunnan, 3,400–4,000m (11,000–13,000ft). Very variable in the wild in height, leaf shape and indumentum. In 1981 on Cangshan, Yunnan, I saw this variation in a small area. Seed from four numbers collected should hopefully give a variety hitherto unknown in cultivation. Found on alpine meadows and as an under-shrub, often under *lacteum*.   May–June

haematodes ssp. *chaetomallum* (Balf.f. & Forr.) Chamb. 1979 H3–4 USDA 7a–6b L2–3 F2–3

Ht 1.2–1.8m (4–6ft). Habit compact to open and leggy. Young shoots mostly *setose*.
L to 11.3cm (4½in) long, 6cm (2½in) wide, obovate to oblong-obovate. Vestiges of indumentum often persistent above, ± densely woolly below, pale to dark fawn.
F usually blood-red, fleshy, about 4cm (1⅝in) long, tubular-campanulate, 4–7 per truss, often hanging between leaves.

Usually distinct from ssp. *haematodes* in cultivation with larger leaves, paler thinner indumentum below, vestiges of indumentum above on a slightly rugulose surface and usually a looser habit. Herbarium specimens point to its merging with ssp. *haematodes* in the wild. We and others find this short-lived in gardens and liable to die off branch by branch. Try placing a mixture of gravel, sand and/or crushed rock under plant. AM 1959 turkey-red. Rootability low to moderate.

Former varieties are either natural hybrids or of no botanical significance. Chamberlain considers var. *hemigynum* to be *pocophorum* × *eclecteum* which could well be correct.

Exceedingly widespread in the wild. Very common in N.W. Yunnan, S.E. Xizang and N.E. Upper Burma, 3,000–4,600m (10,000–15,000ft), open bouldery slopes and meadows, cliffs, thickets, forest or bamboo.
                                                                   March–May

piercei Davidian 1976 (*beanianum* var. *compactum* Cowan) H3–4 USDA 7a–6b L2–3 F2–3

Ht 1.2–2.5m (4–8ft). Habit open bushy. Young shoots tomentose.
L 6–11cm (2⅖–4⅓in) long, 2.7–5.2cm (1⅛–2in) wide, ovate to elliptic, *more shiny* above than *beanianum*, indumentum *paler* below.
F crimson, fleshy, about 3.2cm (1⅓in) long, tubular-campanulate, 6–8 per truss.

Related to *beanianum* but has a more spreading habit plus differences above. A good plant in foliage and flower but very subject to bark-split from spring frosts. Rootability moderate to good.

Only known from type collection from S. Xizang.   March–April or May

pocophorum (Balf.f. ex) Tagg 1927 H3–4 USDA 7a–6b L2–3 F2–3

Ht 1.2–3m (4–10ft). Habit rather erect and can become tree-like.
L 10–16cm (4–6½in) long, 4–7cm (1½–2¾in) wide, *2–3 times as long as broad*, oblong to oblong-obovate, thick and leathery, dark green above, covered below with a thick continuous indumentum.
F light to deep crimson, about 5cm (2in) long, tubular-campanulate, 10–20 per truss, often dense.

A fine and imposing species but all too easily frosted, even in bud, resulting in few perfect trusses. The giant of the Alliance after *mallotum*. Closely related to *coelicum* but larger in all parts with leaves longer and narrower for their size. Rootability low to moderate.

From E. Xizang (Tsarong) where quite plentiful at 3,700–4,600m (12,000–15,000ft), margins of bamboo and fir forest, crags, gullies and meadows.   March–April

pocophorum var. **hemidartum** (Tagg) Chamb. 1978 (*hemidartum* Tagg) rating as var. *pocophorum*

Rather smaller in most parts than var. *pocophorum*. L with *patchy discontinuous indumentum below*. Not to be confused with *floccigerum* which has much narrower leaves, often recurved and usually a more scattered indumentum below. Rootability moderate.

Location, altitude and habitat similar to var. *pocophorum*.

SANGUINEUM ALLIANCE (SANGUINEUM SUBSERIES)

This contains one of the most evolved groups of all rhododendrons. Although distinct enough species, subspecies and varieties occur, equally common are a whole host of intermediaries and obvious natural hybrids, several of which are in cultivation. Chamberlain has wisely attempted to reduce the vast number of subspecies previously recognized, as I predicted in *Dwarf Rhododendrons* (p.141).

Many are slow to start flowering freely and can be classed as connoisseurs' plants. Personally, I find them interesting and worth cultivating when one has patience and some suitable space. All appreciate moisture but perfect drainage. Over-wet roots can lead to semi-deciduous leaves and, here again, a gravel-and-sand base before planting is worth trying. They also dislike too much sunshine and dry roots.

aperantum Balf.f. & Ward 1922 H3–4 USDA 7a–6b L1–2 F2–3

Ht to 60cm (2ft), occasionally more. Habit dense and matted. *Bud scales persistent for several years.* Very slow-growing.
L 3–6.5cm (1⅕–2⅗in) long, 1.4–2.4cm (⅗–1in) wide, obovate to lanceolate, almost in *whorls* at end of shoots, glaucous below.
F usually crimson to pink in cultivation but reported as white, yellow, orange-red, white flushed pink and other combinations in the wild, to 4.5cm (nearly 2in) long, tubular-companulate, 4–6 per truss.

It is sad that this species, greatly acclaimed by those who have seen it in the wild, has behaved so poorly in cultivation. Slow to bloom freely, it often starts to die back when reaching flowering size. Even apparently thriving large 'table top' specimens can suddenly start dying off for no apparent reason. As with *forrestii*, rotting leaves may kill off the foliage if not promptly removed. It just seems to be one of those plants used to maximum exposure in its monsoon-drenched home that cannot really thrive in our fickle climate. I would like to try it *en masse* on a cool, north-facing steep bank with plenty of organic matter and away from trees. Quite successful in S. Scandinavia. Rootability moderate to high.

From N.E. Upper Burma and adjoining N.W. Yunnan, covering miles of open alpine slopes and screes, cliff ledges and under bamboo in a multitude of colours. 3,700–4,400m (12,000–14,500ft).   April–May

citriniflorum Balf.f. & Forr. 1919 (*chlanidotum* Balf.f. & Forr.) H4 USDA 6b L1–2
F1–3

Ht 20cm–1.5m (8in–5ft). Habit compact to leggy with age.
L 4–7.7cm (1½–3in) long, 1.3–2.5cm (½–1in) wide, obovate to elliptic, leathery, with
moderate to *thick* brown to grey indumentum below. Petiole ± winged.
F lemon-yellow, greenish-yellow, often yellow, flushed or margined pink, 3.2–4.5cm
(1⅓–1⅘in) long, tubular-campanulate, 2–6 per truss. Ovary and pedicels usually *glandular*.

Good yellow forms are rather elusive in cultivation although evidently
plentiful enough in the wild. Those in gardens are mostly various shades
of yellow-flushed pink or red. While some clones bloom quite freely, they
may take ages to do so. It needs some shade and perfect drainage. The
best yellow forms could be useful in producing the ever sought after
perfect low yellow elepidote hybrid. Winter hardy but subject to bark-
split from spring frosts. Rootability moderate to high.

Quite common in S.E. Xizang and N.W. Yunnan, 4,000–4,900m
(13,000–16,000ft) on alpine moorland, on boulders, cliffs, screes or among
bamboo.
April–May

citriflorum* var. *horaeum (Balf.f. & Forr.) Chamb. 1979 (*horaeum* Balf.f. & Forr.)

Similar to var. *citriniflorum* but with *non-glandular* ovary and pedicels.
F orangy-red to carmine. F 21850 has striking orange-shot crimson flowers.

There are numerous intermediaries and hybrid swarms containing
citriniflorum with probably *catacosmum* and *temenium* including ×
xanthanthum Tagg & Forr. 1927 and × *hillieri* Davidian 1974. The latter
has discontinuous indumentum and rose-pink to deep crimson flowers.

dichroanthum Diels 1912 H(3–)4–5 USDA (7a–)6b–5 & 6a L1–2 F1–3

Ht 60cm–1.8m (2–6ft). Habit a spreading often compact bush.
L 4–10cm (1½–4in) long, 2–4cm (1–1½in) wide, 2.5–3 times as long as broad, oblanceolate to elliptic, with compacted silvery indumentum below.
F deep orange or various shades of yellow, yellow-flushed rose to carmine, fleshy,
3.5–5cm (1½–2in) long, tubular-campanulate in lax trusses of 3–8. Calyx often large
and usually irregular.

The best orange forms of ssp. *dichroanthum* and the other subspecies
below are well worth growing. We grow a good form of the type under F
6781. Other forms can be of little merit with decidedly unpleasant
shades. Much used in hybridization for orange shades. All are subject to
bark-split from late spring frosts like those of 1981. AM 1923 flowers
orange-red. Rootability moderate to high.

From W. Yunnan, Cangshan Range, 2,700–3,700m (9,000–12,000ft) on
open rocky slopes, near bamboo brakes, ravines and as an under shrub.
May–June

The following ssps. tend to have smaller leaves than ssp. *dichroanthum*.

dichroanthum* ssp. *apodectum (Balf.f. & W.W. Sm.) Cowan 1940
(*jangtzowense* Balf.f. & Forr., *liratum* Balf.f. & Forr.)

L more oval than type, 1.9–2.4 times as long as broad, shiny above, indumentum
silvery to fawn, often a little thicker than other subspecies. W. Yunnan, N.E. Upper
Burma.

dichroanthum ssp. **scyphocalyx** (Balf.f. & Forr.) Cowan 1940 (*herpesticum* Balf.f. & Ward, *torquatum* Balf.f. & Farrer)

L usually obovate, 1.9–2.5 times as long as broad, not shiny above, indumentum thinnish, fawn to grey.

N.E. Upper Burma and adjacent W. Yunnan.

dichroanthum ssp. **septentrionale** Cowan 1940

L often smaller than previous subspecies, 3–3.3 times as long as broad, indumentum whitish to fawn.
F yellow shades.

From N.W. Yunnan and adjacent N.E. Upper Burma.

eudoxum Balf.f. & Forr. 1919 (*trichomiscum* Balf.f. & Forr., *trichophlebium* Balf.f. & Forr., *temenium* ssp. *albipetalum* Cowan & ssp. *rhodanthum* Cowan) H3–4 USDA 7a–6b L1–2 F1–2

Ht 30cm–1.2m (1–4ft) sometimes more in cultivation. Habit fairly dense.
L 3–7cm (1⅕–3in) long, 1–3cm (⅖–1⅕in) wide, elliptic, glabrous above, indumentum below thin, often hardly noticeable. Leaves with thinner texture than that of near relatives.
F rose-pink to rose-carmine, rarely white, 2.5–3.7cm (1–1½in) long, campanulate to tubular-campanulate, 2–6 per truss, often hanging between leaves.

Although often free-flowering once it starts and a good doer, it is not a plant of much merit, the flower colour frequently being rather harsh. Related to *temenium*. Rootability moderate to high. AM 1960.

From S.E. Xizang and N.W. Yunnan, 3,400–4,300m (11,000–14,000ft) on rocky slopes, thickets, gullies and cliffs.   April–May

eudoxum var. **brunneifolium** (Balf.f. & Forr.) Chamb. 1979

L 7–9cm (3–3⅗in) long, indumentum brownish.
F about 4cm (1½in) long, rose-carmine.

eudoxum var. **mesopolium** (Balf.f. & Forr.) Chamb. 1979 (*asteium* Balf.f. & Forr., *epipastum* Balf.f. & Forr.)

L 3.5–7cm (1⅖–2⅘in) long, indumentum whitish.
F pink to rose 3–3.5cm (1⅕–1⅖in) long.

microgynum Balf.f. & Forr. 1919 (*gymnocarpum* (Balf.f. ex) Tagg, *perulatum* Balf.f. & Forr.) H4–5 USDA 6b–5 & 6a L2–3 F2–3

Ht 60cm–1.5m (2–5ft). Habit umbrella-shape, compact when young.
L to 11.5cm (4½in) long, 4cm (1½in) wide, elliptic to oblong-elliptic, dark green above and dense but not thick-felted cinnamon to buff indumentum below, margins recurved.
F pale rose to more commonly deep crimson, often with deeper markings, 3–4cm (1⅕–1⅗in) long, funnel-campanulate, in trusses of 3–10.

An attractive, easily grown species with rich coloured flowers at an earlier age than most of the Alliance.

Formerly and wrongly placed in the Taliense series with which it shows little relationship. *R. gymnocarpum* and *perulatum* have no consistent characters to separate them from this species. Rootability moderate to good.

From N.W. Yunnan and S.E. Xizang at 3,700–4,300m (12,000–14,000ft) in bamboo, conifer forest and stony slopes. Has a limited distribution.   April–May

parmulatum Cowan 1936 H3–4 USDA 7a–6b L1–2 F1–2+

Ht 60cm–1.3m (2–4ft)+. Habit usually erect but neat. Reddish peeling bark, smooth grey underneath.
L 4.5–8cm (1⅘–3⅕in) long, 2–3.8cm (⅘–1in) wide, *rugose* above, rather glaucous below and almost glabrous.
F white, cream, pink to yellow-flushed pink, often heavily spotted, 4–5cm (1½–2in) long, tubular-campanulate, 4–6 per truss.

One of the most distinctive members of the Alliance with unusual coloured and spotted flowers which can take several years to appear. Shows some relationship with *faucium* according to Chamberlain and could be of hybrid origin. Rootability low to moderate.

From a very wet area S. of the Doshing La Pass, S. Xizang, 3,000–3,700m (10,000–12,000ft), steep slopes, cliffs and rocks.   March–May

sanguineum Franch. 1898 H(3–)4(–5) USDA (7a–)6b(–5 & 6a) L1–2 F1–3

Ht 30cm–1.5m (1–4½ft)+ in shade. Habit compact to leggy in shade when old. Thin shoots.
L 3–8cm (1⅕–3⅕in) long, 1.9–2.4cm (¾–1in) wide, elliptic to obovate, glabrous above, rather compacted thin silvery to greyish indumentum below.
F bright crimson, fleshy, 2.5–3.8cm (1–1½in) long, tubular-campanulate, 3–6 per loose truss.

R. sanguineum

The typical plant has bright crimson flowers but there are a whole host of forms, intermediaries and probable natural hybrids. The flowers are rather dark but develop a wonderful glow with the sun shining through them, and are often freely produced on mature plants. Some years it is liable to be semi-deciduous and can look very sparse with age. Coming naturally from wet areas, it needs shade in warmer, drier climates. Rootability moderate.

From N.E. Xizang and N.W. Yunnan, 3,000–4,500m (10,000–14,500ft), in open scrub, rocky slopes and margins of forest and bamboo, common over a fairly limited area.   March–May

sanguineum var. *haemaleum* (Balf.f. & Forr.) Chamb. 1979 (*sanguineum* ssp. *mesaeum* [Balf.f. ex] Cowan)

Very near var. *sanguineum* but with even darker flowers, sometimes almost black when seen under full conditions.

sanguineum var. *himertum* (Balf.f. & Forr.) Chamb. 1979 (*nebrites* Balf.f. & Forr., *poliopeplum* Balf.f. & Forr., *sanguineum* ssp. *aisoides* Cowan)

As above but flowers yellow shades. Rare in cultivation.

sanguineum var. *cloiophorum* (Balf.f. & Forr.) Chamb. 1979 (*leucopetalum* Balf.f. & Forr., *asmenistum* Balf.f. & Forr.)

Flowers white, yellow-flushed pink to pink. Very variable and most likely a hybrid swarm merging with *citriniflorum*.

sanguineum var. *didymoides* Tagg & Forr. 1931 (*roseotinctum* Balf.f. & Forr., *mannopeplum* Balf.f. & Forr., *sanguineum* ssp. *consanguineum* Cowan 1940)

As *sanguineum* but flowers usually a combination of colours such as white and/or yellow-flushed pink, rose or crimson to just pink. Some are very pretty and most delicately coloured. Sad that the name *roseotinctum* had to go as it is much more attractive than *didymoides*.

sanguineum ssp. *didymum* (Balf.f. & Forr.) Cowan 1940

Botanically this ssp. differs from *sanguineum* and its varieties in its glandular ovary and slightly smaller, often shinier leaves. In the wild it may merge with var. *haemaleum* but horticulturally, it is distinct and from my experience, relatively uniform.

The flowering season is much later, June–July and at Glendoick we have found it very difficult to cultivate successfully, often unstable on its roots and liable to severe chlorosis. If only it were easier, it would be a valuable plant but it has been a successful parent for numerous medium- to late-flowering dark red hybrids. Flowers deep to almost black-crimson. Habit usually rather erect and open.

It is said to be partially lime-tolerant so it may not like very acid soil, hence our troubles with it.

temenium Balf.f. & Forr. 1919 (*pothinum* Balf.f. & Forr.) H4(–5) USDA 6b(–5 & 6a) L1–2 F1–3

Ht 30cm–1.5m, rarely over 1m (1–5ft). Habit usually compact, flat-topped or dome-shaped.
L 3.5–8cm (1½–3in) long, 1.2–3cm (½–1⅛in) wide, 2.8–3.5 times as long as broad, elliptic, glabrous and usually *a paler green* than other members of the Alliance above, usually glaucous and glabrous below, perhaps with a vestige of indumentum. Growth bud rather long and pointed. *Petiole very short.*
F scarlet to crimson, fleshy, 3.5–4.5cm (1⅓–1⅔in) long, tubular-campanulate or campanulate, 2–6 or more per truss.

While a well-flowered bush is most attractive, this species often takes even longer to bloom than most of its relatives. Quite distinct in its typical form although natural hybrids occur with *citriniflorum* and other species. Also liable to be semi-deciduous due to poor soil conditions.

From the borders of S.E. Xizang and N.W. Yunnan where it is not so common as *sanguineum* and its allies. 3,700–4,600m (12,000–15,000ft). On open moorland, cliffs and scrub.   April–May

temenium var. **gilvum** (Cowan) Chamb. 1979 (*chrysanthemum* Cowan)

As above but with pale yellow to yellow flowers, sometimes tinged pink or red. Also differs in a few minor botanical details.

A clone from R 22272 formerly known as *chrysanthemum* received an AM in 1958 and FCC in 1964 as 'Cruachan'. At its best it is a splendid plant with yellow flowers and wider leaves. Rootability high.

temenium var. **dealbatum** (Cowan) Chamb. 1979 (*glaphyrum* Balf.f. & Forr.)

As above but with white flowers or white-flushed or margined rose to deep rose-pink in trusses of 2–4.

fulvastrum Balf.f. & Forr. 1920

Chamberlain considers this to be intermediate between *sanguineum* var. *himertum* and *temenium* var. *gilvum*. Rare in the wild and in cultivation.

FORRESTII ALLIANCE (FORRESTII SUBSERIES)

A small group of very variable species which form either prostrate, creeping shrublets or mounds. Some grow more erect in shade. Like the Sanguineum Alliance, they are often shy-flowering and appreciate abundant moisture but perfect drainage. They enjoy coolish conditions where they can flow or creep up or down banks or rocks. When happy and free-flowering they are amongst the most satisfying and beautiful of all dwarf rhododendrons. All flower rather early in the season and also grow early so appreciate some frost protection. The frosting of the first growth flush is perhaps one reason why they may only flower spasmodically as second growth rarely sets flower buds. Beware of fallen leaves collecting and rotting out the centre of the plants. Not suitable for hot climates. Much used for hybridizing for low reds.

R. chamae-thomsonii

chamae-thomsonii (Tagg & Forr.) Cowan and Davidian 1951 H4(–5) USDA 6b(–5 & 6a) L1–2 F2–3

Ht 10cm–1m (4in–3ft). Habit often mound-forming and generally compact with creeping outer branchlets. Can become open in shade. Petiole and shoots glandular.
L 2–9cm (⅘–3½in) long, 1.8–4cm (¾–1½in) wide, 1.5–2.1 times as long as broad, obovate to elliptic, usually glabrous above and below; very variable.
F carmine to crimson to scarlet, fleshy, 2.5–4.8cm (1–2in) long, campanulate, 1–5 per truss.

A very variable species which merges into *forrestii* and differs from that species in its more upright habit, often larger leaves and more flowers to the truss. Rootability high.

From S.E. Xizang and adjacent N.W. Yunnan 3,400–4,600m (11,000–15,000ft) but nearly all 4,000m+ (13,000ft+) in dense thickets on steep hillsides, on or among boulders, cliffs, often found near *forrestii*.

March–May

chamae-thomsonii var. **chamaedoron** (Tagg & Forr.) Chamb. 1979

Similar to the above but leaves have a thin discontinuous indumentum below, when mature; petiole and shoots eglandular. Also S.E. Xizang and adjacent N.W. Yunnan.

chamae-thomsonii var. *chamaethauma* (Tagg) Cowan & Davidian 1951

Similar to var. *chamae-thomsonii* but with *pale to deep pink flowers*. The forms I have grown and seen tend to be freer-flowering than many clones of the red var. *chamae-thomsonii* but I still prefer those with red flowers. Flower buds liable to abort. Closer to and probably merges with *forrestii*.

From S. Xizang and N.E. Arunachal Pradesh.

erastum Balf.f. & Forr. 1918 (*porphyrophyllum* Balf.f. & Forr., *serpens* Balf.f. & Forr.) probably not in cultivation

Ht 5–50cm (2in–1½ft). Habit usually creeping.
L 2.5–4.7cm (1–1⅞in) long, 0.7–1.7cm (⅓–⅔in) wide, elliptic to narrowly elliptic, young shoots and leaves with loose indumentum, often glabrous on maturity.
F pink to deep rose, 2.5–3cm (about 1in) long, tubular-campanulate.

It is doubtful if this is a good species and only a thorough examination in the wild will decide. Intermediaries occur between this and *chamae-thomsonii*. Three specimens (the majority) show a great variation in leaf width, thus showing the instability of the plant.

S.E. Xizang and N.W. Yunnan, 4,000–4,300m (13,000–14,000ft).

forrestii (Balf.f. ex) Diels 1912 (*repens* Balf.f. & Forr.) H4(–5) USDA 6b(–5 & 6a) L1–2 F1–4

Ht a creeping shrub up to 15cm (6in) high. Perulae persistent.
L 1–5cm (⅖–2in) long, 0.6–3.1 (¼–1¼in) wide, 1.1–2.2 times as long as broad, obovate to orbicular, glabrous when mature.
F scarlet to crimson, 3–3.8cm (1⅕–1½in) long, fleshy, tubular-campanulate, 1–2 per inflorescence.

A frustrating species, it is rarely seen growing and flowering to one's satisfaction but is worth every effort to please. The best form I know is a clone of R 59174 which regularly produces its particularly large, well-coloured (scarlet) flowers. The best specimens I have seen were growing up or down north-facing walls or rocks. Keep free of weeds and the vigorous moss *Polytrichum* as much as possible and it will pay dividends to cover the normally early young growth with a cloche when this is developing. The combination of plenty of light and moisture plus freedom from spring frosts should greatly encourage health and flower buds. It enjoys a good tree-stump or a peaty pocket among rocks, as long as it is not in a sump where water collects. Do not apply much nitrogen (ammonia), which induces scorch.

R. forrestii formerly only included those plants with a persistent purple tinge to the leaf underside. This is a common juvenile state in rhododendrons and occasionally, as in this case, persists to maturity. Chamberlain considers this to be of no taxonomic significance and I am inclined to agree. Therefore to name the purple underside of leaf form, we shall have to use the peculiar name *forrestii* Forrestii Group (if the Group system is accepted). This plant has a reputation of being shyer-flowering than Repens Group (green leaf underside) but I really doubt if there is any real difference horticulturally or botanically between the two Groups.

I long to see this plant in flower on the heights of N.W. China with its glowing carpets of fire showing through the swirling mist, as KW reported.

From N.W. Yunnan, S.E. Xizang and adjacent N.E. Upper Burma, 3,000–4,600m (10,000–15,000ft), habitat as *chamae-thomsonii* usually on non-calcareous rocks. April–May

forrestii ssp. *papillatum* Chamb. 1979. Ratings probably as var. *forrestii*

Differs from ssp. *forrestii* in the pale fawn glaucous-papillate leaf underside, with conspicuous glands. *Leaves 2.2–3.2 times as long as broad.* This looks like a good, distinct subspecies usually with narrower leaves than ssp. *forrestii* and a strikingly different colour on leaf under-side. Several herbarium specimens are intermediaries between ssp. *papillatum* and *chamae-thomsonii* including the type of *forrestii* var. *tumescens* Cowan & Davidian. This last named, which should keep at least Group status, includes many mound-forming plants which in habit fall between typical *chamae-thomsonii* and *forrestii*. We grow several of these and some are good horticultural forms. Other unusual forms and hybrids have been found in the wild.

NERIIFLORUM ALLIANCE (NERIIFLORUM SUBSERIES)

Fairly closely allied species. Leaves with a ± glaucous underside and sometimes a loose sparse to moderately thick indumentum below. Ovary densely hairy. Flowers fleshy, usually unspotted and scarlet to crimson but also pink or mixtures of yellow, orange, pink and so on. The elon-gated ovary gradually tapers into the style.

Many inclined towards the tender side for the cooler parts of Britain. As with the rest of the subsection, excellent drainage is appreciated.

albertsenianum Forr. 1919 H3–4 USDA 7a–6b L1–2 F2

Ht 1–2m (3–6ft). Habit stiff straight branches.
L 6–9.5cm (2½–4in) long, 1.5–2.5cm (⅗–1in) wide, *c.* 4 times as long as broad, nar-rowly elliptic, almost glabrous above, loose woolly brown indumentum below.
F bright crimson-rose, about 3cm (1⅛in) long, tubular-campanulate, 5–6 per truss.

Part of a mixed gathering and only known from type specimen. Close to *sperabile*. Is probably a natural hybrid or part of a cline. Rare in cultivation.

From N.W. Yunnan at around 3,000m (10,000ft) in open forest. April

bijiangense Ming 1981 not in cultivation

Recently described in China.
Ht *c.* 1m (3ft). Young shoots bristly-glandular.
L 7–10cm (3–4 in) long, 2–2.5cm (⅘–1in) wide, narrowly lanceolate, largely glabrous below.
F reddish-purple *c.* 3cm (1⅕in) long, campanulate.

Probably close to *neriiflorum*. W. Yunnan.

euchroum Balf.f. & Ward 1916 probably not in cultivation

Ht to 70cm (2ft 4in). Habit dwarf shrub with tomentose and glandular young shoots.
L 4.5–7.5cm ($1\frac{3}{4}$–3in) long, 1.7–2.3cm ($\frac{2}{3}$–1in) wide, glabrous above, fulvous indumentum below.
F brick-red to scarlet, 2.5–3cm (1–$1\frac{1}{5}$in) long, tubular-campanulate.

Close to *albertsenianum* but differs in its glands and smaller leaves, and to *sperabile*.

From N.E. Upper Burma, 3,000–3,400m (10,000–11,000ft) as an under shrub in thickets.

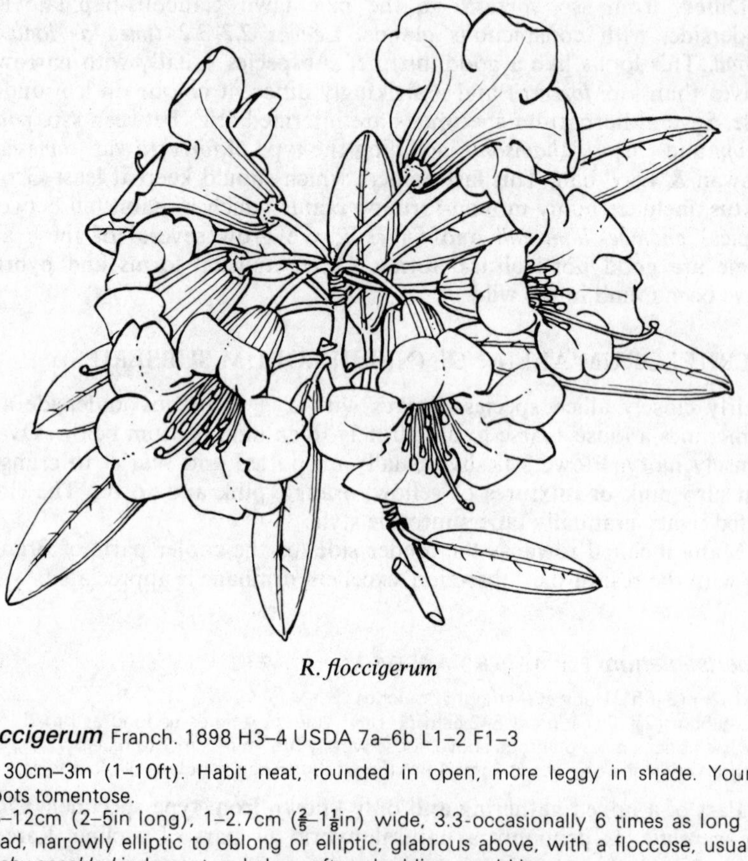

R. floccigerum

floccigerum Franch. 1898 H3–4 USDA 7a–6b L1–2 F1–3

Ht 30cm–3m (1–10ft). Habit neat, rounded in open, more leggy in shade. Young shoots tomentose.
L 5–12cm (2–5in long), 1–2.7cm ($\frac{2}{5}$–$1\frac{1}{8}$in) wide, 3.3-occasionally 6 times as long as broad, narrowly elliptic to oblong or elliptic, glabrous above, with a floccose, usually *patchy speckled* indumentum below, often shedding on old leaves.
F usually rose to deep crimson or scarlet, sometimes mixtures of orange, yellow, and pink, 3–4cm ($1\frac{1}{5}$–$1\frac{3}{5}$in) long, tubular campanulate, 4–7 per truss. Calyx small, rounded lobes.

The scarlet to crimson forms are the best, many others are decidedly muddy-coloured and, due also to their habit of hanging their flowers between the leaves, are not very desirable. Easily identified by the scattered indumentum which may also be found in *sperabiloides*, which is a dwarfer plant with shorter leaves. *R. neriiflorum* ssp. *phaedropum* is very similar to this species but with a glabrous, often glaucous leaf underside. Liable to bark-split and flowers early. Rootability moderate to high.

Common in S.E. Xizang and adjacent N.W. Yunnan, 2,700–4,000m (9,000–13,000ft) in open scrub and thickets or on cliffs, in open conifer forest or bamboo. March–April

neriiflorum Franch. 1886 (*euchaites* Balf.f. & Forr., *phoenicodum* Balf.f. & Farrer) H3–4 USDA 7a–6b L1–2 F2–4

Ht 1–6m (3–20ft). Habit dwarf and compact to loose and straggly, especially in the wild in shade.
L 4–9cm (1½–3½in) long, 1.9–3.5cm (⅔–1⅖in) wide, 1.7–7 times as long as broad, elliptic to oblong, glabrous above, *usually glabrous below and often glaucous.*
F bright scarlet to crimson, 3.5–4.5cm (1⅖–1⅘in) long, tubular-campanulate, 5–12 per truss. Calyx fleshy, coloured and very variable in size.

A well-known and widespread species quite common in gardens and deservedly so. Some introductions are hardier than others and some are of considerable horticultural value, while those formerly grown under *phoenicodum* tend to be inferior. Those under *euchaites* were regarded as being the tallest but this has no botanical significance. It differs from ssp. *phaedropum* in its eglandular pedicels, calyx and ovary. AM as *euchaites* 1929. 'Rosevallon' AM is a curious clone probably referable to this species; it always retains a crimson leaf underside and yet blooms freely. It is said to come true from seed. Rootability moderate for the species.

Found over a wide area of S.E. Xizang, W. Yunnan and N.E. Upper Burma, 2,100–3,400m (7,000–11,000ft) on open meadows, in thin pine forests, among scrub, and in dense rhododendron forest. April–May

neriiflorum ssp. phaedropum (Balf.f. & Farrer) Tagg 1930 (*floccigerum* var. *appropinquans* Tagg & Forr., *tawangense* Sahni & Naithani) H3 USDA 7a

Differs from ssp. *neriiflorum* in its glandular pedicels, calyx and/or ovary, and longer and narrower leaves, 8–11cm (3¼–4½in) long, 3 to rarely 7 times as long as broad. The flowers are sometimes rose to straw-yellow or tawny orange in addition to shades of red. They can be muddy as in the related *floccigerum*. Often more tender than ssp. *neriiflorum*. Shows some geographical variation.

From an extensive area from C. Bhutan through Arunachal Pradesh into Upper Burma, S. Xizang and mid-W. Yunnan, 2,000–3,400m (6,500–11,000ft).

neriiflorum ssp. agetum (Balf.f. & Forr.) Tagg 1930

L reticulated below caused by more prominent veins.

Botanical significance not known. W. Yunnan.

sperabile Balf.f. & Forr. 1922 H3(–4) USDA 7a(–6b) L2–3 F2–3

Ht 1–2m (3–6ft). Habit often dense but sometimes leggy with age. Young shoots tomentose.
L 5–10cm (2–4in) long, 1–2.6cm (⅖–1⅛in) wide, usually 2.5–4 times as long as broad, elliptic, sometimes sparse white indumentum at first above, semibullate, *dense woolly indumentum below*, white to cinnamon.
F scarlet to crimson, 3.5–4cm (about 1½in) long, tubular-campanulate, 3–5 per truss.

One of the neatest of the Alliance but alas not suitable for cold areas. Needs some protection and shade in most places to produce its pretty foliage and flowers. AM 1925 to Farrer 888 scarlet flowers. Rootability moderate.

From a limited area of N.E. Upper Burma and adjacent N.W. Yunnan, 3,000–3,700m (10,000–12,000ft) an under shrub on boulders, slopes, screes and cliffs, in scrub and bamboo.   April–May

sperabile var. *weihsiense* Tagg & Forr. 1927 H3–4 USDA 7a–6b L1–2 F2–3

Differs from var. *sperabile* in its *paler* (whitish) indumentum on leaf underside, its larger, wider leaves and its taller more open habit. A little hardier than var. *sperabile*, just surviving the 1981–2 winter at Glendoick.

From N.W. Yunnan, slightly north of var. *sperabile*, 2,700–4,000m (9,000–13,000ft) on cliffs and rocky slopes.   April–May

sperabiloides Tagg & Forr. 1927 H3(–4) USDA 7a(–6b) L1–2 F2–3

Ht 1–1.5m (3–5ft). Habit compact and spreading. Branchlets with scurfy indumentum when young.
L 3–7cm (1½–2¾in) long, 1.8–2.5cm (¾–1in) wide, 1.6–3 times as long as broad, elliptic, semi-bullate above, *discontinuous indumentum below*.
F crimson to deep red, 2.5–3.5cm (1–1⅜in) long, tubular-campanulate.

Similar to *sperabile* but a little dwarfer, less thick indumentum, larger calyx and lacks the glands of that species. Differs from *floccigerum* in its smaller, broader leaves. Shows some relationship with the rest of the subsection outside the Neriiflorum Alliance owing to its tendency to veer away from a tapering style. Rootability moderate.

From a small area of S.E. Xizang, 3,700–4,000m (12,000–13,000ft) in alpine scrub.   April–May

PONTICA SUBSECTION (PONTICUM SERIES)

Only partially included in this volume due to size of plant. For the rest, see *The Larger Species of Rhododendron*. This is a widely distributed subsection now combining both Ponticum and Caucasicum subseries. Chief characters are the usually long rachis leading to a candelabroid inflorescence, the long erect fruiting pedicels and the deeply lobed corolla. Distribution of the whole subsection is N. America, Europe, W. Asia, Taiwan, Japan and E. Asia. There is considerable disagreement over the classification of this subsection. The American, Frank Doleshy, who has travelled widely studying Japanese rhododendrons, disagreed with Chamberlain's original classification and since these two have thrashed it out, some changes have been made, more on the lines of Japanese botanists like Yamazaki (see *AMRS-J*, Spring 1983, p.81).

aureum Georgi 1775 (*chrysanthum* Pallas 1776, *officinale* Salisbury) H5 USDA 5 & 6a L1–2 F1–2

Ht 20cm–1m (8in–3ft), generally under 30cm (1ft) in cultivation. Habit mound-shaped or creeping. Persistent perulae for up to four years.

L very variable, even on one plant, 2.5–10cm (1–4in) long, 1.2–5cm ($\frac{1}{2}$–2in) wide, ovate to broadly elliptic, glabrous above and below when mature.
F cream to pale yellow, usually lightly flecked, 2.5–3cm (1–1$\frac{1}{8}$in) long, widely campanulate on erect pedicels 2.5–3.5cm (1–1$\frac{2}{8}$in) long, 5–8 per truss.

A very distinct species which forms carpets of generally pale rather unattractive foliage in sun, darker in shade. Coming from windswept mountains of E. Asia, it is very hardy and with careful use; it could become a parent of a race of new, low hybrids although the initial results are not all that promising. It blooms and grows early, typical of Siberian species used to having a short growing season. It stands wind and mineral soil in cold areas better than most species. Very slow-growing as a seedling, it increases its vigour with age. Closest relative is *caucasicum*. It has been suggested that this is the oldest elepidote species. It comes from further north than any other elepidote and is capable of surviving extremely low temperatures, with or without snow. Japanese forms are said to be the easiest to grow. All those I have seen have had very pale-coloured flowers of thin texture; some Siberian forms are said to be yellower. Perhaps more plants in the wild than any other Rhododendron species. Rootability moderate.

From huge areas of E. Asia (C. and E. Siberia), N. China, Kamtschatica, Sakhalin, Kuriles, Korea, C. Honshu and Hokkaido, 1,500–2,700m (5,000–9,000ft) alpine slopes, boulder scree, exposed or in shelter of dwarf pine. March–April

aureum var. *hypopitys* (Pojarkova) Chamb. 1979

L longer than var. *aureum*, 9–15.5cm (3$\frac{1}{2}$–6$\frac{1}{4}$in) long. Perulae usually deciduous. These characters could just be due to growing in shade although on the little material available, the leaves are substantially larger.

× *nikomontanum* (Komatsu) Nakai 1917

Formerly considered to be a species by the Japanese, this was recognized as a hybrid by Ohwi in 1965. Usually mid-way between its putative parents *aureum* × *brachycarpum*. Much more vigorous than the former but with the same yellowish flowers. From Honshu, Japan.

× *kurohimense* Arakawa

Another natural hybrid from Honshu of *aureum* × *degronianum*. Normally these two species do not meet but on Mt Kurohime *aureum* occurs much lower than usual, possibly due to coolness created by air currents blowing through holes in the lava rocks. Leaves mid-way in size between parents. Flowers pink buds opening to white-lined pink.

caucasicum Pallas 1784 H5 USDA 5 & 6a L1–2 F1–2

Ht 30cm–1m (1–3ft). Habit usually compact, broader than tall, slow-growing.
L 5–10cm (2–4in) long, 2–4cm ($\frac{4}{5}$–1$\frac{3}{5}$in) wide, 2.3–3 times as long as broad, obovate to elliptic, glabrous above, compacted fawn to pale rust-coloured below.
F cream to pale yellow, sometimes flushed-pink, spotted, of thin texture, 3–3.5cm (1$\frac{1}{5}$–1$\frac{3}{8}$in) long, broadly campanulate, 6–15 per fairly upright truss.

R. caucasicum

An attractive though not spectacular hardy species, much used in early hybridization and now rare in cultivation. I reintroduced this from N.E. Turkey in 1962 and since then seed has been collected in the Caucasus. These introductions do not appear to vary much.

Susceptible to bud-blast which can cause serious tip die-back and leaf spot as well as loss of buds. Worst in wet areas like W. Scotland. Susceptible to root-rot in E. USA. Enjoys full sun and relatively dry conditions. Seed ripens early. 'Cunningham's Sulphur' could be *caucasicum* × *aureum*. Rootability surprisingly low in my experience.

From N.E. Turkey and adjacent Caucasus area, 1,800–2,700m (6,000–9,000ft) covering wide areas about and above the tree-line, often with little organic matter. Forms large mats, flowing downhill. April–May

× **sochadzeae** Char. & Davlian 1967 *ponticum* × *caucasicum* see *The Larger Species of Rhododendron* pp.251–2.

R. caucasicum apparently also crosses naturally with *smirnowii* although I have not seen plants of this cross.

Mountain peaks in Bhutan
with dwarf rhododendrons in
foreground (photo: G.
Sherriff)

Takpa Shiri S.E. Xizang 1936
(photo: G. Sherriff)

3 Members of the Lapponica subsection in the wild, Chungtien Plateau, Yunnan (photo: G. Forrest)

4 North peat walls, Royal Botanic Garden, Edinburgh

5 'Blue Diamond' and other dwarf rhododendrons. Glendoick, Perthshire

6 *megeratum*, Boothia subsection in the wild (photo: G. Sherriff)

7 *campylogynum* salmon-pink form, Campylogyna subsection

8 *campylogynum* Myrtilloides, Campylogyna subsection

9 *charitopes* ssp. *tsangpoense*, Glauca subsection

10 *impeditum*, Lapponica subsection in wild (photo: G. Forrest)

11 *lowndesii*, Lepidota subsection

12 *ciliatum*, Maddenia
subsection in wild, (photo:
G. Sherriff)

13 *moupinense*, Moupinensia
subsection

14 *hirsutum*, Rhododendron
subsection

15 *calostrotum*, Saluenensia
subsection

16 *saluenense* ssp. *chameunum*
Prostratum, Saluenensia
subsection

17 *hanceanum* ' Nanum ',
Tephropepla subsection

18 *lepidostylum*, Trichoclada
subsection

19 *mekongense*, Trichoclada
subsection

20 *keiskei* dwarf form, Triflora
subsection

21 *uniflorum*, Uniflora subsection

22 *santapauii*, Pseudovireya subsection

23 *anthopogon* 'Betty Graham' L&S 1091, Pogonanthum section

24 *cephalanthum,*
Pogonanthum section

25 *trichostomum,*
Pogonanthum section

26 *camtschaticum,* subgenus Therorhodion

27 *campanulatum* ssp. *aeruginosum,* Campanulata subsection

28 *callimorphum,* Campylocarpa subsection

29 *pseudochrysanthum,*
Maculifera
subsection

30 *haematodes* ssp.
chaetomallum, Neriiflora
subsection, Haematodes
alliance

31 *temenium* ssp. *gilvum*
'Cruachan' FCC R. 22272,
Neriiflora subsection,
Sanguineum alliance

32 *forrestii* Repens, Neriiflora subsection, Forrestii alliance, in wild (photo: G. Forrest)

33 *neriiflorum*, Neriiflora subsection, Neriiflorum alliance

34 *aureum*, Pontica subsection

35 'Degronianum', Pontica subsection

36 *makinoi*, Pontica subsection

37 *yakushimanum*, Pontica
subsection

38 *roxieanum*, Taliensia sub-
subsection

39 *williamsianum*,
Williamsiana subsection

40 *kaempferi*, Tsutsusi section

41 *macrosepalum*,
  'Linearifolium', Tsutsusi
  section

'**Degronianum**' Carriere 1869 (*metternichii* var. *pentamerium* [Maxim.] Hutch. 1911 *nakaii* Komatzu) H(4–)5 USDA (6b–)5 & 6a L1–3 F1–3

Ht 60cm–1.5m (2–5ft). Habit usually compact and rounded, wider than high.
L 7–15cm (3–6in) long, 2–4cm ($\frac{3}{4}$–1$\frac{1}{2}$in) wide, oblong to oblong-elliptic to obovate, margins recurved, deep green above and clad with thick felty fawn to rufous indumentum below.
F soft pink to rose, often with deeper lines on the corolla, about 3.5cm (1$\frac{2}{8}$in) long, funnel-campanulate in fairly loose to dome-shaped truss of 9–15, lobes usually 5 but can vary to as much as 8.

An unholy muddle in naming this group of Japanese species has occurred recently of which I will not go into details here. As the correct names have not been finally settled upon, I am using those most likely to be accepted and am placing them in quotation marks pending the result. The Japanese themselves have classified them in various ways.

This plant differs from var. 'Metternichii' in its usually 5-lobed corolla, and generally smaller leaves and more compact habit. It differs from var. 'Hondoense' which has a thin, pale-plastered indumentum and commonly a 7-lobed corolla. Var. 'Degronianum' has inferior forms with poor trusses and colour and can become a very scrappy plant if not growing healthily. It has been more commonly cultivated in Britain than the other varieties in the past. 'Gerald Loder' AM 1974 flowers white, lined rose, 'Rae's Delight' AE 1956 low habit, deep pink flowers.

From N. Honshu, Japan, around and below 1,800m (6,000ft), forming thickets near the tree-line.   April–May

'**Degronianum**' var. '*Hondoense*' Nakai 1924

Differs from var. 'Degronianum' and var. 'Metternichii' in its thin pale-plastered indumentum and from var. 'Degronianum' only in its 7-lobed corolla. Good forms come from Oki Island. Var. *kyomaruense* Yamazaki is similar with 5 lobes from one peninsula, C. Honshu. = *metternichii* var. *metternianum* Wada.

Found wild in W. Honshu and Kyushu.

'**Degronianum**' var. '*Metternichii*' (Siebold & Zuccarine 1870) (*japonicum* [Blume] Schneider 1909) H(4–)5 USDA (6b–)5 & 6a L1–3 F2–3

Ht 1–3.7m (3–12ft). Habit rounded and compact to more upright and open. Young shoots sparsely tomentose. Perulae deciduous.
L 10–15cm (4–6in) long, 2.5–4cm (1–1$\frac{3}{8}$in) wide, elliptic to oblanceolate, 3–4 times as long as broad, glabrous above and often glossy, a dense, compacted to felted indumentum below, variable in colour, from fawn grey, yellowish, orange, to rust, margins sometimes recurved. Young leaves often attractively red or pink-tinged.
F pink, rose to nearly red, sometimes bluish-tinged and flushed darker, occasionally white, 3.8–5cm (1$\frac{1}{2}$–2in) long, funnel-campanulate, 9–15 per compact to loose truss. Lobes *typically* 7 but can vary from 5–9.

This variable plant has been thoroughly studied in its native Japan by both the Japanese and Doleshy. Many fine forms have been introduced recently, several with excellent foliage. The best foliage usually develops in shade although it is naturally freer-flowering and compact in the sun. According to Doleshy, isolated mountain populations have evolved and tend to be relatively uniform. So-called var. *micranthum* Nakai is one of these fairly distinct forms (also known as forma *micrantha* Takeda) and has a very low compact habit, usually dark thick indumentum and fine pink flowers, smaller than type. Limited to Yamato Area, Kirki Dist.

All good in E. USA. Rootability low to high.

Wild only in S. Japan on various mountains, 200–1,200m (700–4,000ft) in forest or open slopes, often rocky. April–May

hyperythrum Hayata 1913 H5 USDA 5 & 6a L2–3 F1–3

Ht.to 1.7m ($5\frac{1}{2}$ft). Habit compact and rounded to fairly erect.
L 7–12cm (3–5in) long, 2–3.5cm ($\frac{4}{5}$–$1\frac{3}{5}$in) wide, 3.2–3.4 times as long as broad, elliptic to elliptic-lanceolate, glabrous when mature above, superficially glabrous below. Recurved.
F white to off-white, 3.5–4.5cm ($1\frac{2}{5}$–$1\frac{4}{5}$in) long, funnel-campanulate, 7–10 per truss.

A beautiful white-flowered species in its best large-flowered forms. Interesting recurved foliage which apparently remains flat in the wild. A wild collected plant arrived with flat leaves but all young growth at once became recurved. Patrick confirms this. It enjoys open situations and stands −26°C (−15°F) in E. USA, surprising considering its low natural habitat. Not closely related to other members of the subsection; some people suggest moving it elsewhere. Rootability moderate.

Endemic to N. Taiwan in lower mountains, 900–1,200m (3,000–4,000ft) in broad-leaved forest. Very local. April–May

makinoi Tagg 1927 (*metternichii* var. *pentamerium* forma *angustifolium* Makino, *stenophyllum* Makino, *yakushimanum* ssp. *makinoi* Chamb. 1979) H4–5 USDA 6b–5 & 6a L2–3 F1–2

Ht occasionally to 2.4m (8ft), usually much less. Habit usually compact and mounded when well grown. *Persistent perulae.*
L 7–18cm (3–7in) long, 1–2.5cm ($\frac{2}{5}$–1in) wide, *linear-lanceolate, 7.5–10* times as long as broad, margins recurved. Loose white indumentum at first above, thick tawny indumentum below.
F rose to off-white, 4cm ($1\frac{3}{5}$in) long, funnel-campanulate, 6 to occasionally 30 per truss, often compact.

This plant and the narrowest leaf forms of *roxieanum* are the narrowest-leaved members of Subgenus Hymenanthes (elepidotes). Although Chamberlain at first placed it with *yakushimanum*, he has now returned it to specific status. They are very different plants horticulturally. I found it difficult to grow at Glendoick until attempting it in pure peat which it evidently enjoys. An alternative is to graft it on to an easily grown under stock. When unhappy, the root system is poor and the foliage inclined to chlorosis. It grows very late in the season, August-September. Doleshy tells me that it often grows wild on north-facing slopes in shade and appears to resent full sun in cultivation, but does sometimes grow in full sun. On his 1982 trip, he reported that wild plants grow in practically neutral soil (pH 7), so my success in pure peat seems odd. Also of interest is that the peak rainfall is during August, corresponding with the growing period. Buds not as frost-hardy as *yakushimanum*. Rootability moderate to high.

Common in a limited area of C. Honshu, Japan, 180–700m (600–2,300ft), among ferns and rocks in forest.   June

yakushimanum Nakai 1921 (sometimes known as *metternichii* var. or ssp. *yakushimanum*) H5 USDA 5 & 6a L2–4 F2–4

Ht to 2.5m (8½ft) or taller in the wild, not usually over 1m (3ft) in cultivation. Habit (dwarfer forms) rounded and dense, slow growing; (lower elevation forms) more open. Young shoots tomentose.
L 6–20cm (2⅖–8in) long, to 5cm (2in) wide, 2.3–6 times as long as broad, narrowly to broadly elliptic, margins usually recurved, ± thin indumentum above, thick to very thick white to fulvous indumentum below.
F pale rose, usually fading to near white to pure white, occasionally pure white in the bud, 3–4cm (1⅕–1⅗in) long, funnel-campanulate, 5–10 per loose to compact truss.

This fabulous plant is now becoming so well-known that it hardly needs describing. Now known by most rhododendron enthusiasts as 'yak', it is considered by many the most perfect species known. There are many selected and several named clones. Some of the latter may in fact be hybrids and have been raised from seed off cultivated plants. Nearly everyone dabbling in hybridizing has used it as a parent. It was first introduced to Exbury, England in 1934 (two plants from Wada) and several new introductions have been made from wild seed by various collectors since. These have produced considerable variation, some from forest habitats with an open habit and large leaves.

The following are the best-known clones: 'Exbury Form' and 'Koichiro Wada' FCC are the two original introductions and are as good as any with a tight habit and splendid foliage and flowers, 'Ken Janeck' AE is a stronger-than-average grower with unusually flat pink flowers. Probably a hybrid. 'Mist Maiden' large flowers heavily flushed-pink on a strong plant. 'Pink Parasol' larger leaves and deeper pink flowers than average. 'Yak-ity-Yak' larger leaves. Flowers satiny white. 'Yaku Angel' leaves longer and narrower and more recurved. A good doer with good foliage.

Other clones are 'Phetteplace Tall Form', 'White Velvet', 'Rhodoland's Silver Mist', 'Church Lane', Dr Serbin after his visit to Yakushima attempted to classify the plants he saw into four groups; *convexum*, *montanum*, *parvum* and *planum* according to leaf shape and habit.

It enjoys full sun in most localities where most forms develop into very tight bushes but also grow well in some shade. It is very fine grown en masse. Hardy in much of E. USA. Rootability moderate to high but frequently grafted.

Only from Yakushima Island, S. Japan, 1,200–1,800m (4,000–6,000ft), very dwarf on exposed tops sheltering amongst rocks with recurved leaves, taller and more open in the shelter of conifers where it flowers less freely. Now carefully protected by the Japanese Government.   May

TALIENSIA SUBSECTION (TALIENSE AND LACTEUM SERIES)

This is very difficult to divide into dwarfs and otherwise. In *Dwarf Rhododendrons* I just included the majority of the old Roxieanum and

Wasonii sub-series which were entirely false divisions although they tended to include most of the lower-growing members of the whole series.

Long neglected, these plants, particularly the dwarfest, are becoming very much collectors' pieces and eagerly sought after. While slow-growing and slow to start blooming, they are very long-lived and full of character. Many are rare in cultivation and some have never been introduced. I will cover those species not described in *The Larger Species of Rhododendron* which included all the species of the old Lacteum series.

Usually dense shrubs with rough bark.

L thick with compacted to woolly indumentum underneath on most species on maturity. Sometimes patchy when semi-mature. Indumentum in one or two layers, often a good character for identifying certain species. It is easy to see if there is an under-layer by rubbing off the indumentum on the leaf underside.

F generally in compact trusses, small, usually white to pink to purplish, often spotted and/or blotched.

These are generally hardy plants, well suited to cold areas although some come into growth early enough to suffer from frost. Not very particular as to soil. I am very fond of most of them and would never be without them even if banished to a small garden. Some are not as hard to root as first thought and are gradually becoming available while others are grafted or produce excellent plants from hand-pollinated seed plus a few from wild seed.

Distribution: the species covered here are from W. and N.W. Yunnan, adjacent S.E. Xizang and Sichuan, usually from high elevations in dryish areas.

I have attempted to produce a key for the complete subsection in cultivation, and I should be pleased to hear what readers think of it and whether they consider it would be of use for the whole genus as it is or modified. Known as a multi-access key, this is, I feel, much more simple to use and yet more detailed than most keys commonly met with. Letters in parentheses refer to characters occasionally found within that species.

To make full use of this key, it is desirable to have a specimen taken off a mature, healthy plant in flower so as to use all nine characters on p. 181. With such a complex and varying group of species, many of which merge botanically into one another, it may not be possible to get every characteristic to fit. The most important characteristics are 1, 2, 3, 5, 6 and 8. 4, 7 and 9, while useful, may often be too indefinite. Extra help is given by a supplementary description after the letter for each species. An incomplete specimen, say lacking flowers, may still prove to be identifiable.

Go through each number one at a time in the correct order, attempting to fit the specimen into a letter under each number, and list these. For indumentum layers, carefully scratch off the visible layer to see if there is another underneath. For leaf size and shape and calyx size, try to select average sizes.

Many specimens may not fit definitely into certain characteristics so put down the one you think it might be and add an alternative in brackets. Once you have a complete set of letters for each number 1 to 9, check it against the sets of letters on pp.181–3. If the characters nearly all fit one set, and especially if those that match include 1, 2, 3, 5, 6 and 8, it is still likely to be a correct identification.

1 A   Indumentum one layer
  B   Indumentum two layers, under-layer usually compacted
2 C   Indumentum thick, distinctly woolly
  D   Indumentum fairly thick and dense, finer texture than C
  E   Indumentum fine-textured, thin, not agglutinated
  F   Indumentum agglutinated (plastered)
3 G   Indumentum continuous, rarely patchy or split
  H   Indumentum often discontinuous or becoming partly glabrous
  I   Indumentum splitting, often into patches
  J   Indumentum thin, compacted, loose and liable to become glabrous
4 K   Indumentum on maturity dark brown or deep cinnamon
  L   Indumentum on maturity brown to rust red to olive brown
  M   Indumentum on maturity grey, fawn, pinkish, light brown
  N   Indumentum on maturity cream to light fawn
5 O   Leaf size sometimes over 15cm (6in) long
  P   Leaf size often over 10cm (4in) but not over 15cm (6in) long
  Q   Leaf size between 5cm (2in) and 10cm (4in) long
  R   Leaf size under 5cm (2in) long
6 S   Leaves about 2 times as long as broad
  T   Leaves about 2.5 times as long as broad
  U   Leaves about 3 times as long as broad
  V   Leaves about 4 times as long as broad
7 W   Flowers usually white
  X   Flowers usually white flushed pink
  Y   Flowers usually pink
  Z   Flowers usually white to rose
  AA Flowers usually (sometimes) yellow or yellowish
8 BB Calyx length 3–15mm
  CC Calyx length 0.5–2mm
9 DD Mature height often over 3m (10ft)
  EE Mature height usually 1–2m (3–6ft)
  FF Mature height usually under 1m (3ft)

1 ACGKPTXBBDD
  one-year shoots with rusty indumentum   *bureavii*
2 ACGKPUYBBEE
  indumentum leaf underside at first pink   *elegantulum*
3 ACG(H)KPUZCCDD
  leaves bullate above   *wiltonii*
4 ACGLPTXBBEE
  indumentum leaf underside olive brown on maturity   *adenogynum*
5 ACHKPTXBBDD
  leaves and flowers larger than *bureavii*   Bureavioides Group
6 AD(F)(I)MPSYBBDD
  indumentum more plastered than Aganniphoides Group   *balfourianum*
7 ADGMOUYCCDD
  resembles a larger leaved *rufum*   *nigroglandulosum*

8 AE(F)GLOTAACCDD
flowers yellow in one-sided truss   *wightii*

9 AE(F)GLPTW(XY)CCDD
indumentum felted, very variable   *phaeochrysum* var. *phaeochrysum*

10 AEG(H)KQSAACCDD
leaves ovate-lanceolate   *wasonii*

11 AEGLPTWCCDD
indumentum finer-textured than *phaeochrysum* var. *phaeochrysum*
                                                        traillianum var. *traillianum*

12 AEGLPTWCCDD
indumentum coarser and looser, ribbon-like hairs   *traillianum* var. *dictyotum*

13 AEGLPTWCCDD
as *wasonii* but flowers pale pink   *wasonii* var. *rhododactylum*

14 AEGMP(Q)SXCCEE
indumentum rarely splitting   *aganniphum* var. *aganniphum*

15 AEGMPTWCCDD
indumentum felted continuous   *phaeochrysum* var. *levistratum*

16 AEIL(K)P(Q)SXCCEE
indumentum heavily split   *aganniphum* var. *flavorufum*

17 AFG(H)MOUYCCDD
branches stiff and stout   *beesianum*

18 AFG(I)LPTWCCDD
indumentum darker than *aganniphum*   *phaeochrysum* var. *agglutinatum*

19 AFGLOSAACCDD
flowers yellow, branches very stout   *lacteum*

20 AFGMPSYBBEE
indumentum more spongy than type   *balfourianum* Aganniphoides Group

21 AFJMQSZCCEE
indumentum very plastered or absent, yellow petiole and midrib   *przewalskii*

22 BCG(H)K(L)PTZCCEE
loose woolly indumentum   *rufum*

23 BCGKQ(P)UWCCEE
wider leaved *roxieanum*, near to *taliense*   *roxieanum* var. *cucullatum*

24 BCGKQ(P)VWCCEE
narrowest leaves of the subsection   *roxieanum* var. *roxieanum*

25 BCGKRUXCCFF
smallest leaves of the subsection   *proteoides*

26 BCGNPSZCCEE
7-lobed corolla   *clementinae*

27 BCGNPUZCCDD
thick pale indumentum   *principis*

28 BCGNQUZ(AA)CCFF
young leaves glaucous, very low habit   *pronum*

29 BCHLPSXBBDD
upper rust-red indumentum non-persistent   *faberi* ssp. *faberi*

30 BDG(K)LOU(V)ZCCDD
resembles *adenogynum* with small calyx   *alutaceum* var. *alutaceum*

31 BDGK(L)PSWCCDD
dense usually rusty indumentum   *sphaeroblastum*

32 BDGK(L)Q(P)TWCCEE
dense dark indumentum on maturity   *taliense*

33 BDGKQUXCCFF
densely tomentose eglandular ovary   *bathyphyllum*

34 BDGLOU(V)WCCEE
felted ramiform hairs   *alutaceum* var. *iodes*

35 **BDHL(K)OU(V)WCCDD**
    indumentum discontinuous; ramiform hairs   *alutaceum* var. *russotinctum*
36 **BD(H)LPTZBBEE**
    indumentum usually continuous   *mimetes*
37 **BD(I)LPTXBBEE**
    indumentum usually splits   *simulans*
38 **BFJMOSWBBDD**
    large wide leathery leaves   *faberi* ssp. *prattii*

alutaceum var. **russotinctum** (Balf.f. & Forr.) Chamb. 1978 (*triplonaevium* Balf.f. & Forr., *tritifolium* Balf.f. & Forr.) H4–5 USDA 6b–5 & 6a L1–3 F1–2

Ht 1.5–3.7m (5–12ft). Habit compact and dome-shaped to leggy with age. Branchlets with thin indumentum at first. Perulae sometimes persistent.
L 5–18cm (2–7in) long, 1.5–4cm ($\frac{3}{5}$–1$\frac{3}{5}$in) wide, 3–6.2 times as long as broad, glabrous above, *discontinuous* upper layer of indumentum below, fawn to rusty. Margins often slightly recurved.
F white or white, flushed rose with crimson spots and sometimes a blotch, 3.1–3.8cm (1$\frac{1}{4}$–1$\frac{1}{2}$in) long, campanulate to funnel-campanulate, 10–20 per usually compact truss.

Often pretty in flower with neat trusses, it does not often have quite the foliage appeal of those species and varieties with a thicker and/or darker indumentum. It intergrades with var. *alutaceum* and var. *iodes*. Rather tall for inclusion in this book. Rootability medium to low.

Common in N.W. Yunnan and less so in S.E. Xizang, 3,000–4,300m (10,000–14,000ft), open rocky slopes, bamboo, thickets and open conifer forest.   April–May

alutaceum var. **iodes** (Balf.f. & Forr.) Chamb. 1982

Differs from the above in its more felted upper layer of indumentum on the leaf underside with a tendency towards smaller leaves, paler indumentum. Perulae not persistent. S.E. Xizang.

bathyphyllum Balf.f. & Forr. 1919 H4–5 USDA 6b–5 & 6a L2–3 F1–2

Ht 60cm–1.5m (2–5ft). Habit dense and compact.
L 4–7cm (1$\frac{3}{5}$–2$\frac{4}{5}$in) long, 1.5–2cm ($\frac{3}{5}$–$\frac{4}{5}$in) wide, 2.7–3.5 times as long as broad, elliptic to oblong. Dense two-layered indumentum below, dense rufous on top, brown compacted underneath.
F white, flushed rose with crimson spots, 3–3.5cm (1$\frac{1}{5}$–1$\frac{2}{5}$in) long, campanulate, 10–15 per truss.

This is a rare plant in cultivation and the average typical form may not be in cultivation at all although there are plants under this name. It is closely related to *roxieanum* and var. *cucullatum* and *alutaceum* var. *russotinctum* but differs from all three in its densely tomentose eglandular ovary. Woollier, thicker indumentum than *alutaceum* var. *russotinctum*. Leaves tend to be a little smaller than *roxieanum* var. *cucullatum* which has paler indumentum.

From S.E. Xizang and N.W. Yunnan, 3,400–4,300m (11,000–14,000ft), on rocky slopes, forest margins, thickets and cliffs.   April–May

comisteum Balf.f. & Forr. 1919 not in cultivation

Ht 60cm–1m (2–3ft).
L 3–5cm (1$\frac{1}{5}$–2in) long, 1.2–1.5cm ($\frac{1}{2}$–$\frac{3}{5}$in) wide, elliptic to obovate, two-layered indumentum below, dense pale red-brown on top, compacted brown underneath.
F deep rose, lightly spotted, *c.* 3.5cm (1$\frac{2}{5}$in) long.

This looks an interesting plant from the herbarium specimens, with foliage resembling *proteoides*, but if differs in its less thick, paler indumentum, deep-pink flowers and slightly larger and less recurved leaves.

From S.E. Xizang and N.W. Yunnan, 4,000–4,200m (13,000–14,000ft), on open stony slopes.

dumicola Tagg & Forr. 1930 H4 USDA 6b L1–2 F1–2

Ht 1–2.5m (3–8ft).
L 6.5–7.5cm (2$\frac{3}{5}$–3in) long, 3–4cm (1$\frac{1}{5}$–1$\frac{3}{5}$in) wide, 1.8–2.2 times as long as broad, obovate to broadly elliptic, thin brown indumentum below, shedding on maturity.
F white, flushed rose, purple spots, *c* 4cm (1$\frac{3}{5}$in) long. *Calyx large* 0.7–1cm ($\frac{1}{4}$–$\frac{2}{5}$in).

It seems likely that this is a natural hybrid, perhaps with the Thomsonia subsection as the calyx bears a resemblance to those of that subsection.

N.W. Yunnan, 4,300m (14,000ft).

pronum Tagg & Forr. 1927 H5 USDA 5 & 6a L3 F?

Ht 15–60cm (6in–2ft). Habit *creeping, prostrate and compact.* Perulae persisting for several years.
L 4–7.5cm (1$\frac{3}{5}$–3in) long, 1.8–2.8cm ($\frac{2}{5}$–1$\frac{1}{5}$in) wide, 2.7–3.5 times as long as broad, elliptic, *glaucous* above, *convex*, dense greyish to fawn indumentum below in two layers.
F white, creamy yellow to pink, heavily spotted crimson or purple, 3.5–4.5cm (1$\frac{2}{5}$–1$\frac{4}{5}$in) long, funnel-campanulate, 6–10 per truss.

This distinct species has always been very rare in cultivation, in fact there are probably only two clones. One was at Kilbryde, Northumberland and was moved to the RBG, Edinburgh in 1981–2. The other was in the species collection at Windsor and is the same as the American clone known as the Ben Nelson form. The former has very glaucous young foliage and a prostrate habit, the latter has less glaucous leaves and a more mounded habit. The former and at least one of its layers have, I believe, flowered occasionally and the old plant had three flower buds in autumn 1983. It has not flowered in USA yet. No close allies but might be considered as a dwarf *clementinae*.

While it is reasonably easy to grow, growth comes early and is easily frosted so some protection in late April and May is advisable. Rootability moderate. A connoisseur's item.

From W. Yunnan, 3,700–4,600m (12,000–15,000ft), moist rocky slopes, humus-covered boulders and cliffs.   Said to be April–May

proteoides Balf.f. & W.W. Sm. 1916 (*lampropeplum* Balf.f. & Forr.) H5 USDA 5 & 6a L2–3 F2–3

Ht 15–30cm (6–12in), said to reach 1m (3ft) in the wild. Habit *slow-growing* and very compact but not freely branching. Persistent perulae.

L 2–4(–5)cm ($\frac{4}{5}$–1$\frac{3}{5}$(–2)in) long, 0.7–1cm ($\frac{1}{3}$–$\frac{2}{5}$in) wide, 3–4 times as long as broad, elliptic, margins strongly recurved, partly glabrous above on maturity with some white to brown indumentum persisting, two-layered indumentum below, thick woolly brown to rufous upper layer.

F white to pale yellow, flushed rose, purple spots, 2.5–3.5cm (1–1$\frac{2}{5}$in) long, campanulate, 5–10 per truss.

This is perhaps even more of a connoisseur's plant than *pronum*. First flowered in cultivation (to my knowledge) in Cecil Smith's splendid garden in Oregon about 1967 and has in all flowered about ten times. Very occasional buds have been set on one or two British plants. Mr Smith's grows on a tree stump and when I saw it in 1982, it had over 30 flower buds but looked sick, probably due to squirrels digging underneath. Possibly needs some stress to make it bloom although Mr Smith waters his plant very regularly. There are several clones, some with wider leaves than others but beware of any named *proteoides* with leaves over 4cm (1$\frac{2}{5}$in) long which are forms of *roxieanum*. Several hybrids have been raised from it. All plants in cultivation probably come from Rock's 1948–9 expedition. Many buds on my biggest plant, autumn 1984.

Appreciates peat beds or stumps; look out for damage to young growth, a delicacy to slugs, weevils etc. Rootability easier than at first considered.

Quite widespread and common in the wild, often flowering freely, from S.E. Xizang, N.W. Yunnan and S.W. Sichuan, 3,700–4,600m (12,000–15,000ft), on open rocky slopes and on rocks and cliffs. April

roxieanum Forr. 1915 (*recurvum* Balf.f. & Forr., *aischropeplum* Balf.f. & Forr., *poecilodermum* Balf.f. & Forr.) H5 USDA 5 & 6a L2–3 F2–3

Ht very variable, 15cm–4m (6in–13ft), usually 30cm–1.2m (1–4ft). Habit dwarf and compact to leggy and upright. Woolly branchlets.
L 4–12cm (1$\frac{3}{5}$–4$\frac{3}{4}$in) long, 0.6–2cm ($\frac{1}{4}$–$\frac{4}{5}$in) wide, more than 4 times as long as broad, linear to narrowly elliptic, two-layered indumentum below, upper layer thick woolly fawn to rufous, margins recurved.
F creamy-white or white with rose flush, ± crimson spots, 2–4cm ($\frac{4}{5}$–1$\frac{3}{5}$in) long, funnel-campanulate, 6–15 per truss, usually compact.

The narrow-leaved forms known as Oreonastes Group are remarkable for their porcupine-like appearance and look delightful topped with their neat rounded trusses. A variable plant which appears to flower more freely in woodland conditions than when dwarfed in the open. Even one plant can produce quite a variation of leaf widths. One of my favourites. Rootability low but is easily grown from hand-pollinated seed. *R. roxieanum* merges with *proteoides* (which has shorter leaves) and *roxieanum* var. *cucullatum* (with wider leaves).

From wide areas of S.E. Xizang, N.W. Yunnan and S.W. Sichuan, 3,400–4,300m (11,000–14,000ft), open rocky pastures, in and around conifer forests, bamboo and cliffs. April–May

roxieanum var. **cucullatum** (Hand.-Mazz.) Chamb. 1978 (*coccinopeplum* Balf.f. & Forr., *porphyroblastum* Balf.f. & Forr.)
L 2.2–4 times as long as broad.

This variety has a less dense (but still very woolly or spongy) indumentum than var. *roxieanum* and merges with *proteoides* and *bathyphyllum*. It differs from the latter in its paler indumentum and slightly larger leaves.

We found it on Cangshan where it almost certainly intergrades with neighbouring *taliense*. As small seedlings, they are impossible to tell apart except that var. *cucullatum* has a slightly thicker indumentum. Very neat and compact with a striking indumentum. Introduced by us under SBEC 0350.

Very common in the wild. Location and habitat as above plus W. Yunnan. Chamberlain has now placed *roxieanum* var. *globigerum* (Balf.f. & Forr.) Chamb. 1978 under *alutaceum* var. *alutaceum*.

roxieodes Chamb. 1982 not in cultivation

Ht *c.* 2.5m (8ft). Young shoots densely tomentose. Perulae persistent.
L 6.5–7.5cm (2$\frac{3}{5}$–3in) long, 1.3–1.8cm ($\frac{1}{2}$–$\frac{3}{4}$in) wide, *linear*, two-layered indumentum below, thick brown.
F deep pink, spotted, *c.* 3cm (1$\frac{1}{5}$in) long, funnel-campanulate, 12–16 per truss.

Differs from *roxieanum* in its deeper-coloured flowers and glandular style. Known only from type locality in E. Sichuan.

R. wasonii

wasonii Hemsl. & Wils. 1910 H4–5 USDA 6b–5 & 6a L2–3 F2–3

Ht 60cm–1.5m (2–5ft). Habit compact when young, becoming open with age.
L 5–10cm (2–4in) long, 2.5–4.5cm (1–1$\frac{4}{5}$in) wide, 1.6–3 times as long as broad, ovate-lanceolate, dark green above, sparse to dense one-layered indumentum below, reddish brown.
F yellow to white to pink, lightly spotted, 3–4cm (1$\frac{1}{5}$–1$\frac{3}{5}$in) long, openly campanulate, in a fairly loose truss of 8–15.

A distinct species with pretty flowers produced younger than most of the subsection and fine foliage. Easily grown and highly recommended. This species and *wiltonii* apparently have no close relations and do not fit into this subsection happily. A plant known as *bureavii* aff. McL AD 106 is undoubtedly nearer to or a form of *wasonii* with thicker indumentum. Anyway it is doubtful if *bureavii* (*bureavioides*) and *wasonii* meet in the wild. Rhododactylum Group with pink flowers has even darker leaves; the Group's status is doubtful until re-studied in the wild but could be a natural hybrid. Rootability low to moderate.

From C. Sichuan, 2,300–3,000m (7,500–10,000ft) and probably higher, in forest, on cliffs and boulders.   April–May

THOMSONIA SUBSECTION (THOMSONII SERIES)

thomsonii ssp. *lopsangianum* (Cowan) Chamb. 1982 H3–4 USDA 7a–6b L2–3 F2?

Ht 60cm–1.8m (2–6ft). Habit low and compact to upright.
L 2.7–6cm (1–2$\frac{2}{5}$in) long, 1.6–4cm ($\frac{3}{5}$–1$\frac{3}{5}$in) wide, 1.1–2 times as long as broad, glabrous above, variable below, sometimes glaucous, sometimes just glabrous, sometimes with a thin fine indumentum or occasional hairs.
F deep crimson, 3–4.2cm (1$\frac{1}{5}$–1$\frac{3}{5}$in) long, campanulate to funnel-campanulate, 3–5 per loose truss. Calyx 2–4mm long, usually crimson.

I cannot accept Chamberlain's interpretation of this plant, placing it in a different subsection from *sherriffii*. They are extremely closely related and are often impossible to tell apart except by looking at the indumentum. Apparent intermediaries with thin indumentum occur both in herbarium specimens and in cultivation and I would say that while *lopsangianum* is undoubtedly related to *thomsonii*, it is closer to *sherriffii* which has no connection with *fulgens*. The indumentum of *sherriffii* is of a very fine texture which appears to approach the thin scurf on some *lopsangianum*. Both *lopsangianum* and *sherriffii* come from the same area in the wild and horticulturally behave in a very similar manner. *R. lopsangianum* is slow to bloom but this may be partly due to the frequency of the first growth flush being frosted. It is the probable parent of *thomsonii* var. *pallidum* Cowan, now treated as a synonym of × *candelabrum* (*thomsonii* × *campylocarpum*). Rootability moderate to high.

From S. Xizang, 2,600–4,300m (8,500–14,000ft), rocky hillsides, cliffs, stream sides, conifer and rhododendron forest, often in wet zone.   April

FULGENSIA SUBSECTION (PART CAMPANULATUM SERIES)

miniatum Cowan 1936 not in cultivation

Ht 1.5–2m (5–6ft).
L 4–5cm (about 2in) long, 2–2.6cm (about 1in) wide, glabrous above, dense fulvous indumentum below.
F crimson, 3–3.5cm (1$\frac{1}{5}$–1$\frac{2}{5}$in) long, funnel-campanulate, *c.* five flowers per truss. Calyx 0.8–1.5cm ($\frac{1}{3}$–$\frac{3}{5}$in) long.

Probably related to *sherriffii* and/or *thomsonii* spp. *lopsangianum*. Indumentum is coarser than *sherriffii*. Seed was not collected.

From S. Xizang, *c*. 3,700m (12,000ft) beside cliffs on edge of rhododendron zone.

LANATA SUBSECTION (PART CAMPANULATUM SERIES)

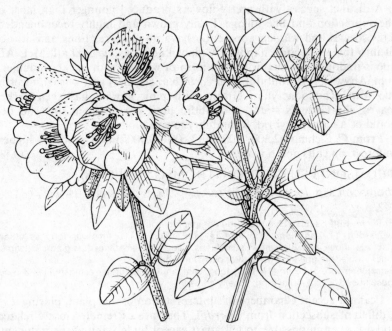

R. tsariense

tsariense Cowan 1937 H4 USDA 6b L2–3 F2–3

Ht 1–3m (3–10ft) but rarely over 1.5m (5ft) in cultivation. Habit fairly compact but rarely dense. Branchlets densely woolly.
L 2.3–6.2cm ($\frac{7}{8}$–2$\frac{1}{2}$in) long, 1–3cm ($\frac{2}{5}$–1$\frac{1}{5}$in) wide, 1.6–2.2 times as long as broad, indumentum ± persistent above, dense fawn to rust-coloured indumentum below.
F pale pink or white-flushed pink, crimson spots, 2.5–3.5cm (1–1$\frac{2}{5}$in) long, open campanulate, 3–5 per truss.

This species is a treasure both in and out of flower. Fairy-like flowers contrast beautifully with the dark foliage. While fairly hardy, both flower and growth buds may be easily frosted in spring. It may be grown in sun or shade. It is more easily cultivated than its close relative, *lanatum*, with which it merges and/or hybridizes in the wild. Some of these intermediaries are in cultivation. *R. lanatum* has yellow flowers and is generally bigger all round. 'Yum Yum' AM 1964. Rootability low to sometimes moderate.

From S. Xizang, Arunachal Pradesh and E. Bhutan, 3,000–4,400m (10,000–14,500ft), in and on edges of conifer forest, rhododendron thickets, bamboo, open hillsides and cliffs, fairly widespread and common.　　　　　　　　　　　　　　　　　　　　　　　　March–May *circinatum* Cowan & Ward 1936 not in cultivation

Close to *lanatum* but owing to poorness of specimen, its status is not clear. S. Xizang, 4,000–4,300m (13,000ft).

lanatoides Chamb. 1982 not in cultivation

Ht 2–4m (6–13ft).
L 9–11cm (3⅜–4⅝in) long, 2.1–2.7cm (about 1in) wide, lanceolate, slightly persistent indumentum above, dark fawn to light brown indumentum below.
F white, flushed pink, lightly spotted, 3.5–4cm (about 1½in) long, campanulate, 10–15 per truss.

Leaves narrower than *lanatum*, apparently its closest ally. Rather beyond our dwarf limit.

WILLIAMSIANA SUBSECTION (THOMSONII SERIES, SUBSERIES WILLIAMSIANUM)

williamsianum Rehd. & Wils. 1915 H4–5 USDA 6b–5 & 6a L2–3 F2–3

Ht 60cm–1.5m (2–5ft). Habit dense and spreading but ultimately dome-shaped. Branchlets thin and glandular.

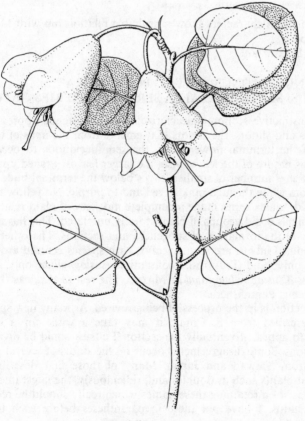

R. williamsianum

L 1.5–4.5cm ($\frac{3}{5}$–1$\frac{4}{5}$in) long, 1.3–3.5cm ($\frac{1}{2}$–1$\frac{2}{5}$in) wide, *c. 1.3 times as long as broad, ovate orbicular*, glabrous above and below.
F pale pink to rose, occasionally white, spotted, 3–4cm (1$\frac{1}{5}$–1$\frac{3}{5}$in) long, campanulate, 2–3 rarely to 5 per truss, corolla lobes 5 occasionally to 7. Calyx small.

A superb and most distinct species. We at Glendoick find it does best in full sun, resulting in a tight, compact free-flowering bush. Early growth is its only fault so frost pockets should always be avoided. While it is hardy, bark-split may affect young plants. Otherwise easily grown. Hardy in coastal S. Sweden but barely so in E. USA. Some forms have extra large flowers and these usually have extra corolla lobes. Much used in hybridizing. AM 1938.

It is probably related to *martinianum. The Species of Rhododendron* suggests *souliei* and *callimorphum.* Rootability mostly high.

From two or more mountains in C. Sichuan only, 2,400–3,000m (8,000–10,000ft), in isolated places on cliffs. April–May

leishanicum Fang & S. S. Chang not in cultivation

A possible relation of *williamsianum.*
Ht *c.* 3m (9ft).
L with dense indumentum on petioles and midrib below.
F purple, openly campanulate, 3 per truss.

Indumentum characters show a probable relationship with Maculifera subsection.

From E. Guizhou.

SUBGENUS TSUTSUSI (SWEET) POYARKORA
TSUTSUSI SECTION (AZALEA SERIES, SUB-SERIES OBTUSUM)

A very distinctive section characterized by the flattened appressed hairs on leaves and shoots, the shoots that emerge from the axils of the lower scales of the terminal flower buds, the semi-deciduous to occasionally deciduous nature of the leaves also, the larger leaves ± shed up the stem retaining a ± number of smaller leaves below the terminal bud. F colour varies from white through pink to red and to purple. No yellow tones.

The old Azalea series made a complete mockery of plant relationships, containing as it did groups of plants totally unrelated. This has now been put right in the formation of subgenera and sections. The other sections in subgenus Tsutsusi are: Brachycalyx, with species centred around *reticulatum* only; and Tsusiopsis, containing *tsusiophyllum* only, formerly known as *Tsusiophyllum tanakae* Maxim. The rest of 'Azaleas' belong to the subgenus Pentanthera.

This section is in the process of being revised. As many new species are being described from S. China, it may take a while for a complete revision to appear. Eventually the section Tsutsusi could be divided into sub-sections. Some disagreements occur on the status of several so-called species from Taiwan and Japan. Many of those first described were cultivated plants such as doubles and, ridiculously, the latest international rules insist on retaining these names which really should be reduced to cultivar status. I have put these in parentheses before each true wild species.

Hybrids derived from within this section have become perhaps the most widely cultivated part of the genus Rhododendron. The majority of species come from warm, sunny climates, thus rendering them suitable for hot areas which the cooler and/or more moisture-loving remainder of the genus cannot tolerate. In contrast, we in Scotland are at the extreme edge of the area where these azaleas can flourish out-of-doors owing to our cool summers not ripening the wood, more than to the severity of our winters. Enormous quantities of the more tender hybrids are of course used as pot plants.

Distribution mostly in Japan, Taiwan and S. China with outliers in the Philippines, Korea, W. China and just into E. Burma.

In this section, I am only describing those species in cultivation. The only information generally available on those not in cultivation at the moment is in *The Species of Rhododendron* and *Rhododendrons of China* and both are far from complete. The latter has line drawings of each species. Also see the newly published *A Survey of Genus Rhododendron in South China*.

In northern Britain, these azaleas should be planted in full sun to flower freely, while in the south some shade may not greatly reduce their floriferousness. Most species and hybrids root easily from softish to semi-hard cuttings taken in July–August.

As these plants come from climates completely alien to the Scottish one, I have not attempted to give them all the usual H5–1 rating for hardiness but have given an estimated minimum temperature in fahrenheit which they will tolerate. Many, quite useless to us, will thrive in climates with considerably colder winters but much hotter, longer summers.

breviperulatum Hayata 1914 +5–10°F

Recently introduced from Taiwan into USA by Creech.
L about 2.5cm (1in) long, 1–1.5cm ($\frac{2}{5}$–$\frac{3}{5}$in) wide, ovate-elliptic to oblong-ovate. Glossy brown when young.
F reddish, to 2.5cm (1in) across, 3–6 per truss.

eriocarpum (Hayata) Nakai (*tamurae* [Makino] Masamane? *simsii* var. *eriocarpum* Wils.) H2–3? +10°F?

Habit often prostrate.
L evergreen, 2–4cm ($\frac{4}{5}$–1$\frac{3}{5}$in) long, 0.8–1.5cm ($\frac{1}{2}$–$\frac{3}{5}$in) wide, elliptic to obovate.
F red to purple, rose, pink or white, 3–4cm (1$\frac{1}{5}$–1$\frac{3}{5}$in) across, broadly funnel-shaped, 1–2 per truss. Stamens 9 or fewer.

The Gumpo azaleas probably originate from this plant. Considered a full species by Ohwi but under *tamurae*. Late-flowering and generally tender for us in E. Scotland.

Grows on Yakushina, S. Japan at sea level and low elevations in gravelly soil or in granite fissures, also Kyushu and other S. Japanese islands in thickets and thin woods.
July

indicum (L) Sweet 1833 (*breynii* Planch., *danielsianum* Planch., *hannoense* Nakai, *lateritium* Planch., *macrantha* Bunge) −5°F with warm summers, +5°F with cool summers L1–2 F2–3

Ht occasionally to 1.8 (6ft) but often low and compact. Habit dense with rigid branches.
L evergreen, to 3.8cm (1½in) long, lanceolate to oblanceolate, scattered hairs on both surfaces. Often dark green above.
F rose-red to bright scarlet, 5–6.3cm (2–2½in) across, broadly funnel-shaped, 1–2 per truss.

A fine plant where warm summers ripen the wood, so of little use in Scotland. Not to be confused with 'Indica' azaleas grown as pot plants which largely have *simsii* as a parent. Flowers tend to open over a long period.

From S. Japan in rocky ravines, stream sides and open country. Satsuki azaleas mostly originate from this species and probably *eriocarpum*.   June–July

kaempferi Planch. (*obtusum* var. *kaempferi* Wils.) −5°F L1–2 F2–4

Ht up to 3m (10ft) often less. Habit loosely branched with erect growth. Cinnamon-brown trunks with age.
L semi-evergreen to deciduous, to 7.6cm (3in) long, hairy both sides. Often turn scarlet in autumn.
F pink through salmon-red to rosy-red or white, spotted, 4.4–6.3cm (1⅘–2½in) long, funnel-shaped, 1–4 per truss. Stamens 5.

The commonest (Tsutsusi) azalea in Japan and hence very variable. Many selected clones occur including ones with no corolla, stripes and doubles. These odd forms are revered by the Japanese; some are now introduced into USA. One named form, f. *tubiflorum*, has long-lasting flowers which eventually turn light green and crimson in autumn resulting in flowers for half the year. How would people appreciate these curiosities in Europe?

This species hybridizes with many other Japanese species in the wild such as *kiusianum*, *macrosepalum* and *komiyamae*, resulting in vast hybrid swarms in a multitude of different colours and shades.

One of the tallest species, it can become almost tree-like in habit. Much used in hybridizing. The flowers are liable to bleach in the sun. *kaempferi* forma *latisepalum* is the northern form from Hokkaido. We are testing several seedlings of this for hardiness and possible use in hybridization. Most have light salmon-coloured flowers.

'Eastern Fire' FCC 1955, AM 1953, AGM 1968.

Wild on all main islands of Japan, often very common from sea-level to 800m (2,600ft), usually on sunny hillsides, also in conifer or deciduous forest and on volcanos.   May–June

kanehirae Wils. 1921 +10°F

Habit usually prostrate in wild.
L evergreen to semi-evergreen, dark green, shiny, to 5.6cm (2½in) long, 0.6cm (¼in) wide, *narrowly oblanceolate to narrowly obovate*.
F pink, carmine to red, scarlet spots, 2.5–4.3cm (1–1¾in) long, funnel-shaped, 1–3 per truss.

Recently introduced from Taiwan. Looked interesting but too tender for us (killed at Glendoick).

From Taiwan, on river banks and rocks.

April–May

R. kiusianum

kiusianum Makino H4 USDA 6b L1–2 F1–3

Ht to 75cm (2½ft) usually less. Habit flat-topped and spreading to compact and bushy.
L semi-deciduous to evergreen, to 1.9cm (¾in) long, 1.3cm (½in) wide, elliptic to narrowly obovate.
F purple mauve, orange-red, carmine to soft pink to white, 1.8–2.5cm (¾–1in) across, funnel-shaped, 2–4 per truss, usually 2. Stamens 5.

This is proving one of the most reliable species for cool summer/ coldish winter areas like Scotland and coastal E. Canada. Many new clones are being introduced of various clear colours. All are hardy and free-flowering and thoroughly recommended. Their spreading habit makes them ideal for ground cover and they are excellent subjects for bonsai. Many new hybrids are likely to be raised from these clones for northern climates.

Confined to the high peaks of Kyushu Is., Japan. On some peaks typical *kiusianum* occurs while on others, only plants tainted with *kaempferi* blood are present. It often grows on volcanos where it can be wholly or partially destroyed by eruptions. Grows on bare meadows, pumice flats and among dwarf pines, at 1,200–1,700m (4,000–5,600ft). Below 1,200m, hybrid swarms often occur.

May

× **komiyamae** Makino (*indicum* var. *mikawanum*, *kaempferi* var. *mikawanum*)
−5°F? H4? USDA 6b? L1−2 F

Habit fairly upright.
L almost deciduous, appressed brown hairs on both surfaces.
F reddish-purple, 2−3.5cm (⅘−1⅖in) across, 1−4 per truss. Stamens *10*.

Comes from the furthest north in Japan of any Tsutsusi azalea except *kaempferi* so could be useful for breeding. The 10 stamens (Ohwi says 6−9) are the chief character separating it from *kaempferi* which has 5. Chamberlain considers it to be a synonym of *tosaense* but I am doubtful.

From Mt Ashitaka, C. Honshu only, occurring above *kaempferi* to the summit at 1,505m (5,000ft). In between are a multitude of natural hybrids.   May

macrosepalum Maxim. 1870 H2−3 USDA 7b & 8a−7a L1−2 F2−3

Ht 1−2m (3−6ft). Habit spreading.
L Semi-evergreen, to 6.3cm (3½in) long, ovate to lanceolate, rather hairy, *slightly rugose above*.
F pale lavender to rose-purple, often heavily spotted, sometimes scented, 3.8−5cm (1½−2in) across, funnel-shaped, 2−10 per truss. Calyx green, *large*. Stamens usually 5, sometimes more.

Quite pretty in its better forms but definitely rather tender with foliage and flowers liable to frost damage.

From C. and S. Japan in the open or in pine woods and thickets, often on gravelly soil. Frequently associated with *kaempferi* resulting in hybrid swarms. 'Linearifolium' is a curious Japanese selection with narrowly linear leaves and pink flowers of the same shape. Quite widely cultivated and slightly hardier than the type. There are other related Japanese selections.   April−May

microphyton Franch. 1886 H3 USDA 7a +5°F? L1−2 F1−2+

Ht to 1m (3ft), rarely to 2m (6ft). Habit bushy and spreading.
L evergreen, 0.6−5cm (½−2in) long, oval to lanceolate.
F rose-purple through pink to almost white, 1.3−1.9cm (½−¾in) across, funnel-shaped, 3−6 per truss, often forming multiple buds. Stamens 5.

A pretty little azalea, very variable in colour even in one place in the wild. Common on warm, dry slopes and probably too tender for all but the S. and W. of Britain. Recently reintroduced by SBEC and others.

Common in Yunnan. It is said to come from 1,800−3,000m (6,000−10,000ft)—although we did not see it above 2,500m (8,250ft)—on dry banks, thickets, cliffs and shady gullies.   April−May

nakaharae Hayata 1908 −5°F H3−4 USDA 7a−6b L1−2 F2−3

Ht to 30cm (1ft) usually less. Habit prostrate, often mound-forming, sometimes with occasional erect shoots.
L evergreen, to 1.8cm (¾in) or rarely 2.5cm (1in) long, oblanceolate to oblong-ovate, medium to dark green above.
F brick-red to rose-red, 3.8cm (1½in) across, funnel-campanulate, 1−3 per truss. Stamens 6−10.

This is proving to be one of our best new introductions of recent years. Quite hardy in Scotland and only suffering a little die-back in hard winters, it is an invaluable ground cover creeper with plentiful flowers produced late in the season. As a parent of a new race of hybrids with a low compact habit, late-flowering, reliable and hardy, it is doubly valuable, especially for the north. Used for hybridizing in Japan, Germany, USA, and Canada and by ourselves in Scotland. Enjoys full sun on banks, peat walls and in the rock garden. 'Mariko' AM is an exceptionally dwarf, compact clone with dark leaves while 'Mount Seven Stars' is more vigorous with paler foliage. Some clones known as *nakaharae* pink are hybrids.

Endemic to N. Taiwan at 300–800m (1,000–2,500ft), surprisingly low for a relatively hardy plant, growing around hot springs on sandstone.

All out at once or spasmodically, June–August.

noriakianum T. Suzuki 1935 +5°F H3 USDA 7a L1 F1–2

Ht to 1m (3ft). Habit twiggy and often open.
L semi-deciduous, *c.* 1.3cm ($\frac{1}{2}$in) long, ovate to ovate-oblong.
F pale to deep purple on the plants we grew but reported as being red, 2.5cm (1in) across, funnel-shaped, 3–4 per truss.

As we grew this, it was untidy, twiggy and rather tender and of little merit although it seemed quite distinct in habit and foliage.

From N. Taiwan, 2,000–3,000m (6,500–10,000ft), in thin conifer forest and *Miscanthus* (tall grass).   May

'*Obtusum*' (Lindl.) Planch. 1854 nom. illegit.

Introduced by Fortune in 1844 from China, this plant is called by the illegitimate name 'Obtusum' which was previously used for some form or hybrid of *ponticum* by Wats. in 1825. It is most probably a natural or garden hybrid anyway, possibly from *kaempferi* × *kiusianum*. Consequently it was a most unfortunate choice for the type-species for the sub-series Obtusum. For named clones, see listed hybrids.

oldhamii Maxim. 1870 +10°F H2–3 USDA 7b & 8a–7a L1–2 F2–3

Ht. 1.2–3m (4–10ft). Habit spreading. Young shoots clothed with red-brown hairs.
L evergreen, to 8.8cm (3$\frac{1}{2}$in) long, elliptic to oval, slightly rugose above, dull green and noticeably hairy.
F salmon-red to brick-red, spotted, 3.8–5cm (1$\frac{1}{2}$–2in) across, 1–4 per truss. Stamens 10.

This is the commonest red azalea on Taiwan and makes a fine plant, often with a long flowering season both in cultivation and in the wild. Alas, it is only suitable for the mildest of British gardens. Differs from *simsii* in its glandular nature and more abundant hairs.

Endemic to Taiwan and Liukiu from sea-level to 2,700m (9,000ft) on windswept grassy slopes and sandstone cliffs and around lakes and streams.   Mostly May (*yedoense* Maxim var.) *poukhanense* (Lévl.) Nakai (*hallaisanense* Lévl., *coreanum* Rehd.) −15°F H4 USDA 6b L1–2 F1–3

Ht to 1.8m (6ft), usually much less. Habit semi-upright to spreading or even prostrate (in the wild).
L deciduous to semi-deciduous, to 8.8cm (3½in) long, usually less, oblanceolate to ovate-lanceolate.
F rose to pale lilac, about 5cm (2in) across, broadly funnel-shaped, slightly fragrant, 2–4 per truss. Stamens 10.

One of the hardiest azalea species and much used in hybridizing. Often quite showy and attractive with large flowers. New introductions have come in recently. AM 1961. Not the easiest to root.

According to the ridiculous international rules, the name *yedoense* has preference over *poukhanense* even though the former is a double-flowered cultivar, also known as 'Yodogawa'. Although described many years before *poukhanense*, *yedoense* should only be considered as a clone and for horticultural purposes ignored.

Wild in C. and S. Korea and islands off coast on rocks and in scrub, stream sides to hilltops.   April–May

(*mucronatum* G. Don var.) *ripense* (Makino) Wils. 1914 +5°F H3–4 USDA 7a–6b L1–2 F2–3

Ht to 1.8m (6ft) or more. Habit spreading.
L semi-evergreen, 1.1–5.7cm (⅖–2¼in) long, lanceolate to oblanceolate, clothed with grey or grey-brown hairs.
F pale mauve to white, about 3.8cm (1½in) across, rarely to 11.4cm (4½in) in some cultivated forms, widely funnel-shaped, 1–3 per truss. Scented? Stamens 8–10.

This is thought to be the wild parent of *mucronatum*, another plant described from cultivated material. Probably close to *macrosepalum* which could be included in the parentage of *mucronatum*. The wild plant is worth growing in mild areas while *mucronatum* in its commonest clone (also known as 'Ledifolium') is hardier. AM 1933 flowers pink. Chamberlain retains the name *mucronatum* as the species as he regards it as a typical white variant of the wild *ripense*.

From S. Honshu, Shikoku and Kyushu, Japan.   April–May

rubropilosum Hayata 1911 (*caryophyllum* Hayata, *randaiense* Hayata) +5°F? H2–3(–4?) USDA 7b & 8a–7a(–6b) L1–2 F1–3?

Ht to 3m (10ft). Habit upright to spreading. Densely hairy.
L to 5cm (2in) long, convex, oblong-lanceolate to elliptic-lanceolate, crowded at ends of branchlets.
F pink to lavender, spotted mauve, 1.4–2.5cm (⅗–1in) across, funnel-shaped, 2–4 per truss. Stamens 7–10.

This species has been introduced several times recently and it remains to be seen whether any are hardy enough for anywhere but the warmest parts of Britain. Wilson thought highly of it and plants I have seen or grown indoors I considered pretty. Perhaps the most variable species on Taiwan.

Endemic to Taiwan at 2,000–3,200m (6,500–10,500ft) on sunny hillsides, common and widespread.   May–June

sataense Nakai 1949 H3? USDA 7a?

Habit dense mound.
F pink to purple

Recently given specific status by the Japanese (not by Ohwi) but changed to *kaempferi* var. *sataense* (Nakai) Chamb. by Chamberlain. This apparently includes plants that resemble *kaempferi* but have smooth and generally smaller leaves. It has flower colours outside the usual orange-red to salmon range of *kaempferi*. Not all that different from *kiusianum* × *kaempferi* intermediaries of Mt. Kirishima but may have evolved by isolation caused by lava flows. Seedlings I grew proved rather tender.

From S. Kyushu, from 500m (1,500ft) on open meadows.

scabrum G. Don 1834 (*sublanceolatum* Miq., *liukiuense* Komatsu, *sublateritium* Komatsu) +15°F H2 USDA 7b & 8a L1–2 F2–3

Ht 1–2m (3–6ft). Habit stiff to loosely branched.
L up to *10cm (4in) long*, oblanceolate to oval.
F rose-red to brilliant scarlet, spotted purple, about 6.3cm (2½in) across or larger, broadly funnel-shaped, 2–6 per truss. Calyx green, often large. Stamens 10.

This fine species is barely hardy anywhere in Britain with flower buds even liable to be frosted in mild areas. Probably used in the parentage of many indoor azaleas. AM 1911.

From Ryukyu Archipelago, S. Japan on scrubby hillsides and south-facing cliffs. May

serpyllifolium (A. Gray) Miq. 1865–6 −10°F H3–4 USDA 7a–6b L1–2 F1–2

Ht to 1.2m (4ft). Habit thin and twiggy, much branched.
L semi-deciduous to deciduous, 0.6–1.2cm (¼–½in) sometimes to 1.8cm (¾in) long, obovate to elliptic, bright green.
F pale to rose-pink or white, with or without spots, about 1.3cm (½in) across, 1–2 per truss. Calyx small. Stamens 5.
F pale to rose-pink or white, with or without spots, about 1.3cm (½in) across, 1–2 per truss. Calyx small. Stamens 5.

The combination of perhaps the smallest leaves in the genus and tiny, often solitary flowers make this a dainty, though hardly showy plant. Subject to autumn and spring frost damage due to soft growth. Better with warmer summers than ours in Scotland. The white form is attractive (*albiflorum*).

From C. and S. Japan on volcanic soil and moss-covered boulders. April–May

simsii Planch. 1854 (*indicum* var. *ignescens* Sweet, *indicum* Hemsl. part, *calleryi* Planch.) +15°F H2 USDA 7b & 8a L1–2 F2–3

Ht to 2.4m (8ft). Habit much-branched and sometimes straggly.
L semi-evergreen to evergreen, to 5cm (2in) long, elliptic to oblanceolate.
F various shades of red, spotted, 3.8–6.3cm (1½–2½in) across, broadly funnel-shaped, 2–6 per truss. Stamens usually 10, rarely 8–9.

The chief ancestor of our popular indoor azaleas wrongly known as 'Indian' or 'Indica' azaleas. Barely hardy anywhere in Britain. Does well in climates like S.E. USA, FCC 1933. I shall never forget seeing the fiery red flowers of this species appearing out of the swirling mist in Hong Kong's New Territory mountains.

From a wide area stretching from N.E. Upper Burma to Thailand, Taiwan and Hong Kong and much of C. and S. China, 300–2,400m (1,000–8,000ft) in forests, on dry slopes, scrub, boulders, cliffs and river banks.   May

sikaytaisanense Masanune 1939

I believe this has been introduced but I have not seen it. Rather small, narrow leaves and small flowers. Taiwan, one valley only.

sublanceolatum Miq.

Usually considered as a synonym of *scabrum* but still classed as a species by some Japanese. According to Wada, this has been crossed successfully with *amagianum*.

subsessile Rendle 1896 +15°F? H2? USDA 7b & 8a?

L evergreen, 1.5–3.8cm ($\frac{3}{5}$–1$\frac{1}{2}$in) long, elliptic to lanceolate, densely clothed with white hairs.
F lilac to violet-purple, about 2.5cm (1in) across, funnel-campanulate, 2–4 per truss. Stamens 6–10.

We grew this indoors for a number of years but did not attempt it outside. It appeared to be close to *rubropilosum*.

Endemic to Philippines, N. Luzon highlands in pine, oak and mossy forest.   May

taiwanalpinum Ohwi 1937 +5°F? H3? USDA 7a? L1–2 F1–2

Ht small shrub under 1m (3ft).
L evergreen? 1.6cm ($\frac{2}{3}$in) long, ovate to oblong-lanceolate, recurved, very hairy below.
F pink, spotted rose, 1.6cm ($\frac{2}{3}$in) across, widely funnel-shaped, 2–3 per truss. Stamens 10.

Newly introduced and often confused with *rubropilosum* of which it seems to be an alpine form. I am not sure if we have the correct plant or not.

Endemic to N. Taiwan, 2,700–3,000m (9,000–10,000ft), on rocks or in grass, often associated with *pachysanthum*.   May or later

tamurae (Makino) Masamune

Often considered synonymous with *eriocarpum* and as one of the parents of the Satsuki azaleas.
L broad. F red to purple. Stamens 8–10.

From Kyushu and Yakushima.

tosaense Makino 1892 0–+5°F H3–4 USDA 7a–6b L1 F1–2

Ht 1.5 to rarely 2.1m (5–7ft). Habit much-branched, often erect, shoots slender.
L evergreen to deciduous, 1.3–3.8cm ($\frac{1}{2}$–1$\frac{1}{2}$in) long, lanceolate to elliptic-lanceolate, crowded at ends of branchlets, sometimes purplish in autumn.
F pink to rose to lilac-purple, about 3.1cm (1$\frac{1}{4}$in) across, funnel-shaped, 1–6 per truss. Stamens 5–10.

Pretty in its better forms and admired by Wilson in Japan where it flowers very freely in the wild. Best in climates warmer than Scotland. 'Barbara' is a good pink-flowered clone. Chamberlain regards *komiyamae* as a synonym of *tosaense* as does *The Species of Rhododendron*.

Abundant in S. Japan, 0–300m (0–1,000ft) on exposed slopes or in forest.   April–May

tschonoskii Maxim. 1870 (*trinerve* Franch.) −15°F H4 USDA 6b L1–2 F1

Ht 30cm–1.5m (1–5ft), rarely to 2.4m (8ft). Habit erect to mat-forming. Shoots densely hairy.
L largely deciduous, 0.5–3.8cm ($\frac{1}{5}$–1$\frac{1}{2}$in) long, narrowly lanceolate to elliptic-lanceolate, turning orange-red to reddish-brown in autumn.
F white, about 0.8cm ($\frac{1}{3}$in) across, funnel-shaped, 3–6 per truss. Pedicels very short. Stamens 4–5.

Very hardy but the tiny flowers almost hidden in the leaves are of little significance. Only worth growing for its autumn colour.

From S. Japan north to Sakhalin and Korea, widespread and common, forming large colonies on mountain tops, on rocks and cliffs and in moist forest.   June

yakuinsulare (not described?) H2–3 USDA 7b & 8a–7a

Ht perhaps to 2m (6ft).
L up to 6.3cm (2$\frac{1}{2}$in) long, 2.5cm (1in) wide, elliptic to ovate-oblong.
F rosy-red, to 3.8cm (1$\frac{1}{2}$in) long, funnel-shaped, 1–3 per truss.

We used to grow a very narrow-leaved clone sent to us from Japan under this name which only occasionally produced its red flowers. It was rather tender. Apparently *yakuinsulare = kaempferi* in Yakushima although our plant did not resemble *kaempferi* as we know it at all. It looked nearer to *indicum*.

TSUSIOPSIS SECTION

tsusiophyllum Sugiomoto (*tanakae* (Maxim.) Ohwi, *Tsusiophyllum tanakae* Maxim.)

Ht to 45cm (1$\frac{1}{2}$ft). Habit spreading to prostrate.
L semi-evergreen to 1.8cm ($\frac{3}{4}$in) long, ovate to lanceolate to oblanceolate, appressed hairy on both sides.
F white, 9mm ($\frac{3}{8}$in) long, 6mm ($\frac{1}{4}$in) across, tubular, one or more per truss.

Formerly in the monotypic genus *Tsusiophyllum* as *T. tanakae*, Sleumer and the Philipsons have placed this in *Rhododendron* in its own section Tsusiopsis of the subgenus Tsutsusi. Its chief characters are its anthers opening by slits instead of pores and three-celled ovary (generally five-celled in the rest of the genus). It differs from the closely related *Menziesia* in the three-celled ovary and hairy exterior of corolla.

This is a dainty little creeper, very suitable for the peat garden, which forms wide mats covered with pretty little tubular white flowers. Rootability moderate but should be taken early (June–July). AM 1965.

Rare in the wild, confined to a few areas in Honshu.   June

SUBGENUS PENTANTHERA (AZALEA SERIES, SUBSERIES CANADENSE) (PLUS LUTEUM AND NIPPONICUM) RHODORA SECTION

canadense Torrey 1839 (*Rhodora canadensis* L., *rhodora* S. F. Gmelin) −25°F H5 USDA 5 & 6a L1–2 F1–2

Ht to 1m (3ft). Habit upright and bushy, often stoloniferous.
L deciduous, 1.9–5.7cm (¾–2¼in) long, 0.8–1.9cm (⅓–¾in) wide, elliptic to oblong, dull bluish-green above, autumn colour bluish-purple on rosy-purple-flowered forms, yellowish on white-flowered forms.
F pale to deep rosy-purple or white, about 1.9 (¾in) long, *corolla deeply divided*, 3–6 per truss.

A dainty little azalea which is easily grown on a moist site. Extremely hardy and worth planting more often, especially in cold areas. The darkest-coloured forms and the lovely pure white are the most desirable; the latter comes true from seed off isolated plants.

It has been crossed with *luteum* and 'glabrius' (*japonicum* [sic]) and further breeding experiments with this species seem a worthwhile project.

From N.E. North America from Labrador southwards to N.E. Pennsylvania and New Jersey, W. to C. New York. The most northerly of all azalea species, from river banks, moist woods and swamps.   April–May

5 *Hybrids*

Introduction to hybrid lists

These lists include all dwarf (below 1.5m [5ft] on average) hybrids that are well established in commerce plus a selection of the most promising new hybrids. They are divided into two major sections, Elepidote (within the subgenus Hymenanthes) and Lepidote (within the subgenus Rhododendron). I have included a higher proportion of lepidote hybrids reaching 1.5m (5ft) or a little over as these are more suitable for the small garden and are also more easily kept small by pruning. These are further divided into colours. Some colours are hard to place in any group so are put into the nearest colour range.

Key to abbreviations and descriptions in order used

1–5/ = flower ratings (1 = poorest, 5 = best)
/1–5 = foliage + habit ratings (1 = poorest, 5 = best)
0°F = nought degrees fahrenheit (zero) and so on, − indicates degrees below zero. These figures indicate the average minimum a given plant can tolerate in mid-winter. Unseasonable frosts are not taken into account.

Flowering seasons

VE = very early	January–February on average
E = early	
EM = early mid-season	
M = mid-season	
ML = medium-late	
L = late	
VL = very late	July–August on average

Height (average ultimate)
low = 1–1.5m (3–5ft)
semi-dwarf = 50cm–1m (1½–3ft)
dwarf = below 50cm (1½ft)
F = flower(s)
person's name = hybridizer and/or introducer. I have attempted to give credit to the hybridizer.
date = date hybridized and/or introduced

Country raised

Can = Canada
Ger = West Germany
GB = Great Britain
Ho = Holland
NZ = New Zealand
USA = United States of America

A brief description follows where possible
L = leaves
Abbreviations of awards—see Introduction

Temperature conversion table
degrees

Fahrenheit	Centigrade
−10	−23
−5	−21
0	−18
5	−15
10	−12
15	−9
20	−7
25	−4
30	−1
32	0

Elepidote hybrids (subgenus Hymenanthes)

Pink Hybrids Elepidote

Many good pinks but avoid early-growing *williamsianum* crosses in bad spring frost areas.

April Glow (*williamsianum* × 'Wilgens Ruby') 4/4, −10°F, EM, low, F rosy-pink, Wilgen, Ho, compact, coppery young growth, gold medal and award of merit Holland, HC 1975.

Arthur J. Ivens (*williamsianum* × *fortunei* ssp. *discolor* (*houlstonii*) 3/3, −10°F, M, low, F pale pink, Hillier 1944, GB, compact, good in sun but slow to bud, AM 1944.

August Lamken (*williamsianum* × Dr. V. H. Rutgers) M, F dark rose, Hobbie, Ger, compact, exceptionally hardy flowers.

Bashful (*yakushimanun* × ?) 3/2 0°F? ML, low, F pale pink, brown blotch, Waterer, GB, no indumentum.

Bowbells ('Corona' × *williamsianum*), 3/4, −5°F, M, low, F pink, Rothschild 1934, GB, bushy, one of the most popular pink hybrids with attractive coppery young growth and red buds, AM 1935.

Brickdust (*williamsianum* × 'Dido') 3/4 −5°F M, low, F dusty orange-rose, R. Henny 1959, USA, compact, roundish L, bronzy young growth and plentiful F.

Bruce Brechtbill (sport of 'Unique') 3/5, −5°F, M, low, F pink, yellow-ish throat, Brechtbill 1974, USA, identical to 'Unique' apart from the pink instead of pale yellow-tinged peach F, compact.

Carlene ('Lems Goal' × *williamsianum*) 3/3 5°F, M, low, F cream-flushed glowing pink, Lem, USA, compact, very prone to bark-split in Scotland but striking F.

Concorde low, F carmine-pink, brown blotch, gold medal Flora Nova.

Doc (*yakushimanum* × 'Corona') 3/3, 0°F, or lower, low, F pink, Waterer, GB, fairly compact, little indumentum.

Dormouse ('Dawn's Delight' × *williamsianum*) 3/4, 0°F, low, F pale pink-flushed deeper pink, Rothschild GB, compact, very good young foliage, late growth.

Elizabeth Lockhart (sport of 'Hummingbird') 2/4, 0°F, EM-M, low, F deep rose-pink, Lockhart 1972 GB, compact, the foliage always creates great admiration, at first deep glossy red, then reddish-chocolate-brown; unfortunately it is liable to revert partially to green, HC 1972 for foliage.

Gartendirektor Glocker ('Doncaster' × *williamsianum*) 3/4 −10°F, M, low, F deep pink, Hobbie 1952, Ger, one of the hardiest *williamsianum* hybrids with good, shiny, curved foliage, compact.

Hummingbird (*haematodes* × *williamsianum*) 2/3, 0°F, EM-M, low, F rose-pink to near red, Williams, Rothschild, Aberconway, compact, slow to start flowering and subject to bark-split, different forms vary considerably in foliage, flowers and hardiness.

Hydon Dawn (*yakushimanum* × 'Springbok') 4/4, 0°F, M-ML, low, F pale pink, frilled, George 1969, GB, free-flowering, downy young L, one of the best 'yak' hybrids, AM 1977.

Jacksonii (*caucasicum* × 'Nobleanum') 3/2, 0°F, EM, semi-dwarf, F pink with deeper-lines, Herbert 1835 GB, spreading habit, free-flowering but rather poor foliage.

Jackwill ('Jacksonii' × *williamsianum*) low, F cherry-red, Hobbie 1967 Ger, buds red, young L bronze.

Jock (*griersonianum* × *williamsianum*) 2/4, −5°F, EM, low, F dark pink, Stirling Maxwell 1939 GB, compact, best in full sun.

Karen ('Britannia' × *williamsianum*) 4/4, −15°F, EM, low, F pink, ruffled in full truss, Boskoop Research Station before 1966, Ho, compact, earlier than 'Linda' but just as good and reliable, gold medal Boskoop, award of merit Boskoop 1968.

Kimberly (*williamsianum* × *fortunei*) 3/4, −10°F, EM, low, F pastel-pink, Greer 1964 USA, compact, very free-flowering, slightly fragrant but early into growth, PA 1963.

Kimbeth ('Kimberly' × 'Elizabeth') 3/4, −10°F, EM, low, F clear pink, Greer 1979 USA, very free-flowering with attractive flower buds.

Kristin (*yakushimanum* × 'Bowbells') 0°F, M, low, F pale pink, Bovee 1973 USA, compact, dark foliage, very free-flowering.

Linda ('Britannia' × *williamsianum*) 4/4, −15°F, M, low, F deep rose, Boskoop Research Station 1953, Ho, compact, so far we have found this the best newer *williamsianum* hybrid, attractive, hardy and reliable, award of merit Boskoop.

Lissabon ('Nova Zembla'? × *williamsianum*) 0°F, low, F carmine-rose, v. von Martin 1964, L deep green, survived 1981–2 winter well.

Lori Eichelser (*forrestii* Repens × 'Bowbells') 4/4, 0°F, EM, semi-dwarf, F cherry-pink, Brandt USA, very compact, Greer speaks very highly of this tight grower with comparatively large F.

Lovely William (*neriiflorum* Euchaites × *williamsianum*) F deep rose, Horlick 1950 GB

Marion Street (*yakushimanum* × 'Stanley Davis') F bright pink fading once open, Street GB, good foliage, brown indumentum, F colour near 'Pink Pearl', can be good but liable to chlorosis, AM 1978.

Moerheim's Pink ('Genovera' × *williamsianum*) 4/3, 0°F or lower, M, low, F deep pink, Hobbie 1965 Ger, large F, hardy and reliable, AM 1972.

Molly Ann ('Elizabeth' × garden hybrid) 4/4, −12°F, EM, low, F rose, Freimann 1974 USA, compact, F of heavy substance in upright truss, round L, free-flowering from a young age.

Morgenrot (*yakushimanum* ×) M, low, F rose-red, Hachmann 1978 Ger, L dark green, brown indumentum, habit wider than high.

Noyo Brave ('Noyo Chief' × *yakushimanum* 'Koichiro Wada') 0°F, low, F bright pink, red blotch, C. Smith 1978 USA, compact, very fine foliage.

Oudijk's Sensation ('Essex Scarlet' × *williamsianum*) 0°F or lower, EM, low, F rose, paler throat, Hobbie 1958 Ger, named Le Feber 1965, not the best-coloured *williamsianum* hybrid.

Pink Bountiful (*williamsianum* × 'Linswegeanum') EM, low, F pink, paler throat, Hobbie 1974 Ger, AM 1975.

Pink Pebble (*callimorphum* × *williamsianum*) 4/3, 0°F, EM, low, F pale pink, Harrison 1954 GB, very pretty and free-flowering with pleasing foliage.

Polaris (*yakushimanum* ×) M, low, F rose, yellow-orange centre, Hachmann 1978 Ger.

Psyche (*fortunei* 'Sir Charles Butler' × *williamsianum*) 0°F or lower, EM, low, F pink, Hobbie 1950 Ger, prone to bark-split and slow to bloom.

Renoir ('Pauline' × *yakushimanum*) 3/3, 0°F or lower M, low, F pale pink deep flair, RHS 1961 GB, compact and free-flowering, AM 1961.

Reve Rose ('Bowbells' × *forrestii* Repens) 3/3, 0°F, EM, semi-dwarf, F rose, Brandt USA, compact, more than one clone.

Royal Pink ('Homer' × *williamsianum*) 4/4, −15°F, M, low, F clear pink, Hobbie Ger named by Le Feber 1965, compact, good foliage, free-flowering with a ball-shaped truss, silver and gold medal winner.

Seven Stars (*yakushimanum* × 'Loderi Sir Joseph Hooker') too large.

Silberwolke (*yakushimanum* ×) M, lower, F red-purple, spotted yellow-green, Hachmann 1983 Ger, compact, spreading.

Sneezy (*yakushimanum* × 'Doncaster') 3/3, 0°F or lower, M-ML, low, F red buds, opening rose-pink rose crimson blotch, fades, Waterers GB, compact rounded, no indumentum.

Surrey Heath (*facetum eriogynum* × 'Fabia') × (*yakushimanum* × 'Britannia'), M–ML, 0°F or lower, low, F salmon-rose, pale yellow-cream centre, Waterers GB, no indumentum, vibrant-coloured F.

Temple Belle (*orbiculare* × *williamsianum*) 3/4, −5°F, EM, low, F soft pink, RBG Kew 1916 GB, usually compact, mid-way between parents.

Tibet (*williamsianum* ×) 2/3, 0°F or lower, M, low, F pale pink fading to white, Ho.

Treasure (*forrestii* Repens × *williamsianum*) 2/3, −5°F, EM, dwarf, F rose, Crosfield 1937 GB, prostrate, good ground cover but can be shy-flowering.

Vintage Rose (*yakushimanum* × [Jaliso Eclipse × Fusilier]) 4/4, 0°F or lower, ML, F clear rose-pink, Waterer GB, compact, very good L, F and indumentum, promising.

Whisperingrose (*williamsianum* × 'Elizabeth') 4/4, 0°F, EM, low, F rose fading to pink, Greer 1982 USA, compact, a good new introduction, easily grown, buds young with very large F, dark L.

Willbrit ('Britannia' × *williamsianum*) 0°F, M–ML, low, F deep pink, Hobbie Ger, (Le Feber Ho 1960), compact, light foliage.

Yaku Princess ('King Tut' × *yakushimanum* 'Koichiro Wada'), −10°F, M, low, F apple-blossom pink, green spots-fading, Shammarello 1977 USA, good habit and foliage.

Yellow Hybrids Elepidote

Much room for improvement in this section.

Buttermint ('Unique' × ['Fabia' × *dichroanthum* ssp. *apodectum*]) 3/4, −5°F, M, low, F white tinged yellow, red spots, Mauritsen 1979 USA, compact, dense foliage, lax truss.

Canary (*campylocarpum* × *caucasicum*) 3/3, −10°F, EM, low, Koster 1920 Ho, fairly compact, a good free-flowering yellow but occasionally the buds do not open properly and the L are yellowish.

Cunninghams Sulphur (*caucasicum* ×) 3/2, 0°F, EM, low, F primrose-yellow, Cunningham 19th century GB, fairly compact, very slow-growing and not easy to please, free-flowering.

Flava (*yakushimanum* × *wardii* L&S) M–ML, low, F light yellow, Hobbie Ger, compact.

Golden Witt (*dichroanthum* ssp. *scyphocalyx* × ['Moonstone × 'Adrastia']), 4/4, 0°F, M, low, F primrose-yellow, red blotch, Witt & Michaud 1977 USA, a promising new yellow.

Moonstone (*campylocarpum* × *williamsianum*), 4/4, −5°F, EM, low, F creamy-yellow, to ivory or pink, J. C. Williams 1933 GB, compact, very popular, different clones.

Serendipity (*yakushimanum* × *aureum*) Potter 1972 USA.

Tidbit (*dichroanthum* × *wardii*) 3/3, 5°F, M, low, red buds opening to straw yellow F, R. Henny 1958 USA, compact, nice dark shining L, free-flowering.

Orange Hybrids Elepidote

Few good plants available in this colour.

Fabia Tangerine (*dichroanthum* ssp. *scyphocalyx* × *griersonianum*) 4/3, 10°F, M, low, F vermilion-orange, Aberconway 1940 GB, compact, lower than 'Fabia' itself, AM 1940.

Golden Gate (*dichroanthum* ssp. *scyphocalyx* × ?) 3/4, −5°F, M, low, orange-edged magenta, USA, compact, L shiny, easy.

Hansel (*bureavii* × 'Fabia') 3/4, −5°F, M, low, F salmon-orange, Lem USA, buff indumentum, loose truss.

Medusa (*dichroanthum* ssp. *scyphocalyx* × *griersonianum*) 3/3, 5°F, M, low, F buff orange & vermilion, Aberconway 1928 GB, upright habit, a good plant.

Sweet Sue (*eriogynum* × 'Fabia' × (*yakushimanum* × 'Fabia Tangerine')) 3/3?, 0°F or lower, ML, low, F light-orange-red, Waterer GB, compact, an unusual colour.

Whitney Orange (*dichroanthum* × ?) 4/2, 0°F, ML, low, F orange, Whitney 1972 USA, twisted L, spreading, poor habit but good F.

Red Hybrids Elepidote

Many good reds now obtainable.

Arthur Osborne (*didymum* × *griersonianum*) 3/3, 5°F, VL, low, F black-red, RBG Kew 1929 GB, dark leaves, AM 1933.

Baden Baden ('Essex Scarlet' × *forrestii* Repens) 4/3, −15°F, M, semi-dwarf, F dark red, Hobbie 1956 Ger, compact with slightly twisted dark green L, one of the best Hobbie reds, HC 1972.

Better Half ('Elizabeth' × ?) 3–4/4, 0°F, EM, low, F red, Whitney (Sather) USA, neat, compact and free-flowering.

Blitz (*haematodes* × 'G.A. Sims') 3/4, 5°F, M, low, F dark red, Clark 1945 USA, compact, heat-tolerant and not very hardy.

Blood Ruby (*forrestii* Repens × 'Mandalay') 3/3, 0°F, M, dwarf, F rich red, Brandt 1954 USA, small L, spreading habit.

Carmen (*sanguineum* ssp. *didymum* × *forrestii* Repens) 3/3, −5°F, M, dwarf, F deep red, Rothschild 1935 GB, compact, neat with waxy F but subject to bark-split, popular.

Cary Ann ('Corona' × 'Vulcan') 3/4, −5°F, M, low, F coral red, Wright Sr & Jr 1962 USA, upright but spreading top, sun-tolerant, widely grown USA.

Charmaine ('Charm' × 'May Day') 3/3, 5°F, EM, dwarf, F blood red, Aberconway 1936 GB, attractive with a thick indumentum but subject to bark-split, AM 1946.

Creeping Jenny (*griersonianum* × *forrestii* Repens) 3/4, 5°F, EM, semi-dwarf, F red, Aberconway 1939 GB, the creeping form of 'Elizabeth' often with prostrate shoots, good ground cover in the open, sometimes called 'Jenny'.

Debbie ('May Day' × 'Carmen') 3/4, 0°F, EM, semi-dwarf, F bright blood-red, Henny & Wennekamp 1963 USA, compact, dark L and free-flowering.

Doncaster (*arboreum* ×) 2/3, −5°F, M–ML, low, F crimson-scarlet, Waterer GB, compact, old but still good and reliable.

Dopey (*facetum* [*eriogynum*] hybrid × 'Fabia') × (*yakushimanum* × 'Fabia Tangerine') 4/4, 0°F, or lower M, low, F rich-red, Waterers GB, compact, large good L, F in well shaped trusses.

Elisabeth Hobbie ('Essex Scarlet' × *forrestii* Repens) 4/4, −5°F, EM–M, low, F glowing red, Hobbie 1945 Ger, compact, very reliable but does not flower as freely when young as 'Baden Baden' or 'Scarlet Wonder', HC 1974. All the following are of the same parentage and too many have been named: 'Baden Baden', 'Elisabeth Hobbie' and 'Scarlet Wonder' fulfil the requirements of most people and are amongst the best. Others are: 'Aksel Olsen', 'Bad Eilsen' HC 1969, 'Bengal', 'Frühlings Zauber', 'Mannheim'. Least popular are 'Antje', 'Spring Dream'.

Elizabeth (*griersonianum* × *forrestii* Repens) 4/4, 0°F, EM–M, low, F red, Aberconway 1939 GB, one of the most popular reds and exceptionally free-flowering, subject to bark-split but usually recovers, FCC 1943 but there are other clones.

Elizabeth Red Foliage (? 'Elizabeth' sport) 4/4, 0°F, EM–M, low, F as 'Elizabeth', Ostbo USA, red new growth lasting for much of the season.

Ems (*forrestii* Repens × 'Purple Splendour') 3/3, −5°F, M, low, F glowing crimson, Hobbie 1951 Ger, compact, free-flowering, a striking colour but not everyone's choice.

Ethel ('F.C. Puddle' × *forrestii* Repens) 3/3, 5°F, EM–M, low, F light crimson scarlet, Aberconway GB, bushy, good F but we do not find it hardy here, FCC 1940, more than one clone.

Firedance (RM 11) (? *forrestii* Repens, *williamsianum* & others) 4/3, −5°F, M, low, F scarlet-red, Whitney USA, round L.

Fireman Jeff ('Jean Marie de Montague' × 'Grosclaude') 4/4, 0°F, M, low, F bright red with large red calyx, Brandt C. 1970 USA, bushy, free-flowering and promising.

Flora's Boy (*forrestii* Repens × 'Jean Marie de Montague') 4/4, 5°F, EM–M, semi-dwarf, F bright waxy red, Markeeta USA, upright habit, glossy L, rather early into growth, large F held in upright trusses.

Grafin Kirchbach (*forrestii* Repens ×) M, low, F red, V. von Martin.

Indiana (*dichroanthum* ssp. *scyphocalyx* × *kyawi*) 3/4, 5°F, L, low, F orange-red, Rothschild GB, good shining dark L, F in loose trusses.

Linswege (*forrestii* Repens × 'Britannia') F dark red, Hobbie 1974 Ger, a selection of 'Linswegianum' grex Boskoop 1974, a good rich colour.

Little Bert (*neriiflorum* Euchaites × *forrestii* Repens) 3/3, 5°F, EM, semi-dwarf, F scarlet, Scrase-Dickens 1939 GB, AM 1939.

Little Gem ('Carmen' × *elliottii* KW 7725) 4/4, 5°F, M, semi-dwarf, F blood-red, Whitney 1957 USA, dark glossy L and fine F, PA 1962.

Little Joe (*forrestii* Repens × 'May Day') 3/3, 5°F, dwarf, F bright red, Brandt USA, slow-growing and creeping.

Martha Robbins (*forrestii* Repens × *sperabile*) 4/3?, 0°F, EM, semi-dwarf, F bright red, Brandt 1971 USA, compact, slightly more vigorous than *forrestii*, free-flowering and showy.

May Day (*haematodes* × *griersonianum*) 4/3, 5°F, M, low, F scarlet-red, A.M. Williams, Aberconway, Rothschild GB, exceptionally free-flowering and easy but not for cold or exposed gardens, tawny indumentum, AM (Williams) 1932.

Oporto (*thomsonii* × *sanguineum*) 3/3, 0°F, EM-M, low, F deep crimson, Collingwood Ingram GB, fine waxy bells freely produced at quite a young age, AM 1967.

Peek-A-Boo (['Carmen' × 'Moonstone'] × *elliottii*) 3/3, −5°F, EM, semi-dwarf, F red, Whitney USA, bushy, not free-flowering or of good habit with us.

Potlatch ('Thor' ×) 4/4?, 5°F, M, low, F bright scarlet-red, Clark USA, compact, thick indumentum and large F.

Red Carpet (*forrestii* Repens ×) EM–M, F red, Hobbie Ger, good foliage, AMT 1983.

Red Velvet ('Fusilier' × *williamsianum*) 3/3, 0°F, M, low, F coral-red, Larson USA, compact, good foliage.

Red Wax (*haematodes* × 'May Day') 3/4, 5°F, M, semi-dwarf, F orient red, R. Henny USA, compact, dark foliage, heavy indumentum, PA 1958.

Robert Louis Stevenson ('May Day' × 'Jester') 4/4, 0°F, L, semi-dwarf, F bright blood-red, Seabrook 1967 USA, glossy L and very late F.

Rödhätte (*williamsianum* × *didymum*) M, low, F blood red, Hobbie Ger, spreading habit.

Royal Windsor ('Jutland' × 'Royal Blood') 0°F, M, F rich crimson, Crown Estate Commissioners GB, AM 1975.

Ruby Heart (['Carmen' × 'Elizabeth'] × *elliottii*) 4/4, 5°F, M, low, F dark red, Whitney 1974 USA, rather upright but well clothed with fine dark L, excellent F but not for the coldest of gardens. Free-flowering.

Satin ('Dr. Rutjers' × *forrestii* Repens) EM, low, F pink, Hobbie Ger, habit wider than high.

Scarlet Wonder ('Essex Scarlet' × *forrestii* Repens) 4/4, −15°F, EM–M, semi-dwarf, F bright red, Hobbie Ger, one of the best of all dwarfish reds with good foliage, habit and F, HC 1970.

Sheila Ann (*sanguineum* × ?) 3/3, 5°F, low, F blackish-crimson, Caperci USA, one of the darkest reds of all.

Sparkler 4/4, ML, low, F rich bright red, does not fade, Waterer GB, F large, like an improved 'Elizabeth', promising.

Stephanie (*forrestii* Repens × ?) 3/3, 0°F, M, low, F light red, Whitney USA, compact, small L.

Thor (*haematodes* × 'Felis') 4/4, 5°F, M, low, F bright scarlet-red, Brandt USA, compact, thick indumentum, calyx large, a possible successor to 'May Day'.

Titian Beauty (*eriogynum* × 'Fabia Tangerine' × [*yakushimanum* × 'Fabia Tangerine']) 3/3 or higher, 0°F or lower, low, F geranium-lake, Waterer GB, erect but compact, a neat plant.

Venetian Chimes (*eriogynum* × 'Fabia' × [*yakushimanum* × 'Fabia Tangerine']) 4/3, 0°F or lower, ML, low, F scarlet, Waterer GB, compact, a promising red.

Whitney Dwarf Red (unknown) 4/4?, 0°F, EM, low, F red, Whitney USA, upright habit, shiny L and red buds.

Pastel Hybrids Elepidote and mixed or changing colours

The colours are becoming more and more popular but avoid muddy tones.

Chelsea Seventy 3/3?, 0°F or lower, ML, low, F orange-pink, pale inside, Waterer GB, F fades, L poor.

Coral Velvet (*yakushimanum* ×) 3/3, −10°F, M, dwarf, F coral to ivory, Japan (Swanson), compact, spreading, thick indumentum on stems and L, long-lasting F open over several weeks.

Cowslip (*williamsianum* × *wardii*) 2–3/3, 0°F, EM, low, F cream-flushed pink, Aberconway 1937 GB, fairly compact, quite popular in GB but largely superseded, AM 1937.

Dusty Miller (*yakushimanum* × un-named ×) 2/3, M, dwarf, F pale shrimp-pink, flushed cream fading, Waterers GB, slow-growing, some indumentum.

Fred Hamilton ([*neriiflorum* × *griersonianum*] × *dichroanthum*) 3/3, −5°F, EM, low, F yellow, lined pink, Van Veen 1972 USA, compact, dense foliage, wide habit.

Goldbug (*wardii* × 'Fabia') 2/3, 5°F, M, low, F red turning to yellowish, spotted, R. Henny USA, F of rather a muddy colour though unusual.

Golden Torch (*yakushimanum* × 'Fabia Tangerine' × 'Bambi' × 'Grosclaude' × *griersonianum*) 3/3?, 0°F or lower, ML, low, F yellow-pink, Waterer GB, compact.

Grumpy (*yakushimanum* × unknown hybrid) 3/3? 0°F or lower, EM, low, F peach fading to cream, Waterers GB, compact, some indumentum.

Jingle Bells ('Lem's Goal' × 'Fabia') 4/4, −5°F, M, low, F red changing to yellow, Lem 1974 USA, compact, truss loose.

Manda Sue ('Vulcan' × 'Elspeth') 4/3, 0°F, M, low, F shell-pink, red picotte edge, yellow throat, Baker USA, compact, dark L.

Molly Miller (*yakushimanum* × 'Fabia Tangerine') 2/3, 0°F?, ML, F creamy-pink-flushed apricot long pedicels, Waterers GB, good indumentum.

Ostbo's Low Yellow (unknown), 4/4, 0°F, M, F cream, apricot and yellow combined, Ostbo 1960 USA, buds young, PA 1960.

Percy Wiseman (*yakushimanum* × 'Fabia Tangerine') 4/4, 0°F or lower, ML, low, F pink and cream turning creamy-white, Waters GB, good F, no indumentum, HC 1977.

Riplet (*forrestii* Repens × 'Letty Edwards') 4/4, 0°F, E–EM, low, F crimson fading to pale salmon, Lem USA, compact, very showy with strikingly large F freely produced, nice red buds, PA 1961, more than one clone.

Rose Point ('Dido' × *williamsianum*) 3/4, 0°F, EM, low, F pastel-pink touched salmon-orange, Lem introduced Elliott 1980 USA, round L, excellent foliage and indumentum.

Shrimp Girl (*yakushimanum* × 'Fabia Tangerine') 2/3, 0°F or lower, M, low, F soft salmon-pink, paling to edge of corolla, Waterers 1971 GB, slow-growing.

Unique (*campylocarpum* ×) 3/5, −5°F, EM, low, F pink buds opening to yellowish-peach, Slocock 1934 GB, compact, very fine stiff foliage, popular, FCC 1935.

White Hybrids Elepidote

There are comparatively few good dwarfish white hybrids of this category to date.

Gartendirektor Rieger (*williamsianum* ×), M, low, F cream, dark blotch, Hobbie Ger.

Hydon Ball (*yakushimanum* × 'Springbok') 2/2, 0°F or lower, ML, low, F pale pink buds opening white, brown spots, George GB, compact, similar to *yakushimanum* and not as good, AM 1977.

Morning Cloud (*yakushimanum* × 'Springbok') 0°F or lower, ML, low, F white, flushed pale pink, George 1971 GB, very compact, dark L with creamy-buff indumentum, AM 1971.

Nestucca (*fortunei* × *yakushimanum*) 4/4, −10°F, M, low, F white, slightly brown throat, Hanger introd. C. Smith 1960 USA, PA 1950.

Rothenburg ('Diane' × *williamsianum*) EM, F pure white, Bruns (V. von Martin) 1971 Ger, dark L and large F, promising but F and L easily frosted.

Lavender Hybrids Elepidote

Some good *yakushimanum* hybrids of this shade are now becoming available.

Caroline Allbrook (*yakushimanum* × 'Purple Splendour') 0°F or lower, ML, low, F lavender, George 1975 GB, free-flowering but perhaps too like *ponticum* in appearance, AM 1977.

Daphnoides ('Imbricatum') (*ponticum* or *catawbiense* × ?) 2/4, −15°F, ML, low, F purple, possibly raised by Methven 1868 GB but this is given as *virgatum* ×, dark shiny rolled L, tight growth, very unusual.

Hoppy (*yakushimanum* × ?) 3/2, 0°F or lower, M, low, F white-tinged lilac, Waterers GB, AM 1977, little indumentum, rather ponticum-like but effective as a large specimen.

Sleepy (*yakushimanum* × 'Doncaster' selfed) M, low, F pale mauve, spotted brown, Waterers GB, little indumentum.

Lepidote hybrids (subgenus Rhododendron)

Blue Hybrids Lepidote

More and more of these are being raised leading to too many. Only the best should be propagated and the rest, especially those with poor foliage, allowed to drop out of commerce.

Augfast (*augustinii* × *fastigiatum*) 3/3, 0°F, EM, low, F shades of violet blue, Magor 1921, GB, different clones, largely superseded by newer hybrids, good in sun.

Azurika (*impeditum* ×) EM, semi-dwarf, F deep blue, Hachmann 1979 Ger, fairly compact, shiny L.

Azurwolke (*russatum* ×) 4/3, 0°F or lower, EM, low, F clear deep blue, Hachmann 1979 Ger, open habit but F in large trusses.

Blue Bird (*intricatum* × *augustinii*) 4/3, 0°F, EM, low, F blue or violet mauve, Aberconway 1930 GB, different clones, foliage often poor and largely superseded, AM 1943.

Blue Diamond ('Intrifast' × *augustinii*) 5/3, 0°F, EM, low, F bright to violet-blue, Crosfield GB, best-known blue but foliage inclined to chlorosis, different clones, FCC 1939.

Blue Star (*impeditum* × 'St Tudy') 0°F?, EM–M, semi-dwarf, F blue, George GB, compact, very promising new blue.

Blue Tit (*impeditum* × *augustinii*) 3/2, 0°F, EM, low, F grey-blue, Williams 1933 GB, compact, foliage often poor, largely superseded.

Blue Wonder (*russatum* × *augustinii*), M, semi-dwarf, F dark blue, Hobbie Ger.

Bluette (*augustinii* × *impeditum*) 3/4, 0°F, EM, low, F hyacinth-blue, Lancaster 1958 USA, dense habit, very free-flowering.

Gletschernacht (*russatum* × 'Blue Diamond') EM–M, semi-dwarf, F blue, Hachmann 1976 Ger.

Gristede (?), 3/4, 0°F or lower, EM–M, low, F medium blue, Bruns Ger, foliage better than 'Blue Diamond' but F slightly inferior.

Ilam Violet (*augustinii* 'Electra' × *russatum*) 0°F, M, low, F deep violet, Stead 1947 NZ, taller and deeper-coloured than 'Blue Diamond' AMT 1983.

Intrifast (*intricatum* × *fastigiatum*) 4/4, 0°F or lower, EM, dwarf, F violet blue, Lowinsky GB, similar to *fastigiatum* but still a first-rate plant, fine glaucous foliage, free-flowering and easy.

Little Imp (*impeditum* ×) 0°F EM, low, F blue-purple, Barber USA, compact, glaucous foliage.

Moerheim (*impeditum* × ?) 0°F or lower, EM, semi-dwarf, F lilac-blue, Moerheim 1969 Ho, sometimes known as *impeditum* 'Moerheim' or 'Moerheim's Blue', compact, floriferous, L maroon in winter, well known in trade in Europe.

Mother Greer (*hippophaeoides* × Triflora SS) 3/4, −10°F, M, semi-dwarf, F purplish-blue, Greer 1982 USA, compact, very floriferous.

Oceanlake ('Blue Diamond' × 'Sapphire') 3/3, −5°F, EM, semi-dwarf, F deep violet-blue, Wright 1966 USA, good in sun.

Oudijk's Favourite (*augustinii* ×) 0°F or lower, EM–M, low, F dark blue, Ho.

Sacko (*russatum* × 'Moerheim') 4/4?, 0°F or lower, M, semi-dwarf, F violet blue, van Vliet 1977 Ho, compact, L shiny.

St Breward (*augustinii* × *impeditum*) 4/3, 0°F, EM, low, F violet-blue, Magor GB, a spectacular taller blue but not the hardiest, drooping L, FCC 1962.

St Merryn (*impeditum* × 'St Tudy') 4/4, 0°F, EM, semi-dwarf, F deep blue, Harrison 1971 GB, very compact, one of the best low blues, AM 1970, AMT 1983.

St Minver (*russatum* × 'St Breward') 0°F, EM, low, F violet-blue, Harrison 1973, compact.

St Tudy (*augustinii* × *impeditum*) 4/3, 0°F, EM, low, F lobelia-blue, Magor 1960 GB, upright habit, similar to St Breward, FCC 1973.

Sapphire ('Blue Tit' × *impeditum*) 3/3, −5°F, EM, semi-dwarf, F light to medium blue, Knaphill GB, different clones, a good low blue, the paler is commoner in the trade, compact, AM 1967.

Songbird (*russatum* × 'Blue Tit') 4/4, −5°F or hardier, EM, low, F clear violet-blue, Horlick 1954, one of the best deep-coloured blues, sometimes blooms in autumn, AM 1957.

Yellow Hybrids Lepidote

A great many of these are now coming onto the market and like the 'blues' they will need sorting out, partly depending on climatic conditions.

Bo-peep (*lutescens* × *moupinense*) 3/3, 5°F, E, low, F pale yellow, Rothschild 1934 GB, upright habit, lovely with pink and white earlies, AM 1937.

Chiff Chaff (*hanceanum* 'Nanum' × *fletcherianum*) 3/4, 0°F, EM–M, semi-dwarf, F yellow, Cox 1976 GB, compact with good dark foliage and plentiful F, AM 1976.

Chikor (*rupicola* var. *chryseum* × *ludlowii*) 4/3, 0°F, EM–M, dwarf, F yellow, Cox 1962 GB, compact, my first real hybridizing success and now perhaps the most popular dwarf yellow, FCC 1968.

Chink (*trichocladum* × *keiskei*) 3/3, 0°F, E–EM, low, F pale yellow, Crown Estate Commissioners GB, upright habit, semi-deciduous with attractive bronzy young growth, more than one clone, AM 1961.

Chrysomanicum (*chrysodoron* × *burmanicum*) 15°F?, E, low, F primrose-yellow, Aberconway 1947 GB, AM 1947.

Cream Crest (*rupicola* var. *chryseum* × 'Cilpinense') 3/3, 0°F, EM, low, F creamy-yellow, Wright 1963 USA, upright habit, popular in USA but like 'Cilpinense' F very frost prone in Scotland.

Curlew (*ludlowii* × *fletcherianum*) 5/4, −5°F, EM-M, semi-dwarf, F yellow lightly spotted, Cox 1969 GB, compact, possibly my best and perhaps the best dwarf yellow yet raised, large F cover the next shiny L, do not over fertilize, FCC 1969, AMT 1981.

Eldorado (*valentinianum* × *johnstoneanum*) 4/3, 15°F, EM, low, F yellow, Rothschild 1937 GB, bushy, bud tender.

Euan Cox (*hanceanum* 'Nanum' × *ludlowii*) 4/3, 0°F, M, dwarf, F yellow, Cox 1981 GB, very compact, one of the latest of our dwarf yellows, neat and very free-flowering, AMT 1981.

Golden Bee (*keiskei* 'Yaku Fairy' × *mekongense* var, *melinanthum* [*semilunatum*]) M?, dwarf?, F deep yellow, Berg 1982 USA, L inclined to be semi-deciduous, one of the deepest yellows yet raised, CA 1983, promising.

Lemon Mist (*xanthostephanum* × *leucaspis*) 3/3, 15°F, E, low, F bright greenish-yellow, Scott 1968 USA, narrow cinnamon-green L, AE 1969.

Mary Fleming (*racemosum* × *keiskei*) 3/3, −15°F, EM–M, low, F bisque-yellow, flushed pink, Nearing 1972, bushy, attractive foliage bronzy in winter, F rather small, AE 1973.

Merganser (*campylogynum* white × *luteiflorum*) 4/3, 0°F, M, semi-dwarf, F yellow, Cox 1980 GB, compact, neat yellow bells and dark L, HC 1981.

Patty Bee (*keiskei* 'Yaku Fairy' × *fletcherianum*) 4/4, 0°F or lower, EM, dwarf, F pale yellow, Berg 1977 USA, compact, large F very freely produced, CA 1983.

Princess Anne (*hanceanum* × *keiskei*) 3/3, 0°F, M, dwarf, F pale yellow, Reuthe 1961 GB, compact mound, a good plant, popular, AM 1978 FCCT 1983.

Quaver (*leucaspis* × *sulfureum*) 3/4, 10°F, E, low, F creamy-yellow, Rothschild 1950 GB, different clones.

Remo (*valentinianum* × *lutescens*) 3/2, 10°F, EM, semi-dwarf, F clear yellow, Stevenson 1943 GB, bushy, grows poorly for us but a good colour, several clones.

Shamrock (*keiskei* dwarf × *hanceanum* 'Nanum') 4/4, −5°F, EM, dwarf, F chartreuse, Ticknor 1978 USA, compact, becoming very popular in USA.

Talavera (*moupinense* × *sulfureum*) 4/3, 5°F, E–EM, low, F golden-yellow, Williams GB, upright habit, does well at Glendoick on a sheltered wall, FCC 1963.

Teal (*brachyanthum* × *fletcherianum*) 4/4, 5°F or lower, M, low, F clear yellow, Cox 1977 GB, fairly compact, a really showy yellow, often with multiple buds, reddish peeling bark, AM 1977.

Towhead (*minus* (*carolinianum*) × *ludlowii*) 3/4, −15°F, M, dwarf, F cream, Leach 1969 USA, compact, good foliage and very hardy.

Valaspis (*valentinianum* × *leucaspis*) 2–3/3, 10°F, E, semi-dwarf, F creamy-yellow flushed deeper, Aberconway 1935, Gibson, GB, several seedlings, AM 1935.

Wren (*ludlowii* × *keiskei* 'Yaku Fairy') 4/4, 0°F, EM, dwarf, F yellow, Cox 1983 GB, spreading prostrate, vigorous, very promising.

Yellow Hammer not a dwarf.

Pink Hybrids Lepidote

There is great scope for improvement here. Few are a really clear pink, many are early-flowering and bud tender.

Anna Baldsiefen ('Pioneer' selfed) 4/3, 0°F, EM, low, F brightest pink, Baldsiefen 1964 USA, upright habit, the most strikingly coloured pink I know, rather tender in E. USA, PC 1978 HC 1979.

Ann Carey (*keiskei* × *spinuliferum*) 3/3, 5°F, EM, low, F chartreuse fading to coral pink, Lem, Anderson 1966, straggly grower with sparse L, long F season, several clones including one with petaloid stamens, PA 1966.

Candi (*campylogynum* Cremastum × *racemosum*) 3/2, 5°F or lower, EM–M, dwarf, F bright rose, Caperci 1963 USA, bad foliage here so we discarded it.

Cilpinense (*ciliatum* × *moupinense*) 4/4, 5°F, E, semi-dwarf, F pale pink flushed deeper pink, Aberconway 1927 GB, compact, a beautiful early hybrid in its best clone, exceptionally free-flowering but bud-tender, AM 1927.

Cutie (*calostrotum* × *racemosum*?) 3/3, −15°F, EM–M, semi-dwarf, F purplish-pink, Greig 1960 Can, compact, free-flowering and reliable but very susceptible to rust fungus, AE 1949.

Fittra (*racemosum* × 'Fittianum') 3/2, 0°F, M, low, F rich pink, Hillier GB, upright habit, good F but straggly and hard to propagate, AM 1949.

Ginny Gee (*keiskei* 'Yaku Fairy' × *racemosum*) 4/3, 0°F, EM, semi-dwarf, F white flushed pink, Berg 1979 USA, very compact and free-flowering, exceptionally promising.

Kim (*campylogynum* ×) 3/4, 5°F, M, dwarf, F pink turning yellow, Caperci 1966 USA, compact, I considered this muddy and tender so threw it out.

Laetevirens (*minus* [*carolinianum*] × *ferrugineum*) said to be a synonym of 'Wilsoni', see 'Wilsoni'.

Multiflorum (*ciliatum* × *virgatum*) 10°F?, E–EM, low, F pink, J. Waterer GB, very old and rather tender.

Myrtifolium (*minus* × *hirsutum*) 3/4?, −15°F, VL, low, F pink, 1917 or earlier GB, bronzy winter foliage, dense habit, sun-tolerant.

Pink Fluff (*racemosum* × *davidsonianum*) 4/3, 5°F, EM, low, F light pink, darkening, Greer 1979 USA, erect habit, good colour but hard to propagate.

Pink Snowflakes (*racemosum* × *moupinense*) 4/4, 0°F, E, semi-dwarf, F white-flushed pink, Scott 1969 USA, has good reports, bronze-red young growth.

Pipit (*lowndesii* × *lepidotum* a natural hybrid from *lowndesii* seed) 4/3, 5°F, M–ML, dwarf, F pink, introduced Cox 1970 GB, almost pros-trate, dainty flat little F, semi-deciduous, needs a little protection. From C. Nepal seed.

Puncta (*minus*? × *ferrugineum*) An old hybrid previously known as 'Punctatum'.

Racil (*racemosum* × *ciliatum*) 3/2, −5°F, EM, low, F pale blush pink, Holland 1937 GB, compact, very free-flowering but foliage often poor, also 'Hariet Noble' AM 1957.

Razorbill (*spinuliferum* chance seedling) 5/4, 0°F, EM–M, semi-dwarf, F bright pink, Cox 1976 GB, compact, surprisingly hardy for *spinuli-ferum* cross, most unusual upright tubular F, very free-flowering and showy, becoming very popular, AM 1981, FCCT 1983.

Rose Elf (*racemosum* × *pemakoense*) 3/4, 0°F, EM, dwarf, F white-flushed pink, Lancaster USA, compact, free-flowering but buds easily frosted, PA 1954.

Rosy Bell (*ciliatum* × *glaucophyllum*) 3/3, 7°F, E–EM, semi-dwarf, F old rose, Davis 1894 GB, compact, rather plant-tender and very bud tender.

Seta (*spinuliferum* × *moupinense*) 4/3, 3°F, E, low, F light pink striped rose, Aberconway 1933 GB, beautiful early flowerer but young plants are tender, upright habit, AM 1933.

Snipe (*pemakoense* × *davidsonianum*) 4/3, 5°F, EM, semi-dwarf, F light pink, Cox GB, very floriferous but a little bud-tender, AM 1975.

Tessa Roza ('Praecox' × *moupinense*) 4/3, 0°F, E, low, F deep rose-pink, Stevenson 1953 GB, upright habit, the brightest-coloured really early pink, AM 1953.

Tiffany ('Anna Baldsiefen' × *keiskei*) 3/3, −15°F, M, low, F pink with apricot and yellow throat, Baldsiefen 1972, USA, star-shaped F and good foliage.

Tottenham (*ferrugineum* ×) 3/3, 0°F or lower, ML, semi-dwarf, F pale pink, Moerheim Ho, compact, a good beginners' plant.

Wilsoni (*minus* [*carolinianum*] × *ferrugineum*) 3/3, −15°F, L, low, F rose-pink, GB, compact when young, old but hardy useful late flow-erer.

Windbean ('Constoga' seedling) 3/2 (E. USA 4/3), −25°F, EM, low, F light pink, Nearing 1943 USA, upright habit, inferior by our standards.

Lavender and Purple Hybrids Lepidote

These colours may be despised by some people but some of the following are excellent plants none the less.

April Chimes (*hippophaeoides* × *mollicomum*) 3/3?, 0°F, E–EM, low, F rosy-mauve, Hillier 1969 GB, upright habit.

Arbutifolium (*ferrugineum* × *minus*) L, F lilac-rose, 1917 GB.

Barto Alpine (Lapponica ×) 2/2?, −10°F, EM, low, F fuchsia-purple, Barto 1964 USA, I discarded this, considering it of little merit.

Caperci Special (like *ferrugineum* × *minus*) 3/2?, −15°F, EM, semi-dwarf, F purple-pink, Caperci 1977 USA, bronze winter L, rounded habit.

Carousel (*minus* [*carolinianum*] × *saluenense*) −15°F, EM–M, semi-dwarf, F lavender-pink, Caperci 1965 USA, upright habit, floriferous.

Conemaugh (*racemosum* × *mucronulatum*) 3/3, −25°F, E, low, F lavender-pink, Gable 1958 USA.

Debijo (*minus carolinianum* × *saluenense*) −15°F, EM–M, semi-dwarf, F lavender-purple, Caperci 1966 USA.

Emasculum (*ciliatum* × *dauricum*) 3/2, −10°F, EM, low, F rosy-lilac, Waterers GB, upright habit, no stamens, later than 'Praecox', often a poor root system.

Ernie Dee (*dauricum* × *racemosum*) 3/3?, 0°F, EM, semi-dwarf, F purple, lightly frilled, Dzurick 1974 USA, compact, F long-lasting and free-flowering.

Lavendula ([*russatum* × *saluenense*] × *rubiginosum*) 3/3, −5°F or lower, M, low, F lavender-rose, spotted, Hobbie Ger, upright but compact, good foliage and attractive large F.

Olive (*moupinense* × *dauricum*) 3/3, −10°F, VE, low, F lavender-pink, Stirling Maxwell GB, upright habit, AM 1942.

Phalarope (*pemakoense* × *davidsonianum*) 3/3, 5°F, EM–M, low, F pale lilac-pink, Cox 1968 GB, very free-flowering, PC 1968, AMT 1983.

Pink Drift (*calostrotum* × *polycladum* [*scintillans*]) 3/4, −10°F, M, dwarf, F pinkish-mauve, Sunningdale Nursery 1955 GB, very compact, hardly pink but very easy and free-flowering.

P. J. Mezitt (P.J.M.) (*minus* [*carolinianum*] × *dauricum*) 3/4, −25°F, E–EM, low, F bright lavender-pink, Mezitt USA, rather similar to 'Praecox' but hardier, more compact, F of a brighter shade and L turn mahogany in winter, several clones in E. USA, very hardy there, PC 1967, AM 1972.

Praecox (*dauricum* × *ciliatum*) 3/3, −5°F, E, low, F rosy-lilac, Davis 1860 GB, so well-known it is included here although it can reach over 2m, AGM 1926, FCC 1978.

Prostigiatum (*saluenense* ssp. *chameunum* Prostratum × *fastigiatum*) 3/2, −5°F, M, dwarf, F deep purple, Magor 1924 GB, very compact but really too slow-growing, a good colour, AM 1924.

Purple Gem (*fastigiatum* × *minus* (*carolinianum*)) 3/4, −20°F, EM, semi-dwarf, F purplish-violet, Gable-Nearing 1958 USA, sister to 'Ramapo', F darker and possibly a better plant, good young L.

Ramapo (*fastigiatum* × *minus* [*carolinianum*]) 3/4, −20°F, EM, semi-dwarf, F pale violet, Gable-Nearing 1958 USA, very fine young foliage, a lovely grey-blue-green, very hardy E. USA.

Tessa ('Praecox' × *moupinense*) 3/3, −5°F, E, low, F deep lilac-pink, Stevenson 1935 GB, upright habit, dark L, stands sun, AM 1935.

Violetta (*impeditum* ×) F violet-lilac, Hachmann 1977 Ger.

Red Hybrids Lepidote

There is little scope here for many more through lack of suitable red species but perseverance should pay off.

Grouse (*campylogynum* Cremastum 'Bodnant Red' × *calostrotum* 'Gigha') 4/2, 0°F, M, semi-dwarf, F dark red, Cox 1977 GB, the reddest lepidote cross yet raised with waxy red bells but L inclined to yellow and turn brown at edges. Subject to rust fungus, AM 1977.

White Hybrids Lepidote

Several good new plants here but more are needed.

Bric-a-brac (*leucaspis* × *moupinense*) 4/3, 5°F, VE, semi-dwarf, F pink turning white, Rothschild 1934 GB, compact, not very hardy.

Cowbell (*ciliatum* × *edgeworthii*) 4/4, 15°F, EM, low, F pure white, large, Rothschild 1935 GB, fine foliage, low habit.

Dora Amateis (*minus* [*carolinianum*] × *ciliatum*) 4/4, −15°F, EM–M, low, F blush opening white, Amateis 1958 USA, a really outstanding plant which never fails to cover itself with its F, hardy blooms, will become one of the most planted of all rhododendrons, very hardy E. USA, AMT 1976, FCCT 1981.

Egret (*campylogynum* white × *racemosum* 'White Lace') 3/4, 0°F, M, dwarf, F pure white, Cox 1982 GB, plentiful little white bells on long pedicels, very compact, good foliage, AM 1982, HCT 1983.

Eider (*minus* [*carolinianum* white] × *leucaspis*) 4/2 (probably) −10°F, EM–M, low, F pure white, dark stamens, Cox GB, smothers itself with exceptionally long-lasting F, much hardier than *leucaspis*, 'Bric-a-brac' etc. L sometimes spot, AM 1981.

Fine Feathers ('Cilpinense' × *lutescens*) 3/3, 5°F, E, low, F cream, Aberconway 1949 GB, very easily frosted.

Lucy Lou (*leucaspis* × [*ciliatum* × *leucaspis*]) 4/4, 5°F?, E, low, F pure white, Larson 1958 USA, compact, attractive hairy L.

Maricee (*sargentianum* ×) 4/3, −5°F, M, semi-dwarf, F creamy-white, Caperci 1962 USA, bushy, a most attractive plant, easier, quicker-growing and freer-flowering than *sargentianum*, AE 1959, AMT 1983.

Ptarmigan (*orthocladum* var. *microleucum* × *leucaspis*) 4/3, −5°F, E–EM, dwarf, F pure white, Cox GB, compact with age, exceptionally free-flowering and is proving surprisingly hardy in cold climates, FCC 1965.

Sarled (*sargentianum* × *trichostomum*) 3/3, 0°F, M, semi-dwarf, F pale pink becoming white, Collingwood Ingram 1942 GB, very compact, easy with freely produced long-lasting F, AM 1974.

Small Gem (*pemakoense* × *leucaspis*) 4/4, −5°F, E, dwarf, F white-flushed pale pink, Frisbie USA, compact, L of *pemakoense*, F of *leucaspis* and no doubt very prone to frost from its parents.

Snow Lady (*leucaspis* × *ciliatum*) 4/4, 5°F, E, semi-dwarf to low, F pure white, Lancaster 1958 USA, compact to upright, excellent early white, often with multiple buds, not for coldest areas, PA 1955.

Tessa Bianca (*moupinense* × 'Praecox') 4/4, −5°F, E, low, F white-flushed pink, Brandt 1965 USA, compact, better habit than 'Tessa', promising.

Wyanokie ('Constoga' ×) 3/3, −25°F, M, low, F white, Nearing 1958 USA, good for cold climates.

Azaleodendrons

Artic Tern (*trichostomum* × *Ledum* sp.?) 4/3, 0°F or lower, ML, semi-dwarf, F pure white, Larson USA, very interesting hybrid, beautiful little upright trusses, very hardy. HC 1982, AM 1984.

Hardijzer's Beauty (*racemosum* × Kurume azalea) 3/3, −5°F?, M, low, F pink, Hardijzer Ho, very floriferous with bright-coloured F, AM 1970. None of these three azaleodendrons are proving hardy or good with us.

Martine (*racemosum* × Evergreen azalea) 3/2, 5°F, M, semi-dwarf, F clear pink, Hardijzer Ho, pretty F, seemed promising but has not proved satisfactory.

Ria Hardijzer (*racemosum* × 'Hinodegiri') 3/1, 0°F, M, semi-dwarf, F bright carmine, Hardijzer Ho, bushy, poor grower with us but has proved vigorous elsewhere, AM 1974.

Principal groups of evergreen azalea hybrids

Aronense Bred by Georg Arends of Wuppertal-Ronsdorf, Germany. Introduced by G. D. Bohlje Nursery of Westerstede, Germany in 1960s. *R. kiusianum* hybrids with large colour range. Very hardy. Low-growing and compact. −10°F, H4.

Back Acre Raised by B. Y. Morrison after he retired from Glenn Dale when he moved to Pass Christian, Miss. Worked for doubles, lateness, shedding of flowers once over and light colours. These are tender and liable to bark-split even in Oklahoma. Probably +10°F, H2–3, USDA 7b & 8a–7a.

Diamant (Diamond) Bred by Carl Fleischmann, Germany. Introduced by Johann Bruns Nursery, Bad Zwischenahn, Germany in 1969. *kiusianum* × Kurumes. Low-growing and compact. Have proved very hardy. −10°F, H4, USDA 6b.

Exbury Not as many evergreens as the famous deciduous strain. Some good reds and pinks. Many said to be hybrids of the tender *oldhamii* (*International Rhododendron Register*) but *The Rothschild Rhododendrons* denies this. However the majority are not suitable for Scotland and N. England. Mostly +5°F, H3, USDA 7a.

Ferndown Bred at D. Stewart & Sons Ltd, Ferndown, Dorset. Few are well known. Most are of the Kurume type. Probably 0° to +5°F, H3–4, USDA 7a–6b.

Gable Bred by Joseph Gable of Stewartstown, Penn., principally from *poukhanense* and *kaempferi*, also *mucronatum*, *indicum* and some Kurumes. Several are excellent and hardy but none I have tried are 100 per cent hardy for us in Scotland. Many hardy to −10°F where the summers are hotter, H4, USDA 6b.

Glendoick A new group mostly based on *nakaharae*, *kiusianum* × the hardiest Glenn Dales and *kaempferi* hybrids. Hopefully this will give us a race of badly needed reliable performers for Scotland and similar climates with cool summers. Four clones named in 1982. Hardy to lower than 0°F, H4, USDA 6b.

Glenn Dale Raised by B. Y. Morrison at Glenn Dale, Maryland. Over 400 clones named (too many) out of 70,000 seedlings. Many are splendid plants, several excellent for the S. of England but few have proved really satisfactory in Scotland. Several have very large flowers including multicolours. Many −5 to 0°F, H3–4, USDA 7a–6b.

Hirado Bred from *ripense, scabrum, simsii, macrosepalum, mucronatum* and so on, on the Island of Hirado, S. Japan. 300 clones recognized. These stand heat including hot nights. Large flowers on dwarfish plants. Likely to be +5 to +15°F, H2–3, USDA 7b & 8a–7a.

Indian (so-called) This includes most of the popular indoor azaleas forced for pot plants. Most of those raised in Britain in the early 1800s died out and it was the Belgian-raised hybrids that became really popular. Parentage is unknown but probably most are derived from *simsii* with *scabrum* and others. By 1880 the Belgian cultivars had taken over. Some of the hardier clones introduced into USA over a century ago became known as Southern Indian hybrids which flourish in S.E. States. Further work is being carried out in Belgium to produce cleaner and different colours, easier forcing and other characters, partly by attempting to incorporate many other azalea species and also dwarf lepidote rhododendrons. +5 to +15°F, H2–3, USDA 7b & 8a–7a.

kaempferi hybrids This species in its many forms has been widely used in the hybridization of evergreen azaleas. The progeny tend to be taller, hardier and later-flowering than Kurumes and many have fine autumn colour on the lower larger leaves which mostly shed. Most are single-flowered and many were raised in Holland by Koster, van Nes and other nurseries. Several are known as 'Malvatica' × *kaempferi.* −10 to 0°F, H4, USDA 6b.

Kurume Originated about 150 years ago in the city of Kurume. E. H. Wilson sent home his selection of the best 50 clones in 1918. These were numbered and all were given alternative English names. The majority do best in climates like S. England. These are mostly dense growers with small flowers and are thought to have come from *kiusianum* × *kaempferi* (which hybridize naturally) and/or from the supposed species *sataense*. Complete collections of the Wilson 50 do still exist and various additions have been made to these by further introductions and hybridizing. −5 to +5°F, H3–4, USDA 7a–6b.

Linwood Breeding started by Charles Fischer and carried on and introduced by G. Albert Reid of New Jersey. The aim was to produce hardy cultivars with flowers as large as the tender 'Indians' to be grown outside and yet be useful to florists. Many are double or partially double with heavy-textured, long-lasting flowers in May. Probably −5 to 0°F, H4, USDA 6b, in Britain.

North Tisbury Raised by Mrs Polly Hill of Martha's Vineyard Is., Mass., mostly from *nakaharae* crosses made by Dr Rokujo of Japan. Hybrids of *nakaharae* are mostly hardier than the species but as parents used include Satsukis, they may not be suitable for the north. Probably −5 to +5°F, H4, USDA 6b.

Pericat Raised by Alphonse Pericat in Penn., probably Kurume × Belgian Indians. Primarily raised for forcing but do well in S. and E. States, USA.

Robin Hill Bred by Robert Gartrell, New Jersey, using hardy selections × Satsukis. These are highly rated with large flowers, late in the

season (June–July), mostly of pastel shades and some have been introduced into Britain. Probably around 0°F, H4, in Britain, USDA 6b.

Satsuki Means 'fifth month' in Japanese. Originally used for Bonsai,
most are low and twiggy with very large flowers. Gumpos (almost pure
eriocarpum) are included here. Those with *simsii* blood are especially
tender. Few if any are likely to do well in any cool summer areas.
Probably +5 to +15°F, H3, USDA 7.

Shammarello In the cold climate of N. Ohio, Shammarello has raised 11
named cultivars, six of which are patented. Many are from 'Hino-
Crimson' × *poukhanense* and all are reckoned hardy from −20 to
−10°F in E. USA.

USDA, Beltsville, Maryland. Raised by Guy E. Yerkes and Robert L.
Pryor for hardiness, forcing and general garden use. Many are known
as Beltsville dwarfs. I tried a selection of these in Scotland and they
proved to be useless here.

Vuykiana Breeding started in 1921 by Aart Vuyk of Vuyk van Nes
Nurseries, Boskoop, Holland. Goal was hardy azaleas with large
flowers. A *kaempferi* × *mucronatum* cross was used as seed parent,
apparently using Mollis as pollen parent. This is most likely impossible and in any case there is no sign of Mollis occurring in the progeny.
A very large percentage of those named have become standard commercial azaleas in Britain. Most are hardy to below 0°F, H4, USDA
6b.

Wada Japan. Mostly from Satsuki hybrid group and bred to withstand
hot climates, especially hot nights. No doubt unsuitable for Britain.

Weagle Bred by John Weagle, a new hybridizer working with the hardiest species and hybrids for areas like coastal E. Canada with coldish
winters and cool summers.

Evergreen azalea hybrids

Owing to lack of space, I can only include a small selection of the most
popular and a few very promising new cultivars out of all those thousands named. I consider that many of the most commonly propagated
cultivars in Britain are now completely surpassed by new introductions,
mostly American and European, and several should be discarded. Many
of these have small red to pink flowers which rapidly fade, even in our
rather weak sunshine. In the north, these azaleas have to be grown in the
sun to make them flower; therefore any that fade readily are of little
merit.

Flower size where given is across the corolla.

(S) = particularly good in cool summer areas such as Scotland.

Addy Wery H4 USDA 6b (Kurume) (H. den Ouden & Son, Holland) F
orange-red, single. 3.8cm (1½in), upright habit. AMT 1950.

Alexander (Polly Hill, USA [Rokujo]) F bright salmon-red, single, very
low and spreading.

Beethoven H4 USDA 6b (Vuyk van Nes, Holland) F lilac-mauve, single,
6.9cm (2¾in), medium height.

Betty Anne Voss (R. Gartrell, USA) F clear pink.

Blaauw's Pink H4 USDA 6b (Kurume × *kaempferi*) (J. Blaauw & Co., Holland) F salmon-pink, hose-in-hose, 3.8cm (1½in), early, quite good in N.

Blue Danube H3–4 USDA 7a–6b (*kaempferi* ×) (Vuyk van Nes, Holland) F rich blue-purple, distinct, low.

Buccaneer H3–4 USDA 7a–6b (Kurume ×) (Glenn Dale, USA) F vivid orange-scarlet with dark flair, 5cm (2in) across, liable to fade in sun. Tall.

Chippewa (S) H4 USDA 6b (*kaempferi* × Indian) (Bobbink & Atkins, USA) F deep pink, single, 6.3cm (2½in), late, very hardy, compact.

Diamant azaleas (S) H4 USDA 6b (Diamond) (C. Fleischmann, Germany) F mauve, pink, purple small. Very hardy, low and compact.

Everest H3–4 USDA 7a–6b (Glenn Dale, USA) F white single, 5cm (2in), showy.

Favorite (S) H4 USDA 6b (*kaempferi* ×) (C. B. van Nes, Holland) F deep pink, single. Generally reliable in N. Upright.

Fedora H3–4 USDA 7a–6b (*kaempferi* ×) (C. B. van Nes, Holland) F dark pink, single, 5cm (2in), a constant bloomer. Liable to bark-split in Scotland. Medium height, FCC 1960.

Florida H3–4 USDA 7a–6b (Vuyk van Nes, Holland) F crimson-scarlet, 5cm (2in), semi-double, no stamens. Not successful with us. Medium height.

Gaiety (S) H4 USDA 6b (*indicum* ×) (Glenn Dale, USA) F pink, 5–7.5cm (2–3in) single, medium-late. Low and compact.

Gumpo H3 USDA 7a (Satsuki) F white, others pink, white and pink and rose, 6.9cm (2¾in) not satisfactory in Scotland. Late.

Hatsugiri H3–4 USDA 7a–6b (Kurume) F brilliant crimson-purple, single. Low and compact. Reasonably good in N. FCC 1969.

Hino Crimson H4 USDA 6b (Kurume) F brilliant red, 2.5cm (1in). Dense habit.

Hinomayo (Hinamayo) H3–4 USDA 7a–6b (Kurume) F soft pink, free-flowering. Reasonably hardy in N. FCC 1945, AGM 1968.

Iroha Yama H3–4 USDA 7a–6b (Dainty) (Wilson Kurume No. 8) F white, margined lavender, compact, AMT 1952.

John Cairns H4 USDA 6b (*kaempferi* ×) (L. J. Endtz & Co., Holland) F dark red, 3.8cm (1½in), rather upright, fairly reliable in N, autumn colour, AGM 1952.

Kermesina (S) H4 USDA 6b (*kiusianum* ×) F glowing rich pink, low and very compact, nice shiny leaves.

Kure-no-yuki H3–4 USDA 7a–6b (Snowflake) Wilson (Kurume No. 2) F white hose-in-hose, compact, leaves shiny, AMT 1952.

Lemur (S) H4 USDA 6b (*nakaharae* ×) (Cox, Scotland) F deep pink, long-lasting, habit prostrate, mound-forming, buds red in winter.

Leo H3–4 USDA 7a–6b (*kaempferi* × ?) (Rothschild, England) F salmon, single, 6.3cm (2½in), late. Habit spreading.

Linwood azaleas (G. Albert Reid, USA) Amongst the best selections are 'Linwood Blush', 'Lustre', 'Pink Giant' and 'Salmon'. F partly double, heavy-textured and long-lasting.

Martha Hitchcock H3–4 USDA 7a–6b (*mucronatum* ×) (Glenn Dale, USA) F white, magenta margins, 7.5cm (3in) late. Habit spreading. One of the hardier of the multicoloured cultivars. AMT 1972.

Mother's Day H4 USDA 6b (Kurume × *indicum*) (van Hecke, Belgium) F crimson. Habit low and compact. A fine red but alas very susceptible to gall fungus. FCCT 1970, AGM 1968.

Mucronatum (see species list)

Naomi H4 USDA 6b (*kaempferi* ×) (Rothschild, England), F salmon-pink, 6.3cm (2½in), late. Medium height.

Nancy of Robinhill (R. Gartrell, USA) F pale pink with slight blotch.

Orange Beauty H3–4 USDA 7a–6b (Kurume × *kaempferi*) (C. B. van Nes), F salmon and orange, 3.8cm (1½in), liable to fade. Subject to bark-split in N. FCCT 1958.

Palestrina H3–4 USDA 7a–6b (Vuyk van Nes, Holland) F white, green markings, 4.4cm (1¾in), medium height, susceptible to tip frosting in N. According to Bean (1976) there is a second hardier clone, much better and freer-flowering in the N. with a lower habit and better leaves.

Panda (S) H4 USDA 6b (*kiusianum* × Glenn Dale) (Cox, Scotland) F pure white. Habit low and compact, hardier than its parent Everest. Nice foliage.

Princess Juliana H3–4 USDA 7a–6b (Vuyk van Nes, Holland) F soft orange-red. Habit low spreading. Best in some shade.

Redmond (R. Gartrell, USA) F salmon-orange, spotted red.

Rosebud H3–4 USDA 7a–6b (*kaempferi* × *poukhanense* and others) (J. Gable, USA) F rose-pink, 4.4cm (1¾in), splendid double. Habit compact. Very popular. AMT 1972.

Squirrel (S) H4 USDA 6b (*nakaharae* ×) (Cox, Scotland) F bright scarlet, sun resistant, long-lasting, late. Habit compact, mound-forming, splendid colour and exceptionally free-flowering.

Stewartstonian H4 USDA 6b (J. Gable, USA) F deep brownish-red, 3.8cm (1½in). Leaves glossy. Hardy but flowers inclined to fade. AMT 1975.

Vida Brown H4 USDA 6b (Kurume ×) (introduced by Stewart of Ferndown, England) F rose-pink, hose-in-hose, 4.4cm (1¾in), late mid-season. Leaves small. Habit low and compact, slow growing. AMT 1960.

Vuyk's Rosy Red H3–4 USDA 7a–6b (Vuyk van Nes, Holland) F rosy-red, 6.9–7.5cm (2¾–3in), low. Fairly reliable in N. but leaves inclined to spot. AMT 1962.

Vuyk's Scarlet H4 USDA 6b (Vuyk van Nes, Holland). F crimson-scarlet 7.5cm (3in), low. Fairly reliable in north. A good plant. FCCT 1966.

White Moon H3–4? USDA 7a–6b (R. Gartrell, USA). F white, green spots, few red markings.

Willy H4 USDA 6b (*kaempferi* ×) (C. B. van Ness, Holland) F clear pink, single, 5.6cm (2¼in). Medium size, leaves often colour in autumn, sometimes suffers bark-split.

Wombat (S) H4 USDA 6b (*nakaharae* ×) (Cox, Scotland). F pink, single, late, very free-flowering. Habit prostrate, vigorous, excellent ground cover.

Hybridizing at home

It is 12 years since I wrote on hybridizing in *Dwarf Rhododendrons*. While many thousands of new hybrids have been made since then, the objects I stated still remain the same and I fully endorse the majority of statements I made then. Rather than repeat myself, I will attempt to go a stage further with some different ideas or advances on previous ones. Those without a copy of *Dwarf Rhododendrons* wishing to read what I wrote then will need to borrow a copy from a friend or library.

How to pollinate and induce seed set is described under 'Seeds' on p.241–2. Before any hybridizing is done, there must be an object in mind such as new colours, hardiness, special foliage, early or late flowers and/or growth, freedom of flowering, good habit, ease of propagation, drought, heat- or cold-resistance, disease-resistance or a combination of several of these goals.

No plant yet produced is perfect and few perform consistently to one's satisfaction year after year. Before selecting any proposed parents, get to know the plants concerned really well. Are they good forms? Do they grow too early or too late? Is the foliage liable to chlorosis, leaf spot or rust? Are the flowers heavy- or light-textured and weather-resistant? Do they grow well in a variety of different soils? Are the buds liable to abort or susceptible to bud-blast? Is the habit leggy or compact? Get to know the answers to these questions and many others.

Direct interspecific crosses (F1) usually produce a relatively even progeny which is to some extent foreseeable in its make-up. This often makes the selection of one clone extremely difficult, especially if there is a large number to choose from. Select a few the first season most of them flower, and then watch their performance over the next few seasons. On the other hand, hybrid × hybrid can give an enormous variation. The American geneticist Dr Gustav Mehlquist once told me that one must grow at least 999 of each hybrid cross to have a good chance of the combination of characters one is looking for. Luckily, many seedlings can be weeded out at various stages of growth from a tiny seedling onwards, discarding those with chlorotic leaves, poor roots, weak growth and bad habit. Crossing two siblings of a species cross in an attempt to combine the best characteristics of both parents can be a good plan (F2).

It so happens that many lepidote interspecific hybrids are wholly or partially sterile. Some, previously considered sterile, have now been proved fertile but often a large number of flowers need to be pollinated to have any hope of seed at all.

The heat treatment described on pp.241 and 243 may help get over this problem and it is especially necessary when attempting 'way out' crosses such as lepidote × elepidote, evergreen azalea × lepidote, Vireya × other rhododendrons, and rhododendrons × other Ericaceae. This type of cross, if it does set any viable seed at all, so often gives weak seedlings which may die in infancy or never bloom. Very few have ever become good commercial plants so far. In contrast, other ericaceous genera such as *Phyllodoce* and *Kalmiopsis*, *Pernettya* and *Gaultheria* may hybridize readily with good results.

Hybridizing is fun and the anticipation of waiting for new seedlings to bloom is something I would not miss for anything. Disappointments are more common than success, but it is a lifetime's work to be enjoyed into old age.

Here are some possible lines of breeding to try in the future. Many of these may be already in the pipeline of some breeders but remember, no two seedlings are identical so it is not necessarily a waste of time remaking crosses done before.

Within the subgenus Hymenanthes (*Elepidote*)

Foliage
Good foliage is now one of the most popular aims of current hybridizers, especially for indumentum. So many indumentumed species are slow to bloom. As indumentum tends to be recessive when 'indumentum' is crossed with 'no indumentum', it is much easier to retain indumentum if crossing is done amongst indumentumed species only. To obtain freedom of flowering, it is necessary to introduce those species that flower quickest from seed. *R. griersonianum* possibly comes first, while *yakushimanum* and its relatives 'Metternichii' and 'Degronianum' are reasonably quick. As many hybrids tend to flower younger than their parents, a little blood of *griersonianum* may be a great help in inducing precocious blooming from seed or a cutting.
    Lines to try for are:–
Persistent indumentum on the upper leaf surface using *pachysanthum, bureavii, elegantulum, tsariense, falconeri* ssp. *eximium, yakushimanum*
Glaucous foliage using *campanulatum* ssp. *aeruginosum, clementinae, thomsonii, callimorphum, souliei, campylocarpum* ssp. *caloxanthum*
Rusty indumentum on leaf underside using *mallotum, falconeri, tsariense, haematodes, arboreum* ssp. *cinnamomium, bureavii, proteoides* and others
Red foliage using *neriiflorum* 'Rosevallon', 'Elizabeth Red Foliage', 'Moser's Maroon', *maximum* 'Mt Mitchell', 'Elizabeth Lockhart'
Perhaps we can raise rhododendrons to rival *Pieris* and *Photinia* for their red young foliage display.
    Let's aim at something new in foliage on dwarfs. Search for species and hybrids with rough and tough leaves. *R. zelanicum* and probable hybrids 'Noyo Chief' and its progeny 'Noyo Brave' have amongst the most outstanding foliage I have seen. Bring in *wiltonii* plus some clones of *forrestii, insigne, falconeri*.

Dwarf yellows
There has been a great effort put into yellows recently but there is still much more to do. Try using *citriniflorum, temenium* ssp. *gilvum* 'Cruachan' F.C.C., *campylocarpum* ssp. *caloxanthum, wasonii, taliense* in its yellow-flowered forms and even *pronum* (when it flowers!). Cross these with existing yellow hybrids to encourage dwarfness and good foliage.

Long-lasting flowers
Large with small. I am surprised how little work has been done crossing big-leaved species with those of intermediate and small stature. Surely species like *falconeri, macabeanum, sinogrande* and *montroseanum* have much to offer in their splendid foliage and heavy-textured, long-lasting flowers. I have *macabeanum* × *wardii* L&S (others have made it) coming on and by incorporating the ubiquitous *yakushimanum* and perhaps *williamsianum* and *forrestii*, we could get something worthwhile.

Attractive buds
There is no doubt that large, coloured flower buds together with good foliage sell a plant in the garden centre. Even an otherwise inferior clone can sell because of its buds but surely outstanding buds can be combined with fine flowers and plant behaviour. To my mind, large fat red buds have the most appeal but any brightly coloured, prominent buds will draw attention. Even red growth buds enhance a plant, especially if contrasting with rich dark foliage. Some hybrids have buds that are too prominent and look incongruous, apart from being easily knocked off.

Other unusual features
Has anyone deliberately bred for the hairiest leaves and stems, the narrowest possible leaves, the shiniest leaves, the frilliest flower, the most upright foliage, or really large leaves on a dwarf plant?

Drought resistance
My trips to Oregon and Washington State, USA plus my recent (1981) expedition to China really brought home to me how tough and resilient rhododendrons can be. There is *macrophyllum*, growing in a climate with infrequent summer rains. It even manages to flourish amongst the ever greedy roots of the Douglas fir. In China, we saw *decorum* and *arboreum* ssp. *delavayi* surviving the most appalling abuse of the axe, fire, and grazing hungry stock including goats, cattle and pigs. After the forest is destroyed, these rhododendrons are left as sentinels while destructive forces act all around them. The organic matter in the soil all but disappears. Before the monsoon rains start, the ground becomes bone dry, yet they survive. Why do we not make use of this ability to survive? I feel sure that plants could be raised that, once established, would never need summer watering or the amount of organic matter we pour into and onto our soil. There must be dwarfer species such as *aureum* which can stand up to equally poor conditions. This species already has a reputation for growing on mineral soils although so far it has not proved to be a very good parent.

Within the subgenus Rhododendron (Lepidote)

Comparatively few hybridizers have seriously turned their hand to the scaly leaved rhododendrons and when they have, only a few lines have been tackled. These have been 'blues', early-flowering, *cinnabarinum* × *maddenii* crosses, *racemosum* hybrids, my own and others' yellows.

Admittedly, incompatability, polyploidy and other barriers make hybrids of these species more difficult to achieve. These are, in the wild, a more versatile group of plants than those of subgenus Hymenanthes, coming from conditions varying from Arctic tundra and mountain tops to sub-tropical jungles. Some are exceedingly heat- and drought-resistant, such as *chapmanii*, *virgatum*, *racemosum*, *spinuliferum*, plus of course many members of subsection Maddenia. So the opportunity is there to produce hybrids for all rhododendron-growing areas. Many people are now realizing how valuable the Maddeniis are in warm climates like coastal California, Australia and much of New Zealand.

Dwarf lepidotes from alpine regions tend to outgrow themselves in these climates but the incorporation of species like those listed above should enable all to enjoy dwarf lepidotes. Try to procure collections from the lowest locations in which they are found growing wild.

Frost-hardy flowers

Here is a case where crossing like with like is all important. While the use of one parent with frost-hardy flowers does produce a cross which improves upon the hardiness of those of the other parent, hardy × hardy should at least be as hardy as either parent. My hybrid 'Eider', *carolinainum* white × *leucaspis* has considerably hardier flowers than *leucaspis* but I feel sure that *carolinianum* × *moupinense* or *dauricum*, both with fairly frost-hardy flowers, will be forerunners in a race of late winter-early spring hybrids that will make this type of plant much more popular in our dreadful frosty British springs. At present, 'Praecox', 'Cilpinense' and their kin just lead to frequent disappointments. No rhododendron hybrid will be entirely frost-hardy when in bloom but even a difference of 2–3°F can avoid frost damage in many seasons. Other parents to use are the majority of the smaller flowered Lapponicums and *mucronulatum*.

Tsutsusi section (Obtusum subseries of Azalea series)

I hate to suggest that any more evergreen azaleas should be raised given the plethora that already exists. However, in certain extreme climates there is still great scope for improvements. For example, places like Scotland, Scandinavia and E. coastal Canada are on the very edge of territory where it is possible to cultivate these plants. We have found that no popular commercial named clones are reliable with us season after season. There is only one answer. We must breed some that are reliable ourselves.

To my knowledge no one has previously hybridized these azaleas in Scotland. I have started a programme to incorporate all the hardiest known species and hybrids, aiming at a full range of colours and sizes including large and small flowers, doubles and multicolours. To everyone's surprise, *nakaharae*, from a low elevation in Taiwan, is a notable parent for hardiness as well as the expected dwarfness.

What is needed in our climates is the ability to ripen growth early, not just winter hardiness, so plants capable of surviving extreme continental cold may be useless to us because they also experience hot, ripening summers. So far, the most promising parents are *kiusianum*, *nakaharae*, *kaempferi* and to a lesser extent *poukhanense*. It is apparent that *nakaharae* crossed with some of the hot-climate Satsuki azaleas from S. Japan, raised by Polly Hill, on an island off Massachussetts, are proving amazingly tough and versatile so the addition of tender blood is in some cases feasible. I hope to try these plants shortly.

6 *Propagation*

Propagation is divided into vegetative and by seed. To produce an exact simile, choose vegetative. Seed is used for quantities of some species and for the results of crossing. All rhododendron propagation requires patience, observance and care.

Vegetative propagation

This can be divided into four parts: cuttings, micro- or *in vitro* propagation, layering and grafting. The simplest is layering followed by cuttings. Grafting requires a little skill with a knife plus some careful looking after. Micropropagation is now proving very successful with many rhododendrons but really needs a small laboratory and is only at present for those needing large quantities of young plants.

Cuttings

Most rhododendrons can now be propagated this way. Many different methods can give good results. The majority take some time to root and they must have optimum conditions at all times. If dry, they shrivel; if too wet or in too little light, they rot. Adequate moisture and light are essential but no direct sunlight. A medium too dry or too wet is hard to adjust. Other basic necessities are cleanliness and good-quality cuttings free from pests and diseases.

Propagating facilities

If few plants are required, old sweet jars, pots enclosed in polythene bags, small propagators or a small frame, should suffice.

For larger quantities, many dwarfs can be rooted in unheated frames out of direct sunlight. Larger plants need more sophisticated equipment. The options include mist, fog, or an airtight structure. In a mist system, mist from special nozzles sprays very fine droplets over cuttings to keep the leaves turgid. It is controlled to come on in short bursts and must only give the foliage just sufficient moisture to avoid run-off, which can soak the rooting medium. The mist bursts can be controlled manually, by a time clock, an electronic 'leaf', a solar control or a moisture balance. I have tried the last three and none is perfect. The moisture balance may be upset by wind turbulence.

An alternative to mist is the use of polythene. This may either be laid direct onto the cuttings or held above them by some means of support. I

226

have been using the former method for several years and provided it is carefully handled, it can be very successful. Thin 80–100 gauge polythene is best, but a thicker 150 gauge will suffice. If the polythene is held off the cuttings by wires or other substances, the resulting air space can give rise to some stress for the cuttings. One advantage of the latter method is that very small cuttings do not have the chance to attach themselves to the polythene when it is being taken off and on. With a cold frame outside, we have had good results by using a combination of glass lights and polythene laid on to the cuttings underneath. An alternative to a simple outdoor frame is the 'Nearing' frame, pioneered by G. G. Nearing in E. USA. It has a hood and sides to keep out all direct sunlight and white painted insides for maximum light reflection. This can be modified as to latitude and it is important to face it exactly north (see *Rhododendrons of the World* by David G. Leach, p.322).

Fogging is an alternative to mist for large propagating units. Water is vaporized by at least three different methods but all aim to give near 100 per cent humidity. Cuttings are best placed in trays on wire mesh for drainage. This system is probably best suited to areas with a high light intensity and plenty of sunshine like S.E. England and E. USA. It is said to be unsatisfactory on a small scale. The fog itself reduces the light intensity by a considerable amount. It also acts as a cooling system giving the desirable 'cool head' to the cuttings. Droplets are very much smaller than with mist.

Heating

Hot bottoms with cool tops is an ideal situation to aim at and is easiest achieved under mist or fog. Bottom heat will speed up the rooting in nearly every case although some small-leaved dwarfs really prefer no heat at all. Heat can be provided by electricity through plastic-coated cables. Plain wire of various types or wire-netting may be used if the voltage is drastically reduced with a transformer. The heat can be thermostatically controlled by rod-type thermostats or more efficiently using sensor probe thermostats which keep the temperature more even. The most rapid rooting may be obtained by temperatures of 21–24°C (70–75°F) but these high temperatures are expensive to run and can also maximize rotting. Electricity bills can be kept down by the reduction of temperatures during the low light period in mid-winter. In many cases, all that is necessary is to keep the frost out. Rooting can be slower but perfectly adequate in time. A considerable saving of heat can also be achieved by insulating the heated beds. Five-centimetre (2in) sheets of polystyrene (kept dry with polythene sheets) around the sides and underneath the beds, plus the use of bubble polythene or aluminized polyester sheets placed over the cuttings at nights and during very cold weather can save electricity by up to 50 per cent. Beds may be similarly heated by hot water or hot air pipes. Electric cables should be buried in moist sand or grit as they may overheat in peat. Hot water or air pipes can be insulated in specially made polystyrene beds with grooves made for the pipes. Wire-netting can be used under cutting trays or in heated beds over the existing source of heat to spread the heat more evenly.

Lighting

Artificial lighting is not usually necessary for the smaller dwarfs. It can, however, be of considerable help for forcing rooted soft wood cuttings into growth and also for supplementing poor winter light for hard-to-root subjects like many Talienses. I have recently found that several deciduous species, and those species and hybrids that have deciduous blood in them, root and grow away easier if treated as soft wood cuttings taken in June or July (earlier if the growth is forced indoors). These should be potted up as soon as well-rooted, and placed under supplementary lighting made up to a 16–18 hour day. Time clocks will need to be altered as the days shorten. This supplementary lighting encourages the very necessary growth before dormancy on deciduous items. The lighting can be turned off about the end of October and the plants should be gradually hardened off to give them a winter rest under cool conditions in a cold house or frame with some frost protection.

I use a mixture of warm white and white tubes set 60cm (2ft) above the rooted cuttings, with the tubes set 23–30cm (9–12in) apart although twin holders will do instead. These give off too much heat in an enclosed space but the new lower-wattage tubes help to alleviate this.

Growing rooms are common in American house basements so why not in Britain? The same tubes, preferably the new low-wattage ones, can be used for a 16–18-hour or even a 24-hour day and are particularly good for the germinating and the early growth of seedlings. The lights themselves are usually all that is necessary for heating in a confined space. As stated above, they can produce too much heat and it may be necessary to ventilate to keep the temperature down to, say, below 18°C (65°F). Higher temperatures can be allowed for the initial germination. Shelves can be erected with sets of lights to each shelf.

Rooted and potted soft wood cuttings are a good source of further soft cuttings once they have made some growth. Cut the tips off and treat as normal soft cuttings although during winter it may be necessary to give supplementary lighting to augment the short days and poor light intensity.

Rooting containers

Most people now use plastic seed trays filled with rooting medium either under polythene or mist. I still like to use whole benches filled with medium for many subjects. We have our own saw-mill and still make wooden boxes. These are treated with wood preservative (green Cuprinol or equivalent only) but they do eventually rot. It is probably true to say that plastic trays are more hygienic and easier to sterilize before re-using. The more water applied to the cuttings, the better the drainage has to be, and some brands of plastic trays have inadequate drainage. Under directly laid polythene sheets, very little watering is required so drainage is not so important. Dwarfs require at least 5cm (2in) of medium to root into while semi-dwarfs need 7.5cm (3in), especially if there is bottom heat. Whatever receptacle is used, it is vital to be able to keep the moisture level correct (not too wet or too dry). Individual or sectional pots, trays, honeycombs etc. may be used, but I feel these are best for items that root quicker than rhododendrons. The same applies to blocks made out of rock wool and other substances.

Always thoroughly clean out and disinfect all containers before re-use.

Rooting medium

If good, clean, sharp sand or grit can be obtained locally, they are still just as good as any available artificially prepared medium. Many nurseries in the S. of England use excellent flint grit mixed with first quality sphagnum peat, usually 50/50, and get good results. We now find it impossible to get good grit or sand locally. To get what we want, we have to riddle and wash what sand we have and this is hopelessly time-consuming. Nearly all our local sand is alkaline and full of silt and clay particles.

We now use super coarse perlite under both mist (60 per cent perlite/40 per cent peat) and polythene (40 per cent perlite/60 per cent peat). Seed-grade perlite is good for the smallest dwarfs. For these dwarfs, washed fine sand may be even better than perlite to add to the peat and can be worth the effort to get it. I have found that a fairly uniform-sized coarse grit is unsatisfactory.

Pure peat is sometimes recommended but its moisture level is very difficult to control. Other suitable ingredients are acid pulverized conifer bark (spruce is inclined to be alkaline), styrofoam and even certain types of sawdust. My experiments with the last failed but others have had good success. Some people just use pure fine sand but the quality, of course, has to be very good.

The pH should be between 4 and 4.5 where possible. Lime should be added if the pH is lower although water of a relatively high pH, especially under mist, may raise the pH considerably. Some people add gypsum to the medium with beneficial results. Whatever the medium chosen, it should not be firmed, just carefully levelled. I like to renew the medium with every batch of cuttings, especially in mist where peat breaks down rapidly. Under polythene, re-use may be feasible if the peat is still in good condition and there has been no trouble with rotting.

Preparation of stock plants

Only healthy, vigorous (where possible) material should be used for propagating. Avoid shoots attacked by insects, slugs, fungi, rabbits and other pests and anything that has been trampled on. Mud-spattered material should be washed. Damaged foliage encourages rotting.

The best cuttings are usually those off pruned and fertilized stock plants. Ordinary garden specimens can produce some cuttings regularly if well looked after. Many nurseries propagate almost entirely off growing on or saleable stock. For pruning to shape, or removal of leading shoots, this is all right, but I have frequently seen and bought plants with as many as half their shoots removed for cuttings, a very bad practice and I hope detrimental to that nursery's future sales. Also, if generation after generation is taken off young stock, eventual weakening or a complete breakdown could result although little trouble has *so far* occurred with rhododendrons. So it is at least advisable to have stock or garden specimens to fall back on every few generations. There is little doubt that cuttings off young plants do generally root easier than those off old specimens, particularly if these have been allowed to become short-growthed and woody. Many old plants will respond to pruning and will be encouraged to grow more vigorously with the addition of fertilizer and a mulch. Do, though, avoid the long whippy soft growth that often comes when plants are newly pruned. This applies especially to lepidotes.

Certain weedkillers like simazine and dichlobenil (Casoron) may affect the rooting potential, so if weedkillers are to be used on stock plants, use minimum effective rates of application. Any foliage burn is disastrous.

For the production of quantities of cuttings, it pays to prune and pinch regularly for the maximum number of suitable shoots. Flower buds and single leaf buds may be removed as they begin to expand in the spring. The greater the percentage of shoots removed annually, the greater attention that will have to be paid to nutrition and watering. Plants heavily stripped cannot be expected to perform as good garden plants as well! Make sure stock plants are adequately moist before the cuttings are collected. If dry, water heavily two days before collection. Containerized stock plants should also be carefully pruned and fertilized and must be well watered and looked after, through the seasons.

Collection and selection of cuttings

Cuttings are best collected in the early morning or on damp days during the summer and early autumn. These should be placed immediately into individual polythene bags and adequately labelled. I use odd scraps of paper or even the backs of leaves (dry) at this stage. Do not leave the bags of cuttings in the sun. Large black polythene bags are good and in a warm climate, damp burlap bags help to keep cuttings cool and moist. It is good practice to disinfect constantly all secateurs, bags and anything else that comes into contact with the cuttings, especially in warm, damp climates where diseases can be such a problem.

Soft cuttings of deciduous and related items should be taken in April–July depending on climate, season and whether they have been forced. Take the majority of dwarf lepidotes in July and early August. First growth flush invariably roots better than second. Take evergreen azaleas as soon as long enough and when tips are firming up, usually late July–early August. Sanguineums are best in late July–early August, although September may be successful. *R. williamsianum, forrestii* and hybrids are best in August–September; semi-dwarf lepidotes, mostly late July–August; the rest of the semi-dwarf elepidotes including the Taliensia subsection, September or preferably October. Some people get good results from February–March cuttings. If cuttings are still in perfect condition by that time they may succeed, but cuttings suffering from leaf spot (due to too much autumn rain), which have turned into their respective winter colour, or have curled up during or as a result of severe weather are almost sure to fail.

Try to avoid long, sappy cuttings, thick leading shoots and where possible, those with flower buds. Cuttings from shaded areas or shady parts of a plant often root easier than those in full exposure.

Preparation of cuttings

Prepare in a cool place away from direct sun. On a commercial establishment, it is suggested that the fewer times the cuttings are put down and picked up again, the faster the operation. If they are stripped to single shoots, then have surplus leaves removed where necessary, large leaves cut, ends trimmed, wounded if necessary (see below), treated with rooting substance when needed and inserted into a tray all in one operation. This will also cut down the danger of the cuttings deteriorating from stress due to desiccation.

I like single-stemmed cuttings, other people often use multi-stemmed ones with dwarfs. Remove flower buds when practicable and cut ends of leaves if 5cm (2in) long or over. At 5cm (2in), remove third of leaf. If 7.5–10cm (3–4in), remove half of leaf. (Growers in parts of USA keep their flower buds on until the spring as they say the removal lets in fungus causing rot; also they remove a minimum of leaf due to the danger of *Pestalotia* fungus attacking the cut edge.) For length of cutting dwarfs, 3.8cm (1½in) is long enough. For semi-dwarfs, 3.8–5cm (1½–2in). Make cuttings of each variety as even in length as possible. Reduce numbers of leaves to four or five on the semi-dwarf elepidotes. Strip

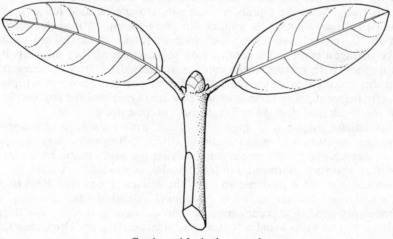

Cutting with single wound

lower leaves off dwarf lepidotes etc., and flush with stem as these may rot if in contact with the rooting medium.

Larger, thicker cuttings all benefit from 'wounding', a slice 1.3–2.5cm ($\frac{1}{2}$–1in) long, at the base of each cutting. The thickest cuttings may be wounded on both sides. Wound down to the cambium layer only (through the bark but not into the wood). Never wound so as to leave a thin point where rotting will invariably start. Do not wound the thinnest dwarfs or any evergreen azaleas, nor the softer, thinner soft wood cuttings. Always cut cleanly, never leaving snags which encourage rotting. While knives and razor blades are commonly used, secateurs are permissible provided they cut cleanly and are not of the anvil type which may crush the stem. Very short-bladed throwaway knives are now available.

Rooting 'hormones' and fungicides

Evergreen azaleas and many of the smaller dwarfs root perfectly well without the assistance of a rooting substance. Of the plants included in this book, only semi-dwarfs, especially elepidote species and hybrids, are likely to benefit from these so called 'hormones'. At their best, these substances do not take the place of a skilled propagator. Most are based on the chemicals indolebutyric (IBA), indoleacetic (IAA) and naphthaleneacetic (NAA) acids. These are applied in powder or liquid forms. Various chemicals, fungicides and diluents are added to the proprietary brands available to the public. Follow instructions with caution and do not use some new brand on a whole batch of valuable cuttings. The commonly available strengths of powder are sufficient to treat most dwarfs. Only species such as *roxieanum* and some other Talienses might succeed better with a stronger mixture. Some stronger liquid brands are available in America and Britain, or one's own mixture can be made up by acquiring the pure chemicals and mixing them with talc for a powder. With liquid, the chemicals can be melted in alcohol and then diluted with water. With the liquids, a weak solution can be used for a 'soak' and a stronger solution for a quick dip. Near-wilting cuttings will absorb more 'hormone' than those which are fully turgid. Be careful not to use the strongest commercial products on soft cuttings as they may rapidly kill them. With powder, if the cuttings are very dry it may be necessary to dip the ends in water to hold sufficient powder. Shake off surplus water before dipping them into the powder. Again remove any surplus, as too much may damage or kill the base of the cuttings.

If careful attention is paid to hygiene with regard to containers, rooting medium and preparation of cuttings, fungicides may not be necessary. Some people recommend soaking the newly prepared cuttings (before applying 'hormone') in a fungicidal solution, others water on a fungicide or use a dust blown over the foliage. I now use Rovral or Captan, one full desert spoon to 4.5 litres (1 gallon) of water. Benomyl is frequently used. Fungicides may be applied once a month; use them alternately so as to avoid a fungal resistance building up. Drenching the medium is often recommended, but this is liable to result in the medium becoming too wet.

Soft-wood cuttings

I am making more and more use of this method for rooting anything with deciduous blood in it. This includes the Trichoclada subsection, dwarf forms of *mucronulatum* and *dauricum* (also taller but outside the scope of this book) plus all hybrids of these species, also *camtschaticum*, *lowndesii*, and *cowanianum*.

These cuttings should be taken when the whole shoot is soft or *just* beginning to firm up at the base and before a terminal bud or adventitious flower buds are formed. If terminal buds have formed, remove them. The above will all root successfully from open ground stock plants, but like deciduous azaleas and many deciduous trees and shrubs, stock plants forced under cover providing cuttings earlier in the season, give still better results. These cuttings should only receive low-strength rooting substances ('hormones') if any. They must not be allowed to wilt at any stage and avoid excessive heat building up where rooting is (hopefully) taking place. Even under mist, fairly heavy shading is desirable; apply frequent bursts of spray, especially when cuttings are newly inserted. I prefer polythene directly over the cuttings plus bottom heat. Rooting should be fairly rapid and the cuttings should be ready for potting by August–September or earlier. Potted cuttings must be kept close in a polythene-covered frame for a while and very gradually hardened off while receiving supplementary light (see p.228) to enhance growth. Tips may be taken off this young growth to make a further batch of cuttings, and with adequate heat and light this process can be carried on over winter. Also, several crops can be taken off the stock plants brought indoors earlier. Again (see pp.228 and 234) I must stress the desirability of giving a resting period from January to spring in a cold house or frame.

Insertion and maintenance of cuttings

Insert cuttings as quickly as possible after preparation. Space them far enough apart so that foliage does not overlap to any extent. Over-shaded and touching leaves often rot and turn black. Insert to only a third to a half of the cutting's length. Too-deep insertion can lead to basal rotting. Be very careful not to put similar varieties next to each other in case they get mixed on removal when rooted, and if necessary divide different batches with clean objects that will not rot. Do not place large cuttings next to small ones that might get overshadowed.

Cuttings should be well watered in but never firmed up or dibbled in like young seedlings. They may be treated with an anti-transpirant like S 600 and/or a fungicide (see previous section) after insertion. Never allow cuttings to dry out once inserted, but try to prevent the medium from becoming over-wet, rapidly deteriorating the peat resulting in poor aeration. Only water (under polythene) when the medium begins to get dry; but if allowed to become too dry, it is hard to re-wet. This can be made easier by using a wetting agent such as *Aqua-gro* (liquid or granules).

Never allow direct sunlight to hit cuttings under polythene but when possible, remove shading during dull weather. In sophisticated propagating houses, thermal screens may be used which combine shading properties with heat retention in cold weather. This shading may be manually or automatically controlled. Under mist, the frequency and length of mist bursts should be reduced once the cuttings have been in for more than two to three weeks.

Inspect cuttings weekly, removing any dead or unhealthy foliage and cuttings. Polythene can be kept off for a while on dull days to allow the leaf surfaces to dry, and during mid-winter it may be left off for whole days at a time. Cut slits in polythene once rooting is well-advanced and then remove polythene altogether.

Attempt to keep the air cool and the base of the cuttings warm (where basal heating is applied) by ventilating and shading. Warming the air is only necessary during very cold weather to keep the frost out.

Transplanting and hardening off of rooted cuttings

Roots should be adequate before transplanting. For dwarfs this means about 1cm ($\frac{2}{3}$in) or more across; 2.5cm (1in) or more for semi-dwarfs. If the roots are smaller than that, the plants may fail to establish.

All dwarfs from high elevations must be handled in one of the following two ways. *Either* leave them in the boxes (trays) or frames in which they were rooted until they start coming into growth in the spring; *or* pot, rebox, or plant them into a frame or bed into a suitable compost (see below) and harden them off. Before the end of January, transfer them (if in pots or trays) into a cold house or frame, with some frost-protection at least in the early stages. If potted or boxed without a following cooling period, losses may be severe with a slow and erratic growth break. Evergreen azaleas and the more tender species and their hybrids from low elevations do not require a cool period.

Nothing is more annoying than cuttings rotting off after they have rooted. This is usually due to excessive moisture and/or inadequate light. If rotting starts, fungicides will never stop it. I find various *forrestii* hybrids such as 'Baden Baden' very susceptible. The prompt removal of all shading and frost-protection during daylight hours, especially on dull days during the winter, should help reduce this problem.

All recently transplanted cuttings need a gradual aclimatization to the less humid conditions of an open greenhouse bench and also to low temperatures. Gradually open frames, reduce mist frequency and length of bursts, or cut slits in the polythene (polythene full of little slits is now available). Insulate heavily when the rooted cuttings are first transferred to cold house or frame, especially during frost. If potted, plunge the pots to the rim in peat, ground bark or similar substance.

Composts should contain a very high organic content. I do not use any loam. Some sand can be added if of good quality. I now use a mixture of peat, acid oak/beech leafmould, ground bark and/or conifer needles. For rhododendrons, use half or less of the amount of fertilizer recommended on the packet or bag, particularly towards autumn. Many species, notably of the Taliensia and Neriiflora subsections, are very easily scorched by too much nitrogen (ammonia). Magnesium (dolomitic) limestone is beneficial as is gypsum, about 14 grams ($\frac{1}{2}$oz) of each per bushel. Special ericaceous composts are now available at many garden centres.

Micropropagation

It is unlikely (at least in the foreseeable future) that anyone other than really large nurseries, and laboratories especially catering for smaller nurseries' requirements, will attempt this method of propagation. It is only really worthwhile when large numbers of young plants are required. Still, one never knows what the future may bring, so a basic description of this process may not go amiss. For those wishing further information, consult ADAS booklet 2413, *Introduction to the micropropagation of horticultural crops.* For those outside Britain, similar booklets should be available.

I will not attempt to describe in detail the equipment that is essential, even for the smallest unit; sterile conditions are always essential.

A 5cm (2in) cutting, semi-ripe (as used for ordinary cuttings) is stripped of leaves and terminal bud, is thoroughly cleaned and sterilized, the base recut and placed in a test tube in sterile media containing cytokinin and placed under artificial light at temperatures between 21 and 27°C (70–80°F). Many die or fail to grow at this stage but those that succeed should start growing in two to eight weeks. Shoots grow from axial buds and these are in turn cut off and placed in tubes for further multiplication. Calluses may form, of which each grain is a potential plant, although very often it is impossible to get anything other than further callous tissue. This dividing can be done up to five times, resulting in a potential of about a million plantlets, or may be stopped at the third or fourth stage if requirements are less.

These minute cuttings may be rooted on another sterile medium of a different formula containing auxin, or rooted in an ordinary type of peat/perlite type of media under humid conditions. Both are successfully carried out in different American nurseries and laboratories. These little cuttings have reverted to a juvenile state which are invariably easier to root than cuttings from adult plants or even off young nursery stock.

Little trouble has been had as a result of mutating, but it is advised not to keep each culture going for more than a year. These cultures can be stored dimly lit for many months without deterioration. So far, those that have reached flowering size have all been true to type.

The commercial production of rhododendrons from micropropagation has just started in Britain.

Layering

While this old method of propagation has now been largely replaced by cuttings and more recently, tissue culture (micropropagation), it still has its uses and, I feel, always will.

Species and a few hybrids that are very difficult to root may be increased this way, either just for one or two extra plants for the amateur or in fair quantities for the nurseryman. I produce several different items this way. Also, it is a very useful way to rejuvenate an old leggy specimen of a dwarf. If the branches are buried with the tips protruding from the soil, they may be left to re-root and then refurbish themselves without actually lifting the layered branches. Alternatively, old plants may be lifted and lain on their sides ('thrown' is the term often used for this) and every shoot tip (where they will bend) bent. These bent shoots are carefully buried with just the tips above soil level. A few items have very stiff branches but the majority of dwarfs, especially the lepidotes, are flexible enough to bend at least 90 degrees into an upright position. This bend helps to encourage roots to form. If one or two shoots are left above ground, these will form the foundation of a plant to relayer after the first crop is removed. Vigorous, relatively young plants are actually easier to layer than very old specimens. The shoots are easier to bend and they root more quickly.

There is quite an art in this layering and making the best use of each branch and shoot, bending them without breaking and spacing them out evenly. A considerable number of young plants may be produced off one flexible twiggy plant. I use stones of various sizes for keeping the branches in place. Roots like to form under these stones which help to retain moisture. A liberal amount of peat and sand thoroughly mixed into the existing soil greatly helps one's success. Try to finish off with a level surface.

While this layering may be done at any time, it is better to avoid the summer and early autumn when young shoots are soft and easily broken off. Most items will root sufficiently with us in two growing seasons. In the spring after they have been down for two seasons, we carefully lift them and chop them up (with secateurs) into as many rooted bits as possible and line them into a partly shaded area of the nursery. Many will benefit from a prune as layers are apt to be straggly. I prune before lining out and again the following spring. Most should be saleable after two seasons' growth. Most of the subjects I layer are the more difficult-to-root members of the subsection Lapponica and the section Pogon-anthum (Anthopogon series).

Low branches on established plants may also be layered, preferably into boxes so as not to damage the parent's root system. Again try to bend the shoot upwards. A slit may be cut in the stem and rooting powder inserted to enhance rooting. Never attempt to root large branches as these may never root and in any case would be harder to establish after severing. Some people sever the layer from its parent a season before lifting but unless the growing conditions are particularly good on that site, I would not advise this. The chief difficulty over this type of layering is in keeping the soil around the layer moist enough during the summer. Under adverse conditions, rooting may take three years or more and some may not root at all.

Air layering is hardly necessary for dwarfs.

Grafting

Grafting need not be considered for the great majority of dwarfs as they can be propagated by the other methods described. Only the most difficult-to-root of the larger dwarfs or new rare material need be grafted. In very cold climates like Germany, very hardy understocks may promote hardiness and special varieties selected for this purpose are propagated from cuttings.

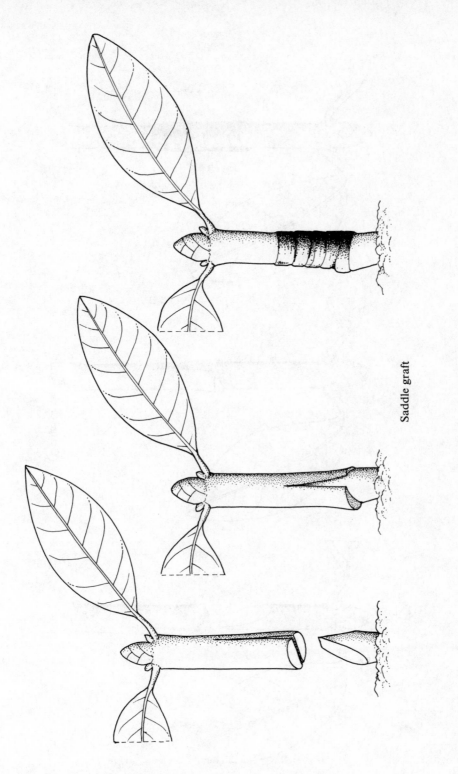

Saddle graft

237

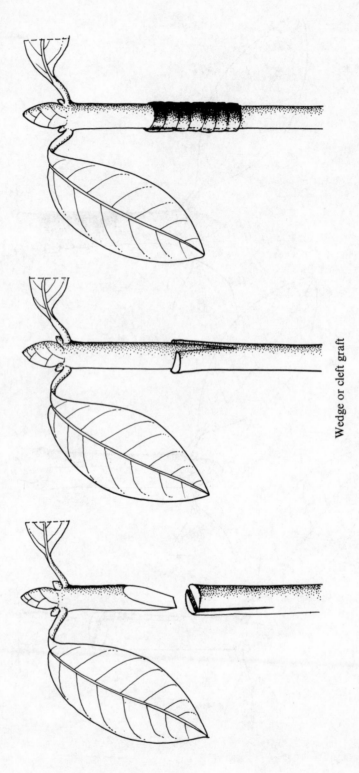

Wedge or cleft graft

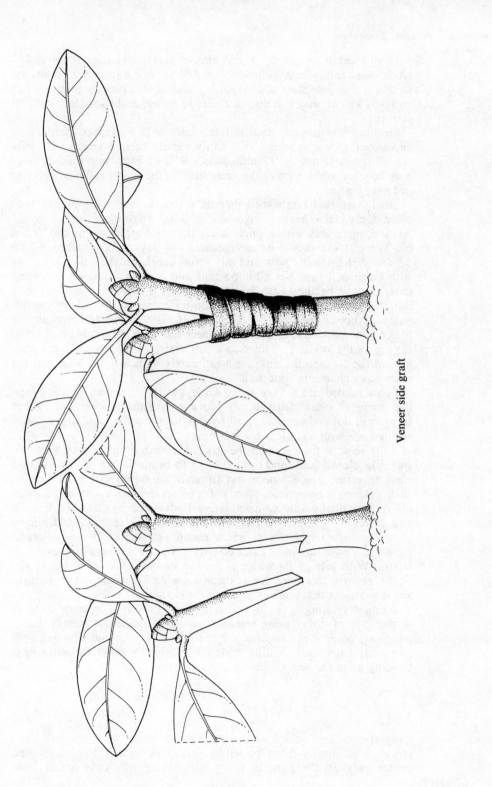

Veneer side graft

Until recently, *R. ponticum* was almost universally used as an understock. Availability, ease of production and possibly more even results led to this undesirable state of affairs. I say undesirable because *ponticum* has two well-known major faults, its ability to sucker and its susceptibility to root rot.

Grafting is commonly done in late winter or late summer. People now endeavour to use seedlings of a fairly closely related species or easily rooted hybrids such as 'Cunningham's White'. Even unrooted cuttings may be used which root at the same time as the union calluses. Treat as ordinary cuttings.

Stocks are best established in pots a year before grafting is to take place. Only clean, healthy, vigorous seedlings or rooted cuttings should be used, preferably with a single straight stem. Surplus stems can be cut off. These stocks should be brought in a few days before grafting. Clean off any dirt from the pots and any loose debris on the soil surface. As with cuttings, hygiene is all-important and a clean frame or polythene cover should be used into which the grafts are to be placed. Several different grafts can be used such as those illustrated. For others, consult reference books such as *The Grafter's Handbook* (see Bibliography). I prefer a saddle, wedge or cleft or a veneer side graft. With the last, part of the top of the stock is retained as a sap drawer. I like to make the graft low on the stem so the union can ultimately be below soil level and the scion has a chance to root itself.

Tools needed are a very sharp knife, plastic or rubber grafting tape (cut strips of clean, fairly heavy-gauge polythene or large cut rubber bands will do) and surgical spirit to sterilize the knife regularly. A fairly strong knife with a straight blade is best.

If the scion is thinner than the stock, it is important to match up one side. Cut cleanly and bind tight enough to bring the wood of scion and stock together. It is not necessary to cover the union with grafting wax. After grafting is completed, place in frame, shade if necessary and harden off very gradually after callusing is well advanced by allowing in more and more air. While some heat may be beneficial, grafts should not be placed in high temperatures which encourages the stock and scion to grow before the union is callused-over properly and usually results in failure. With side grafts where a portion of the stock is left above the union, remove this once the scion is growing vigorously. Also remove any new shoots that might appear on the stock.

Summer grafting is highly rated in the USA. It is usually done in August out of doors using semi-soft wood. If shaded, it is said that a polythene cover is not necessary, but I would recommend covering with polythene bags with shading material on top to avoid excessive heat building up in the bag. Callusing takes place very rapidly.

Seed

Only species and deliberate crosses should be grown from seed. The species seed should either be wild-collected or from a hand-pollinated source only. In the past, so many disappointments have arisen from sowing open (insect) pollinated seed from such sources as the RBG, Edinburgh and Wisley Garden. A very large percentage of open-pollinated seed of species turn out to be hybrids. For instance, I once grew 100 seedlings of a certain species and three were true to type. A few species rarely cross and fewer still never cross with others (such as *camtschaticum*). An occasional plant, or better still a group of one species, may bloom when nothing else is out or be isolated enough not to have contaminated pollen, though remember that bees and other insects can travel a long way. Far too many gardens are full of open-pollinated seedling rubbish. Hand-pollinating is not difficult and if one is not able to do it oneself, an excellent supply of this seed may be obtained by joining the American Rhododendron Society.

Provided good forms of species are selected, there is a really good chance that equally good or even superior forms can be raised from hand-pollinated seed. Most elepidotes are self-sterile and in any case, cross pollination of species produces more vigorous offspring. Lepidotes are more often self-fertile and certain species such as *pumilum* tend to pollinate themselves within each flower. Still, I would advise cross-pollination with two good selections of a species where possible. These *must* be two different clones. Use unopened buds only, cutting off the corolla with scissors down to the base and removing the stamens. This makes the remainder of the flower unattractive to insects so there is no need to cover it.

I use two methods from this stage on.
(1) Pollinate at once by dabbing ripe anthers on to the stigma, then cover the stigma with a small piece of micropore (surgical) tape which keeps the stigma dry, holds the pollen in place and stops any contamination.
(2) Very small dwarfs are hard to treat this way. Having stripped as before, leave for a few days until the stigma becomes noticeably sticky (receptive) and then pollinate. It may increase the chances of success by repollinating after two more days. This process applies to both species seed production and hybridizing. Carefully label all pollinated shoots and record in a notebook.

It is not necessary to have fresh pollen at hand. Pollen (dried) can be sent by post or can be stored in gelatine capsules over calcium chloride (to keep it dry) in a screw-topped jar for several months. For longer storing, place in a freezer, after pre-drying the pollen in a refrigerator for two to three days. It must be warmed before use and can be refrozen several times if desired. Always label carefully.

Even pollinated species frequently set no seed. With species, the poor set may be due to cool, wet weather during pollination or, of course, frost which may ruin all the early pollinations in a season. Cross-pollination to make hybrids often results in failure due to some degree of incompatability. It has been found that the combination of heat and high humidity greatly increases not only the chances of seed being set but increases the amount and size of the actual seed. Stock plants in pots can be brought inside in January and the temperature gradually increased. Allow the greenhouse temperature to get as high as possible (from the sun) and keep up the humidity by frequently damping down the floor. While it is better to go through the same process of stripping and pol-

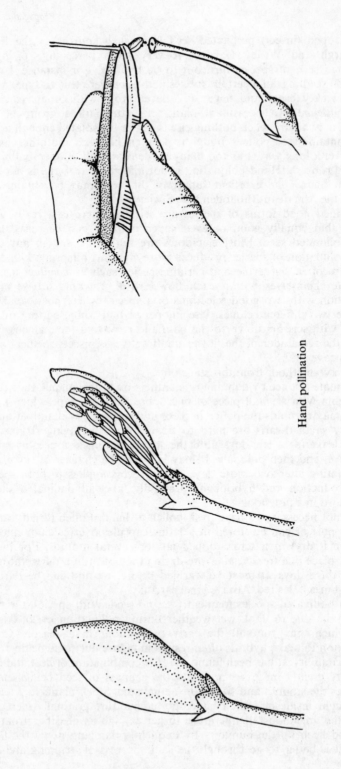

Hand pollination

lination as described earlier, there should be no danger of insect pollination if the ventilators are not opened.

The application of heat to stimulate successful pollination may be taken a stage further by erecting a small growing chamber. It can be made in various different ways but the combination of a framework surrounded by polythene with fluorescent tubes at the top and a hotplate underneath should be adequate. A pan of water should be placed on the hotplate to maintain a very high humidity. Experiments have shown that most rhododendrons will stand 43–45°C (110–114°F) for up to three hours. Pollinate and then place plant inside the chamber. The heat greatly speeds up the actual time of fertilization of the ovaries and three hours should be more than sufficient. Lepidote crosses have been particularly successful using this method.

Seed ripens between August and December. Generally speaking, the more alpine a species is, the earlier it will ripen. *R. pumilum* ripens in August, evergreen azaleas not until late November–December. Capsules may be picked green when full-sized. Open them in gentle heat and sow immediately. If one has growing-room facilities, this can gain at least half a season's growth. Seed picked green is unlikely to be viable for as long as naturally ripened seed. If one does not have suitable facilities under artificial lights, it is better to hold off sowing until January–February. Alternatively, seed can be sown early, put outside in a cold frame and left to germinate naturally when the temperature warms up in the spring. This is often the best method for the highest-elevation species.

Naturally ripened capsules should be picked as they begin to turn brown or black or as they start to split open. During the main ripening season, I like to inspect all capsules weekly. Dry in a sunny window or over gentle heat (on top of a box over a radiator). Most capsules open under these conditions but a few need to be prised open. Try to avoid crushing the capsule to extract the seed as bits of capsule encourage mould when germination is taking place. I use different sizes of riddles or sieves to separate the seed from the chaff. Store seed in folded paper and/or little envelopes. Avoid polythene as the seed sticks to it. I store all our seed in our refrigerator in screw-top jars or air-tight plastic food containers. This increases the life of good autumn-collected seed from an average of two to five or more years. Green or spring-gathered seed may not keep so long.

I use plastic pans for sowing (half pots) but any reasonable containers such as a divided seed tray or old plastic margarine containers are suitable, provided holes are made in the base. Only use thoroughly clean pans etc.

Finely riddled peat (I use a mixture of heather and sphagnum peat) is a perfectly adequate medium on which to sow most rhododendron seeds. For the trickiest dwarfs, very old seed, and many of the epiphytic type species, use fresh riddled sphagnum, preferably from a high elevation as this is more likely to grow slowly and not overtake the growth of the seedlings. I have found that dried sphagnum has lost much of its antibiotic properties leading to mould and a growth of algae.

Fill containers to the rim, gently firm and soak in a trough or basin until thoroughly moist. Allow to drain, refirm carefully around edges and you are ready for sowing.

Most dwarf lepidotes have tiny seed and if the seed is good and fresh, every one should germinate. So sow thinly. Overcrowding encourages that worst killer of little rhododendron seedlings, grey mould (*Botrytis cinerea*). Rhododendron seed should always be germinated under moist, humid conditions with no direct sunlight. Do not germinate them in the dark or under very dull conditions or they will soon become leggy. I now cover them with polythene full of tiny slits (made by Fabro, a Swiss firm) which supposedly open when vigorous seedlings like annuals and vegetables grow. The advantage of the slit polythene is that there is little or no condensation underneath so that it is now unnecessary to turn or remove the covering to allow it to drip. I place the pans under lights in my growing room under this polythene and leave them with very little attention. All that is needed is an occasional inspection for mould, mice and insects and to sift some fine peat over the germinating seeds to help anchor them. Re-soak pans if they start to dry out.

Alternative covers are glass and polythene sheets which should be turned daily. If germination takes place in a greenhouse, cover glass or polythene with newspaper to keep out sunlight. One layer of newspaper is good for shading after germination when the sun is out.

Some people like to prick out seedlings as soon as they are large enough to handle (with two to three true leaves) while others prefer to prick out after a year's growth. If the seedlings are widely spaced, there is no hurry but if crowded, there is. Most seedlings seem to prefer company and not the isolation of individual pots. I use either wooden boxes or plastic trays but they can be pricked out directly into open benches with a peaty compost or into a frame. Handle carefully to avoid damage to leaves and roots. I have yet to find the ideal compost but at present use a quarter peat, a quarter oak or beech leafmould, a quarter spruce needles off the forest floor and a quarter pulverized bark. Other ingredients can be rotten wood (better sterilized), light acid loam, rotten chopped bracken, pine needles and good-quality sand. Be careful that leafmould or needles do not contain pests like weevil grubs and leather jackets. They may need to be sterilized.

Be very sparing with fertilizer at this stage if it is used at all. Liquid fertilizer can be given once the seedlings are established after pricking out, or if left in the seed pans, once a few true leaves have developed. Carefully shade seedings at all times from direct sun, especially when just pricked out and re-cover with polythene if pricked out in a growing room.

Boxes or trays are best watered only from underneath in the early stages. Moisture hanging on the leaves encourages botrytis so water overhead in sunny weather in the morning only, never when it is dull and damp.

Growing on of young plants

Young seedlings (and other plants) grown on steadily without a check always make the best plants. Checks can be caused by too much or too little water, excessive heat or fertilizer, sunburn, fungus and insect attacks. If a fungus develops on the organic matter in the tray or box, re-box into fresh compost. Overcrowding must always be avoided—it leads to botrytis. Vigorous seedlings re-boxed in mid- to late summer will make a good deal more growth before winter. Even dwarfs vary considerably in the amount of growth made per season and those that grow very slowly may require two seasons before being large enough to plant into nursery beds or a cold frame.

Like rooted cuttings, seedlings appreciate a cooling period over winter in a cold frame or greenhouse. Over-wintering seedlings need very careful watering to avoid mould and should only be watered on sunny and/or windy days. Always ventilate during mild weather. Some small seedlings are amazingly hardy and may actually survive better when just given the protection of plastic netting if well-hardened off before frost. Likewise, the majority of small seedlings and rooted cuttings can survive nine seasons out of ten in a cold frame or greenhouse. 1981–2 was different. In a cold house with a paraffin (kerosene) heater plus a bubble polythene cover, I lost many seedlings when the temperature dropped to $-18°C$ ($0°F$) or lower.

Shade houses made out of plastic netting or lath are excellent for growing on young plants. The percentage of shade is important. In C. Scotland, 40 per cent shade is dark enough. Tunnel houses are now available with a combination of polythene tops and net sides for ventilation. Alternatively, shade houses can have polythene placed over them, partially or fully, and in some the polythene can be rolled up and down. Another protection is a low-level hoop covered with polythene or netting. I have not found netting itself a great protection against spring frosts and those items that start into growth early need an additional barrier against the frost. I now use a cloche made out of double rigid plastic which can be bent to form an inverted 'V' shape. I push wire between the two plastic layers to protrude at both ends and act as pins to stick into the ground and anchor them.

Seedlings of dwarfs do not normally need the same degree of pruning as many rooted cuttings do. The latter often tend to grow from terminal buds only and may need at least two pinchings of the tips in the first growing season and at least one in the second.

Feeding twice a season with Hortus GOC No. 1 (ICI, SAI) (analysis: N12 P6 K6) or equivalent in April–May and late June–July at a medium handful (50 grams) per 3 sq m (33 sq ft) is very beneficial to all young plants with the possible exceptions of Neriiflora and Taliensia subsections plus some vigorous hybrids like 'Elizabeth' and 'May Day' which are apt to remain soft into autumn with late growth.

Frames and shade houses should have at least 50 per cent organic matter well mixed in, even if the soil is suitable for rhododendrons. If the soil is heavy, use an entirely made-up mixture. I find pure peat beds plus the fertilizer (above) excellent for tricky dwarfs such as *ludlowii*, *pumilum* and the hybrid 'Pipit'. Some peats can be too acid on their own so it may be necessary to add some dolomitic lime to avoid chlorosis.

Wherever planted, young dwarfs need extra special care during their first season. Make sure the root balls are moist before planting and be sure to plant at the correct depth. Water in thoroughly and never allow the surface to get really dry. Watch out for pests like moles and blackbirds which can play havoc with watered beds in dry weather. Net beds if necessary. I do my planting out of young stock in June–July. Harden off as much as possible before planting, either by leaving ventilators open day and night or preferably by placing out of doors for a week or two. In warm climates, some overhead shading is essential for at least the first few months after planting.

Frost without snow loosens up the soil and usually throws out a large percentage of small plants. This does little harm provided they are all carefully pushed back and re-firmed before any dry weather occurs in spring. All dwarfs of doubtful hardiness should be kept in a frame for their first season or two. With us this includes *valentinianum* and *leucaspis*.

Mycorrhizal association with rhododendrons is normal. By adding a little soil from the root areas of established healthy plants to soil mixes, beneficial results have been reported.

Moss and liverwort can be reduced or controlled using the fungicide Thiram or algicides like Algenex or Algifen. Liverwort in particular can become so dense that it can choke out the smallest dwarfs. Best applied as a preventative rather than a cure on susceptible ground.

I have had little experience with the use of growth-regulating chemicals and they are unlikely to be used by the home gardener in the immediate future. There does seem to be a future for nurseries to treat rhododendrons so as to get extra shoots, short compact growth and a good set of flower buds prior to selling.

7 Lists of Recommendations

These tend to be a personal choice based on my own observations, but I have tried to be as unbiased in my selections as possible. These lists should only be used as a rough guide, especially with the species which are often extremely variable. Closely related species of equal value may have been omitted. Where individual species vary in their merits, those listed refer to superior forms. Many species or hybrids behave differently where climates are dissimilar. Several of the species are hard to obtain while a few of the hybrids are fairly new.

Species

Easy species

calostrotum, dauricum dwarf, *fastigiatum, ferrugineum, keleticum, orthocladum* var. *microleucum, pemakoense, polycladum, racemosum, russatum, yakushimanum*

Full sun in north

camtschaticum, carolinianum, fastigiatum, ferrugineum, lapponicum Parvifolium, *keleticum, moupinense, myrtifolium, racemosum, trichostomum, williamsianum*

Shade

aperantum, aureum, chamae-thomsonii, dichroanthum, forrestii, pseudochrysanthum, recurvoides, sanguineum, tsariense

For the connoisseur

cephalanthum Crebreflorum, *forrestii, kongboense, lowndesii, ludlowii, megeratum, nivale, pronum, proteoides, pumilum, recurvoides, roxieanum, setosum, temenium* 'Cruachan'

Very slow- and low-growing

aureum, campylogynum Myrtilloides, *cephalanthum* Crebreflorum, *forrestii, hanceanum* 'Nanum', *impeditum, keiskei* 'Yaku Fairy', *keleticum* Radicans, *lowndesii, ludlowii, nivale, proteoides, saluenense* Prostratum, *uniflorum* var. *imperator*

Indumentum

anthopogon, beanianum, haematodes, 'Metternichii', *recurvoides, roxiea-num, roxieanum* var. *cucullatum, tsariense, wasonii, yakushimanum*

Beauty of flower

calostrotum 'Gigha', *campylogynum, charitopes, forrestii, hippophaeoides, haematodes, impeditum, leucaspis, moupinense, primuliflorum* Cephalanth-oides

Very hardy Europe

calostrotum (some), *campanulatum* ssp. *aeruginosum, camtschaticum, capi-tatum, caucasicum, dauricum* dwarf, *fastigiatum, ferrugineum* and *hirsutum, lapponicum* Parvifolium, *mucronulatum* dwarf, *polycladum, russatum, yakushimanum*

Very hardy E. North America

aureum, capitatum, carolinianum, caucasicum, dauricum dwarf, *keiskei, mucronulatum* dwarf, *lapponicum* Parvifolium, 'Metternichii' var. *penta-merum, racemosum* (some), *yakushimanum*

Hot areas (drought resistant)

burmanicum, chapmanii, racemosum, scabrifolium and var. *spiciferum, vir-gatum*

For mild gardens

burmanicum, chrysodoron, edgeworthii, kawakamii, luteiflorum, sperabile, sulfureum, tephropeplum, xanthostephanum, valentinianum, virgatum

Early flowering

aureum, beanianum, capitatum, chamae-thomsonii, ciliatum, dauricum dwarf, *lapponicum* Parvifolium, *laudandum* var. *temoense, leucaspis, lutei-florum, moupinense, mucronulatum* dwarf, *sulfureum*

Late flowering

brachyanthum, calostrotum Nitens, *dichroanthum, didymum, ferrugineum, hirsutum, kawakamii* (tender), *lowndesii, mekongense* Rubroluteum and Viridescens, *santapauii* (tender), *trichostomum* (some)

Free-flowering

calostrotum 'Gigha', *campylogynum* (some), *ciliatum, hippophaeoides, impeditum, lepidotum, leucaspis, pemakoense, racemosum, rupicola* var. *chryseum, russatum, trichostomum, yakushimanum*

Alkaline soil

cephalanthum (some), *ciliatum, dichroanthum* ssp. *scyphocalyx, didymum, hippophaeoides, hirsutum, williamsianum*

Epiphytic

edgeworthii, kawakamii, pendulum, santapauii, seinghkuense, vaccinioides vaccinioides

Flower hardy

capitatum, carolinianum, dauricum dwarf, *hippophaeoides, intricatum, lapponicum* Parvifolium, *moupinense, orthocladum* var. *microleucum*

Glaucous foliage

calostrotum, callimorphum, campanulatum ssp. *aeruginosum, campylocarpum* ssp. *caloxanthum, fastigiatum, intricatum, lepidostylum, mekongense* Rubroluteum and Viridescens

My personal choice

calostrotum 'Gigha', *campylogynum, camtschaticum, cephalanthum* Crebreflorum, *edgeworthii, forrestii, keiskei* 'Yaku Fairy', *leucaspis, moupinense, proteoides, recurvoides, roxieanum, russatum, yakushimanum*

Best yellow

anthopogon ssp. *hypenanthum* 'Annapurna', *chrysodoron, fletcherianum, hanceanum* 'Nanum', *lowndesii, ludlowii, luteiflorum, rupicola* var. *chryseum, sargentianum, sulfureum, temenium* 'Cruachan', *mekongense* var. *melinanthum, valentinianum, wasonii*

Best pink

callimorphum, calostrotum Calciphilum, *campylogynum* salmon pink, *cephalanthum* Crebreflorum, *charitopes, glaucophyllum, hirsutum, pemakoense, primuliflorum, pseudochrysanthum, racemosum* F 19404, *tephropeplum, williamsianum*

Best blue

fastigiatum, hippophaeoides, impeditum, intricatum, polycladum

Best purple, violet, magenta and crimson-purple

baileyi, camtschaticum, keleticum Radicans, *lepidotum* 'Reuthe's Purple', *rupicola, russatum, saluenense* ssp. *chameunum, uniflorum* var. *imperator*

Best white

collettianum, edgeworthii, leucaspis, moupinense white, *orthocladum* var. *microleucum, trichostomum* white, *virgatum* white, *yakushimanum*

Best red shades

calostrotum 'Gigha', *campylogynum* 'Bodnant Red', *camtschaticum* red sel., *chamae-thomsonii, ferrugineum* near red, *forrestii, haematodes, microgynum, neriiflorum, sanguineum*

Best young foliage

callimorphum, calostrotum, campanulatum ssp. *aeruginosum, hanceanum, keiskei, lepidostylum, moupinense, saluenense* ssp. *chameunum, tsariense, williamsianum, yakushimanum*

Interesting foliage

camtschaticum, chapmanii, edgeworthii, makinoi, 'Metternichii', *mucronulatum* dwarf (autumn colour), *neriiflorum* 'Rosevallon', *pendulum, pseudochrysanthum, roxieanum, sperabile, tsariense, valentinianum, williamsianum, yakushimanum*

Most aromatic foliage

anthopogon, brachyanthum, calostrotum, campylogynum, glaucophyllum, kongboense, Lapponicums (many), *primuliflorum, saluenense, sargentianum,* Talienses (several)

Hybrids

Most popular 12

Baden Baden, Blue Diamond, Blue Tit, Carmen, Cilpinense, Elizabeth, Hummingbird, Pink Drift, Praecox, Ptarmigan, Ramapo, Scarlet Wonder

Easy

Anna Baldsiefen, Blue Diamond, Carmen, Curlew, Dora Amateis, Elizabeth, Ginny Gee, Intrifast, Lavendula, Linda, Pink Drift, Ptarmigan, Razorbill, Sarled, Scarlet Wonder, Snipe, Tottenham, Wren

Dwarf

Chikor, Euan Cox, Intrifast, *lowndesii* × *keiskei* 'Yaku Fairy', Pipit, Prostigiatum, Ptarmigan, St Merryn, Treasure, Wren

Semi-dwarf

Charmaine, Chiff Chaff, Creeping Jenny, Curlew, Ginny Gee, Maricee, Merganser, Patty Bee, Ramapo, Razorbill, Sarled, Scarlet Wonder, Snipe, Songbird, Wigeon

Low

Arctic Tern (× *Ledudendron*), Blue Diamond, Caroline Allbrook, Dopey, Elizabeth, Moonstone, Pink Pebble, Riplet, Ruby Heart, Teal, Unique, Vintage Rose

Very hardy Europe

Azurwolke, Baden Baden, Dora Amateis, Elisabeth Hobbie, Euan Cox, Linda, Mary Fleming, Olive, Pink Drift, P.J.M., Ramapo, Sacko, Scarlet Wonder, Tottenham, Wilsoni

Very hardy E. North America

Cutie, Dora Amateis, Mary Fleming, P.J.M., Purple Gem, Ramapo, Windbeam, some *yakushinanum* hybrids

My personal choice

Anna Baldsiefen, Arctic Tern, Curlew, Dora Amateis, Egret, Euan Cox, Ginny Gee, Intrifast, Ptarmigan, Razorbill, Riplet, Ruby Heart, Songbird, Vintage Rose, Wren

Best yellow

Canary, Chiff Chaff, Chikor, Curlew, Euan Cox, Merganser, Moonstone, Patty Bee, Princess Anne, Shamrock, Teal, Wren

Best pink

Anna Baldsiefen, Bowbells, Bruce Brechtbill, Cilpinense, Ginny Gee, Linda, Lori Eichelser, Moerheim's Pink, Molly Ann, Pink Pebble, Pipit, Razorbill, Rose Elf, Seta, Snipe, Tessa Roza, Vintage Rose, Whispering Rose, Wigeon

Best blue, purple, and lavender

Azurwolke, Blue Star, Blue Diamond, Caroline Allbrook, Cutie, Gristede, Lavendula, Phalarope, Pink Drift, P.J.M., Purple Gem, Ramapo, St. Merryn, Sapphire, Songbird

Best white

Arctic Tern, Dora Amateis, Egret, Eider, Maricee, Ptarmigan, Sarled, Snow Lady, Tessa Bianca

Best mixed or changing colours

Mary Fleming, Percy Wiseman, Riplet, Unique

Best red

Baden Baden, Charmaine, Creeping Jenny, Dopey, Elisabeth, Elizabeth, Firedance (RM11) Grouse, Oporto, Ruby Heart, Scarlet Wonder, Titian Beauty

Best foliage

Curlew, Egret, Gartendirektor Glocker, Grumpy, Intrifast, P.J.M., Purple Gem, Ramapo, Riplet, Unique, Vintage Rose

Best ground cover

Baden Baden, Carmen, Creeping Jenny, Curlew, Egret, Ginny Gee, Ptarmigan, Sarled, St Merryn, Scarlet Wonder, Treasure, Wren

Best yakushimanum hybrids (smaller)

Caroline Allbrook, Doc, Dopey, Hydon Dawn, Marion Street, Morgenrot, Morning Cloud, Nestucca, Noyo Brave, Percy Wiseman, Serendipity, Silberwolke, Sparkler, Surrey Heath, Vintage Rose

Best new American hybrids

Bruce Brechtbill, Buttermint, Dora Amateis, Ginny Gee, Lori Eichelser, Molly Ann, Patty Bee, P. J. Mezitt, Riplet, Ruby Heart, Shamrock, Whispering Rose

Evergreen (Obtusum) azaleas (Tsutsusi Section)

Species for cool areas

kaempferi, kiusianum, nakaharae, poukhanense, tschonoskii, tsusiophyllum

Species for mild areas with hot summers

eriocarpum, indicum, macrosepalum, microphyton, oldhamii, ripense, rubropilosum, sataense, scabrum, simsii

Hybrid for cold areas with cool summers

Chippewa, Diamant hybrids, Gaiety, Lemur, Panda, Squirrel, Vuyk's Scarlet, Willy, Wombat

Appendix A

Appendix B

Rhododendron Nurseries

Australia
Berna Park Nurseries, 5 Paul St., Cheltenham, Adelaide.
Camellia Lodge Nursery, 348 Prince's Highway, Noble Park, Victoria 3174
Cedar Lodge Nursery, Creamery Rd., Sulphur Creek, Tasmania 7321
Hilton Nursery, Hilton Rd., Ferny Creek, Victoria
Lapoinya Rhododendron Gardens, Lapoinya Road, N.W. Tasmania
Olinda Nurseries, Coonara Rd., Olinda, Victoria
Shrublands, 970 Mountain Highway, Boronia, Victoria 3155
Somerset Nursery & Garden Supplies, Bass Highway, N.W. Tasmania
Tanjenong Garden Centre (formerly Boults), Mt. Dandenong, Tourist Rd., Olinda, Victoria
Yamina Rare Plants, 25 Moores Rd., Monbulk, Victoria 3793

Europe
6.D. Böhlje, Klamperesch, 2910 Westerstede, W. Germany
Joh. Bruns, 2903 Bad Zwischenahn, W. Germany
Firma C. Esveld, Baumschulen-Pepinieres, Boskoop, Holland
Hachmann, J., Marken-Baumschulen, 2202 Barmstedt, in Holstein, Brunnenstr. 68, W. Germany
Hobbie, Dietrich G., Rhododendron Kulturen, 2911 Linswege, über Westerstede, W. Germany
Jørgensen, Tue, Rijvej 10, DK 2830, Virum, Denmark
Nagle, Walter, Baumschulen, 7518 Bretten, Hotzenbaumöfe 4, W. Germany
Seleger, Robert, Baumschule, im Grüt, 8134 Adliswil, Switzerland
Wieting, Joh., BdB-Markenbaumschulen, Omorikastrake 6, Giebelhorst, 2910 Westerstede 1, W. Germany

Great Britain
Glendoick Gardens Ltd, Glencarse, Perth PH2 7NS, Scotland
Hillier & Sons Ltd, Winchester, Hampshire
Hydon Nurseries Ltd, Clock Barn Lane, Hydon Heath, Nr. Godalming, Surrey GU8 4AZ
Knap Hill Nursery Ltd, Barrs Lane, Lower Knaphill, Woking, Surrey GU21 2JW
Millais Nurseries, Crosswater Farm, Churt, Farnham, Surrey
Reuthe Ltd., Crown Point Nursery, Ightham, Nr Sevenoaks, Kent
Wall Cottage Nursery (A. J. Clark), Leonardslee, Horsham, Sussex

New Zealand
Alouette Nursery, Lauriston, No. 2 RD Ashburton, Canterbury
Blue Mountain Nurseries, Tapanui, West Otago
Boswell, Mrs E.D., 518 Hills Rd., Christchurch 5
Campbell, Bruce W., 20A Waireka St., Ravensbourne, Dunedin
Jordan's Nursery, 6 Mekaube St, Ashburton
Opoho Nurseries, Mowat St, Opoho, Dunedin
Riverwood Gardens, Main Rd, Little River, Banks Peninsula, Canterbury
Rutland, Heaton, Stonebridge, South Canterbury

U.S.A.
Ace Garden Center, 3820 Pacific Ave., P.O. Box 306, Forest Grove, OR 97116
Azalea & Rhododendron Test Garden, 10408 Greenacres Dr., Silver Spring, MD 20903
Berryhill Nursery, Rt. 4, Box 304, Sherwood, OR 97140
The Bovees, 1737 S.W. Coronado, Portland, OR 97219
T. E. Bowhan Nursery, 27194 Huey Lane, Eugene, OR 97401
Briggs Nursery Inc., 4407 Henderson Blv., Olympia, WA 98501
Bull Valley Rhododendron Nursery, Rt. 1, Box 134, Aspers, PA 17304
Carlson's Garden, Box 305-AR7, South Salem, NY 10590
V. O. Chambers Nursery, 26874 Ferguson Rd., Junction City, OR 97448
County Gardens Nursery, Rt. 2, Box 150, Mobile, AL 36609
The Cummins Garden, 22 Robertsville Rd, Marlboro, NJ 07746
Dogwood Hills Nursery, Rt. 3, Box 181, Franklyn, LA 70438
Eastern Plant Specialities, P.O. Box 40, Colonia, NJ 07067
Ellanhurst Gardens, Rt. 3, Box 233-B, Sherwood, OR 97140
Farwell's, 13040 Skyline Blvd., (Hwy. 35) Woodside, CA 94062
Flora Lan Nursery, Rt. 1, Box 357, Forest Grove, OR 97116
Frank James Nursery, 700 Pine Flat Rd, Santa Cruz, CA 95060
Garden Valley Nursery, 12960 N.E. 181st, Bothell, WA 98011
The Greenery, 14450 N.E. 16th Place, Bellevue, WA 98007
Greer Gardens, 1280 Goodpasture Island Rd, Eugene, OR 97401
Hager Nurseries Inc., RFD5, Box 641D, Spotsylvania, VA 22553
Stan & Dody Hall, 1280 Quince Drive, Junction City, OR 97448
James Harris Nursery, 538 Swanson Dr., Lawrenceville, GA30245
Harstine Island Nursery, E.3021 Harstone Island North, Shelton, WA 98584
Hillhouse Nursery, Kresson-Gibbsboro Rd., Marlton, NJ 08053
Holly Hills Inc., 1216 Hillside Rd, Evansville, IND 47711
Horsley Rhododendron Nursery, 7441 Tracyton Blvd. N.W., Bremerton, WA 98310
Mowbray Gardens, 3318 Mowbray Lane, Cincinnati, OH 45226
Roslyn Nursery, Dept. A, P.O. Box 69, Roslyn, NY 11576
Sonoma Horticultural Nursery, 3970 Azalea Ave., Sebastopol, CA 95472
Stubbs Shrubs, 23225 Bosky Dell Lane, West Linn, OR 97068
Susquehanna Valley Hybrid Rhododendrons, Rt. 4, Box 173-1, Millboro, DEL 19966
The Sweetbriar, P.O. Box 25, Woodinville, WA 98072

Transplant Nursery, Parkertown Rd., Laronia, GA 30553
Trillium Lane Nursery, 18855 Trillium Lane, Fort Bragg, CA 95437
Van Veen Nursery, P.O. Box 06444, Portland, OR 97206
Verde Vista, RD 3, Box 3250, Spring Grove, PA 17362
Westgate Gardens Nursery, 751 Westgate Dr., Eureka, CA 95501
Whitney Gardens, P.O. Box F, Brinnon, WA 98320
Wileywood Nursery, 17414 Bothell Way, S.E., Bothell, WA 98011

Glossary

aberrant characteristics different from the type
agglutinated indumentum glued or joined together
aggregate (species) closely related species
appressed lying flat
auxin a growth-promoting substance occurring in plants in minute quantities (for the production of roots)
axillary (bud) in the angle between leaf and stem
bract a modified leaf below a flower
bullate blistered or puckered
calcareous limy or chalky
callus healing growth over a wound or cut
calyx the outer whorl of a flower
cambium the layer of actively dividing cells between wood and bark of stems or roots
candelabroid (inflorescence) a truss with several tiers of flowers
chlorosis leaves partially or wholly pale green or yellowed
chromosome rod-like objects in a cell nucleus which hold hereditary characteristics. In multiples of thirteen in rhododendrons
ciliate fringed with hairs
classification system of arranging (plants)
cline plants that merge with every gradation between them
clone the vegetatively produced progeny of a single individual
cotyledon seed leaf
crenulate minutely dentate with rounded teeth
cultivar a cultivated variety as opposed to other varieties
cytokinin a growth-promoting substance favouring shoot formation
deflexed bent downwards
eglandular without glands
elepidote without scales
endemic confined to a given geographical area
epiphyte a plant growing non-parasitically upon another
fastigiate upright
flavonoid certain natural colouring compounds in a plant
genus group of closely related species indicated by the first name of a plant
glabrescent becoming glabrous
glabrous hairless
gland a protuberance on leaves or other parts, often secreting and viscid
glandular possessing glands
glaucous covered with a bluish, grey or white bloom

grex all the seedlings of a given cross

Group name applied to former species, subspecies or varieties to maintain a horticultural status

hard pan hard, impervious layer in soil structure

hormone growth-promoting substance

hybrid swarm a large group of natural hybrids in the wild showing much variation

indumentum woolly or hairy covering found on leaves and stems

inflorescence flowers arising from one bud or an aggregate of flowers

lacerate scale torn or irregularly cleft scale

leaf wax natural substances in leaves useful for classification

lepidote scurfy with minute scales

morphological the study of living things (plants) and their parts

nomenclature mode of naming

pedicel flower stalk

periphery outer wall or margin

perulae leaf bud scales

petaloid resembling petals

petiole leaf stalk

pH the measurement of acidity or alkalinity

pilose covered with fine soft hairs

plastered (indumentum) stuck down leaving a smooth finish

polyploid having more than the usual number of chromosomes

precocious flowering before the leaves appear or flowering young

puberulent covered with very fine, short hair

pubescent clothed with short soft hair

racemose stalked flowers on an unbranched main stem

rachis the principal axis of an inflorescence

reflexed bent abruptly downwards or backwards

revolute rolled backwards or downwards from margins

rotate wheel-shaped, flat and circular in outline

rugose wrinkled or rough

rugulose lightly wrinkled

saprophyte a plant that secures its food from organic matter

scabrid roughened with minute scurfy points

scale small disc-like dots found on leaves, shoots and flower parts of lepidote rhododendrons

scion the shoot or bud grafted on to a stock

section middle division in Rhododendron classification

self-sterile unable to develop seed from its own pollen

series grouping of related Rhododendron species (replaced in this book, largely by subsections)

speciation the development of a new species

stock the under part of a grafted union; a plant from which cuttings are taken

stoloniferous sending out suckers from a central plant

subgenus division of genus into major parts

subrotate nearly rotate

subsection lower division into which rhododendrons are now classified

subseries lower grouping of species (see series)

tapering style a style that gradually tapers into the ovary
taxonomy classification
terminal at the tip of a shoot
tetraploid four sets of chromosomes
truss a single inflorescence
union where the stock and scion meet
vegĕtative any means of reproduction other than by seed
vestige remaining trace of an organ
water sprout long, vigorous, sappy shoots

Bibliography

BEAN, W. J., *Trees and Shrubs Hardy in the British Isles*, Vol. III, 8th Revised Edition, John Murray, London, 1976

BERRISFORD, JUDITH, *Rhododendrons and Azaleas*, Faber & Faber, London, 1964

CHAMBERLAIN, D. F., *Notes from the Royal Botanic Garden, Edinburgh*, Vol. 39 No. 2 1982, 'Revision of Rhododendron II Subgenus Hymenanthes'

COX, P. A., *Dwarf Rhododendrons*, Batsford, London, 1973

COX, P. A., *The Larger Species of Rhododendron*, Batsford, London, 1979

CULLEN, J., *Notes from the Royal Botanic Garden, Edinburgh*, Vol. 39 No. 1 1980, 'Revision of Rhododendron I Subgenus Rhododendron, sections Rhododendron & Pogonanthum'

DAVIDIAN, H. H., *The Rhododendron Species Vol. 1 Lepidotes*, Batsford, London 1982

FLETCHER, H. R., *The International Rhododendron Register*, Royal Horticultural Society, London, 1958

GARNER, R. J., *The Grafter's Handbook*, Faber & Faber, London, 1947

GREER, HAROLD E., *Greer's Guidebook to Available Rhododendron Species & Hybrids*, Offshoot Publications, Eugene, Or., 1980

KRAXBERGER, MELDON (ed.), *American Rhododendron Hybrids*, American Rhododendron Society, Or., 1980

LANCASTER, C. R., *Plant Hunting in Nepal*, Croom Helm, London, 1981

LEACH, D. G., *Rhododendrons of the World*, Allen & Unwin, London, 1962

LEE, F. P., *The Azalea Book*, Van Nostrand, London, 1954

MILLAIS, J. G., *Rhododendron Species and the Various Hybrids* (2 vols.), Longmans, Green, London, 1917 & 1924

OHWI, J., *Flora of Japan*, (English), Smithsonian Institute, Washington, 1965

PHILIPSON, M. N. & W. R., *Notes from the Royal Botanic Garden, Edinburgh*, Vol. 34 No. 1 1975, 'A Revision of Rhododendron Section Lapponicum'

PHILIPSON, M. N., & W. R., *Notes from the Royal Botanic Garden, Edinburgh*, Vol. 40 No. 1 1982, pp. 225–227, 'A Preliminary Synopsis of the Genus Rhododendron III'

ROYAL HORTICULTURAL SOCIETY, *The Rhododendron Handbook*, 'Rhododendron Species in Cultivation 1980'

STEVENSON, J. B. (ed.), *The Species of Rhododendron*, Royal Horticultural Society, London, 1930, 1947

TOGASHI, *Species of Rhododendron in Japan*, Seibundo Shinkosha Publishing Co., Tokyo, 1981

YOUNG, JUDY, & CHONG, LU-SHENG (trans.), (Acadamia Sinica), *Rhododendrons of China*, Binford & Mort, Portland, Or., 1980

Periodicals & Year Books

American Rhododendron Society, *Quarterly Bulletin*, Portland Or., 1947–81

American Rhododendron Society, *Journal*, 1982 onwards

Gardeners' Chronicle, London, 1841–1969, merged to form *Gardeners' Chronicle & Horticultural Trade Journal*

Horticulture, Boston Horticultural Society, Mass., 1904–23, N.S. 1923 onwards

Rhododendron Species Foundation, *Rhododendron Notes & Records*, yearly 1984 onwards

Royal Horticultural Society, *Rhododendron Year Book*, London, 1946–71

Royal Horticultural Society, *Rhododendrons*, 1972–3

Royal Horticultural Society, *Rhododendrons with Magnolias & Camellias*, 1974 onwards

General index

Index of rhododendrons

Note: Main page references of valid sections, subsections, and species and Group names appear in italics. Names of hybrids are given in quotes.